THE WORKS OF JAMES BUCHANAN

THE WORKS

OF

JAMES BUCHANAN

Comprising his Speeches, State Papers,
and Private Correspondence

Collected and Edited

By

JOHN BASSETT MOORE

VOLUME X
1856-1860

ANTIQUARIAN PRESS LTD.

New York

1960

First Published
1908-1911

Reprinted 1960
by
ANTIQUARIAN PRESS LTD.
New York, N.Y.

308.1
B851W
v.10

Edition Limited to 550 Copies
of which
500 Numbered Copies are For Sale.

This is No. 342

Library of Congress Catalog Card Number: 59-15119

Printed in the U.S.A.

NOBLE OFFSET PRINTERS, INC.
NEW YORK 3, N.Y.

58603

CONTENTS *of* VOLUME X

1856.

1859.

CONTENTS OF VOLUME X

THE WORKS

OF

JAMES BUCHANAN

1856.

TO MR. MARCY.[1]

No. 112.   LEGATION OF THE UNITED STATES.
                          LONDON, 4 January, 1856.

SIR:

I have the honor to acknowledge the receipt of your Despatch No. 126, of the 13th ultimo. By this I am instructed to bring the cases of Messrs. Gossler & Co., of Boston, and Messrs. Otto Wm. Pollitz & Co., of New York, "to the knowledge of the British Government" for damages sustained by them in consequence of the order of that Government, of the 1st November last, prohibiting the exportation of Saltpetre, and "found thereon claims to indemnification."

The first of these cases is very much stronger than the second, and the circumstances attending each are naturally different. If my view of the subject be correct, the strongest arguments which can be urged in favor of the claim of Messrs. Gossler & Co. would, by almost necessary implication, exclude that of Messrs. Otto Wm. Pollitz & Co. For this reason and because I know that there are several other cases behind of the same character, I shall simply transmit to Lord Clarendon a copy of your instruction and of the accompanying papers, and leave the sequel to my successor, of whose appointment and departure I have expected to hear by every steamer which has left the

---

[1] MSS. Department of State, 68 Despatches from England.

1

United States since the arrival of Mr. Appleton in Washington. He will doubtless be instructed on the different classes of what may now be called the Saltpetre claims; and as but little could be done by me before the 12th of the next month, I shall not in the mean time incur the risk of embarrassing both him and the Government by presenting an argument to Lord Clarendon on the subject which might not receive their approbation.

Much to my regret, I am still without advices from you in relation to any of my Despatches detailing conversations which have taken place between Lord Clarendon and myself since the sending of the British fleet to Bermuda and Jamaica; and am wholly ignorant in what light the President views my conduct in this matter, whilst I necessarily acted without instructions. Indeed, I have not yet received an acknowledgment of any of my Despatches since my Nos. 96 and 97, of the 25th and 26th October, which were acknowledged in your Despatch, No. 122, of the 12th November. I earnestly hope that my suspense may be relieved by the next steamer and that I may then, also, receive a copy of the President's Message.

I have received a letter from Mr. Alfred Fox, of Falmouth, dated on the 29th ultimo, stating that he had advices from you "that the resignation of A. W. Scharit, Esquire, late U. S. Consul at Falmouth, &c., has been tendered and accepted;" and informing me of his application to be appointed Consul.

In this letter he says, "I act as usual for the American vessels now in this Port, but it may perhaps be more regular, under the present change of circumstances, for me to know that my continuing to do so, until I get a reply from the Secretary of State, meets with thy obliging sanction."

In consequence, on the 31st ultimo, by virtue of the power conferred upon me by my personal instructions, I have authorised Mr. Fox "to act temporarily as Consul of the United States at Falmouth, in place of A. W. Scharit resigned, until the pleasure of the President shall be made known" to him.

I ought to add that I entertain a very favorable opinion both of the character and qualifications of Mr. Fox.

Yours very respectfully,

JAMES BUCHANAN.

HON: WM. L. MARCY,
    Secretary of State.

TO MISS LANE.[1]

LEGATION OF THE UNITED STATES,
LONDON, 4 January, 1855 [1856].

MY DEAR HARRIET/

I have received yours of the 17th ultimo & am pained to learn that you neither see your friends nor take exercise since your return to Philadelphia. Your grief for poor Mary's death, or at least the manifestation of it, exceeds all reasonable limits; & I am truly sorry that you have not more self command. Although I know it is sincere & it ought to be deep, yet you ought to recollect that the world are severe censors.

In regard to the bringing of dear Mary's remains from San Francisco to Lancaster or Franklin county,—I have not a word to say. This must be left to her nearer relatives. She sleeps as sweetly on the distant shores of the Pacific as she could do on any other spot of earth; and her disembodied spirit will be equally near to you, wherever you may wander. Still I know it is a sort of instinct of nature to desire to have the tombs of our friends near us; & even if I had any right to object, I should not exercise it. Do as you please & I shall be content.

I regret that you should have sent an order to Mr. Miller for stationery, as if there were none good enough in the United States for your purpose. I have informed Mr. M. what he knows himself, that I cannot send it through the despatch Bag. Of course he would not think of charging it to the Legation. I am pleased, however, that you sent the order, inasmuch as it is an evidence that you begin to think of the small affairs of life; & I trust you will think more & more, not only of these affairs, but of the duties which you owe yr. surviving friends.

James Henry is with me very busy & persevering in sight seeing. I am sorry I do not feel it proper to detain him with me. The carnival comes so early this year that he must soon be off, especially as he intends to take Naples en route to Rome. I get along very well with Mr. Moran, though the labor is too great for one man to perform. In truth, I cannot answer all the letters I receive & attend to my appropriate duties. I shall, however, endeavor to continue to write you a few lines every week.

[1] Buchanan Papers, private collection. Imperfectly printed in Curtis's Buchanan, II. 161.

Friends here still inquire after you with great kindness.

Give my love to Mrs. Plitt & thank her for her letter. Remember me in the kindest terms to Mr. Plitt, & believe me to be

Yours affectionately

Miss Lane.   James Buchanan.

TO MR. MARCY.[1]

No. 113.   Legation of The United States.
                                    London, 8 January, 1856.

Sir :

I have the honor herewith to transmit the copy of a Notification received from Lord Clarendon, and inserted in the London Gazette of the 28th ultimo, announcing that the blockade of all Russian ports, roads, havens, and creeks on the Baltic was entirely raised on the 10th ultimo; with the request that I would transmit the same to my Government, that it may through that channel become known to the citizens of the United States.

Yours very respectfully,

James Buchanan.

Hon : William L. Marcy,
      Secretary of State.

TO MR. MARCY.[2]

(*Private.*)   Legation of the United States,
                                    London, January 11, 1856.

My Dear Sir :—

I have received your favor of the 23d ultimo, and am greatly disappointed neither to have received the message nor any inkling of what it contains. Long expectation has blunted the edge of

---

[1] MSS. Department of State, 68 Despatches from England.
[2] Curtis's Buchanan, II. 117.

curiosity here, and it will not make the impression it would have
done four weeks ago.

I shall expect your answer to Lord C. with much interest,
and shall do all in my power to give it its proper effect with his
lordship.   For my own part, I should have been inclined to cut
the Gordian knot as soon as I possessed clear proof of Mr.
Crampton's complicity, and I am persuaded this was expected at
the time in this country.   No doubt, however, yours is the more
prudent course.

You say that if I can settle the Central American difficulty,
and you the recruitment question, they may blow what blast they
please on any of their organs.   That you can perform the latter
there can be no doubt; the former is a sheer impossibility during
the administration of Lord Palmerston.   Any attempt of the kind
will only more deeply commit this government and render it more
difficult for a succeeding government to do us justice.   It is still
my impression there will be peace in Europe before the season for
opening the next campaign; and this will leave England in such
a state of preparation for war as she has never been at any former
period.   This may act as a stimulus to the reckless and arrogant
propensities of Lord P., which have been so often manifested by
him in his intercourse with other nations.

I have more than once had occasion to admire your self-
possession and " sang-froid," but never was it more strikingly
illustrated than in the concluding and, as it were, incidental sentence of your letter: " I do not learn that the President has his
mind turned towards any one for your successor, or for secretary
of legation." This is cool.   I had confidently expected that immediately after Mr. Appleton's arrival in Washington, I should hear
of the appointment of my successor, and I felt assured that if
there had been need, you would have " turned " the President's
mind towards a subject in which I felt so deep an interest.

As I have on more than one occasion informed you, I do
believe that had it been possible for the new minister to be here
for a fortnight before my departure this would have been greatly
to his benefit, and perhaps to that of the country.   This is now
impossible.   My nephew left me yesterday for Naples and Rome,
and I was truly sorry not to be able to accompany him, as he
speaks French like a Parisian, and Italian tolerably well, and
would, therefore, have been highly useful.   I am again left with
no person except Mr. Moran (who, to do him justice, performs

his duties to my entire satisfaction), and yet the President's mind
has not been "*turned* towards any one," even for secretary of
legation. I hope, at least, that a secretary may arrive before the
12th February, as it would have a better appearance to leave the
legation in his charge than in that of the consul.

You seem to take it hard that your former assistant should
be acting in concert with Don Magnifico Markoe, still one of
your lieutenants, in favor of the nomination of Mr. Dallas, and
well you may. Such ingratitude towards yourself is a proof of
the depravity of human nature. But there is one consolation.
As somebody says: "The vigor of the bow does not equal the
venom of the shaft." I misquote, and don't recollect the precise
language.

I still think there will be peace. France and Turkey both
desire it, and Russia needs it. John Bull is still for war, but this
only to recover his prestige. He has incurred immense expense in
getting ready and don't want to throw his money away. If peace
should remove Lord P., this would be a most happy consummation. Had Mrs. M. been in your place, the President's mind
would ere this have been "*turned*" towards somebody for my
successor. Please to present her my kindest regards, and believe
me to be,

Yours very respectfully, etc.,

JAMES BUCHANAN.

TO MISS LANE.[1]

LEGATION OF THE UNITED STATES,
LONDON, 11 Jan: 1856.

MY DEAR HARRIET/

I have received your favor of the 25th ultimo together with
an agreeable little note from Mrs. Plitt, for which give her my
thanks. I have now but little time to write to my friends. I

---

[1] Buchanan Papers, private collection. Imperfectly printed in Curtis's
Buchanan, II. 161.

could scarcely answer all the letters I receive from the United States, even if I had not to play the part both of Minister & Secretary.

How fortunate you have been in receiving eight presents on Christmas; but those who receive ought always to give, & you tell me nothing of your own donations. I admire the generous character of Mrs. Plitt much more; but the lady who enjoys the character of giving more than she receives will always have plenty of customers. Long life to Mrs. Plitt! She is a woman after my own heart. All I fear is that she may kill you with kindness.

James Henry left us yesterday afternoon. He had drawn all his plans with mathematical precision & I did not like to mar them. He was to go direct to Naples & be at Rome during the Carnival, so that he had but little time. He is a calculating & I think a determined boy. I am convinced I did him much good during his brief stay here in correcting some of his eccentricities & rubbing off some of his rough corners. He certainly has a peculiar taste in dress. His coats are either too long or too short; but his hands were always clean. He speaks French beautifully. I gave a dinner on Wednesday last, chiefly to members of the Diplomatic corps, & he acquitted himself much better than I had expected. He has certainly made a favorable impression here on the persons with whom he has been in company, especially on the Mrs. Plitt of London & Lady Holland.

The dinner went off extremely well; some of them said, *almost* as well as if you had been present. As you would probably like to know the company, I will tell you:

Mr. & Madam Tricoupi, the Count & Countess de Lavradio, Count Bernstorff, the Brazilian Minister & Madam Moreiro, the Swedish Minister & Baroness Hochschild, the Danish Minister & Madam D'Oxholm, Mr. & Mrs. Comyn, Sir Henry & Lady Holland, Lady Talbot de Malahide, R. Monckton Milnes, & J. Buchanan Henry, Esquire.

Count Colloredo had the commands of the Queen & could not attend. Countess Bernstorff was ill. Baron Bentinck had an engagement in the country & so had Mr. & Mrs. Musurus. So you have the list of invitations as well as of those who attended. I expect to leave the house next week.

I very often think of poor Mary & shall always cherish her memory with deep affection. I trust that ere this your grief has moderated & that you begin to bear your loss with the philosophy of a Christian & with humble resignation to the divine will.

James desired me to send his love to you & say that he would write to you from Rome.

With my love to Mrs. Plitt & my kindest regards to Mr. Plitt, I remain

Yours affectionately

Miss Lane.   James Buchanan.

FROM MR. SLIDELL.[1]

Washington, 17 Jany. 1855 [1856].

My dear Mr. Buchanan.

I fear that I shall lose the steamer & must be very brief in acknowledging the receipt of yours of 28 Dec. I have shewn it only to Cobb & Forney. They are very much pleased with it but doubt the policy of communicating it to any but most reliable friends. Cobb suggests the propriety of your writing to me or some other reliable person [a letter] which may be published after consultation with such friends as you may wish & designate. He finds the letter of 28 Dec. only deficient in one point; he thinks that you should make some allusion to the fact that the Missouri Compromise was repudiated by all our Northern opponents, that the South would have been willing to adhere to it if there had been any disposition shewn by its enemies to carry out its principles in good faith; but as it was only invoked to exclude Southern emigration & labor from the territories, there was no reciprocity in its operation. That although Congress might legislate to that effect without violating the letter of the Constitution, yet it would be in derogation of its spirit &c. However, I am by no means certain that it is expedient for you to write anything for the public eye. You cannot well be in a better position than you are now, & those who are not satisfied with your antecedents cannot be made so by any explanations. Excuse this hasty scrawl. I will write more fully by next steamer.

Very faithfully your friend &c.

John Slidell.

Hon. James Buchanan,
&c. &c. &c. London.

---

[1] Buchanan Papers, Historical Society of Pennsylvania.

TO MR. MARCY.[1]

LEGATION OF THE UNITED STATES,
LONDON, January 18, 1856.

I have an hour ago received your despatch of the 28th ultimo, and have only had time to give it a cursory perusal.[2] I have not yet read the despatch of Lord Clarendon to which it is an answer. It appears to me to be of characteristic clearness and ability, and its tone is excellent. Still its conclusion will startle this government. I have had an appointment with Lord Clarendon postponed more than once, on account of the dangerous illness of his mother. She died on Sunday morning last, and his lordship informed me through his private secretary that as soon after the event as possible he would appoint a time for our meeting.

The Central American questions are well and ably stated in the message received two or three days ago. I know from reliable authority that Lord Palmerston " has very strong views on the subject." The *Times* is a mighty power in the State; and I have adopted means, through the agency of a friend, to prevent that journal from committing itself upon the questions until after its conductors shall have an opportunity of examining the correspondence. These means have hitherto proved effectual. The correspondence has now arrived, and the *Times* may indicate its views to-morrow morning. The tone of the other journals has not been satisfactory; and the *Daily Telegraph* has been evidently bought over, and become hostile to the United States within the last four days, as you will perceive from the number which I send. Should the *Times* take ground against us, it is my purpose to have an edition of that part of the message relating to Central America, and the correspondence, published in pamphlet form, and circulated among members of Parliament and other influential persons. Should the expense be great, I may call upon you to pay it out of the contingent fund.

A few hasty remarks upon the present condition of affairs

---

[1] Curtis's Buchanan, II. 119.

[2] For Marcy's comments on his own despatch, here referred to, see his "private and confidential" letter to Buchanan of Jan. 3, 1856; Curtis's Buchanan, II. 116.

in this country. The Austrian proposals, as you will see by the papers, have been accepted by the czar. This is distasteful to the British people who have made vast preparations, at an enormous expense, to recover their military and naval *prestige* in the next campaign. But peace is evidently desired by Louis Napoleon and the French, by the Turks and by the Sardinians. It still continues to be my opinion that peace will be made. In this state of affairs, the British people being sore and disappointed and being better prepared for war than they have ever been, Lord Palmerston, whose character is reckless and his hostility to our country well known, will most probably assume a high and defiant attitude on the questions pending between the two countries. The British people are now in that state of feeling that I firmly believe they could be brought up to a war with the United States, *if they can be persuaded that the territory in dispute belongs to themselves.* This, absurd as it is, may be done through the agency of a press generally, if not universally, hostile to us. I make these remarks because you ought to know the truth and be prepared for the worst. *Certainly not with a view of yielding one iota of our rights to Great Britain or any other power. Most certainly not.*

I understand from friends that it is now stated by British individuals in conversation, how easy it would be for them in their present state of preparation, and with our feeble navy, to bring a war with us to a speedy and successful conclusion. In this they would be wofully mistaken.

I have great hopes, however, that the peace will upset Lord Palmerston. The session of Parliament will commence with a powerful opposition against him.

Do contrive by some means to hasten the construction of a railroad to the Pacific and to increase our navy. Such a road is as necessary for war purposes as the construction of a fort to defend any of our cities.

I have not time to write more before the closing of the bag.

I deeply regret to find that so late as the 3d of January you are *unable* to say one word to me in regard to my successor. For this cause, I think I have good reason to complain.

With my kind regards always to Mrs. Marcy, I remain

Yours very respectfully,

JAMES BUCHANAN.

P. S. I ought not to forget to say that the President's message has received great commendation among enlightened people in this country. I am sorry you did not inform me at an earlier period that it was the President's intention to demand the recall of Mr. Crampton, etc., that I might have prepared them for such a result.

TO MR. CAPEN.[1]

LEGATION OF THE U. STATES,
LONDON 18 Jan: 1856.

MY DEAR SIR/

On the receipt of your favor of the 31st ultimo, I addressed a note to Mr. Peabody inquiring whether he had received the package to which you refer; & in answer he informs me that he did, and would write to you by the Steamer which will leave Liverpool to-morrow.

Many thanks for your friendly wishes! They are cordially reciprocated. Your kindly feelings towards myself have doubtless greatly magnified my popularity at home, but were the Presidency within my reach, which I am far from believing, I might then exclaim:

> " Will fortune never come with both hands full?
> She either gives a stomach and no food,
> Or else a feast and takes away the stomach."

I cannot yet say when I shall return home; but I expect by every Steamer to hear of the appointment of my successor. Indeed, I have been greatly disappointed in being detained here so long. After my relief, it is my purpose to pay a brief visit to the Continent. At the latest, God willing, I expect to be at home some time in April,—possibly before the end of March.

Without a Secretary of Legation, my letters to my friends must be brief; & for this I know you will excuse me.

[1] Buchanan Papers, Historical Society of Pennsylvania. Incompletely printed in Curtis's Buchanan, II. 120.

With my best wishes for your health and happiness, I remain always

Very respectfully your friend

JAMES BUCHANAN.

NAHUM CAPEN, ESQ.

TO MR. MARCY.[1]

No. 114.   LEGATION OF THE UNITED STATES.

LONDON, 22 January, 1856.

SIR:

In my private letter of Friday last, I informed you that I had adopted means, through the agency of a friend, to prevent *The Times* from committing itself upon the Central American questions until after its conductors should have an opportunity of examining the correspondence on the subject which had been sent to Congress with the President's Message. That friend is Dr. James Robert Black, of Kentucky, who has been long a resident of London, and is intimately acquainted with several of the persons who control the course of this Journal. He is an able man, and is true to his native country.

No person who has not resided in England can form an adequate idea of the influence of *The Times* in forming public opinion in this country, and in this manner acting effectually on the Ministry. It has of late given a decided support to Lord Palmerston; and up till the very last moment, I had *good reason* to apprehend it would come out against us on the Central American questions. I was, therefore, agreeably surprised upon the perusal of its Leader of yesterday morning. In the present state of public feeling in this country, it would be difficult to estimate the beneficial effect of that article on public opinion.

On yesterday I had an interview with Lord Clarendon, which had been previously postponed on account of the illness and death of his mother at his family residence.

---

[1] MSS. Department of State, 68 Despatches from England.

His Lordship commenced the conversation by observing that we had at length received the President's Message. I asked him how he liked it, and he replied he was sorry to observe its unfriendly tone towards England. I asked in what particulars, and he designated the remarks on the Central American questions. I expressed a contrary opinion, and told him that I thought the President had treated this subject in an able and discreet manner. This led to a very long conversation on the true construction of the Clayton and Bulwer Treaty. It would be a vain labor to report this conversation in detail, neither of us having advanced any new argument. Towards its conclusion, I pressed upon him the question, Why should Lord Palmerston have been so anxious to exclude Belize from the operation of the Treaty, if he had not felt conscious that, without such exclusion, Great Britain would have been bound to retire from this possession? I told him I had never heard from his Lordship or any other person an answer to this argument. All the answer he made to me was, that he would again examine into this point. He then, as he had more than once done before, referred at some length to the propriety of settling these questions by arbitration. In answer, among other things, I observed that I had sometimes been almost sorry that the Treaty was so plain and explicit as not to justify a resort to this course. But even if this were not the case, I asked him to name the sovereign to whom the United States could with safety refer these questions, considering the relation in which Great Britain stood towards the different Powers of the earth. His Lordship was silent; and I then remarked that if this were not impossible, I would rather take my chance before the Court of Queen's Bench than before any sovereign whom they would be willing to select. He said, laughingly, it was just as likely as not Campbell, (meaning the Lord Chief Justice,) would decide against them.

As I am fond of repeating agreeable things, I ought not to omit that in this long, and upon the whole, pleasant conversation, his Lordship expressed a very favorable opinion of yourself, which would not have been increased had I read to him, at the moment, your Despatch of the 28th ultimo, directing me to ask the recall of Mr. Crampton and of the British Consuls at Cincinnati, Philadelphia, and New York. The truth is, that the hour then becoming late, the Prussian Minister being in waiting in the ante-room, and your Despatch being none of the shortest, I felt it would be more appropriate and produce a better effect to postpone the reading of it to his Lordship until our next interview. There shall, however, be no unnecessary delay in this matter.

I then told his Lordship that I had expected when I asked this interview to be able to inform him of the appointment of my successor and when he would arrive in London; but in this I had been disappointed.

After some brief conversation on the Saltpetre cases and other topics, some of which I shall bring to your notice in my next Despatch, I gave way to the Prussian Minister.

Every day brings more prominently into view the distaste of the British people for peace with Russia; and this presents a striking contrast with the joy manifested in France on the receipt of the news that the Czar had accepted the Austrian propositions. Indeed, French journals begin to comment with some severity upon the reluctance manifested by the English Press to the conclusion of peace. It is quite certain that the pride of the British people recoils from the idea of terminating the war without having acquired equal glory with the French. Even on their own element they have done comparatively little. There has been no Waterloo nor Trafalgar during the present war. Had the British forces captured the Redan when the French captured the Malakoff, the feeling of this country in regard to peace would have been very different from what it is at present.

In order to reinstate the glory of their arms and to redeem their character as a military nation, they have made vast preparations, at an enormous expense, for the next campaign. Yet still, notwithstanding their reluctance to terminate the war, I continue to be convinced that peace will be concluded; because peace is desired both by Louis Napoleon and the Sultan. This event will leave the British people with their pride mortified, and with a vast military and naval force on hand ready for action; and this too, under the control of a statesman whose conduct has generally been arrogant rather than pacific towards foreign nations. All this will not have, and ought not to have, the least effect in preventing us from firmly and steadily maintaining our just rights, though it may prove a temptation to Lord Palmerston's government to act towards us in a different manner from what they might have done under other more propitious circumstances. It was for this reason that I attached so much importance to the course which *The Times* might take on the Central American questions.

Yours very respectfully,

JAMES BUCHANAN.

Hon : WILLIAM L. MARCY,
　　Secretary of State.

TO LORD CLARENDON.

(Enclosure in No. 115.[1])

LEGATION OF THE UNITED STATES.
LONDON, 24 January, 1856.

My LORD :

In obedience to instructions from the Secretary of State, I have the honor to transmit to your Lordship the copy of a letter addressed to the Department of State by Messrs. Gossler & Co., of Boston, Massachusetts, with a copy of the accompanying papers, relative to 418 bags of Saltpetre shipped at London on the 25th October last, on board of the American ship " Catherine," Edmunds, Master,—which Saltpetre was relanded and detained in England, under the order of the British Government of the 1st November last prohibiting the exportation of that article.

I also transmit to your Lordship the copy of a letter of the 26th November last, from Messrs. Otto Wm. Pollitz & Co., of New York, addressed to the Secretary of State, concerning a quantity of Saltpetre which they allege was purchased on their account in London prior to the issuing of the order above referred to, the shipment of which Saltpetre to the United States was in like manner prevented.

And I am further instructed by the Secretary of State to

---

[1] Despatch to Mr. Marcy, No. 115, Jan. 25, 1856, *infra*.

bring these cases to the knowledge of Her Majesty's Government and found thereon claims to indemnification.

In our interview on Monday last, I had the honor of bringing these cases to your Lordship's notice, and of informing you that other claims of a similar character would most probably be presented under instructions from the State Department.

Yours very respectfully,

(Signed)   JAMES BUCHANAN.

THE RIGHT HONBLE. THE EARL OF CLARENDON,
&c. &c. &c.

TO MR. MARCY.[1]

No. 115.   LEGATION OF THE UNITED STATES.
LONDON, 25 January, 1856.

SIR:

I have the honor to acknowledge the receipt of your Despatches Nos. 127, 128, 129, 130, and 131.

In regard to your No. 127, of the 17th ultimo, I have made application to Lord Clarendon for copies of the papers for the Secretary of the Treasury, therein referred to; but have not yet received an answer. I have, of course, offered to pay any expense which might be incurred for preparing these copies.

In respect to your No. 129, of the 24th ultimo, I have addressed a note to Lord Clarendon, communicating the thanks of the President to Captain W. J. Williams, of Her Majesty's ship "Sans Pareil," for repairing to the assistance of the ship "America," off Cabrita Point, &c. &c.

In regard to your No. 131, of the 29th ultimo, I confess I feel somewhat embarrassed. The Secretary of the Treasury, in his note to you of the 24th ultimo, after referring to the complaint of O. K. Ware, Esqr., in regard to "the difficulties experienced in carrying on the trade in Palm oil with Africa," re-

---

[1] MSS. Department of State, 68 Despatches from England.

quests, " if you snall consider the subject one for remonstrance to the British Government, that such remonstrance may be made." I infer from your instructions to me, simply stating that I shall do any thing which I can with propriety towards remedying the grievance complained of, that you do not consider this a case for remonstrance : and I agree with you in this conclusion.

What is the grievance as stated by Mr. Ware? That " the British authorities (on the Coast of Africa) allege that any vessel arriving in British waters with casks on board more than sufficient to contain water for the crew or company of such vessel is liable to seizure on suspicion of being engaged in the Slave Trade under the Consolidated Slave Act."

Mr. Redfield, the Collector of the Port of New York, very justly and properly remarks that it seemed to him proper " that any vessel arriving on the coast of Africa with empty casks, or the material of which empty casks are composed, on board, more than sufficient to hold water for the crew, should be an object of suspicion to all the Powers in league to suppress the Slave Trade." The reason is manifest. Such casks are indispensable to a slaver. Without them it would be impossible to carry a cargo of slaves across the Atlantic. Is it then unreasonable to require that when these casks are intended for the lawful purpose of holding palm oil, instead of water for slaves, that a vessel clearing from an American port shall be furnished with some evidence of the fact similar to that which is required from a vessel clearing from a British port? Mr. Ware's Bark, the " S. W. Nash," when she entered the port of Bathurst on the River Gambia, had no such evidence on board, and she was treated in the same manner as if she had cleared from the port of London. Whilst, in accordance with your presumed opinion, I do not consider this a case for a remonstrance, I shall nevertheless address Lord Clarendon a note on the subject which may have a good effect on our trade in palm oil on the Coast of Africa.

On Monday last I had some general conversation with Lord Clarendon on the Saltpetre claims, in which, without going into the merits of particular cases, I objected strongly to the order of the British Government of the 1st of November last, prohibiting the exportation of Saltpetre; *because it was to go into effect immediately and without any previous notice to those engaged in the trade.* There were, as I informed him, several

cases in which vessels having saltpetre actually on board previous to the date of the order, and this under the authority of
the Custom House officers, had been compelled to reland it; and
there had been a case at Liverpool where a vessel, which had
actually obtained her clearance, was arrested and obliged to
unload the Saltpetre on board. He observed that at the date of
the order, Saltpetre was leaving the country so fast that they
found it absolutely necessary to prohibit its export. I replied
they had no reason for prohibiting its export to the United
States, as the powder manufactured out of it was all furnished
to England and France, and could not reach Russia. He said
that in this I was mistaken,—that a large quantity of it found its
way to Russia through Hamburg.

I informed his Lordship I should, under your instructions,
in the course of the week send him two of these claims, & I knew
of a number that would follow. These, I informed him, I should
leave to my successor, who might now be expected by every
steamer. There will be many similar cases from the East Indies.

I send a copy of my note addressed to Lord Clarendon under
your instructions, No. 126. You will of course, have these claims
thoroughly investigated, and decide which of them are of such
a character as to justify an urgent pressure on the British Government for indemnity.

I thought I had done with the affair of Tal. P. Shaffner, and
it is no longer a case of any public importance; but, in fairness
to the parties concerned, it is my duty to transmit you the copy
of a Manifest left at the Legation some days ago by Mr. Cyrus
W. Field, of New York, in company with Mr. T. B. Smithies,
of the Gutta Percha Company, London. Mr. Field alleges that
the " six cases insulated telegraph wire " therein mentioned consisted of the very wire obtained from the Company by Mr.
Shaffner, and that he had no authority whatever for using the
name of Cyrus W. Field & Co. in this manifest; and that he had
taken this liberty was never known to them until the month of
December last.

I transmit the copy of a note from Lord Clarendon of the
10th Inst., "with copies of Despatches from Rear Admiral
Sterling, and from Commander Fellowes of Her Majesty's ship
' Rattler,' relative to the zealous coöperation which the latter
officer met with from Captain McCluney of the United States

steam Frigate ' Powhatan,' in an attack upon a piratical fleet "
in the Chinese waters.

It is but justice to observe that the gallant and efficient conduct of our officers, Lieutenants Pegram and Rolando, as well
as their men, on the occasion referred to, has elicited much and
well deserved commendation in this country. Lord Clarendon
himself speaks of it in the highest terms; and Sir Charles Wood,
the first Lord of the Admiralty, is quite enthusiastic in his praise
of our brave countrymen.

Yours very respectfully,

JAMES BUCHANAN.

HON: WILLIAM L. MARCY,
    Secretary of State.

TO MR. MARCY.[1]

LONDON, January 25, 1856.

MY DEAR SIR:—

From present appearances the Central American questions
can lead to no serious difficulties with England. Public opinion
would here seem to be nearly altogether in favor of our construction of the treaty. Such, I learn, is the conversation at the clubs
and in society; and with the *Times*, as well as the *Daily News* on
our side, and this in accordance with public sentiment, we might
expect a speedy settlement of these questions, if any statesman
except Lord Palmerston were at the head of the government. He
cannot long remain in power, I think, after peace shall have been
concluded. I expect to go to Paris after the 12th of February,
and may write to you from there, should I have a conversation
with Louis Napoleon. I shall see Lord Clarendon early next
week, and you may expect by the next steamer to hear the result
of my reading your despatch to his lordship.

I still continue firm in the belief that peace will be concluded,
though it is manifestly distasteful to the British people.

---

[1] Curtis's Buchanan, II. 121.

I met Sir Charles Wood, the first lord of the admiralty, at dinner the other day, and had some fun with him about sending the fleet to our shores. He said they had only sent a few old hulks, and with such vessels they could never have thought of hostilities against such a power as the United States; and asked me if I had ever heard that one of them approached our shores. I might have referred him to the Screw Blocks. The conversation was altogether agreeable and afforded amusement to the persons near us at the table. He said: " Buchanan, if you and I had to settle the questions between the two governments, they would be settled speedily." I know not whether there was any meaning beneath this expression.

I consider this mission as a sort of waif abandoned by the Government. Not a word even about a secretary of legation, though Mr. Appleton left me more than two months ago. With the amount of business to transact, and the number of visits to receive, I have to labor like a drayman. Have you no bowels?

The reports, concerning our officers, received from the Crimea, are highly complimentary and satisfactory, and the people here are much gratified with the letter received from the Secretary of War, thanking General Simpson for his kindness and attention towards them.

Before I go away I intend to get up a letter from Lord Clarendon and yourself, manifesting your sense of the manner in which Mr. Bates performed his duty as umpire. As he will accept no pay, it is as little as you can do, to say, " thank you, sir."

I am informed there is a publisher in London about to publish the Central American correspondence in pamphlet form, believing it will yield him a profit.

I have just received a letter from Mason, written in excellent spirits, praising Mr. Wise, his new secretary. For poor me, this is sour grapes. Never forgetting my friend Mrs. Marcy,

I remain yours very respectfully,

JAMES BUCHANAN.

TO MISS LANE.[1]

LEGATION OF THE UNITED STATES,
LONDON 25 January 1856.

MY DEAR HARRIET/

Without a Secretary of Legation, I have so much business to transact & so many persons to see that I must give great offence by necessarily failing to answer the letters of my friends on your side of the Atlantic.　I have not yet heard of the appointment of my successor from Washington; but the last steamer brought out a report, on which some of the passengers thought reliance might be placed, that Governor Toucey either had been or would be appointed.　It would be difficult to make a better selection.　In all this matter, they have treated me discourteously & improperly. By every steamer since the return of Mr. Appleton to the United States, I had a right to expect news of a new appointment.　I have written more than once *emphatically* upon the subject; and they are now fully apprised that I shall leave the Legation next month & entrust its affairs to General Campbell, should neither Minister nor Secretary in the mean time appear.

The Central American questions might now, I think, be easily settled with any other Premier than Lord Palmerston. Since the publication of the correspondence here & the articles in the Times & Daily News in our favor, there would seem to be a general public opinion that we are right.　This, I think, renders it certain that serious difficulties between the two Countries cannot grow out of these questions.　I enclose you an article from the " Morning Advertiser," but little calculated to do me good in the United States.　What on earth could have induced the editor to write such an article is a mystery.　So far as regards any effect it may produce upon the Presidency, I feel quite indifferent.　There is profound wisdom in a remark of Rochefoucauld with which I met the other day :—" Les choses que nous desirons n'arrivent pas, ou, si elles arrivent, ce n'est, ni dans le tems, ni de la manière que nous auraient fait le plus de plaisir."—I had a letter yesterday from Judge Mason dated on the 23d, brought by our old friend Mooney, giving me a pressing & cordial invitation

---

[1] Buchanan Papers, private collection.　Imperfectly printed in Curtis's Buchanan, II. 162.

to stay with him when I visited Paris. This I believe I shall accept, at least for part of my brief visit. He is very much pleased with Mr. Wise, his new Secretary of Legation. James B. Henry, he says, who took the despatches to him, " remained but a few hours in Paris, hurrying to Marseilles to take a steamer for Italy." I have not heard from him since he left me, nor did I expect to hear so soon.

Mrs. Shapter has been quite unwell; but is now down stairs again. I have not seen her since the date of my last.

We had quite an agreeable dinner party at Lord Woodehouse's on Wednesday last. I had a very pleasant conversation with the Countess Persigny, who speaks English very prettily though not yet fluently. She is evidently proud of being the grand-daughter of Marshal Ney; & well she may be. We had quite a *tête à tête*. She, or rather the Count, has been *very civil to me of late*. The woman-killer, for whom, as you know, I have very little respect & with whom I have had no intercourse for a considerable period, seems determined that I shall be on good terms with him. I suffered, as usual, the penalty of this dinner,— a sleepless & uncomfortable night. Dinner invitations are again becoming numerous; but I shall accept none except from those to whom I feel under obligations for past kindness.—Your name still continues to be mentioned with kindness by your friends & acquaintances. I dine tomorrow with the Torrances & on Wednesday next with the Hankeys. I sent the other day by the " Frigate Bird " to Charles Brown the collector a portrait of the justly celebrated John Hampden, from our friend MacGregor,[1] intended to be presented to Congress, & have requested Mr. Brown to keep it for me till my return. I also sent two boxes containing books & different articles,—one of them champagne & other wine. These might be sent to Eskridge. Please to tell Mr. Plitt about them, who, if he will call on Mr. Brown, will hear all about the picture. I have neither room nor time to write more.

With my love to Mrs. Plitt, & my kindest regards to Mr. Plitt I remain

Yours affectionately

JAMES BUCHANAN.

MISS HARRIET LANE.

---

[1] James MacGregor, Esq., M. P.

FROM MR. SLIDELL.[1]

WASHINGTON, 30 Jany. 1856.

MY DEAR MR. BUCHANAN,

I wrote you a hurried letter about ten days since & then promised that my next should enter more into details. It now seems that you will soon be released from your prison house, & I shall consequently reserve what I had to say of a confidential character until we meet. There is not the slightest reason to apprehend that a declaration of the unconstitutionality of the Missouri Compromise or any other doctrine to which you cannot fully subscribe will be adopted at Cincinnati. Every one feels the imperative necessity of selecting our best man for the Presidency, & there is no disposition to encumber him with makeweights. The Georgia platform will satisfy the South, & the democracy of the free states will not object to it. Indeed, several conventions have already gone quite as far in their declarations. Cobb says that the delegates from Georgia will be right, & I have reason to believe that those from Alabama will not be disposed to give more than a complimentary vote to Pierce & will be ready to leave him so soon as their instructions will permit them to do it decently. Cave Johnson writes me that the Tennessee delegation will *certainly* go for you. As for Massachusetts, Vermont, &c., whatever may be their professions, their mandatories will be for a man who can win, & they know that Pierce cannot. So make up your mind, my dear Sir, that the cup will not be permitted to pass from you, & endeavor to bear your cross with as much patience as you can command. Mrs. S. thanks you for your kind recollections & promises herself much satisfaction when you shall occupy the White House.

Very faithfully your friend &c.

JOHN SLIDELL.

HON. JAMES BUCHANAN,
&c. &c. &c. London.

TO MR. MARCY.[2]

No. 117.   LEGATION OF THE UNITED STATES.

LONDON, 1 February, 1856.

SIR:

I had an interview by appointment on Tuesday last with Lord Clarendon at the Foreign Office. After some preliminary conversation on the subject of the approaching peace with Russia,

---

[1] Buchanan Papers, Historical Society of Pennsylvania.

[2] MSS. Department of State, 68 Despatches from England. An extract from this despatch is printed in S. Ex. Doc. 35, 34 Cong. 1 Sess. 65.

I informed him I had come on purpose to read to him your Despatch to me of the 28th ultimo, in reply to his Despatch to Mr. Crampton of the 16th November last. Before proceeding to this, however, I expressed my desire to correct an error, or rather an omission, in his report of a remark made by myself contained in his Despatch to Mr. Crampton. He said he would be very sorry if any such error had been committed by him,—that nothing certainly was further from his intention.—I replied that I had not the most remote idea he had done this intentionally, and I had no doubt it was a mere inadvertence; but still it was proper for me to correct it. I then read to his Lordship the following paragraph from his Despatch to Mr. Crampton of the 16th November:—

" Before I proceed to offer any remarks upon this despatch [your No. 118, of the 13th October,] it will be proper to state that when it was read to me by Mr. Buchanan, I had no cognizance of Mr. Marcy's Despatch of the 15th July to which it alludes, and of which a copy was also transmitted to you; and upon my observing this to Mr. Buchanan he said he had not thought it necessary to communicate it to me, as before it had reached him he had received my note of the 16th July, which he thought would finally settle the question that had arisen between the two Governments."

I then observed that his Lordship's omission consisted in not having added the qualification which I made at the time to his remark, that when I received your Despatch of the 15th July, I had not the least idea of Mr. Crampton's complicity in the business of recruiting. [In truth, I never had, until I received your private letter of the 2d September.]

His Lordship said he did not recollect that I had made this remark at the time, though this was quite probable, as he did recollect I had previously informed him more than once, when speaking in reference to the satisfaction I had expressed in transmitting to you his note to me of the 16th July, that I had no idea at the time of Mr. Crampton's complicity in the affair. I stated it was quite certain I had made this remark to him at the time,— I had always been on my guard in conversing with him on the subject from the time I first heard from you of Mr. Crampton's alleged complicity. He said he had no doubt I was correct in my recollection; and I told him that in this I could not be mistaken, not only because my memory was distinct, but because I had made notes of our conversation soon after it occurred. He said, for his own part, he never had time to make such notes; and repeated, he had no doubt my statement was correct, and expressed his regret that he had not embraced my remark in his Despatch to Mr. Crampton; but observed that he did not see its importance. I told him it might possibly be of some consequence to myself; and I had ever considered Mr. Crampton's complicity in the affair a matter of very grave importance. I then mentioned that in other respects his statement was not altogether correct, and I repeated to him the language which I had employed on the occasion, as follows:—

" I did not deem it necessary to communicate this Despatch (that of the 15th July) to your Lordship until I should hear from Mr. Marcy on the subject of your note of the 16th July, which I thought at the time would finally settle the question, because I had not then the least idea of Mr. Crampton's complicity in the business of recruiting."

I said, I shall now proceed to read to your Lordship Mr. Marcy's Despatch. (This I much desired to do for obvious reasons.) Upon taking it up for this purpose, and when about to commence, he asked me if it was long; and I said it was of considerable length, but I should be pleased to read it to him. He said he would be glad to hear it, but he had several other engagements for the evening;—I would of course leave him a copy, and he would himself read it over carefully that night. I then delivered him the copy. He asked me, as I had anticipated he would, what was the purport of the Despatch; and I informed him that after giving the reasons at length, you had instructed me to request the recall of Mr. Crampton and of the British consuls at Cincinnati, Philadelphia, and New York. This evidently took his Lordship by surprise, and he replied with emotion, " We will not do it." This emotion, however, appeared instantly to subside, and he said, This Despatch is the work of Mr. Cushing and shews the unfriendly sentiments of your Government towards us. I observed that the Despatch was altogether written by Mr. Marcy,—was a very able document, and gave strong reasons, as he would discover when he came to examine it, for asking for the recall of Mr. Crampton and the consuls. He said that Mr. Crampton had never engaged in violating our neutrality laws, and he considered his simple declaration to that effect far more worthy of credit than the confession of such a man as Hertz. I told him that without reference to Hertz's confession, there was the testimony of Captain Strobel, fortified by authentic documents, which could, in my opinion, leave little doubt of Mr. Crampton's complicity in the affair. He asked, where were those documents? I told him he would find them in the trial of Hertz, a copy of which I had given him some time since, and asked him if he had not read it. He said he had only found time to look at it very cursorily; but repeated his strong conviction of the correctness of Mr. Crampton's conduct.

I then observed that if the same things had been done in England which had been done in the United States, they would probably realize the reason why we were so sensitive on the subject. For example,—not to speak of other cities,—a recruiting rendezvous had been established in 3d Street, a public Street of Philadelphia; men were there openly engaged to go to Halifax to be enlisted for the Crimea, their expenses were paid, and they were furnished with free passages on board steamers and other vessels; and all this was done in pursuance of advertisements published in our newspapers.

I proceeded to say I was sorry I had not seen his Despatch to Mr. Crampton of the 16th November before it was sent. If I had done so, I thought I could have called his Lordship's attention to some inconsistencies between it and his note to me of the 16th July. He requested me to point them out. I told him he would find this done in your Despatch; but I would bring some of them to his notice by mentioning one or two of the reasons why I had expressed satisfaction in transmitting to you his note of the 16th July. I said, In this note, your Lordship expressed your regret that the laws of the United States had been violated by any persons, whether British officials or not. He replied, certainly he had done so. You, also, declared that from friendly feelings towards the United States you had arrested enlistments altogether in North America. He said, Certainly,— this was done to remove all causes of offence towards the United States. I then said, You declared substantially that if the laws of the United States had been violated by British officials, this had been done contrary to your positive instructions and against your wishes. He said this was all correct. I then observed, Mr. Crampton being out of the question, & at the time I had no idea of his complicity,—this left the road open to the Government of the United States, in case they should ascertain that British Consuls had been engaged in recruiting contrary to their instructions, to withdraw their Exequaturs, if not to punish them as had been done with the British Consul at Cologne, and thus any direct issue between the two Governments would have been avoided. To these last observations, his Lordship neither signified his assent nor dissent. I then added that upon reading your Despatch he would find that in his Despatch of the 16th November, he had departed from the ground taken in his note to me of the 16th July, and occupied new ground, inconsistent with the positions I had just stated. He smiled (as I understood, incredulously,) but gave no answer. He then said he would soon answer your Despatch either in a note to me or one addressed to Mr. Crampton, and in the latter case I should see it before it was sent.

The conversation continued for some time, and until I took my leave; in a pleasant and good natured manner about indifferent topics.

There can be no doubt but that the British Government will refuse to recall Mr. Crampton and the Consuls; and that your request to this effect will produce much excitement and ill-feeling in this country. In proof of this, I refer you to an article in the *Post* of Wednesday morning on the subject, and I can scarcely doubt but that its author had information of the interview on Tuesday evening between Lord Clarendon and myself. This Journal is notoriously under the direct influence of Lord Palmerston. An article in it on Tuesday morning contains some atrocious suggestions in regard to the mode of carrying on war against our country, in the event of hostilities.

I have been agreeably disappointed at the just light in which the Central American questions seem to be viewed by the British Press & people, although Lord Derby in last night's debate agrees with the British Government's construction of the Clayton and Bulwer Convention. Indeed, public opinion in this country would at the present moment appear to be decidedly favorable to our construction of that Convention. *The Daily News* first and *The Times* the day after, as you will have observed, came out in judicious and friendly articles on the subject; and it is difficult to overestimate the influence of the latter journal. Still, I regret to say we can place but little reliance upon its consistency.

Lord Clarendon does not entertain the least doubt of peace with Russia. At the commencement of our interview on Tuesday last, he gave me a full account of the present state of the negotiation and informed me he would go to Paris as the negotiator on the part of Great Britain. He is fully sensible of how much the British people dislike to make peace at the present moment and how anxious they are to try their fortune in another campaign; and is also perfectly aware that a different sentiment animates the French Emperor and people. Indeed, his Lordship hinted, in unmistakable terms, that the peace might cause the present Ministry to lose their places; but he said he thought it was right in itself and he did not care for the consequences to himself personally.

I transmit a copy of the Queen's speech delivered yesterday, furnished me from the Foreign Office. It was believed by many that an allusion would be made in it to the questions in dispute between the two countries; but in this they, and among the rest several members of the Diplomatic Corps, were disappointed.

I had intended to offer some speculations on these questions, but on reading the debate in *The Times* this morning between Lords Derby and Clarendon, I deem this unnecessary for the present.   Yours very respectfully,

JAMES BUCHANAN.

HON: WILLIAM L. MARCY,
    Secretary of State.

TO MISS LANE.[1]

LEGATION OF THE UNITED STATES,
        LONDON, 1 February, 1856.

MY DEAR HARRIET/

I have received your favor of the 14th ultimo & have sent the one enclosed to Mrs. Shapter, whom I have not seen for some time, though I have called there more than once.

---

[1] Buchanan Papers, private collection. Imperfectly printed in Curtis's Buchanan, II. 163.

I have but little time to write to-day.

Parliament was yesterday opened by the Queen. I need not describe the ceremony to you, as you have already witnessed it. What struck me most forcibly was the appearance in the Diplomatic Box of a full blooded black negro as the Representative of his Imperial Majesty of Hayti.

I have received a letter from James Henry, dated at Rome on the 20th ultimo. He does not seem to be as much pleased with the Eternal City as he had anticipated, though he writes in good spirits. Realities never correspond with the expectations of youth.

I had confidently expected to receive by the Atlantic, whose mails & Despatch Bag have just come to hand, an answer to my last most urgent request for the appointment of my successor & the immediate appointment of a Secretary of Legation; but in this I have been disappointed. Not one word in relation to the subject.

Give my love to dear Mrs. Plitt & thank her for her kind letter. I am glad so favorable an opportunity as that presented by her, Mrs. Billings, & Mrs. Mason has occurred for you to visit New York. You ought by all means to embrace it. I shall begin to believe that I have been mistaken in your character. I thought it possessed more strength. Grief for the loss of a beloved sister is natural, proper, & praiseworthy; but carried to an extreme is a rebellion against Providence, as well as a violation of your duty to the living.

I wish I had time to write you more. This steamer will carry a most important Despatch to Washington.

With my love to Edward & his family & my kindest regards to Mrs. Plitt, I remain always yours affectionately

JAMES BUCHANAN.

MISS HARRIET LANE.

TO MR. MARCY.[1]

No. 119.   LEGATION OF THE UNITED STATES.
LONDON, 5 February, 1856.

SIR:

I have kept you advised, both in my public Despatches and in my private letters, of the state of feeling in this country in regard to the questions now in dispute between the two Governments. These questions now seem to be approaching a diplomatic, if not a belligerent rupture; and I deem it almost certain that as soon as the news shall arrive in this country, that you have sent Mr. Crampton his passports, I shall receive mine from Lord Clarendon.

You will observe in the leading article of *The Times* of yesterday morning the following remarks: "Every day we expect to hear that our Minister at Washington has received his passports and is on his way home. That, of course, will compel a similar proceeding on our part with regard to the American Minister, and Mr. Crampton and Mr. Buchanan, the two inoffensive gentlemen representing their Governments at Washington and London, will probably cross each other on the Atlantic."

I doubt not but that this article indicates the course which the British Government has determined to pursue.

A significant incident in this connection has recently occurred which will prove worthy of notice, should it not appear to be a mere mistake. On Saturday evening last, Lady Palmerston gave her first reception for the season; and to this I was not invited along with the other Foreign Ministers. This omission, if intentional, cannot be explained by any reasons personal to myself, unless, indeed, it was caused by your publication of my opinion that had Lord Aberdeen remained in power, the differences between the two countries on the Central American questions would have been satisfactorily adjusted.

I have ever been on fair terms personally both with Lord and Lady Palmerston.

Ere this can reach Washington, you will have read the speeches of Lord Derby and Lord Clarendon in the House of Lords on Thursday evening last, which will speak for themselves.

---

[1] MSS. Department of State, 68 Despatches from England. Extracts printed in S. Ex. Doc. 35, 34 Cong. 1 Sess. 247–248.

Lord Clarendon says in relation to the Centra American questions:—" In such a case, correspondence is useless, and I lost no time in offering to refer the whole question to the arbitration of any third Power, both sides agreeing to be bound by the decision. That offer has not yet been accepted; it has been renewed, and I hope that upon further consideration the Government of the United States will agree to it."

The evident purpose of his Lordship was, by these remarks, to convey the idea to the country that a formal offer had been made and reiterated by the British Government to our Government to refer these questions to arbitration. As this is a favorite method among the Manchester School of politicians of settling international disputes, the statement of his Lordship is well calculated to produce an effect upon Messrs. Cobden, Bright, and Gibson, as well as many others, in the main friendly to the United States.

It is, therefore, proper for me to state, as a matter of fact, that I have reported to you, in the most faithful manner, every conversation which has passed between Lord Clarendon and myself on the subject of a reference of these questions to a friendly Power. As I have never learned that the British Government has made any such offer to the Government of the United States through Mr. Crampton, I infer that his Lordship must have referred to the general conversations between him and myself, which would by no means justify the broad terms of his statement. Thus much merely to vindicate the truth of history.

Had not the Central American questions been complicated with the recruitment question, I should have entertained, Lord Derby to the contrary notwithstanding, fair hopes of their satisfactory adjustment. An opinion exists in England to a considerable extent in favor of our construction of the Clayton and Bulwer Convention, and this has elicited a spirit of inquiry and investigation which cannot fail to prove advantageous to our cause. Indeed, a leading Bookseller in London has published a pamphlet (price 1 shilling or 25 cents) containing the convention itself, the correspondence between Messrs. Bulwer and Clayton on the exchange of Ratifications, and that between Lord Clarendon and myself; which promises, as I am informed, to have a considerable circulation. I may add, on the information of a Member of Parliament, which, however, I can scarcely credit, that Sir Henry Bulwer himself favors our construction of the

Treaty.   I shall learn more of this in the course of the present
week.

In regard to the anticipated dismissal of Mr. Crampton and
the consuls, I regret to say that public opinion in England seems
at present to be decidedly against our Government.   This you
will learn from the public journals.   Independently of these, I
may state from information derived from our own citizens in
London, that in conversations at the Clubs and in society, the
almost universal expression of opinion is to the following purport:—" We have made the amende honorable to the United
States;—if we have unintentionally violated their laws, we have
tendered them such an apology as one gentleman ought to accept
from another in private intercourse;—we have done everything
in our power to satisfy their susceptibility, and still they are not
satisfied.   It is evident they design ' to pick a quarrel ' with us,"
&c. &c. &c.   Of course, no person talks to me in this manner.

How are these erroneous impressions to be removed?   In
conversation with those on whom I can rely, I have done all that
I could for this purpose; but I have no access to the public journals.   The correspondence will, probably, be published too late
in the United States to produce its proper effect in this country;
and it may not & probably will not be republished in England.
Even if this should be done, the masses of the English people,
unlike our own, do not think for themselves, but are prone to
follow their leaders without much inquiry.   I would suggest that
if this be possible, you should send at least one hundred copies of
the printed correspondence by the same conveyance which will
bring the news of Mr. Crampton's dismissal.

Under ordinary circumstances, no danger of war between
the two countries could result from the dismissal of Mr. Crampton.   For my own part, I do not participate, to any great extent,
in the apprehensions seriously entertained on this subject by our
countrymen engaged in business in London.   The news that you
have sent Mr. Crampton his passports will, beyond all question,
produce an intense sensation throughout England.   This will
doubtless be followed, on the principle of the *lex talionis,* by my
dismissal; and I shall be made the peace offering—a most willing
victim so far as I am personally concerned.

A mere suspension of Diplomatic intercourse, of itself,
cannot be attended with very serious danger, though it will place
the two countries in such a menacing attitude towards each other

that the occurrence of any untoward event may produce hostilities.

Still there are considerations involved in the question on which the American Government ought not to shut their eyes.

Peace with Russia is almost universally unpopular in England. This is not so much for the reason that they dislike the terms, as because they feel deeply mortified that they have not acquired more glory in the war. Their pride is mortified, because they feel that they have not sustained their rank among nations as a first rate military Power. At a moment when their hopes were high,—when they had made vast preparations at an enormous expense to recover their *prestige,* which they doubtless would have done in another campaign, Austria and the inevitable Louis Napoleon have intervened and peace will be concluded. In society I have often heard the expression:—" All we want is another round; and then no matter what may be the result, we shall be willing to make peace." They are now peculiarly sore and sensitive, and are just in that irritable state that they will quarrel for a cause which, under other circumstances, would not have given them serious offence. If they can be made to believe their honor is concerned in the question of Mr. Crampton's dismissal, and that our Government, in a hostile spirit, are pressing them to make unreasonable concessions, I am convinced from my own observation, as well as from the general popular tone, that the Government and the Press could influence them to embark in a war against the United States. They are in a condition at the present moment not to count the cost, the suffering and the pecuniary losses which such a step would entail upon them. Besides, it is believed, and such is my own opinion, that Lord Palmerston's administration cannot long survive the peace; but as a war minister, he is considered a necessity. And whilst I do not for a moment believe, unfavorably as I may think of him as a public man, that he would intentionally involve his country in a war with the United States to perpetuate his own power, yet human nature is too prone honestly to believe that course of public policy the best which chimes in with selfish interest.

You cannot fail to have observed the vain boastings and the threats contained in the British public journals. In the event of a war, according to them, our cities on the sea-board are to be bombarded; our ports blockaded; our commerce swept from the ocean; our Union divided, and a servile war excited by the land-

ing of Black Regiments in the South. Their perfect preparation
—and it is true they have never been so well prepared for war at
any former period of their history—is contrasted with our alleged
want of preparation. They do not know that all their threats, so
far from intimidating the American people, are well calculated to
arouse into action that glorious, indomitable, self-relying, and
patriotic spirit which animates the hearts and would nerve the
arms of our countrymen, and in the end assure them the victory,
in case Great Britain should attempt to carry her vain boasts into
effect. I have deemed it my duty, however, as a faithful sen-
tinel, to present to you these " signs of the times," which ought
not in prudence to be altogether disregarded by the President and
Cabinet.

Another observation which I have to make is, that the delay
to organise the House of Representatives has done much injury
to our national character in England, and as I believe, throughout
Europe. No man who has not resided in this country can appreciate the ignorance, even of otherwise well-informed people, concerning our country and its institutions. This I have every day
occasion to observe. Indeed, considering the intercourse between
the two countries, this ignorance is amazing. The inference most
generally drawn from the failure to elect a speaker is that the
House is divided on the question of abolishing slavery throughout the United States; and that this obstinate struggle portends
civil war between the North and the South and a division of our
Union.

I had hoped to be able in this Despatch to report to you the
result of another interview between Lord Clarendon and myself,
which I had requested; but his Lordship has appointed the time
of meeting for to-morrow.[1]

Yours very respectfully,

JAMES BUCHANAN.

HON: WILLIAM L. MARCY,
    Secretary of State.

---

[1] On a scrap of paper, inserted after the foregoing despatch, is the following extract from the London *Advertiser* of Feb. 1, 1856, under the head
of " America and Great Britain ":

" We regret to hear that at an interview which Lord Clarendon and Mr.
Buchanan, the American Minister, had together, at the Foreign Office, on
Tuesday, very angry words passed between His Excellency and the Noble

TO MR. MARCY.[1]

No. 120.   LEGATION OF THE UNITED STATES.
                              LONDON, 8 February, 1856.

SIR:

On Wednesday last, the 6th Instant, I had an interview with Lord Clarendon at the Foreign Office. I told him I desired to ascertain whether the statement he had made in the House of Lords on the evening of Thursday the 31st ultimo, that the British Government had made to the American Government an offer, which has been recently renewed, to arbitrate the Central American questions, was founded on what had passed between him and myself in conversation; or whether he had instructed Mr. Crampton to make to you in writing a formal proposal for arbitration. He replied that his statement was founded on our different conversations, and that in these he had several times proposed to me a reference of these questions to arbitration; and he expressed the hope that I had communicated his propositions to my Government. I informed him that I had faithfully reported to you all the conversations we had held in reference to an arbitration; but I had not believed that what he had said on these occasions amounted to such an offer as could be recognized by our Government as a foundation for specific action on so grave a matter. I added that I did not doubt you were of the same opinion, as I had never received a line from you on the subject. He observed that before holding these conversations with me, he had consulted the Cabinet, and spoke their sentiments as well as his own. I remarked that this fact had now for the first time been communicated to me. If he had informed me of it at the time, this would have given his conversation a more serious character and caused it to make a deeper impression on my mind. He said he had thought that, as a matter of course, I would consider what

Lord, relative to the Central American question. If what has come to our knowledge be correct, Lord C. did not altogether demean himself on the occasion in such a manner as became his own position in society and the high office he fills in the service of his country."

On the other side of the sheet, there is the following endorsement, in Buchanan's handwriting: "Lord Clarendon has always been most courteous & kind in all his intercourse with me. J. B."

[1] MSS. Department of State, 68 Despatches from England. An extract from this despatch is printed in S. Ex. Doc. 35, 34 Cong. 1 Sess. 248–250.

he had said to me had been said after consultation with the Cabinet. In reply, I observed that I had thought, when one nation desired to propose to another the submission of an international dispute to arbitration, this would be done by writing and in due form. Such had been their own course when they proposed to arbitrate the Oregon question. Besides, the President might, if he thought proper, consult the Senate on the question; and what would be thought by that Body, if such a proposition were presented to them in the loose form of various conversations between him and myself, which, after all, I might, through mistake or inadvertence, not have reported correctly? He said that what he had done he considered the preliminary step; and if our Government had indicated any satisfaction with it, they would have been prepared to proceed further; but from what I had said to him, he did not think they had received much encouragement. I told him that whenever I had spoken to him upon the subject, I had always been careful to assure him that I was expressing my own individual sentiments, without any instructions or information from my Government; and that these remained unchanged. I also observed that his last letter to me, finally denying our construction of the Treaty, and forming an issue between the two Governments, might appropriately have contained a proposition for arbitration; and in this manner the question might have been brought in regular form before our Government. He then, for the first time, informed me that he had addressed a Despatch to Mr. Crampton on the subject, with instructions to him to read it to you. He then sent for it, and read it to me. I believe it is dated in November, but a copy being doubtless in your possession, it will speak for itself; and he informed me that all you had said about it to Mr. Crampton was, that the matter was in Mr. Buchanan's hands.

He proceeded to express a decided opinion in favor of arbitration, and said that when two friendly Governments disagreed upon the construction of a Treaty, the natural and appropriate course was to refer the question to a third friendly Power. He had ever firmly believed their construction of the Treaty to be correct. He then requested me to communicate to you their proposal for an arbitration, and how anxious they were that the question might be settled in this manner. I told him I should cheerfully comply with his request; but repeated that my own individual opinions remained unchanged. I considered the language of the Treaty too clear for serious doubt, and such I believed was the opinion of public men of all parties in the United States. This had been evinced by the recent debate in the Senate on the President's Message. Besides, the difficulty of selecting a suitable sovereign as an arbitrator seemed insurmountable. But, I said, this was a question for my own Government and not for myself.

I then proceeded to observe, that as there might soon be a suspension of diplomatic intercourse between the two Governments, it was the duty of each during the period this might continue carefully to avoid all causes of irritation, as any spark might then produce an explosion. To this sentiment he very cordially responded. With this view, I said I desired to talk to him seriously about a matter which had recently occurred at Antigua. (Vide your Despatch No. 134.) We then held a conversation upon this subject which I do not deem it necessary to repeat. He had been made acquainted with it before, and his promises were altogether fair and satisfactory. In the same connection, I brought to his notice the subject of your Despatch No. 108, concerning a similar occurrence at Savana la Mar. When I receive the report of Captain Fairfax of the Cyanne, which I presume has been sent to me, I shall probably address his Lordship a note in regard to these two cases, and especially the occurrence at Antigua.

After the conclusion of this conversation, he expressed a wish to know why I thought we were about to have a suspension of Diplomatic relations. I informed him I had derived this information from high authority—that of *The Times* and *Morning Post*, the latter the acknowledged organ of Lord Palmerston. According to these, I was to receive my passports as soon as the news should arrive in England that you had sent his passports to Mr. Crampton; and we were to cross each other on the Atlantic. He denounced the newspapers in strong terms and said he had not seen the article either in the *Post* or *Times;* but he neither admitted nor denied the truth of their assertion, though expressing a warm regard for myself, which I must in justice say I reciprocate towards him personally. This led to a general conversation about the course of these journals and the threats contained in them against the United States, which he condemned in strong and emphatic terms, and expressed a warm desire, on their part, to cultivate the most friendly relations with our country. In the course of this conversation, I denounced in most decided terms the injustice so frequently done to President Pierce in these and other English journals, in attempting to make the British public believe that he had brought forward the great questions now in contest between the two Governments for mere electioneering purposes. Nothing, I said, could be more false and unfounded; and on these questions the people would rally round their President. He agreed with me in opinion that such charges against President Pierce were unjust and unbecoming, and he was sorry they had ever been made; but observed that Mr. Cushing's conduct and publications, calculated to inflame the American people against England, whilst standing in the confidential relation of a member of the Cabinet, evinced anything but those friendly feelings towards them which they entertained for the United States; and this conduct, so far as he knew, had never been marked by any sign of disapprobation from the President. We then went into a discussion of Mr. Cushing which became quite animated, especially on the part of his Lordship; but which it could do no possible good to repeat. One thing is certain: that his Lordship is kept informed, doubtless with great exaggerations, of every thing which Mr. Cushing says in regard to this country.

I then asked his Lordship if he had yet sent to Mr. Crampton an answer to your Despatch of the 28th December. He said he was sorry he had not been able to do this. He thought it due to Mr. Crampton, as well as to themselves and the Government of the United States, first, to afford him an opportunity of explaining or answering some things contained in your Despatch, which he was glad to say had been written in a proper and praiseworthy tone and spirit, and with this view he had sent a copy of it to him by the last steamer. I stated he had informed me at our interview that they would not recall Mr. Crampton, and had said he would soon answer your Despatch, and this I had written to you. He asked, What did you tell Mr. Marcy I had said in relation to Mr. Crampton's recall? and I replied I had repeated his own words: " *We will not do it.*" He asked, Did I say so? and I answered, Yes,—these were your very words. He then appealed to me to say whether it was not right and fair to give Mr.

Crampton an opportunity of being heard. I replied, such a course was always right; but intimated that the opportunity might have been offered to him at an earlier day. My memory does not recall the words he then employed; but I understood him rather to intimate than express an apprehension lest you might act before receiving his answer; and I told him I did not think you would take any decisive action in the matter until you had received it; and then the interview ended. He will go to Paris the latter end of next week to attend the peace conferences.

I have been a good deal in society since the meeting of Parliament and have conversed with a number of members of both Houses on the Central American and recruiting questions; but never except when introduced by themselves. On the former I have expressed my opinions pretty freely; but on the latter with more reserve, as the correspondence has not yet been published. Upon the whole, I may venture to say, that appearances have assumed a more favorable or rather a less unfavorable aspect than when I last wrote. I have reason to believe that our construction of the Clayton and Bulwer Treaty will be ably sustained in the House of Commons, and probably also in the House of Lords. I shall carefully watch " the signs of the times," during the brief period I may remain here, and I earnestly hope that a successor may yet arrive before my departure. Within the last day or two I have heard a suggestion from an influential and friendly quarter, that it would be best to submit the construction of the convention to two citizens of our own country and two British subjects, all of eminent character and abilities, with authority to them, should this prove necessary, to select an umpire. I have given this suggestion no encouragement, but the reverse; though it would be less hazardous than a reference to any European sovereign. I fear that the proposal of arbitration may withdraw public attention from the merits of the question; but my impression daily gains strength that the people of Great Britain will not consent to a war with the United States to maintain their contested possessions in Central America.

I have some reason to believe I was mistaken in the speculation contained in my last Despatch, that the Manchester School would advocate arbitration. I know that at least one of them, and he the most distinguished, is in favor of an immediate settlement and an abandonment of their claims in Central America.

I have delivered to Lord Clarendon the tenth volume of Little & Brown's edition of the United States Statutes at Large, in conformity with your instructions (No. 133).

Yours very respectfully,

JAMES BUCHANAN.

HON: WILLIAM L. MARCY,
  Secretary of State.

TO MISS LANE.[1]

56 HARLEY STREET,
LONDON, 8 Feb: '56.

MY DEAR HARRIET/

Our latest dates from New York are to Saturday the 19th of January. We have had no Collins or Cunard steamer during the present week. Since the first spell of cold weather, the winter has been open, damp, & disagreeable.

I have gone a good deal into Society since the meeting of Parliament; because it is my duty to embrace every opportunity of conversing with influential people here on the relations between the two Countries. "The Morning Advertiser" has been publishing a series of articles,—one stating that high words had passed between Lord Clarendon & myself at the Foreign Office & that he had used violent expressions to me there;—another that I had because of this declined to attend Lady Palmerston's first reception, & a third, which I have not seen, that Sir Henry Bulwer & myself had been in conference together with the view of settling the Central American questions. Now all this is mere moonshine & there is not a shadow of truth in any one of these statements. *Should this become necessary, not otherwise,* Mr. Plitt may have them contradicted.

I went to Count Persigny's on the evening of Shrove Tues-

---

[1] Buchanan Papers, private collection. Imperfectly printed in Curtis's Buchanan, II. 164.

day & had quite an agreeable time of it. There were a number of distinguished persons present though not a crowd. Many kind inquiries were made respecting yourself. I dine to-day at Sir Henry Holland's on purpose to meet Macaulay should his health enable him to be present. On Tuesday at Mr. Butt's & on Wednesday at Lord Granville's where there will be a party in the evening.

I have met the " woman-killer " (D'Azeglio) in the ante-chamber of the Foreign office on Wednesday last. He now seems determined to be such friends with me that in good manners I must treat him kindly. Knowing my tender point, he launched out in your praises & said such extravagant things of you as I could scarcely stand notwithstanding my weakness on this subject. Fortunately for me, before he had concluded, he was summoned to Lord Clarendon, greatly to my relief.

I think they will hesitate about sending me away, even if Mr. Crampton should receive his passports. Mr. Cobden told me the other evening at the Reform Club that Mr. Willcox, the member of Parliament from Southampton had said to Lord Palmerston:—" Well, you are about to send Buchanan away; " & his reply was, " If Buchanan should remain until I send him away, he will be here to all eternity."—This however, is *à la mode de* Palmerston & means but little one way or the other. I only repeat it as one of his jokes; & my hesitation on the subject is not, in the slightest degree, founded on this remark.

I should infer that my Presidential stock is declining in the market. I do not now receive so many love letters on the subject as formerly, always excepting the ever faithful Van Dyke & a few others. Heaven bless them! I see the best face has been put on Bigler's election, but still it is an ugly symptom. Declining prospects give me no pain. These would rather afford me pleasure, were it not for my friends. Pierce's star appears now to be in the ascendant, though I think it is not very probable he will be nominated. Heaven only knows who will be the man.

With my kindest love to Mrs. Plitt & my warmest regards to her excellent husband, I remain

Yours affectionately,

JAMES BUCHANAN.

MISS LANE.

TO MR. MARCY.[1]

No. 121.   LEGATION OF THE UNITED STATES.

LONDON, 12th February, 1856.

SIR:

I was somewhat surprised at the broad statement made by Lord Palmerston in the House of Commons on Friday night last, (vide the *Times* of Saturday morning,) " that when the communication to which I have referred [that contained in Lord Clarendon's note to me of the 16th July last,] was made to the American Minister in London, he expressed himself satisfied with the explanation and said that he felt confident that his Government would entertain a similar feeling in regard to it."

Fortunately the expression, and the only expression, verbal or written, which I employed upon the occasion is contained in my note to Lord Clarendon of the 18th July acknowledging the receipt of his note of the 16th, and is in the following language: " And the Undersigned will have much satisfaction in transmitting a copy of his Lordship's note to the Secretary of State by the next steamer."

From this you will perceive that I made no allusion whatever to what might be the opinion of my Government in regard to Lord Clarendon's note, nor did I express any opinion of my own, except what might have been inferred from the statement that I would have much satisfaction in transmitting a copy of this note to the Secretary of State.

I have never had any conversation at any time with Lord Palmerston on the subject, and the matter thus rested between Lord Clarendon and myself until after the 24th September, on which day I received your Despatch No. 107, of the 8th September, with the documents implicating Mr. Crampton in the recruitment question. From this Despatch I learned that you had resolved to conduct the subsequent correspondence yourself directly with Mr. Crampton at Washington, and this on account of his personal complicity in the affair.

Under these circumstances I had no occasion of sufficient importance to see Lord Clarendon from the 24th September until

---

[1] MSS. Department of State, 68 Despatches from England. An extract from this despatch is printed in S. Ex. Doc. 74, 34 Cong. 1 Sess. 1–3.

the 29th October, this being a season of the year when, according to the current phrase, " everybody is out of town," and all public business is suspended except in urgent cases.

On the 29th October, I called upon his Lordship by appointment for the purpose of bringing to his serious attention the question of sending a British fleet to Bermuda and Jamaica; and on this first opportunity which had presented I informed him, " That when in acknowledging the receipt of his note to me [of the 16th July,] on the subject of enlistments, I had expressed the satisfaction I should feel in forwarding it to Washington, I had not the most distant idea that Mr. Crampton was implicated in these enlistments," &c. [Vide my Despatch No. 98, of the 30th October.]

Again, at an interview with his Lordship on the 1st November, I employed substantially the same language; adding thereto that I was " sorry to say satisfactory proof existed that Mr. Crampton and other British officers had before and since [the date of his note of the 16th July,] been engaged in aiding and countenancing these proceedings and recruitments," &c. [Vide my Despatch No. 99, of the 2d November.]

I need scarcely refer to my recent Despatch No. 117, of the 1st Inst., wherein I reported to you the correction I had made in conversation with Lord Clarendon, of the statement contained in his Despatch to Mr. Crampton of the 16th November, because he had omitted from his statement the qualification which I made at the time, that when I had received his note of the 15th July I had not the least idea of Mr. Crampton's complicity in the business of recruiting.

Had Lord Palmerston, therefore, been careful to consult accuracy, he would have said:—" When the communication to which I have referred was made to the American Minister in London he expressed the satisfaction he would have in communicating it to his Government; but having subsequently learned that the British Minister at Washington was implicated in the transaction, he informed Lord Clarendon more than once that he did not know that fact when he expressed this satisfaction."

When in December last I informed you of my intention to present my letter of recall and leave the Legation on the 12th February, (this day) the President's Message had not been received, and I could not have anticipated the threatening aspect which the relations between the two countries have since assumed. Of course, urgent as are my private affairs at home, I shall not retire from the post of duty at such a moment as the present, when my unwearied exertions are every day required in attempting to do service to my country. I would, however, respectfully reiterate my request to the President that he would, as soon as may be, send out my successor. I shall expect him here in time for me to reach Lancaster, if possible, on the 1st April, where business engagements for that day require my presence.

A favorable change has taken place within the last fortnight in public opinion here, in regard to the relations between the two countries. The friendly tone of Lord Palmerston's speech on Friday night last is perhaps the best evidence of this change. Wilful and determined as he is, no man has a quicker perception of the state of public opinion than himself, or yields to it more gracefully when he cannot control it. A war with the United States, on either or both the questions pending between the two countries, would not be popular in England, unless the people could be made to believe that their honor was involved in them. That his Lordship is still sore on these questions I should infer from a brief half jocular and half serious conversation I had with him casually at a party on the next evening after he had made his speech.

On Tuesday, February 5th, when "Mr. Cobden asked whether it was the intention of the Government to lay upon the table of the House any correspondence explanatory of our present relations with the United States," &c., &c., Lord Palmerston declined to do so for the present.

On Friday evening the 8th, when Mr. Cobden again introduced the subject, referring to the pamphlet in his hand, published by Trübner & Co., to which I adverted in my Despatch No. 119, of the 5th Inst., his Lordship consented to lay the Central American Correspondence before Parliament. This change was probably produced from deference to public opinion and a knowledge of the fact that the correspondence was already before the public and in the hands of the members.

Yours very respectfully,

JAMES BUCHANAN.

HON: WILLIAM L. MARCY,
    Secretary of State.

TO GOVERNOR BIGLER.[1]

LONDON, February 12, 1856.

MY DEAR SIR:—

I did not receive your kind and friendly letter of the 21st ultimo until last evening, and although oppressed by my public duties to-day, I cannot suffer a steamer to depart without bearing you an answer.

We had been friends for many years before our friendship was suspended. The best course to pursue in renewing it again is to suffer bygones to be bygones. In this spirit I cordially accept your overtures, and shall forget everything unpleasant in our past relations. When we meet again, let us meet as though no estrangement had ever existed between us, and it shall not be my fault if we should not remain friends as long as we both may live. I wish you an honorable and useful career in the Senate.

I had hoped to return home with Miss Lane in October last, but a succession of threatening incidents has occurred in the relations between the two countries which has kept me here until the present moment. And even now I do not know when I can leave my post. My private business requires that I should be at home on the 1st of April, but no pecuniary consideration can induce me to desert my public duty at such a moment as the present. I trust, however, that by the next steamer I shall hear of the appointment of my successor.

In regard to the Presidency to which you refer, if my own wishes had been consulted, my name should never again have been mentioned in connection with that office. I feel, nevertheless, quite as grateful to my friends for their voluntary exertions in my favor during my absence, as though they had been prompted by myself. It is a consolation which I shall bear with me to my dying day, that the Democracy of my native state have sustained me with so much unanimity. I shall neither be disappointed nor in the slightest degree mortified should the Cincinnati Convention nominate another person; but in the retirement, the prospect of which is now so dear to me, the consciousness that Pennsylvania has stood by me to the last will be a delightful reflection. Our friends Van Dyke and Lynch have kept me advised of your exertions in my favor.

---

[1] Curtis's Buchanan, II. 122.

I am happy to inform you that within the last fortnight public opinion has evidently undergone a change in favor of our country. The best evidence of this is perhaps the friendly tone of Lord Palmerston's speech on Friday night last. His lordship has, however, done me injustice in attributing to me expressions which I never uttered, or rather which I never wrote, for all is in writing. All I said in relation to the matter in question was that I should have much satisfaction in transmitting a copy of Lord Clarendon's note to the Secretary of State. I never had a word with Lord Palmerston on the subject.

The moment has arrived for closing the despatch bags, and I conclude by assuring you of my renewed friendship.

Yours very respectfully,

JAMES BUCHANAN.

TO MR. MARCY.[1]

No. 122.   LEGATION OF THE UNITED STATES.
LONDON, 15 February, 1856.

SIR:

On yesterday morning, by the Baltic, I received the gratifying intelligence through the newspapers that my successor, Mr. Dallas, had been appointed and may be expected here about the end of the present month.

In reference to your Despatch No. 132, of the 11th ultimo:—I have to state that from information which I have received from J. Rodney Croskey, Esquire, United States Consul at Southampton, the American bark "Kleber," though she may touch at Cowes, will be permitted to proceed wherever she may be ordered, provided this be to the Port of a friendly Power. I have not learned that she has yet reached Cowes.

Col: Seibels, our Minister at Brussels, is now in London on a brief visit. He informs me that at Brussels, where the Russians are numerous, they and the French are on the most friendly

---

[1] MSS. Department of State, 68 Despatches from England.

terms, visiting and complimenting each other; whilst both are reserved in their intercourse with the English. He says that on the continent Lord Palmerston's speech on Friday night last is considered as an ample apology and atonement on the recruiting question. Indeed, the common conversation among the Diplomatists at Brussels was that he had gone further than it was ever supposed he would do; and had treated us much more respectfully than he had done Prussia and other neutral Powers on the continent.

Count Creptowitch, the Russian Minister at Brussels, said to Colonel Seibels that this apology of Lord Palmerston was all that we could reasonably require, and asked what more we wanted. The Colonel replied, that if an apology had been made of the character Lord Palmerston had stated, he supposed himself it would be sufficient. Then the Count remarked, it ought to be considered amply sufficient, for it was the most humiliating apology that England had ever made to any nation; and that, although he was their enemy, he thought we ought not to exact from them more than was conceded in that apology. He added that he thought we were disposed to bear down more severely on England than on any other nation.

I send you a Duplicate copy of my Despatch No. 121, of Tuesday last, the 12th Inst., which was sent to Southampton on that day to be transmitted by the Arago on Wednesday; because we have not yet (on Friday,) heard of the departure of that vessel.

Yours very respectfully,

JAMES BUCHANAN.

HON: WILLIAM L. MARCY,
    Secretary of State.

TO MR. MARCY.[1]

Private and Confidential.

LEGATION OF THE UNITED STATES,
LONDON 15 February 1856.

MY DEAR SIR:

I have received your favor of the 27th ultimo; and although the contents are very acceptable, yet, like a lady's letter, its pith and marrow are in the two Postscripts informing me that Mr. Dallas had been offered and would probably accept this Mission. By the newspapers I learn that his nomination had been sent to the Senate. It is long since I have heard such welcome news. But there is some alloy in almost every good; and in my own joy I cannot but sympathise with you for the loss of Mr. Markoe, who, the papers say, is to be appointed Secretary of Legation. Pray bear it with Christian resignation.

I need not say that I shall do all I can to give Mr. Dallas a fair start.

I have two things to request of you:—

1. Although I have no doubt the omission of Lady Palmerston to invite me to her first party was both intentional and significant *at the time,* yet I should be unwilling to leave the fact on record in a public Despatch. I will, therefore, send you by the next steamer, the same Despatch, No. 119, of the 5th Instant, with that portion of it omitted. When you receive this, please to withdraw the first Despatch and keep it for me until my return.

2. Should you, in your friendly discretion, deem it advisable under the circumstances, please to have an editorial prepared for the Union, stating the facts in my last Despatch (a duplicate of which is now sent you) in relation to the remarks of Lord Palmerston as to my expression of satisfaction with the apology contained in Lord Clarendon's note of the 16th July. I send you with this a Pamphlet which has just been published here on this subject. I know the author. He is an Englishman of character. Several members of Parliament have called upon me for information; but my position requires that I should be very chary. I have furnished some of them with copies of Hertz's trial, among

---

[1] Buchanan Papers, Historical Society of Pennsylvania; Curtis's Buchanan, II. 123.

the rest Mr. Roebuck. I met him afterwards in society, and it was evident the pamphlet had strongly impressed him with Mr. Crampton's complicity. Still, it is not to be denied that Lord Palmerston's speech on Friday last, in relation to this subject, has made a strong impression here, as it has done on the Continent, judging by the facts stated by Colonel Seibels contained in my Despatch.

I know from the tone of your letter that you would consider me in a state of mental delusion if I were to say how indifferent I feel in regard to myself on the question of the next Presidency. You would be quite a sceptic. One thing is certain: that neither by word nor letter have I ever contributed any support to myself. I believe that the next Presidential term will perhaps be the most important and responsible of any which has occurred since the origin of the Government; and whilst no competent and patriotic man to whom it may be offered should shrink from the responsibility, yet he may well accept it as the greatest trial of his life. Of course, nothing can be expected from you but a decided support to your chief.

Never forgetting my excellent and esteemed friend whose influence, I shrewdly suspect, put you in motion in regard to the appointment of a successor, I remain, as always,

　　　　　　　　Yours, very respectfully,

　　　　　　　　　　　　　JAMES BUCHANAN.

HON: WILLIAM L. MARCY.

TO MISS LANE.[1]

LEGATION OF THE UNITED STATES,
　　　　　　　LONDON 15 February 1856.

MY DEAR HARRIET/

I have received yours of the 28th ultimo, together with the valued favor of Mrs. Plitt of the same date; & also, by the Baltic, afterwards, yours of Jan: 18 & Feb: 1st.

------

[1] Buchanan Papers, private collection. Imperfectly printed in Curtis's Buchanan, II. 165.

Nothing of much importance has occurred since I wrote you last. I have been out a good deal, deeming it my duty at the present crisis to mingle with influential Society as much as possible. Everywhere you are kindly remembered. Lord & Lady Stanhope have been very particular in their inquiries about you & say much which it would be gratifying to you to hear. I promised to Mr. & Mrs. Butt that I would transmit you their kind compliments. The Duchess of Somerset begged me to say to you that at the date of her letter to you, she had not heard of your affliction.

I trust that Mr. Dallas may soon make his appearance in London; as I am exceedingly anxious to be relieved from my present position. You seem to bear " malice prepense " against that gentleman. What will you say to my reconciliation with Governor Bigler? He addressed me *such a letter* as you have scarcely ever read. It was impossible for me to avoid giving it a kind answer. I accepted his overtures & informed him that it would not be my fault if we should not always hereafter remain friends. He had often made advances to me indirectly before, which I always declined. This seems to be the era of good feeling in Pennsylvania. Davy Lynch's letters for some months past have been quite graphic & amusing. He says that " the Eleventh hour Buchanan Legion " at Harrisburg have unanimously elected him a member, for which he kindly thanked them, & at the same time advised them to work hard & diligently to make up for lost time. They responded that their exertions should be directed with a view to throw my old Fogy friends into the shade.

Notwithstanding all this, the signs of the Times are not very auspicious to my experienced eye & I shall be neither disappointed nor sorry should the Cincinnati Convention select some other person. It will, however, be always a source to me of heartfelt gratification that the Democracy of my native State have not deserted me in my old age but have been true to the last.

I am truly sorry to hear of Mr. Randall's affliction. He is an able & true hearted man to whom I am much attached. Please to remember me to him & Mrs. Randall in the kindest terms.

Your uncle John has died at a good old age with a character for integrity which he well deserved. He had a kind & excellent heart. As he advanced in life his peculiarities increased & apparently obscured his merits, in his intercourse with his relations & friends. But still he possessed [them]. For many years after he came to Lancaster we were intimate friends & we always continued friends.

I trust that Mr. Dallas may arrive by the next Collins steamer. It is my intention to act handsomely towards him. I thank Heaven that a successor has at last been appointed. Whether I shall return home soon after his arrival or go to the continent I cannot at present determine.

On the 18th December last I paid Mr. Randall for six shawls & have his bill & receipt.

At Lord Granville's dinner on Wednesday the Marquis of Lansdowne & Mr. Ellice said very pretty things about you. I know you love praise from the Aristocracy.

Colonel Seibels, our minister at Brussels, is now here with me, & I am delighted to see him. He will remain until after the Queen's Levee on the 20th. I shall leave the house on Tuesday next, on which day the inventory is to be taken; & shall most probably go to the Clarendon.

With my kindest love to Mrs. Plitt & my kindest regards to Mr. Plitt, I remain

Yours affectionately

JAMES BUCHANAN.

TO LORD CLARENDON.

(Enclosure in No. 123.[1])

LEGATION OF THE UNITED STATES,
LONDON, 16 February, 1856.

MY LORD:

Considering what has been said in the two Houses of Parliament in relation to myself, in advance of the publication of the correspondence between the two Governments on the recruitment

[1] Despatch to Mr. Marcy, No. 123, Feb. 19, 1856, infra. This note is printed in S. Ex. Doc. 74, 34 Cong. 1 Sess. 3.

question, I have deemed it a duty to communicate to your Lordship, as you are the only individual in this country to whom I could make such a communication with propriety, an extract from my Despatch of Tuesday last, the 12th Instant, to the Secretary of State upon this subject, which was transmitted to Washington on Wednesday by the steamer "Arago" from Southampton.

Yours, very respectfully,

(Signed)   James Buchanan.

The Right Honble. The Earl of Clarendon, &c., &c. &c.

TO MR. MARCY.[1]

No. 123.   Legation of The United States.
London, 19 February, 1856.
Sir:

I.have the honor to transmit to you the copy of a note which I addressed to Lord Clarendon on the 16th Instant.

Your attention has doubtless been attracted to the debate on American affairs in the House of Commons on Friday last, [15th] and reported in *The Times* the next morning, in which Mr. Roebuck, Lord Palmerston, Mr. Disraeli, and Mr. Gibson participated.

From this you will observe that Lord Palmerston, whilst refusing to lay upon the table the correspondence relating to British recruitments in the United States, has stated such facts in regard to its contents as would favor his own side of the question without the necessary and inseparable qualifications which could alone present these facts in their true character. This course of proceeding was well calculated to make an erroneous impression on the House.

---

[1] MSS. Department of State, 68 Despatches from England. The first four paragraphs of this despatch, relating to recruitment, are published in S. Ex. Doc. 74, 34 Cong. 1 Sess. 3.

This was the first official information to the British people that you had demanded the recall of Mr. Crampton and the Consuls, whilst entirely suppressing the reasons on which this demand was founded. This announcement has produced a marked impression upon the public; although well informed people had reason to know the fact previously from the American journals.

It'is now, I think, generally believed that his Administration cannot long survive the peace, which is considered a necessity. I have been informed on good authority that Lord Clarendon left London for Paris to attend the Conference, with rather gloomy forebodings as to the fate of the Ministry.

The Editorials in the *Morning Post* are far from being in the pacific spirit of Lord Palmerston's remarks in the House of Commons.

It has been stated to me by the member of the House of Commons to whom I referred in a former Despatch that Sir Henry Bulwer is quite decided in our favor so far as the surrender of Ruatan and the Bay Islands to Honduras is concerned; but although this information proceeds from a highly respectable source, I do not deem it worthy of implicit credit..

When I had progressed thus far with my Despatch, Lord Aberdeen called to see me and we had a long conversation concerning the existing state of the relations between the two countries. There is but one portion of it, however, which I have time to insert, even if I should deem it proper to make the rest the subject of a public Despatch.

I reminded him of the conversation between us on the 28th December, 1854, which I reported to you in my Despatch No. 54, of the 30th December; and informed him that, from motives of delicacy towards himself, I had requested you not to publish this Despatch with the other Central American documents, to which you had kindly assented. He thanked me for having done this; and I then informed him that I would, with his permission, be pleased to read this Despatch (No. 54) to him for the purpose of ascertaining whether my report had been correct. He replied that he would be very glad to hear it read; whereupon I sent for it and read it over to him. At the end, his Lordship said it was altogether correct;—he could not have reported it more correctly, if as correctly, himself; and that he would not hesitate to express the very same opinions in the House of Lords.

His visit was one of considerable length; and before his

departure I made him fully acquainted with the true state of the recruitment and Crampton question in contrast with the statements and suppressions of Lord Palmerston. I have communicated more to him on this subject than to any other person. His conversation throughout this interview afforded me additional evidence of his sound and mature judgment, as well as the frankness and justice of his character.

Yours very respectfully,

JAMES BUCHANAN.

HON: WILLIAM L. MARCY,
    Secretary of State.

FROM LORD CLARENDON.

(Enclosure in No. 124.[1])

FOREIGN OFFICE, February 20, 1856.

SIR:

I have the honor to acknowledge the receipt of your letter of the 16th Instant, inclosing a copy of a Despatch which you had addressed to your Government on the 12th Instant, with reference to a statement made by Viscount Palmerston on Friday the 8th Instant, "that when the communication to which I have referred (that contained in my note to you of the 16th July,) was made to the American Minister in London, he expressed himself satisfied with the explanation, and said that he felt confident that his Government would entertain a similar feeling in regard to it."

I have not failed to communicate your letter and its inclosure to Viscount Palmerston, who has requested me to state to you, in reply, that he should feel much regret if he had unintentionally misrepresented the tenor of any communication which you had made to Her Majesty's Government, but it seems to him that there is no essential difference between the substance and the effect of what he said in the House of Commons and the statement which you now make in regard to the same point.

Although it appears that he did not correctly quote the words you had used, Viscount Palmerston said in the House of Commons that you had expressed yourself satisfied with my note of the 16th of July, and that you had expressed your expectation that your Government would be so also.

You say that you only said that you had *much satisfaction* in transmitting to the United States Government a copy of my note; I cannot but

---

[1] Despatch to Mr. Marcy, No. 124, Feb. 22, 1856, infra. This note is printed in S. Ex. Doc. 74, 34 Cong. 1 Sess. 5.

think, however, that this comes to the same meaning, because you could not have felt *much satisfaction* in transmitting a copy of that note, if that note had not appeared to you to be satisfactory, and if you had not expected that it would have been so considered by your Government also.

Viscount Palmerston, moreover, with reference to that part of your Despatch to Mr. Marcy which adverts to your communication to me in October last, would beg to observe that the accuracy of his statement as to the impression produced upon your mind in July by my note of the 16th of that month cannot be affected by the tenor of your statement to me three months afterwards, on the 29th of October, founded upon communications, whether correct or incorrect, which you had then recently received from Washington.

Viscount Palmerston adds that he would be much obliged to you, if you will have the goodness to transmit to your Government a copy of this explanation on his part.

With reference to a passage in your Despatch to Mr. Marcy as to the suspension of Public Business in the Autumn when "everybody is out of town," I beg leave to observe that, with the exception of a few days when I was in attendance on the Queen during Her Majesty's visit to Paris, I was accessible during the whole of the Autumn to any of the Representatives of Foreign Powers who wished to see me, being invariably in the habit of coming to the Foreign Office for several days in each week from my country seat only a few miles from London.

I have the honor to be, with high consideration, Sir, Your most obedient humble servant,

(Signed)   CLARENDON.

THE HONBLE. JAMES BUCHANAN,
&c. &c. &c.

TO LORD CLARENDON.

(Enclosure in No. 124.[1])

LEGATION OF THE UNITED STATES,
LONDON, 22 February, 1856.

MY LORD:

I have the honor to acknowledge the receipt of your note of the 20th Instant, in answer to mine of the 16th, enclosing to your Lordship the copy of part of a Despatch addressed by me to my

---

[1] Despatch to Mr. Marcy, No. 124, Feb. 22, 1856, infra. This note is published in S. Ex. Doc. 74, 34 Cong. 1 Sess. 6.

Government on the 12th Instant; And I shall have much satisfaction in complying with the request of Viscount Palmerston and transmitting a copy of this note to the Secretary of State by to-morrow's steamer.

Your Lordship's note, I am happy to observe, proves that we are entirely agreed upon the facts of the case; and I am quite willing to leave, without further comment, the difference of opinion between Viscount Palmerston and myself, on the question as to whether the expression, that I should have much satisfaction in transmitting a copy of your note of the 16th July last to the Secretary of State, justified the statement of his Lordship in the House of Commons, that I had expressed myself satisfied with the explanation contained in that note and said I felt confident my Government would entertain a similar feeling in regard to it.

So in like manner am I willing to leave, without further comment, the question whether it was altogether just to myself in Viscount Palmerston, whilst prominently presenting his construction of what I had written in July, to be entirely silent in regard to my communication to you in October, thus unintentionally, I have no doubt, creating the impression on his audience that my opinion still remains unchanged, notwithstanding the information I had received in September and communicated to you at our next interview thereafter, respecting Mr. Crampton's complicity in the recruitment of soldiers for the British army within the territory of the United States.

But I am not willing to leave without further explanation your Lordship's notice of the reason which I assigned for not asking an interview with you in October. I did not doubt for a moment that if I had requested such an interview, even at that season of recreation, it would have been promptly granted; and this I should have done had my business been of urgent character. And I am glad to avail myself of the present occasion to express to you my grateful sense of your uniform attention to all my requests and of your invariable courtesy and kindness. These have made an impression upon me which will be enduring.

Yours, very respectfully,

JAMES BUCHANAN.

THE RIGHT HONBLE. THE EARL OF CLARENDON,
&c. &c. &c.

TO MR. MARCY.[1]

No. 124.   LEGATION OF THE UNITED STATES.
                        LONDON, 22 February, 1856.

SIR:

I have the honor to transmit to you a copy of the answer of Lord Clarendon, or rather of Lord Palmerston, (for the former is now in Paris) dated on the 20th Instant, to my note to Lord Clarendon of the 16th Instant, (a copy of which I transmitted to you with my Despatch No. 123, of the 19th Instant,) together with a copy of my reply of this date.

In this reply, I have truly said it would afford me much satisfaction to comply with Lord Palmerston's request and to transmit a copy of Lord Clarendon's note to you by to-morrow's steamer. And why? Because this note is an admission that Lord Palmerston had no other foundation for all he has said on the subject of my satisfaction with Lord Clarendon's note of the 16th July, except the fact that in acknowledging its receipt I had stated I would have much satisfaction in transmitting a copy of it to you.

The note itself, to which Lord Clarendon has signed his name, is evidently the production of a person who has placed himself in such a dilemma that every attempt he makes to escape from it only involves him in greater difficulties.

Lord Palmerston has left the impression upon his audience in the House of Commons that up to the present moment I am satisfied with the explanation of the 16th July, by remaining entirely silent in regard to the communication which I made to Lord Clarendon in October; and the excuse which he makes for this conduct is most extraordinary. According to his mode of reasoning, if you had informed me three months ago that the character of an individual was good, notwithstanding you might have afterwards called upon me and told me you had come to the knowledge of a fact which materially injured his character, I would yet be perfectly justified in publishing to the world, and this on your authority, that the character of the individual was

---

[1] MSS. Department of State, 68 Despatches from England. The first four paragraphs of this despatch, relating to recruitment, are printed in S. Ex. Doc. 74, 34 Cong. 1 Sess. 4.

still fair, without the most remote allusion to your subsequent change of opinion.

In reference to your Despatch No. 127, of the 17th December last,—I informed you in my No. 115, of the 25th January, that I had made application to Lord Clarendon for copies of the papers for the Secretary of the Treasury therein referred to. I now transmit to you the copy of a note from E. Hammond, Esquire, Under Secretary of State for Foreign Affairs, dated on the 21st Instant, in answer to my application.

Some time since, Mr. Fred'k M. Kelley, of New York, presented to me a letter of introduction from yourself; and explained the object which had brought him to Europe. This was to induce the British and French Governments, in conjunction with our own, if this could be obtained, to make a survey of the Atrato route for a thorough cut ship canal between the Atlantic and Pacific oceans. Mr. Kelley, with commendable public spirit and liberality, had caused a survey of this route to be made at his own expense, and he feels a great desire that the accuracy of this survey should be tested by a survey undertaken by the three Governments.

I had a purely private and unofficial conversation with Lord Clarendon some time since on the subject; and we entirely agreed in opinion that such parts of the Isthmus as were not already well known ought to be thoroughly explored; and if any practicable route could be found for a thorough cut canal through which vessels of burden might continue their voyages from the Atlantic to the Pacific, the interests of the commerce of the world required that it should be constructed, no matter what might be the cost. His Lordship seemed to be perfectly willing to join the United States and France, without delay, in causing this exploration to be made and the correctness of Mr. Kelley's survey to be ascertained; but I informed him I had no instructions on the subject, and I did not believe that whilst the Central American questions remained in their present situation, my Government would feel disposed to unite with the British Government in such an undertaking. I have deemed it proper thus to bring the subject to your notice.

Yours very respectfully,

JAMES BUCHANAN.

HON: WILLIAM L. MARCY,
    Secretary of State.

TO MISS LANE.[1]

LEGATION OF THE UNITED STATES,
LONDON, 22 Feb: '56.

MY DEAR HARRIET/

Another week has passed & I am happy to inform you that you are still freshly remembered by your friends & acquaintances on this side of the Atlantic. I delivered up possession of the House to the agent of Mrs. Lewis on Tuesday morning last with the exception of the offices & went to Fenton's, because I could not obtain comfortable apartments at the Clarendon. I retain the offices for the present at the rate of £10 per month, awaiting the arrival of Mr. Dallas. I earnestly hope he may be here in the Pacific which is expected at Liverpool on Wednesday or Thursday next. The two house agents, on the part of Mrs. Lewis & myself, respectively, have been employed on the inventory ever since Tuesday morning & have not yet finished.

I expect to be all ready upon the arrival of Mr. Dallas either to go home or go to the Continent, according to the then existing circumstances. At present I am quite undetermined which course I shall pursue.

You will see by the *Morning Post* that I presented Col. Seibels at the Levee on Wednesday. He paid me a visit for a week & his society afforded me great pleasure. He is both an honorable & agreeable man, as well as a tried & sincere friend. I dine with Lord & Lady Palmerston to-morrow, & with the Lord & Lady Mayoress on Wednesday, & on Thursday attend the wedding of Miss Sturgis & Mr. Coleman at 11 o'clock at the Church of " St. John, Robin Hood," close to the Robin Hood Gate of Richmond Park. Mr. Sturgis's country residence is close to this church.

I receive letters from home some of which say with reference to the Presidency,—come home immediately, & others,—stay away a while longer. I shall not regulate my conduct with any view to this office. If it be the will of Providence to bestow upon me the Presidency, I shall accept it as a duty, a burden, & a trial, & not otherwise. I shall take no step to obtain it.

---

[1] Buchanan Papers, private collection. Imperfectly printed in Curtis's Buchanan, II. 166.

Mrs. Shapter's health is delicate & John has been quite unwell. I shall not fail to leave her some token of my great regard before I leave London. She richly deserves it.

With my love to Mrs. Plitt & my warm regards to Mr. Plitt, I remain always,

Yours affectionately,

JAMES BUCHANAN.

MISS LANE.

TO MR. MARCY.[1]

No. 125.   LEGATION OF THE UNITED STATES.

LONDON, 29 February, 1856.

SIR:

Referring to your No. 123 of the 16th November, and my No. 110 of the 18th December, I have now to inform you that on Wednesday last I received from the Foreign Office the Commission and Exequatur of Mr. James Winter, appointed consul of the United States at Turk's Island, and have forwarded the same to him at his post.

Referring to your Despatch No. 93, of the 16th June last, and my No. 88, of the 4th September, I have the honor to transmit to you the copy of a letter which I addressed to the Hon: John Y. Mason, on the 6th December last, upon the request of Mr. Juan B. Alberdi, Chargé d'Affaires of the Argentine Confederation to Great Britain and France; and also an original letter in Spanish from Mr. Alberdi, dated on the 21st Instant, with a translation of the same communicated by himself.

The favorable change in the public opinion of this country towards the United States, to which I took occasion to refer in my No. 121, of the 12th Instant, has since continued to advance. Indeed, no person, unless he has been upon the spot, can appreciate the extent of this change since the meeting of Parliament on the last day of January. The savage editorials of *The Times, Morning Post,* and other London journals a few weeks ago are

----

[1] MSS. Department of State, 68 Despatches from England.

in perfect contrast with the speeches and proceedings at the Lord Mayor's dinner on Wednesday last.

Without reporting the conversation at length between Lord Aberdeen, now a private gentleman, and myself on the 19th Instant, I deem it proper to inform you that he expressed a decided opinion, under existing circumstances, in favor of arbitration. In answer to my objections, he said that in his opinion no arbitrator could be selected who would not decide the question of the Bay Islands in our favor; and for his own part, after peace was made, he should be quite willing to agree that the Emperor of Russia might be the Arbitrator. It is but just to him to add, that he thought it far from clear that the Treaty abolished the Mosquito Protectorate, though he freely admitted that it had essentially limited its use. He, however, considered this Protectorate a matter of small importance, which might be easily arranged to the satisfaction of both Governments. They were anxious to get clear of it. All they desired was that the Mosquitos should have secured to them the same right of occupancy, over a limited portion of the territory, which Indians enjoyed under the practice of Great Britain and the United States.

Although Lord Aberdeen is now out of power, and I am persuaded at his advanced age (now in his 73d year) would be unwilling to return to it, yet his opinions will always exercise great influence, especially among the governing classes of this country. He is esteemed by all as an honest, able, and wise statesman; and in regard to personal character, that of no man in England stands higher.

Mr. Appleton left this Legation on the 16th November last; and since that day, through a trying and laborious period, Mr. Benjamin Moran, the Clerk employed by myself, has performed the duties of Secretary of Legation to my entire satisfaction. He is, therefore, justly entitled to the salary, already appropriated by Congress, from that date until the arrival of another Secretary. If you should feel any difficulty, under the existing law, in ordering this to be paid to him by the Bankers of the United States in London, I trust you may be kind enough to ask authority for this purpose from Congress.

Not having heard either from yourself or Mr. Dallas since the appointment of the latter as my successor, I am left in a state of uncertainty as to the time of his arrival. I shall be prepared, however, to deliver up the Legation to him as soon after I shall hear of his arrival at Liverpool as I can possibly obtain my audience of leave from Her Majesty.

Yours, very respectfully,

JAMES BUCHANAN.

HON: WILLIAM L. MARCY,
    Secretary of State.

(Enclosure in No. 125.)

PARIS, 21st Feby. 1856.

To THE HONOURABLE JAMES BUCHANAN.
    &c. &c. &c.

DEAR SIR,

I have the honour to communicate to you that the reclaims of the Argentine Confederation on the French Government have been attended to in a satisfactory manner for the general interests of commerce and fluviatic navigation in yonder country.

The Emperor of the French has agreed to change his Legation in the river Plate, recalling Mr. Le Moyne, which had accredited himself near the province of Buenos Ayres as well as the capital of the Confederation.

Monsieur Lefebvre de Becour has been appointed in his stead as Minister Plenipotentiary, in order to reside in the city of *Paraná,* Capital of the Confederation, without accrediting himself in Buenos Ayres.

This change has been communicated to me on the 8th of the present month by Monsieur Le Comte Walewski, Minister for foreign affairs.

I have reasons to believe that the motives which the French Governmt. has had in view, for causing this modification in his policy in the river Plate, one of them has been the example lately given by the Governmt. of the United States and also the desire of being uniform.

May it then please you, Sir, to accept the thanks that I present you in the name of my country, for the co-operation of the United States, whose organ you had the goodness to be in London & Paris. I also believe to have made use of this kindness with the greatest discretion.

Lord Clarendon has equally communicated to me that the Government of H. B. M. would send a Minister Plenipotentiary to the Paraná, and no longer a Chargé d'Affaires as was first appointed.

I hope you will allow me to express the desire that you will have the goodness to acquaint the Government of the United States with this news.

Concerning you, Sir, I have the honour to wish you the greatest felicity in returning to your country, and to consider me as one of your most respectful servants, with which sentiment I have the honour to be &c. &c.

(signed)   JUAN B. ALBERDI.
Chargé d'Affaires of the Argentine Confederation.

TO MR. REED.[1]

Private.   LEGATION OF THE UNITED STATES,

LONDON 29 February 1856.

MY DEAR SIR/

Many thanks for your kind letter of the 7th Instant!

It rarely happens that a party man can change his party name, even although his principles may remain unchanged, without reproach. In regard to yourself, however, & the gentlemen you have named, such a change of name can expose you to no censure. It is quite impossible that you should become Know Nothings or Free Soilers; & you have no place to go except to the Democratic party, which has now become the only true conservative party of the Country. We have differed upon several important public questions; but these have been all decided, & I know not the practical political question existing at the present moment on which we hold contrary opinions. You will, therefore, pardon me for saying, if I had been a whig in your situation, I should without hesitation act with the party holding my principles, just as though I had been called a Democrat all my life. In this I should adopt no half-way measures, but would, in a prudent manner, make myself be felt for what I was worth. From what I have said, you will infer my opinion in regard to the question whether you should act in a separate organised form or individually.

I should do injustice to my own feelings were I not to express my pride & gratification in the knowledge that you & those whom you represent entertain an opinion so favorable to myself. You may be assured that this, on my part, is warmly & gratefully reciprocated. In regard to the connection of my name with the Presidency in the present canvass, strange as it may seem to you, I have had no part, either directly or indirectly. In the beginning I did all I could to prevent any movement in my favor; & what has since been done has been entirely spontaneous, at least so far as I am personally concerned. I had hoped & believed that my public life would terminate with my present mission, but events must now take their course at the Cincinnati Convention. Never, however, did any man in my position care so little as to

---

[1] Buchanan Papers, Historical Society of Pennsylvania.

what this may be. I make these remarks to excuse myself for saying I scarcely know to what friend I can refer you, in compliance with your suggestion. I shall name Arnold Plumer, the Canal Commissioner, to whom you may, if you think proper, read this letter. He is prudent, sagacious, & discreet, & perfectly faithful & honest. I believe I have received but one letter from him since I have been in Europe, & this not upon the subject of the Presidency. He has been my devoted friend, personally & politically, for more than a quarter of a century, & is so at the present moment.

I am warmly attached to James C. Van Dyke, the District Attorney. He is able & energetic & is as true as steel. I have the most perfect confidence in him. I do not think he stands as high among you in Philadelphia as he deserves, but he will yet make his mark. You may speak to him with perfect unreserve. I shall neither write to Plumer nor Van Dyke, because this might in some degree commit you; *but I am quite willing you should shew them this letter, if you think proper, or rather make known to them such parts of its contents as you may deem expedient.* Should you have an opportunity, you might converse with Senator Slidell at Washington.

The time of my return home is uncertain, though I am very anxious to be relieved from the mission. Should Mr. Dallas arrive here by the middle of March, as I confidently expect, I shall then, Deo volente, pass a month in Paris & on the continent, & return home some time in April.

Yours very respectfully

James Buchanan.

Wm. B. Reed, Esquire.

TO MISS LANE.[1]

LEGATION OF THE UNITED STATES,
LONDON, 29 Feb: 1856.

MY DEAR HARRIET/

   . . . .[2] I dined with the Queen on Wednesday last, & had a pleasant time of it. I took the Duchess of Argyle in to dinner; & sat between her & the Princess Royal. With the latter I had much pleasant conversation. She spoke a great deal of you & made many inquiries about you; stated how very much pleased she had been with you. The Queen, also, spoke of you kindly & inquired in a cordial manner about you. Indeed, it would seem you were a favorite of both. There has been a marked & favorable change of feeling here within the last month towards the United States. I am now made something of a lion wherever I go;—& I go much into society as a matter of duty. The sentiment & proceeding at the Mansion House on Wednesday last were quite remarkable. Perhaps it is just as well I received the command to dine with the Queen on that day.

   I am yet in ignorance as to the time when Mr. Dallas may be expected to arrive. The moment I learn he has arrived in Liverpool I shall apply for my audience of leave & joyfully surrender the Legation to him with the least possible delay. . . .

Yours affectionately

JAMES BUCHANAN.

MISS LANE.

FROM LORD CLARENDON.

(Enclosure in No. 126.[3])

FOREIGN OFFICE, March 3, 1856.

SIR: I have the honor to acknowledge the receipt of your further letter of the 22d instant, respecting Viscount Palmerston's language in the House of Commons on the subject of the communication, with regard to the recruiting

---

[1] Buchanan Papers, private collection; Curtis's Buchanan, II. 166.

[2] The first sheet of this letter is missing.

[3] Despatch to Mr. Marcy, No. 126, March 7, 1856. This note is printed in S. Ex. Doc. 74, 34 Cong. 1 Sess. 7.

question, which you addressed to me on the 18th July, in reply to my letter of the 16th of that month.

I have communicated your letter to Viscount Palmerston, who has observed upon it that you are mistaken in supposing that he had made no mention of your communication on the same subject in October last, for he distinctly stated that in the autumn, and a considerable time after your communication of July, the United States government had reopened the matter which her Majesty's government had been led to believe had been closed in a satisfactory manner by my letter of the 16th of July.

I beg to thank you for your kind expressions towards myself, and to assure you that I shall always look back with sincere satisfaction to the friendly and agreeable relations which have subsisted between us during your residence in England.

I have the honor to be, with the highest consideration, sir, your most obedient humble servant,

CLARENDON.

HON. JAMES BUCHANAN, &c., &c., &c.

TO MR. MARCY.[1]

No. 126.   LEGATION OF THE UNITED STATES.
                                LONDON, 7 March, 1856.

SIR:

I have the honor to transmit to you the copy of a note dated on the 3d Instant, which I have received from Lord Clarendon in answer to mine of the 22d ultimo, addressed to his Lordship, a copy of which was forwarded to you with my No. 124.

Upon the perusal of this note, I think you will agree with me that this last effort of Lord Palmerston to extricate himself from the dilemma in which he has placed himself by his speeches in the House of Commons has served only to make the awkwardness of his position still more conspicuous.

I transmit a Duplicate of my Despatch (No. 114) of the 22d January last, the original having been forwarded to you by

---

[1] MSS. Department of State, 68 Despatches from England; S. Ex. Doc. 74, 34 Cong. 1 Sess. 7.

the Pacific; though I trust in Heaven that the next steamer will bring us advices of her safe arrival in the United States.

Yours, very respectfully,

JAMES BUCHANAN.

HON: WILLIAM L. MARCY,
    Secretary of State.

TO MISS LANE.[1]

LEGATION OF THE UNITED STATES,
LONDON 7 March 1856.

MY DEAR HARRIET/

I received your two letters of February 15th & 19th on Monday last, on my return from Mr. Lampson's, where I went on Saturday evening. Both Mr. & Mrs. L. talked much & kindly of you & desired to be remembered to you. . . .[2] I shall expect Mr. Dallas about the middle of next week & intend soon after his arrival to cross over to Paris. I hope to be at home some time in April; but when I cannot now inform you.

I am glad to learn that you purpose to go to New York.

It was very kind in you to jog my memory about what I should bring you from Paris. I know not what may be the result. *Nous verrons.*

Becky Smith is a damsel in distress, intelligent & agreeable & a country-woman in a strange land. Her conduct in London has been unexceptionable, & she is making her way in the world. She has my sympathy, & I have given her "a lift" whenever I could with propriety.

I delivered your letter to the Duchess of Somerset on Monday last, & she was delighted with it. She handed it to me to read. It was well & feelingly written. I was sorry to perceive

---

[1] Buchanan Papers, private collection. Imperfectly printed in Curtis's Buchanan, II. 167.
[2] A sentence is here omitted.

that you complained of your health; but you will, I trust, come out with the birds in the spring, restored & renovated. I am pleased with what you say concerning Senator Welsh.

In writing to me I think you had better direct to me at Paris to the care of Mr. Mason, giving him his appropriate style, & you need not pay the postage. Better not, indeed. But you will scarcely have time to write a single letter there before I shall probably have left. I shall continue to write to you; but you need not continue to write to me more than once after the receipt of this letter, unless I should advise you differently by the next steamer.

Mr. Bates is quite unwell, & I fear he is breaking up very fast. At the wedding of Miss Sturgis the other day as I approached to take my seat beside Madame Van de Weyer, she said, "Unwilling as you may be, you are now compelled to sit beside me." Of course I replied that this was no compulsion but a great privilege. Mrs. Bates complains much that Mrs. Lawrence has not written to her.

With warm affection to Mrs. Plitt & my kindest regards to Mr. Plitt, I remain yours affectionately

JAMES BUCHANAN.

MISS LANE.

TO LORD CLARENDON.

(Enclosure in No. 127.[1])

LEGATION OF THE UNITED STATES,
LONDON, 10 March, 1856.

MY LORD:

I have the honor to acknowledge the receipt of your note of the 3d Instant, on which I beg to make a single remark.

I am content that my note to your Lordship of the 22d ultimo shall speak for itself. It relates to myself personally and

---

[1] Despatch to Mr. Marcy, No. 127, March 14, 1856, infra. This note is printed in S. Ex. Doc. 74, 34 Cong. 1 Sess. 8.

not in the slightest degree to the conduct of my Government.
For this reason, justice to them requires I should state, that they
never " reopened," because they never had closed the recruitment
question, neither did they, to my knowledge, at any period express
their satisfaction with your Lordship's note of the 16th July, nor
did I ever say or intimate, on any occasion, that they had been
thus satisfied.

Yours, very respectfully,

(Signed)   JAMES BUCHANAN.

THE RIGHT HONBLE. THE EARL OF CLARENDON, &c. &c. &c.

TO LORD CLARENDON.

(Enclosure in No. 127.[1])

LEGATION OF THE UNITED STATES,
LONDON, 10 March, 1856.

MY LORD:

On the 13th May 1854, the American bark " S. W. Nash,"
owned by Mr. O. K. Ware, a respectable merchant of New York,
cleared from the port on a voyage to Africa, with a quantity of
casks on board *" shooked "* in bundles, for the purpose of bringing back Palm oil.   In July, 1854, this vessel was seized by the
British authorities at Bathurst, and was detained more than a
month during the most sickly season of the year, in consequence
of which the Master, first mate, and several of the crew died and
the voyage was much deranged, greatly to the loss of the owner.
The reason assigned for this seizure was that the number of
casks on board being more than sufficient to contain water for
the crew, a suspicion arose that the vessel might be engaged in
the slave trade.   Whilst it cannot be denied that this circumstance
afforded some ground of suspicion, yet, standing alone, it is
conceived that if the authorities at Bathurst had made proper

---

[1] Despatch to Mr. Marcy, No. 127, March 14, 1856, infra.

inquiries into the case, they might easily have discovered that this vessel was engaged in a fair and lawful trade, and that the casks were intended to contain Palm oil and not water for slaves. And this more especially, as I am informed it is quite usual to carry these casks on board of vessels, both from England and the United States, for the purpose of holding Palm oil; because they cannot be obtained on the Coast of Africa.

Without presenting any claim for damages in this case, I have been instructed to bring the subject to the notice of your Lordship; and I would respectfully suggest the propriety of intimating to the British authorities on the Coast of Africa to be more careful hereafter, in regard to the seizure and detention of American vessels under such circumstances. The very fact that the " S. W. Nash " sought a British Port was in itself strong evidence that she had not been fitted out for the slave trade and did not intend to pursue it.

Yours, very respectfully,

(Signed)   JAMES BUCHANAN.

THE RIGHT HONBLE. THE EARL OF CLARENDON,
    &c. &c. &c.

TO LORD CLARENDON.

(Enclosure in No. 127.[1])

The Undersigned, Envoy Extraordinary and Minister Plenipotentiary of the United States, has the honor to inform the Earl of Clarendon, Her Majesty's Principal Secretary of State for Foreign Affairs, that he has been entrusted with the delivery of a Letter of Recall, addressed to Her Majesty by the President of the United States, stating that he had acceded to the wish of the Undersigned and granted him permission to retire from his Mission,—a copy of which is herewith transmitted to the Earl of Clarendon. In consequence thereof, the

---

[1] Despatch to Mr. Marcy, No. 127, March 14, 1856, infra.

Undersigned would respectfully request that Her Majesty may be graciously pleased to grant him an audience of leave for the purpose of delivering the original of this letter, and assuring Her Majesty of the sincere desire of the President to foster and extend the amicable intercourse happily subsisting between the two nations, and his most earnest wishes for Her Majesty's happiness, as well as for the prosperity of the British Empire.

The Undersigned has the honor to renew to the Earl of Clarendon the assurance of his distinguished consideration.

(Signed)   JAMES BUCHANAN.

LEGATION OF THE UNITED STATES,
    LONDON 14th March, 1856.

THE RIGHT HONBLE. THE EARL OF CLARENDON,
    &c. &c. &c.

TO MR. MARCY.[1]

No. 127.   LEGATION OF THE UNITED STATES.
                        LONDON, 14 March, 1856.

SIR:

I have the honor to transmit you a copy of my note of the 10th Instant, in reply to Lord Clarendon's note of the 3d.

In reference to your No. 131, of the 29th December last, and my No. 115, of the 25th January, 1856, I transmit a copy of a note addressed by me to Lord Clarendon on the 10th Instant.

Having learned the arrival of Mr. Dallas at Liverpool on yesterday afternoon by a Telegraphic despatch from Mr. Hawthorne, and that it was his intention to set out for London to-morrow morning, I addressed a note this morning to Lord Clarendon requesting from Her Majesty an audience of leave,

---

[1] MSS. Department of State, 68 Despatches from England. The first paragraph of this despatch, with the copy of the note therein mentioned, is printed in S. Ex. Doc. 74, 34 Cong. 1 Sess. 8.

(a copy of which I now transmit;) and took it to the Foreign Office in person. In the absence of Lord Clarendon, I made a personal request to Lord Wodehouse, Under Secretary of State for Foreign Affairs, to have this audience granted, if possible, on to-morrow, Monday, or Tuesday next; which I hope may be accomplished.

I have this morning received from you a number of copies of the Correspondence on the Recruitment Question, submitted to the Senate on the 28th ultimo, and also of that on the Arbitration Question, submitted on the 29th; of which I shall make the best use in my power during the two or three days I may remain in the Legation.

Yours very respectfully,

JAMES BUCHANAN.

HON: WILLIAM L. MARCY,
  Secretary of State.

TO MISS LANE.[1]

LEGATION OF THE UNITED STATES,
LONDON, 14 March, '56.

MY DEAR HARRIET/

I tell you the simple truth when I say I have no time to-day to write to you at length. Mr. Dallas arrived at Liverpool yesterday afternoon & is to leave there to-morrow at 9 for London. So the consul telegraphed to me. I have heard nothing from him since his appointment. I expect an audience of leave from the Queen early next week, & shall then, God willing, pass over to the Continent.[2]

I have this morning received your two letters of the 25th & 29th & congratulate you on your arrival in New York. I hope you may have an agreeable time of it. Your letter of the 25th

---

[1] Buchanan Papers, private collection; Curtis's Buchanan, II. 168.

[2] Two sentences of a personal nature are here omitted.

is excellent.   I like its tone & manner very much; & am sorry
I have not time to write you at length in reply.   I am, also,
pleased with that of the 29th.   I send by the Bag the Daguerreo-
type of our excellent friend Mrs. Shapter.   I have had mine
taken for her.   I think hers is very good.   I saw her yesterday
in greatly improved health & in fine spirits.

With my love to Mrs. Plitt & my kindest regards to Mr.
Plitt, I remain always yours affectionately

JAMES BUCHANAN.

MISS LANE.

TO MR. MARCY.[1]

No. 128.   LEGATION OF THE UNITED STATES.

LONDON, 17 March, 1856.

SIR:

Referring to my No. 127, of the 14th Instant, and your No.
131, of 29th December last, I have the honor to transmit to you
the copy of a note which I received on Saturday last from Lord
Wodehouse, Under Secretary of State for Foreign Affairs.

On Saturday last, (the 15th Inst.) I had my audience of
leave of the Queen and delivered to Her Majesty my Letter of
Recall.   In presenting it I assured Her Majesty, in obedience
to its purport, of the sincere desire of the President to foster
and extend the amicable intercourse happily subsisting between
the two nations and his earnest wishes for Her Majesty's happiness, as well as for the prosperity of Her Empire.   To this I
added the expression of my own individual wishes that the most
friendly relations might always exist between the two countries,
and also my grateful sense of the uniform kindness with which
Her Majesty had treated me whenever I had enjoyed the privilege
of being in Her presence.

Her Majesty, in a feeling and kind manner, responded to
the sentiments of the President, expressing a strong desire on
Her part to cultivate the most friendly relations with the United

---

[1] MSS. Department of State, 68 Despatches from England.

States.   Her Majesty then made a request to me of a purely private nature, with which I promised to comply, and after some further brief conversation, of no public importance, I took leave of Her Majesty and Prince Albert.

At this interview, Lord Palmerston officiated for the Earl of Clarendon, now absent in Paris, and Sir Edward Cust, as Master of the Ceremonies, was also present.

I have this day delivered up the Legation with the books and archives to Mr. Dallas.

Mr. Moran has ceased to perform the duties of Secretary of Legation.   His claim, therefore, for salary will be from the 16th November, 1855, until the 16th March, 1856, at $2500 per annum, amounting to $833.33⅓,—to which, in my opinion, he is fairly and justly entitled.

Every item of business has been brought up by Mr. Moran until the present moment, so that Philip N. Dallas, Esquire, the new Secretary of Legation, will not be encumbered with any remnants.   He has, also, made a full and perfect inventory of the Books, archives, and papers belonging to the Legation, which he will deliver to Mr. Dallas.   This will, therefore, serve both for Mr. Dallas and myself.

I transmit the copy of a note of the 15th Instant, this moment received from the Foreign Office, acknowledging the receipt of mine of the 10th, signed by E. Hammond, Under Secretary of State for Foreign Affairs, but no doubt dictated by Lord Palmerston, now acting for Lord Clarendon during the absence of the latter in Paris.

I also send the copy of a note from Lord Clarendon, of the 15th February, preparatory to his departure for the Paris Conference.

Yours, very respectfully,

JAMES BUCHANAN.

HON: WILLIAM L. MARCY,
    Secretary of State.

(Enclosure in No. 128.)

FOREIGN OFFICE, March 15th, 1856.

SIR:

I have the honor to acknowledge the receipt of your letter of the 10th Instant, stating, with reference to my Letter of the 3d, that your Government never " reopened," because they never had closed, the recruitment question;

neither did they, to your knowledge, at any period express their satisfaction with my note of the 16th of July, nor did you ever say or intimate on any occasion that they had been thus satisfied.

I am with great truth and regard, Sir,

Your most obedient humble servant,

(Signed) E. HAMMOND.

In the absence of the Earl of Clarendon.

THE HONBLE. JAMES BUCHANAN,
&c. &c. &c.

TO MISS LANE.[1]

FENTON'S HOTEL

LONDON 18 March 1856.

MY DEAR HARRIET/

The arrival of the Steamer which left New York on the 5th Instant has not yet been announced.

The Queen, at my audience of Leave, on Saturday, desired to be kindly remembered to you.

The Marquis of Lansdowne at parting from me said:—
" If Miss Lane should have the kindness to remember me, do me the honor to lay me at her feet."

I have seen the Dallases & treated them with gentlemanly civility & kindness. I expressed much solicitude about your health (which I had some reason for doing from your letter to the Duchess of Somerset) & asked if any of them had happened to see you a short time before their departure. This inquiry evidently produced embarrassment. Mrs. D. regretted extremely that when they had called to see you, you were out; & that when you had returned their call, they were out. Mr. Dallas, or some of them, mentioned that he had seen you at the theatre & that you were looking well & healthy. Mr. Dallas had told Mr. Plitt he should be most happy to bring any thing from you to me.[2]

---

[1] Buchanan Papers, private collection.
[2] Two sentences of a personal nature are here omitted.

Old Robert Owen came in & has kept me so long that I must cut this letter short.   I go to Paris, God willing, on Thursday next in company with Messrs. Campbell & Croskey, our Consuls. ––I send a letter from James which I have rec'd––open.

Yours affectionately

JAMES BUCHANAN.

MISS LANE.

————————

TO MISS LANE.[1]

LEGATION OF THE UNITED STATES,

BRUSSELS 27 March '56.

MY DEAR HARRIET/

I write this in the Legation of Col: Seibels.   He & I intend to go to-morrow to the Hague on a visit to Mr. Belmont, from which I propose to return to Paris on Tuesday or Wednesday next.   It is my purpose, God willing, to leave for Havre for home in the Arago on Wednesday the 9th of April.   I do not believe that a more comfortable vessel or a better or safer Captain . exists.   All who have crossed the Atlantic with him speak in the same terms both of his ship & himself.

I shall return to Mr. Mason's at Paris; because I could not do otherwise without giving offence.   What a charming family it is!   Judge Mason, though somewhat disabled, has a much more healthy appearance, & in the face resembles much more his former self, than he did when attending the Ostend conference. The redness & sometimes blueness of his face have disappeared & he now looks as he did in former years.   I shall defer all accounts of my doings on the continent until after we meet.   I may or I may not write to you once more before embarking.

With my kindest love to Mrs. Plitt, & my warm regards to Mr. Plitt, I remain always yours affectionately

JAMES BUCHANAN.

MISS LANE.

————————

[1] Buchanan Papers, private collection.   Imperfectly printed in Curtis's Buchanan, II. 168.

P. S.　You might let Eskridge & Miss Hetty know at what time I shall probably be at home,—though I do not wish it to be noised abroad.　You cannot calculate our passage to be less than two weeks.　Should I reach my native shore on my birthday the 23 April, I shall thank God & be content.　The Arago takes the Southern route to keep clear of the Ice.

TO MISS LANE.[1]

PARIS 3 April 1856.

MY DEAR HARRIET/

I returned from the Hague last evening after a most agreeable visit, & now have only time to say that, God willing, I shall leave Havre by the Arago for home on the 9th Instant.—I recd. a very large packet of letters from London this morning, among the rest two from yourself, none of which I have time to answer before the departure of the mail.　I shall send yours to Mrs. Shapter to London to-day.

With my love to Mrs. Plitt & my kind regards to Mr. P. I remain always

Yours affectionately

JAMES BUCHANAN.

MISS LANE.

SPEECH, APRIL 24, 1856,

AT NEW YORK.[2]

FRIENDS AND FELLOW-CITIZENS: I can scarcely describe the emotions I feel at the present moment, in view of the vast crowd of my fellow-citizens of the great commercial emporium of the

---

[1] Buchanan Papers, private collection.

[2] Horton's Life of Buchanan, 401. Horton refers to this speech in these words: "A brief speech delivered by Mr. Buchanan from the balcony of the Everett House, where he stopped, to a large crowd of persons who had assembled to serenade him, is so full of earnest feeling, that we give the principal portion."

Union. I have been for years abroad in a foreign land, and I like the noise of the democracy! My heart responds to the acclamations of the noble citizens of this favored country. I have been abroad in other lands; I have witnessed arbitrary power; I have contemplated the people of other countries; but there is no country under God's heavens where a man feels to his fellow-man, except in the United States. If you could feel how despotism looks on; how jealous the despotic powers of the world are of our glorious institutions, you would cherish the Constitution and Union to your hearts, next to your belief in the Christian religion—the Bible for Heaven and the Constitution of your country for earth.

TO PRESIDENT PIERCE.[1]

(*Private.*)   WHEATLAND, near LANCASTER,

29th April, 1856.

MY DEAR SIR:

I arrived at home on Saturday night last.

It was my desire to proceed directly to Washington & wait upon you without delay; but such was the condition of my private affairs here, or rather of others committed to my charge, that I found this would be highly prejudicial to their interests.

I am not aware that I have any information to communicate to you not already in your possession. Nevertheless, as you may have some questions to propound in regard to our relations with Great Britain which have not occurred to me, it is my purpose to visit Washington for a few days about the end of next week. Besides, I have my accounts to settle. I should go sooner but for an important engagement on Thursday week.

I saw Lord Clarendon twice during my brief visit to Paris, & conversed with him as a private citizen. He is evidently well posted up concerning what passes at Washington & who are the authors of the articles in the Union against England, & either

----

[1] Buchanan Papers, Historical Society of Pennsylvania.

believes or affects to believe that a settled hostility exists on the part of your administration towards that country.   I did not much like the tone of his conversation.

With my kindest regards to Mrs. Pierce, I remain as ever, very respectfully your friend,

JAMES BUCHANAN.

HIS EXCELLENCY FRANKLIN PIERCE.

TO MR. CLAYTON.[1]

WHEATLAND, near LANCASTER
30 May 1856.

MY DEAR SIR,

I know you will pardon me for not having called at your Lodgings whilst I was at Washington.   I fully intended to do this, but found it impracticable.   Had there been any necessity for it, I should have run away from my friends; but we are in such perfect accord on the Construction of the Clayton and Bulwer Treaty, that any conference between us was quite unnecessary.   I desire to repeat my thanks to you for the very able and kind manner in which you have sustained my diplomatic course on this question.   "Laus est a te laudari."

With sentiments of the highest respect
I remain yours truly

JAMES BUCHANAN.

HON: JOHN M. CLAYTON.

---

[1] Clayton MSS. Library of Congress.

SPEECH, JUNE 8, 1856.[1]

Gentlemen :—

I thank you, with all my heart, for the kind terms in which, under a resolution of the late Democratic State Convention, you have informed me that I am " their unanimous choice for the next Presidency."

When the proceedings of your convention reached me in a foreign land, they excited emotions of gratitude which I might in vain attempt to express.   This was not because the Democracy of my much-loved State had by their own spontaneous movement placed me in nomination for the Presidency, an honor which I had not sought, but because this nomination constitutes of itself the highest evidence that, after a long course of public services, my public conduct has been approved by those to whom I am indebted, under Providence, for all the offices and honors I have ever enjoyed.   In success and in defeat, in the sunshine and in the storm, they have ever been the same kind friends to me, and I value their continued confidence and good opinion far above the highest official honors of my country.

The duties of the President, whosoever he may be, have been clearly and ably indicated by the admirable resolutions of the convention which you have just presented to me, and all of which, without reference to those merely personal to myself, I heartily adopt.   Indeed, they met my cordial approbation from the moment when I first perused them on the other side of the Atlantic.   They constitute a platform broad, national, and conservative, and one eminently worthy of the Democracy of our great and good old State.

These resolutions, carried into execution with inflexibility and perseverance, precluding all hope of changes, and yet in a kindly spirit, will ere long allay the dangerous excitement which has for some years prevailed on the subject of domestic slavery, and again unite all portions of our common country in the ancient bonds of brotherly affection, under the flag of the Constitution and the Union.

---

[1] Curtis's Buchanan, II. 169. This speech was made to a committee which waited upon Mr. Buchanan at Wheatland, to present to him certain resolutions unanimously adopted by the Democratic State Convention, declaring him to be the first choice of the Pennsylvania Democracy for the Presidency.

SPEECH, JUNE 9, 1856.[1]

GENTLEMEN OF THE KEYSTONE CLUB: I give you a most hearty and warm welcome to my abode. I congratulate you, not upon my nomination, but upon the glorious privilege of being citizens of our great Republic. Your superiority over the people of other countries has been fully demonstrated by the conduct of a vast concourse assembled during the past week at Cincinnati. Upon any similar occasion in Europe, the voluntary expression of the people would have been drowned in martial music, and their actions controlled by an army with banners. How unlike the spectacle at Cincinnati, where delegates from the people of the different States met in convention under protection of the Constitution and laws, and harmoniously deliberated upon subjects of vital importance to the country! Gentlemen, two weeks since I should have made you a longer speech, but now I have been placed upon a platform of which I most heartily approve, and that can speak for me. Being the representative of the great Democratic party, and not simply James Buchanan, I must square my conduct according to the platform of the party, and insert no new plank, nor take one from it. That platform is sufficiently broad and national for the whole Democratic party. This glorious party, now more than ever, has demonstrated that it is the true conservative party of the Constitution and of the Union.

TO THE COMMITTEE OF NOTIFICATION.[2]

WHEATLAND (near LANCASTER), June 16, 1856.

GENTLEMEN: I have the honor to acknowledge the receipt of your communication of the 13th instant, informing me officially of my nomination by the Democratic National Conven-

---

[1] This speech was made to the Keystone Club of Philadelphia, at Wheatland. (See Cong. Globe, June 9, 1856, 34 Cong. 1 Sess., Appendix, 1200.)

[2] Horton's Buchanan, 414-418.

tion, recently held at Cincinnati, as the democratic candidate for the office of President of the United States. I shall not attempt to express the grateful feelings which I entertain towards my democratic fellow-citizens for having deemed me worthy of this, the highest political honor on earth—an honor such as the people of no other country have the power to bestow. Deeply sensible of the vast and varied responsibility attached to the station, especially at the present crisis of our affairs, I have carefully refrained from seeking the nomination either by word or by deed. Now that it has been offered by the democratic party, I accept it with diffidence in my own abilities, but with an humble trust that, in the event of my election, I may be enabled to discharge my duty in such a manner as to allay domestic strife, preserve peace and friendship with foreign nations, and promote the best interests of the republic.

In accepting the nomination, I need scarcely say that I accept in the same spirit the resolutions constituting the platform of principles erected by the convention. To this platform I intend to confine myself throughout the canvass, believing that I have no right, as the candidate of the democratic party, by answering interrogatories, to present new and different issues before the people.

It will not be expected that in this answer I should specially refer to the subject of each of the resolutions, and I shall, therefore, confine myself to the two topics now most prominently before the people.

And, in the first place, I cordially concur in the sentiments expressed by the convention on the subject of civil and religious liberty. No party founded on religious or political intolerance towards one class of American citizens, whether born in our own or in a foreign land, can long continue to exist in this country. We are all equal before God and the Constitution; and the dark spirit of despotism and bigotry which would create odious distinctions among our fellow-citizens will be speedily rebuked by a free and enlightened public opinion.

The agitation of the question of domestic slavery has too long distracted and divided the people of this Union and alienated their affections from each other. This agitation has assumed many forms since its commencement, but it now seems to be directed chiefly to the territories; and, judging from its present character, I think we may safely anticipate that it is rapidly approaching a " finality." The recent legislation of Congress respecting domestic slavery, derived, as it has been, from the original and pure fountain of legitimate political power, the will of the majority, promises ere long to allay the dangerous excitement. This legislation is founded upon principles as ancient as free government itself, and, in accordance with them, has simply declared that the people of a territory, like those of a State, shall decide for themselves whether slavery shall or shall not exist within their limits.

The Nebraska-Kansas act does no more than give the force of law to this elementary principle of self-government, declaring it to be " the true intent and meaning of this act not to legislate slavery into any Territory or State, nor to exclude it therefrom, but to leave the people thereof perfectly free to form and regulate their domestic institutions in their own way, subject only to the Constitution of the United States." This principle will surely not be controverted by any individual of any party professing devotion to popular government. Besides, how vain and illusory would any other principle prove in practice in regard to the Territories! This is apparent from the fact admitted by all, that, after a Territory shall have entered the Union and become a State, no Constitutional power would then exist which could prevent it from either abolishing or establishing slavery, as the case may be, according to its sovereign will and pleasure.

Most happy would it be for the country if this long agitation were at an end. During its whole progress it has produced no practical good to any human being, whilst it has been the source of great and dangerous evils. It has alienated and estranged one portion of the Union from the other, and has even seriously threatened its very existence. To my own personal knowledge, it has produced the impression among foreign nations that our great and glorious confederacy is in constant danger of dissolution. This does us serious injury, because acknowledged power and stability always command respect among nations, and are among the best securities against unjust aggression, and in favor of the maintenance of honorable peace.

May we not hope that it is the mission of the democratic party, now the only surviving conservative party of the country, ere long to overthrow all sectional parties, and restore the peace, friendship, and mutual confidence which prevailed in the good old time among the different members of the confederacy? Its character is strictly national, and it therefore asserts no principle for the guidance of the federal government which is not adopted and sustained by its members in each and every State. For this reason it is the same determined foe of all geographical parties, so much and so justly dreaded by the Father of his Country. From its very nature it must continue to exist so long as there is a Constitution and a Union to preserve. A conviction of these truths has induced many of the purest, the ablest, and most independent of our former opponents, who have differed from us in times gone by upon old and extinct party issues, to come into our ranks and devote themselves with us to the cause of the Constitution and the Union. Under these circumstances, I most cheerfully pledge myself, should the nomination of the convention be ratified by the people, that all the power and influence Constitutionally possessed by the Executive shall be exerted, in a firm but conciliatory spirit, during the single term I shall remain in office, to restore the same harmony among the sister States which prevailed before this apple of discord, in the form of slavery agitation, had been cast into their midst. Let the members of the family abstain from intermeddling with the exclusive domestic concerns of each other, and cordially unite on the basis of perfect equality among themselves, in promoting the great national objects of common interest to all, and the good work will be instantly accomplished.

In regard to our foreign policy, to which you have referred in your communication, it is quite impossible for any human foreknowledge to prescribe positive rules in advance to regulate the conduct of a future administration in all the exigencies which may arise in our various and ever-changing relations with foreign powers. The federal government must, of necessity, exercise a sound discretion in dealing with international questions as they may occur; but this under the strict responsibility which the executive must always feel to the people of the United States, and the judgment of posterity. You will, therefore, excuse me for not entering into particulars; whilst I heartily concur with you in the general sentiment, that our foreign affairs ought to be conducted with such wisdom and firmness, as to assure the prosperity of the people at home, whilst the interests and honor of our country are wisely, but inflexibly, maintained abroad. Our foreign policy ought ever to be based upon the principle of doing justice to all nations, and requiring justice from them in return; and from this principle I shall never depart.

Should I be placed in the executive chair, I shall use my best exertions to cultivate peace and friendship with all nations, believing this to be our highest policy, as well as our most imperative duty; but, at the same time, I shall never forget that in case the necessity should arise, which I do not now apprehend, our national rights and national honor must be preserved at all hazards and at any sacrifice.

Firmly convinced that a special Providence governs the affairs of nations, let us humbly implore His continued blessing upon our country, and that He may avert from us the punishment we justly deserve for being discontented and ungrateful while enjoying privileges above all nations, under such a constitution and such a Union as has never been vouchsafed to any other people.   Yours, very respectfully,

JAMES BUCHANAN.

HON. JOHN E. WARD, W. A. RICHARDSON, HARRY HIBBARD, W. B. LAWRENCE, A. G. BROWN, JOHN L. MANNING, JOHN FORSYTH, W. PRESTON, J. RANDOLPH TUCKER, . and HORATIO SEYMOUR, Committee, &c.

TO MR. REED.[1]

Monday morning 7 July '56.

MY DEAR SIR/

I return Mr. Stevenson's letter with thanks. He appears to be "a marvellous proper man." There never was a more unfounded falsehood than that of my connection with the bargain, or alleged bargain. At the time I was a *young* member of

---

[1] Buchanan Papers, Historical Society of Pennsylvania; Curtis's Buchanan, II. 178.

Congress, not on terms of intimacy with either Jackson or Clay. It is true I admired both, & wished to see the one President & the other Secretary of State; & after Mr. Clay had been instructed by the Kentucky Legislature to vote for Jackson, I believed my wish would be accomplished. It must have been then that I had the conversation with Mr. Clay, in Letcher's room, to which Colton refers; for I declare I have not the least trace on my memory of any such conversation. Had I known any thing of the previous history of Jackson & Clay, I could not have believed it possible that the former would appoint the latter Secretary. A conversation of a few minutes with Jackson on the street on a cold & stormy day of December, fully related by me in 1827, & a meeting with Mr. Clay in Letcher's room, & a conversation perfectly harmless as stated, have brought me into serious difficulties.

Yr. friend, very respectfully,

JAMES BUCHANAN.

W. B. REED, ESQ.

TO MR. DOBBIN.[1]

WHEATLAND 20 August 1856.

MY DEAR SIR/

Your favor of the 13th Instant did not reach me at the Bedford Springs until I was about leaving,—hence the delay of my answer. I did not reach home until the night before the last.

I congratulate you, with all my heart, on the result of your election. The population of the old North State is steady & conservative. Of it you may be justly proud. The Southern States now promise to be a unit at the approaching Presidential election. Maryland is still considered doubtful; but the changes in our favor have been great within the last three weeks. The letters of Messrs. Pierce & Pratt have had a happy effect.

---

[1] Buchanan Papers, Historical Society of Pennsylvania; Curtis's Buchanan, II. 179. Mr. Dobbin was Secretary of the Navy.

I am glad to learn that our foreign affairs are assuming a favorable aspect. I most heartily approved of the dismissal of Mr. Crampton, & would have been quite as well satisfied had he been sent home in the last Autumn. About the present condition of the Central American questions I knew nothing until the receipt of your letter, except from the revelations in the British Parliament, which I know, from experience, are not reliable. Mr. Dallas said nothing to me about his instructions or the views of the President; & of course I did not solicit his confidence. The question of the Bay Islands is too clear for serious doubt. Lord Aberdeen, the purest & most just of British Statesmen, when Premier gave it up, as is shewn by my correspondence with the State Department; & it is highly probable Great Britain may make a virtue of necessity & surrender these islands to Honduras, to whom they clearly belong.

I am glad to learn that the President enjoys good health, notwithstanding the fatigue, troubles, & responsibility incident to his position. I concur with you in opinion as to the character of his manly and excellent address on the receipt of the intelligence from Cincinnati. It was no more than what might have been expected from him by all who knew him. My aspirations for the Presidency had all died four years ago, & I never felt the slightest personal interest in securing the nomination. It was easy to foresee the impending crisis & that the Union itself might depend on the result of the election. In this view, whilst we all have every thing near & dear to us of a political character at stake, the President of all men has the deepest interest in the result. My election so far as I am personally concerned is a very small matter; but as identified with the leading measures of his administration,—the preservation of the Constitution & the Union, and the maintenance of the equality of the States and of the right of the people of a territory to decide the question of Slavery for themselves in their constitution before entering the Union,—it is a subject of vast and transcendent importance.

Most cordially reciprocating your friendly sentiments towards myself, & wishing you all the blessings which you can desire, I remain as ever, very respectfully
                              Your friend,
                                        JAMES BUCHANAN.

HON: JAMES C. DOBBIN.

TO MR. CAPEN.[1]

WHEATLAND 27 Aug: '56.

MY DEAR SIR/

On my return from Bedford Springs on Monday night I found your favor of the 22d Inst. & your manuscript. The latter I have endeavored to find the time to read with care; but this has been impossible. I have, therefore, only been able to glance over it. It is written with characteristic ability, and that portion of it which gives extracts from my speeches has been prepared with much labor & discrimination. I have not seen the manuscript of any biography of mine before publication, nor have I read any one of them since; & this simply because I did not choose to be identified with any of them.

For my own part, I consider that all incidental questions are comparatively of little importance in the Presidential question, when compared with the grand & appalling issue of union or disunion. Should Fremont be elected, he must receive 149 Northern Electoral votes at the least; & the outlawry proclaimed by the Black Republican convention at Philadelphia against 15 Southern States will be ratified by the people of the North. The consequence will be *immediate* & inevitable. In this region the battle is fought mainly on this issue. We have so often cried " wolf," that now when the wolf is at the door, it is difficult to make the people believe it; but yet the sense of danger is slowly & surely making its way in this region.

After reflection & consultation, I stated in my letter of acceptance substantially that I would make no issues beyond the platform; & have, therefore, avoided giving my sanction to any publication containing opinions with which I might be identified & prove unsatisfactory to some portions of the Union. I must continue to stand on this ground. Had it not been for this cause. I should have embraced your kind offer & asked you to prepare a biography for me, & furnished the materials. Indeed, I often thought of this.

I am deeply & gratefully sensible of your friendship; & therefore most reluctantly adopt the course towards you which I have done to all other friends under like circumstances.

---

[1] Buchanan Papers, Historical Society of Pennsylvania; Curtis's Buchanan, II. 180.

In the cursory glance I have been able to take of your manuscript, I observed one or two errors.   In page 37 of No. 1, my allusion was to Mrs. Adams, and not to Mrs. Jackson.   I entered college at the age of 16, not of 14, having been previously prepared for the Junior class.

It is not the fact that I accepted no compensation for trying the widow's cause.   " Millions for defence, but not a cent for tribute," was not original with me.

I am so surrounded I regret I cannot write more, & still more deeply regret that my omission to sanction your very able manuscript may give you pain.   I sincerely wish you had referred it to the National Committee or to the Committee in your own State.

We are fighting the battle in this State almost solely *on the great issue,* with energy & confidence.   I do not think there is any reason to apprehend the result, certainly none at the Presidential election, so far as Pennsylvania is concerned.

In haste, I remain always very respectfully
Your friend,
JAMES BUCHANAN.

NAHUM CAPEN, ESQ.

TO MR. MARCY.[1]

WHEATLAND, near LANCASTER,
August 27th, 1856.

MY DEAR SIR:

I returned home the night before last, and then received your note of the 21st instant with your letter to Count Sartiges. Like your other productions, it is clear and able; but it will fail to convince Great Britain at least that she ought to refrain from capturing private property on the ocean.   When I made this suggestion to Lord Clarendon and informed him of our old

---

[1] From the editor's collection of Marcy Papers.

Treaty with Prussia to this effect, he was silent and ceased for the time to urge the question of abolishing privateering.

I should have been sorely tempted, had I been the President, to let the Black Republicans bear the consequences of their own outrageous conduct in refusing to pass the Army Bill without the proviso. This would beyond question have decided the fate of the Presidential election in our favor, and thus have prevented the danger to the constitution and the Union which would exist should Fremont be elected. It was a choice between two great evils, about which I have formed no decided opinion.

With my kindest regards to Mrs. Marcy, I remain
Yours very respectfully,
JAMES BUCHANAN.

HON. WILLIAM L. MARCY.

TO MR. REED.[1]

WHEATLAND 8 Sep: '56.

MY DEAR SIR/

I have received your favor of the 5th Instant. I do not recollect the names of the two members of the Society of Friends to whom you refer; but should you deem it important, I can, with some trouble, find the original letter. I have no doubt Dr. Parrish was one of them. He, William Wharton, & Joseph Foulke were the three gentlemen referred to in my remarks on the 25th April, 1836, in presenting the petition of the Society of Friends against the admission of Arkansas &c. They not only acquiesced in my course, but requested me to procure for them a number of copies of the National Intelligencer containing my remarks, & left Washington entirely satisfied. Vide the volume of the Register of Debates to which you refer, pages 1277 & 78.

---

[1] Buchanan Papers, Historical Society of Pennsylvania; Curtis's Buchanan, II. 181.

I can procure the London Quarterly in Lancaster. I took the Reviews in England, but have neglected to order them since my return. I have no doubt it does me great injustice. I was so popular personally in England that whenever I appeared at public dinners, &c., I was enthusiastically cheered; but now they are all for Fremont (who left London under a cloud) & a dissolution of the Union.

I am gratified that you have sent me Mr. Stevenson's letter. I have no doubt he is a gentleman of fastidious honor as well as much ability. Although a patient & much enduring man, I have never had patience about " the Bargain & Sale story." So far as I am concerned, it all arose from the misapprehension by General Jackson of as innocent a conversation on the street, on my part, as I ever had with any person. I cannot charge myself even with the slightest imprudence. And then, as a re-butter, a conversation equally innocent, in Letcher's room, about the particulars of which I have no more recollection than if it had never taken place. Still, I have not the least doubt it has been stated accurately; because it is just what I would have said under the circumstances & in entire ignorance of the nature of the personal relations between Gen: Jackson & Mr. Clay. Blair's exposé has fallen dead, so far as I can learn.

Yr. friend, in haste,

JAMES BUCHANAN.

WILLIAM B. REED, ESQ.

TO MR. REED.[1]

Private & Confidential.

WHEATLAND 14 Sep. '56.

MY DEAR SIR/

I have at length found & now enclose the letter to which you refer. I have very often spoken in the Senate on the subject of Slavery in the different forms which the question has

---

[1] Buchanan Papers, Historical Society of Pennsylvania; Curtis's Buchanan, II. 182.

assumed; but have not the time at the present moment to look over the debates.

I have recently received a letter from Gov: Wright of Indiana, who informs me it would be of great importance in that State should the National Intelligencer come out in favor of the Democratic candidates.   He had heard, as we have done, that such was the intention of its editors, after the adjournment of Congress.   But they have at length come out in favor of Fremont.   I say this, because they scout the idea that the Union would be in danger from his election; & from their neutral position this will do us much harm.   Better they had at once raised the Black Republican flag.   This opinion they have expressed, notwithstanding I am in the daily receipt of letters from the South which are truly alarming; & these from gentlemen who formerly opposed both nullification and disunion.   They say explicitly that the election of Fremont involves the dissolution of the Union, & this immediately.   They allege that they are now looking on calmly for the North to decide their fate.   When I say from the South, I refer to the States south of the Potomac.   These evidences of public determination first commenced in the extreme South; but now the same calm & determined spirit appears to pervade Virginia.   Indeed, the most alarming letter I have received has been from Virginia, & this, too, from a prudent, tranquil, and able man who has for some years been out of public life from his own choice.   The remarks of the National Intelligencer will either serve to delude the Northern people, or the Southrons are insincere.   God save the Union!   I do not wish to survive it.

From your friend, very respectfully,

JAMES BUCHANAN.

WILLIAM B. REED, ESQ.

P. S.   I refer to the article in the Intelligencer of the 11th Instant, headed " The Balance Wheels of the Government."   One gentleman informs me that the men who were our contemporaries when the States lived in peace with each other, before the slavery excitement commenced, have passed away, & they have been succeeded by a new generation who have grown up pending the Slavery agitation.   He says that they have been constantly assailed by the North, & now have as much hatred for the people of New England as the latter have for them; & many now deem that it would be for the mutual advantage of all parties to have a Southern Confederation in which they can live at peace. I have received such communications with regret & astonishment.

TO MR. WASHINGTON.[1]

WHEATLAND, near LANCASTER, PENNA.

17 September 1856.

To B. F. WASHINGTON, ESQUIRE, Chairman of the Democratic State Central Committee of California.

SIR/

I have received numerous communications from sources in California entitled to high regard, in reference to the proposed Pacific Rail Road. As it would be impossible for me to answer them all, I deem it most proper & respectful to address you a general answer in your official capacity. In performing this duty to the citizens of California I act in perfect consistency with the self imposed restriction contained in my letter accepting the nomination for the Presidency, not to answer interrogatories raising new & different issues from those presented by the Cincinnati Convention; because that Convention has itself adopted a Resolution in favor of this great work. I then desire to state briefly that, concurring with the Convention, I am decidedly favorable to the construction of the Pacific Rail Road; and I derive the authority to do this from the Constitutional power " to declare war " and the Constitutional duty " to repel invasions." In my judgment, Congress possess the same power to make appropriations for the construction of this Road, strictly for the purpose of national defence, that they have to erect fortifications at the mouth of the harbor of San Francisco. Indeed the necessity, with a view to repel foreign invasion from

---

[1] Buchanan Papers, Historical Society of Pennsylvania; Curtis's Buchanan, II. 183.

California, is as great in the one case as in the other. Neither will there be danger from the precedent; for it is almost impossible to conceive that any case attended by such extraordinary & unprecedented circumstances can ever again occur in our history.

Yours very respectfully,

JAMES BUCHANAN.

TO MR. BROWN.[1]

WHEATLAND, near LANCASTER, PENNA.

30 Sep: 56.

MY DEAR SIR

I sincerely regret that I have only time to acknowledge the receipt of your kind and interesting letter of the 21st Instant and to say that I cordially reciprocate all the friendly sentiments which you have expressed towards myself. I recollect, with peculiar pleasure, our intercourse in "the auld lang syne" and have watched your wanderings from your native soil with all the interest of warm personal and political friendship. I am convinced that your own happiness will be promoted by your return to the "Old North State" in which I shall always feel much interested.

The shrewdest and most experienced Democratic politicians in this State firmly believe they will carry it in October against all the "isms" now thoroughly fused and combined; but in November they entertain no doubt.

from your friend

very respectfully

JAMES BUCHANAN.

HON : BEDFORD BROWN.

---

[1] An Annual Publication of Historical Papers; published by the Historical Society of Trinity College, Durham, N. C.; Series VI., 1906, pp. 91-92.

TO MR. BENNETT.[1]

WHEATLAND, Monday morning 20th October 1856.

MY DEAR SIR/

I have this moment received, when about to leave home for Philadelphia, a letter from our mutual friend Mr. W. which has afforded me great satisfaction. I rejoice that our former friendly relations are about to be restored. I can assure you I am truly sorry they were ever interrupted; & this not only for my own sake but that of the Country. The New York Herald, exercising the influence which signal ability & past triumphs always command, can contribute much to prostrate the Sectional party which now so seriously endangers the Union & to restore the ancient friendly relations between the North & the South.

Mr. W. refers to something about a letter from Mr. Dillon which I do not exactly comprehend. I never received a letter from that gentleman for you; but I did receive one from him about you which gratified me much. The truth is that when I parted from you in Paris I had neither the purpose nor the desire again to become a candidate for the Presidency. A ground swell, however, in this State among a noble people who had sustained me for more than thirty years forced me reluctantly into the field.

I confess I had calculated with the most perfect confidence you would be as you had been my friend. It has been throughout between us a Comedy of errors, in which I have been the sufferer. But let by-gones be by-gones; & when we again get together, I feel that we shall never separate.

Yours very respectfully

JAMES BUCHANAN.

JAMES GORDON BENNETT ESQ.

P. S. It is too late for our Mail. I shall have to take this with me & post it in Philadelphia, where I go for only two days.

-----

[1] Buchanan Papers, Historical Society of Pennsylvania.

SPEECH AT WHEATLAND.[1]

[Nov. 6, 1856.]

MY FRIENDS AND NEIGHBORS:

I am glad to see you and to receive and reciprocate your congratulations upon the triumph of the Democrats in Pennsylvania and Indiana.

It is my sober and solemn conviction that Mr. Fillmore uttered the words of soberness and truth when he declared that if the Northern sectional party should succeed, it would lead inevitably to the destruction of this beautiful fabric reared by our forefathers, cemented by their blood, and bequeathed to us as a priceless inheritance.

The people of the North seem to have forgotten the warning of the Father of his Country against geographical parties. And by far the most dangerous of all such parties is that of a combined North against a combined South on the question of slavery. This is no mere political question—no question addressing itself to the material interests of men. It rises far higher. With the South it is a question of self-preservation, of personal security around the family altar, of life or of death. The Southern people still cherish a love for the Union; but what to them is even our blessed confederacy, the wisest and the best form of government ever devised by man, if they cannot enjoy its blessings and its benefits without being in constant alarm for their wives and children.

The storm of abolition against the South has been gathering for almost a quarter of a century. It had been increasing by every various form of agitation which fanaticism could devise. We had reached the crisis. The danger was imminent. Republicanism was sweeping over the North like a tornado. It appeared to be resistless in its course. The blessed Union of these States—the last hope for human liberty on earth—appeared to be tottering on its base. Had Pennsylvania yielded, had she become an abolition State, without a special interposition of Divine Providence, we should have been precipitated into the yawning gulf of dissolution. But she stood erect and firm as her own Alleghanies. She breasted the storm and drove it back.

---

[1] Curtis's Buchanan, II. 175.

The night is departing, and the roseate and propitious morn now breaking upon us promises a long day of peace and prosperity for our country.   To secure this, all we of the North have to do is to permit our Southern neighbors to manage their own domestic affairs, as they permit us to manage ours.   It is merely to adopt the golden rule, and do unto them as we would they should do unto us, in the like circumstances.   All they ask from us is simply to let them alone.   This is the whole spirit and essence of the much abused Cincinnati platform.   This does no more than adopt the doctrine which is the very root of all our institutions, and recognize the right of a majority of the people of a Territory, when about to enter the Union as a State, to decide for themselves whether domestic slavery shall or shall not exist among them.   This is not to favor the extension of slavery, but simply to deny the right of an abolitionist in Massachusetts or Vermont to prescribe to the people of Kansas what they shall or shall not do in regard to this question.

Who contests the principle that the will of the majority shall govern?   What genuine republican of any party can deny this? The opposition have never met this question fairly.   Within a brief period, the people of this country will condemn their own folly for suffering the assertion of so plain and elementary a principle of all popular governments to have endangered our blessed Constitution and Union, which owe their origin to this very principle.

I congratulate you, my friends and neighbors, that peace has been restored to Kansas.   As a Pennsylvanian I rejoice that this good work has been accomplished by two sons of our good old mother State, God bless her!   We have reason to be proud of Colonel Geary and General Smith.   We shall hear no more of bleeding Kansas.   There will be no more shrieks for her unhappy destiny.   The people of this fine country, protected from external violence and internal commotion, will decide the question of slavery for themselves, and then slide gracefully into the Union and become one of the sisters in our great Confederacy.

Indeed, viewed in the eye of sober reason, this Kansas question is one of the most absurd of all the Proteus-like forms which abolition fanaticism has ever assumed to divide and distract the country.   And why do I say this?   Kansas might enter the Union with a free constitution to-day, and once admitted, no human power known to the Constitution could prevent her from establishing slavery to-morrow. No free-soiler has ever even contended that she would not possess this power.

TO MR. BATES.[1]

WHEATLAND, near LANCASTER, PENNSYLV.

6 Nov. 1856.

MY DEAR SIR,

I received in due time your kind congratulatory letter of the 10th July, which I should have immediately answered had I been able to express a decided opinion as to the result of the Presidential election. It was one of the most severe political struggles through which we have ever passed. The Preachers & Fanatics of New England had excited the people to such a degree on the Slavery questions, that they generally prayed & preached against me from their Pulpits on Sunday last throughout that land of " isms." Your information from Massachusetts was entirely unfounded. Boston is a sad place. In that city they have re-elected to Congress a factious fanatic, by name Burlingame, who, in a public Speech, [said] that we must have an anti-Slavery Constitution, an anti-Slavery Bible, and an anti-Slavery God.

Whilst the British Press by their violent attacks did me much good service, I very much regretted their hostile publications, because it was and is my sincere desire to cultivate the most friendly relations with that country. The Times does England much injury, at least in Foreign nations; it has made the English unpopular throughout the Continent and keeps alive the ancient prejudice which still exists in large portions of our Country. In very many of the Democratic papers, throughout the late canvass, beautiful extracts from the Thunderer, the Chronicle, & other English journals were kept standing at the head of their columns. But enough of this. I most sincerely

---

[1] Buchanan Papers, Historical Society of Pennsylvania. Imperfectly printed in Curtis's Buchanan, II. 183.

hope the Central American questions may be settled before the 4th of March. I know nothing of their condition at present. I never doubted in regard to the true construction of the Treaty, nor did I ever consider it doubtful. The purest and the wisest Statesmen I met in England agreed with me in regard to the construction of the Treaty. If we are to be as good friends as I desire we may be, your Government ought to be careful to select the proper man as Minister, and not send us some Government pet simply because they have no other provision for him. I have said much to Lord Clarendon on this subject before I had the slightest idea of becoming President. By the bye, I like his Lordship personally very much, as well as Lord Palmerston. They are both agreeable & witty companions, as well as great Statesmen. I should like them much better, however, if their friendly feelings were a little stronger for this Country. I have no doubt they both, as you say, expressed their satisfaction at the prospect of my becoming President. This was, however, at an early day. They have probably since changed their opinion. I have been a good deal quizzed by private friends since I came home, [because] I spoke in strong & warm terms of the kindness & civility which had been extended to me in England, and of the vast importance to both Countries & to the world that friendly feelings between the two Countries should be cherished by the Governments & people of each. How often have the articles from British newspapers been cast up to me as a comment upon my remarks! They have, however, produced no effect upon my feelings. I was delighted to see Sir Henry Holland & to gossip with him about valued friends & acquaintances on the other side of the water. Please to remember me very kindly to Mrs. Bates, & Miss Lane desires me to present her warm regards to you both. It is long since I have heard from Mr. & Mrs. Lawrence.

From your friend, very respectfully,

JAMES BUCHANAN.

JOSHUA BATES, ESQ.,
    London.

TO MR. MASON.[1]

WHEATLAND, near LANCASTER, PENNA.

29 December 1856.

MY DEAR SIR/

Ere this can reach Paris, you will doubtless have received my letter to Miss Wight. I shall not repeat what I have said to her, because such is the pressure now upon me that I have scarce time to say my prayers. This I can say, in perfect good faith, that the man don't live whom it would afford me greater pleasure to serve than yourself. In this spirit I have determined that you shall not be disturbed during the next year, no matter what may be the pressure upon me. I am not committed, either directly or indirectly, to any human being for any appointment; but yet I cannot mistake the strong current of public opinion in favor of changing public functionaries both abroad & at home who have served a reasonable time. They say, & that too with considerable force, that if the officers under a preceding Democratic administration shall be continued by a succeeding administration of the same political character, this must necessarily destroy the party. This perhaps ought not to be so; but we cannot change human nature.

The great object of my administration will be to arrest, if possible, the agitation of the Slavery question at the North & to destroy sectional parties. Should a kind Providence enable me to succeed in my efforts to restore harmony to the Union, I shall feel that I have not lived in vain.

I beg of you to say nothing to any of your colleagues in Europe about your continuance in office during the next year. Had it been announced I had informed you, in answer to Miss Wight, that you should continue indefinitely in office, this would have done both you & myself injury. We know not what may transpire in 1857; & therefore in reference to the mission after that period I can say nothing. " Sufficient unto the day is the evil thereof."

Even if I had the time, I could not communicate any news to you which you will not see in the Papers. The pressure for

---

[1] Buchanan Papers, Historical Society of Pennsylvania; Curtis's Buchanan, II. 185.

office will be nearly as great as though I had succeeded a Whig administration.

With my kind & affectionate regards to Mrs. Mason & your excellent family, & cordially wishing you & them many a happy Christmas & many a prosperous New Year, I remain, always,
Very respectfully your friend,

JAMES BUCHANAN.

HON. JOHN Y. MASON, Paris.

P. S.   In reading over my letter I find it is quite too cold in reference to Mary Ann, & therefore I beg to send her my love.

1857.

TO MISS LANE.[1]

Sunday Evening 25 Jan: 57.

MY DEAR HARRIET/

Yours of last Sunday reached me yesterday.   It is my purpose, God willing, to leave here tomorrow for Washington in company with Mr. Robert Magraw.   I enclose a letter from Mr. Appleton to yourself, received yesterday.   I opened it, because I was very anxious to receive late news from Washington & thought it might be intended for me.   I am ignorant of the character of the letter except so much of it as to discover I had no concern with it.

It's an ill wind that blows nobody good, & the snow storm has enabled me to do much necessary work.   I do not intend to pass more than one week in Washington.

I received a letter for you from Lady Chantrey.   It came enclosed in a note to me, but has been mislaid.   I cannot find it; but James will send it.

With my affectionate regards to Mr. & Mrs. Plitt, I remain yours affectionately

JAMES BUCHANAN.

MISS HARRIET LANE.

---

[1] Buchanan Papers, private collection.

TO LORD CLARENDON.[1]

Personal, Private & Confidential.

WHEATLAND, near LANCASTER, PENNA.

23 February 1857.

MY DEAR LORD CLARENDON/

The communication which you made to me in December last through Mr. Bates afforded me very great satisfaction, though in regard to any desire on my part to obtain the nomination for the Presidency I perceive you are still laboring under a mistake. Since the nomination of Gen. Pierce, in 1852, I never felt any such desire; & whilst in England I wrote in this spirit to all my friends. *I therefore require no allowance for anything I said or did throughout the Canvass.* I am content to stand before my own country & the world on my letter accepting the nomination; & this is my only committal. My position is quite as independent as that of the best of my predecessors.

What I said to your Lordship in our conversation at Paris was uttered in perfect frankness & sincerity, as I doubt not all you said to me was in the same spirit. England & the United States & the English & American people owe it to their own dearest principles & interests to cultivate the most friendly relations with each other. Ever since the American Revolution we have had a succession of angry negotiations; & when these have been concluded by Treaties, we have immediately begun to wrangle about their true meaning. I trust, as the hymn says,— " there's a better day a-coming."

It is more than doubtful whether your Treaty with Mr. Dallas can obtain the Constitutional majority of two thirds of the Senate. This I infer solely from what I see in the Public Papers, having declined to converse with any Senator on the subject. I have never seen the Treaty itself; but if its contents have been correctly published in the New York Herald, it does not accord with Gen. Washington's maxims,—never to interfere with the domestic concerns of any nation & to avoid entangling alliances with all. Of one thing you may rest perfectly assured,

---

[1] Buchanan Papers, Historical Society of Pennsylvania.

that should the Senate, in the exercise of its constitutional right, withhold its consent to the Treaty, this will be done with great reluctance & from an imperative sense of public duty. There never has been a period, within the last forty years, when the people of the United States were so generally & so cordially desirous of being on friendly terms with Great Britain as at the present moment.

The Clayton & Bulwer Treaty never was popular, & as I have assured your Lordship, would not have received a single vote in the Senate had they supposed at the time it could bear your construction. The late Treaty proceeds upon the same principles, according to the version in the New York Herald, & goes still further. Should it not be ratified, I trust we shall still be able to get along with the Clayton & Bulwer Treaty. As Lord Aberdeen says,—" where there's a will there's a way." Besides, the late Treaty would seem to be so long & complicated that I fear it might prove " an entangling alliance," & like several of its predecessors become a source of future dissension between the two nations.

Gen. Cass is to be my Secretary of State, & no Englishman need feel the least uneasiness on this account. His Anglophobia, as you used facetiously to term it, if it ever existed, no longer exists. His age, his patriotism, his long & able public services, his unsullied private character, & the almost universal feeling in his favor rendered his appointment peculiarly appropriate.

I hope Lord Napier may prove to be the right man for the place, & may come to this country in the proper spirit.

With my kindest regards for Lady Clarendon, I remain always very respectfully your friend

JAMES BUCHANAN.

P. S. Miss Lane desires to be kindly remembered to Lady Clarendon & yourself.

TO COLONEL FORNEY.[1]

WHEATLAND 28th February 1857.

MY DEAR SIR/

Grateful for the signal services which you have rendered to the Democratic party, I deem it proper to offer you the Naval Office in Philadelphia or the Consulate at Liverpool, in the earnest hope that you may find it convenient to accept the one or the other.

In making you this tender, whilst I perform an act of public duty, I at the same time gratify my own warm feelings of friendship for yourself. I ought to observe that the Consulate at Liverpool will not be vacant till August.

From your friend, very respectfully,

JAMES BUCHANAN.

COL: JOHN W. FORNEY.[2]

---

[1] Buchanan Papers, Historical Society of Pennsylvania.

[2] The reply of Col. Forney to this letter is among the Buchanan Papers of the Historical Society of Pennsylvania. It is dated March 6, 1857, and, after referring approvingly to the appointment of Judge Black as Attorney General, says:

"While several considerations, not unknown to you, will prevent me from accepting either of the alternatives contained in your offer of the 28th of February (among which is the fact that I have become committed to two old-time friends of yours for the places referred to in that letter), I shall be found hereafter as I always have been found heretofore under the Democratic flag, and especially when that flag is borne by a man to whose cause I have given the best years of my life, and upon whose election to the Presidency I have expended every effort I could command, and nearly every dollar I had in the world.

"I am about to embark once more upon the ocean of the future. I am no applicant for position at your hands. I have suffered deep and bitter humiliation since you have been elected, the gibes of false friends and the open exultation of open foes. Yet I can still appreciate all your difficulties and embarrassments, and from my heart I wish you God speed.

"Your friend,

"J. W. FORNEY."

INAUGURAL ADDRESS, MARCH 4, 1857.

Fellow-citizens:

I appear before you this day to take the solemn oath " that I will faithfully execute the office of President of the United States, and will, to the best of my ability, preserve, protect, and defend the Constitution of the United States."

In entering upon this great office, I most humbly invoke the God of our fathers for wisdom and firmness to execute its high and responsible duties in such a manner as to restore harmony and ancient friendship among the people of the several States, and to preserve our free institutions throughout many generations.   Convinced that I owe my election to the inherent love for the Constitution and the Union which still animates the hearts of the American people, let me earnestly ask their powerful support in sustaining all just measures calculated to perpetuate these, the richest political blessings which Heaven has ever bestowed upon any nation.   Having determined not to become a candidate for re-election, I shall have no motive to influence my conduct in administering the government except the desire ably and faithfully to serve my country, and to live in the grateful memory of my countrymen.

We have recently passed through a presidential contest in which the passions of our fellow-citizens were excited to the highest degree by questions of deep and vital importance; but when the people proclaimed their will, the tempest at once subsided, and all was calm.

The voice of the majority, speaking in the manner prescribed by the Constitution, was heard, and instant submission followed.   Our own country could alone have exhibited so grand and striking a spectacle of the capacity of man for self-government.

What a happy conception, then, was it for Congress to apply this simple rule—that the will of the majority shall govern —to the settlement of the question of domestic slavery in the Territories!   Congress is neither " to legislate slavery into any Territory or State, nor to exclude it therefrom, but to leave the people thereof perfectly free to form and regulate their domestic institutions in their own way, subject only to the Constitution of the United States."   As a natural consequence, Congress has also prescribed that, when the Territory of Kansas shall be admitted as a State, it " shall be received into the Union, with or without slavery, as their constitution may prescribe at the time of their admission."

A difference of opinion has arisen in regard to the point of time when the people of a Territory shall decide this question for themselves.

This is, happily, a matter of but little practical importance. Besides, it is a judicial question, which legitimately belongs to the Supreme Court of the United States, before whom it is now pending, and will, it is understood, be speedily and finally settled.[1] To their decision, in common with all good citizens, I shall cheerfully submit, whatever this may be, though it has ever been

---

[1] In connection with this statement, the following letters are of interest:

"Thursday, Feby. 19th [1857].

" MY DEAR SIR:

" The Dred Scott case has been before the Judges several times since last Saturday, and I think you may safely say in your Inaugural,

" ' That the question involving the constitutionality of the Missouri Compromise line is presented to the appropriate tribunal to decide; to wit, to the Supreme Court of the United States. It is due to its high and independent character to suppose that it will decide & settle a controversy which has so long and seriously agitated the country, and which *must* ultimately be decided by the Supreme Court. And until the case now before it, (on two arguments) presenting the direct question, is disposed of, I would deem it improper to express any opinion on the subject.'

" A majority of my Brethren will be forced up to this point by two dissentients.

" Will you drop Grier a line, saying how necessary it is—& how good the opportunity is, to settle the agitation by an affirmative decision of the Supreme Court, the one way or the other. He ought not to occupy so doubtful a ground as the outside issue—that admitting the constitutionality of the Mo. Comp. line of 1820, still, as no domicile was acquired by the negro at Ft. Snelling, & he returned to Missouri, he was not free. He has no doubt about the question on the main contest, but has been persuaded to take the smooth handle for the sake of repose.

" Sincerely yr. frd.   " J. CATRON.

" To MR. BUCHANAN."

"WASHINGTON, Feby. 23d 1857.

" MY DEAR SIR

" Your letter came to hand this morning. I have taken the liberty to shew it in confidence to our mutual friends Judge Wayne and the Chief Justice. We fully appreciate and concur in your views as to the desirableness at this

my individual opinion that, under the Nebraska-Kansas act, the appropriate period will be when the number of actual residents in the Territory shall justify the formation of a constitution with a view to its admission as a State into the Union. But be this as it may, it is the imperative and indispensable duty of the government of the United States to secure to every resident inhabitant the free and independent expression of his opinion by his vote. This sacred right of each individual must be preserved. That being accomplished, nothing can be fairer than to leave the people of a Territory free from all foreign interference, to decide their own destiny for themselves, subject only to the Constitution of the United States.

The whole territorial question being thus settled upon the principle of popular sovereignty—a principle as ancient as free

time of having an expression of the opinion of the court on this troublesome question. With their concurrence, I will give you in confidence the history of the case before us, with the probable result. Owing to the sickness and absence of a member of the court, the case was not taken up in conference till lately. The first question which presented itself was the right of a negro to sue in the courts of the United States. A majority of the court were of the opinion that the question did not arise on the pleadings and that we were compelled to give an opinion on the merits. After much discussion it was finally agreed that the merits of the case might be satisfactorily decided without giving an opinion on the question of the Missouri compromise; and the case was committed to Judge Nelson to write the opinion of the court affirming the judgment of the court below, but leaving both those difficult questions untouched. But it appeared that our brothers who dissented from the majority, especially Justice McLean, were determined to come out with a long and labored dissent, including their opinions & arguments on both the troublesome points, although not necessary to a decision of the case. In our opinion both the points are *in* the case and may be legitimately considered. Those who hold a different opinion from Messrs. McLean & Curtis on the powers of Congress & the validity of the compromise act feel compelled to express their opinions on the subject, Nelson & myself refusing to commit ourselves. A majority including all the judges south of Mason & Dixon's line agreeing in the result but not in their reasons—as the question will be thus forced upon us, I am anxious that it should not appear that the line of latitude should mark the line of division in the court. I feel also that the opinion of the majority will fail of much of its effect if founded on clashing & inconsistent arguments. On conversation with the chief justice I have agreed *to concur with him.* Brother Wayne & myself will also use our endeavors to get brothers Daniels & Campbell & Catron to do the same. So that if the question must be met, there will be an opinion of the court upon it, if possible, without the contradictory views which would weaken its force.

government itself—everything of a practical nature has been decided.   No other question remains for adjustment; because all agree that, under the Constitution, slavery in the States is beyond the reach of any human power, except that of the respective States themselves wherein it exists.   May we not, then, hope that the long agitation on this subject is approaching its end, and that the geographical parties to which it has given birth, so much dreaded by the Father of his Country, will speedily become extinct?   Most happy will it be for the country when the public mind shall be diverted from this question to others of more pressing and practical importance.   Throughout the whole progress of this agitation, which has scarcely known any intermission for more than twenty years, whilst it has been productive of no positive good to any human being, it has been the prolific source of great evils to the master, the slave, and to the whole country.   It has alienated and estranged the people of the sister States from each other, and has even seriously endangered the very existence of the Union.   Nor has the danger yet entirely

---

But I fear some rather extreme views may be thrown out by some of our southern brethren. There will therefore be six if not *seven* (perhaps Nelson will remain neutral) who will decide the compromise law of 1820 to be of *non-effect*. But the opinions will not be delivered before Friday the 6th of March. We will not let any others of our brethren know any thing about *the cause of our anxiety* to produce this result, and though contrary to our usual practice, we have thought due to you to state to you in candor & confidence the real state of the matter.

" Very Truly Yours

" D. Grier.

" Hon. James Buchanan.

"P. S.—It is the weak state of the Chief Justice's health which will postpone the opinion to that time."

Mr. Justice Catron, by whom the first of these letters was written, was, as abundantly appears by the contents of the present work, an old personal friend of Mr. Buchanan. The pendency of the Dred Scott case at this time was a matter of public notoriety, and the possible outcome was a frequent subject of conjecture in the press. It was in these circumstances that both the confidential communications above printed were written. They are obviously inconsistent with and tacitly refute the charge that the Dred Scott case was the result of a "conspiracy" in which the Kansas-Nebraska bill was the first step. As the facts are narrated by Mr. Justice Grier, the action eventually taken in the case seems to have been brought about by the activity of the minority rather than of the majority of the court.

ceased. Under our system there is a remedy for all mere political evils in the sound sense and sober judgment of the people. Time is a great corrective. Political subjects which but a few years ago excited and exasperated the public mind have passed away and are now nearly forgotten. But this question of domestic slavery is of far graver importance than any mere political question, because, should the agitation continue, it may eventually endanger the personal safety of a large portion of our countrymen where the institution exists. In that event, no form of government, however admirable in itself, and however productive of material benefits, can compensate for the loss of peace and domestic security around the family altar. Let every Union-loving man, therefore, exert his best influence to suppress this agitation, which, since the recent legislation of Congress, is without any legitimate object.

It is an evil omen of the times that men have undertaken to calculate the mere material value of the Union. Reasoned estimates have been presented of the pecuniary profits and local advantages which would result to different States and sections from its dissolution, and of the comparative injuries which such an event would inflict on other States and sections. Even descending to this low and narrow view of the mighty question, all such calculations are at fault. The bare reference to a single consideration will be conclusive on this point. We at present enjoy a free trade throughout our extensive and expanding country, such as the world has never witnessed. This trade is conducted on railroads and canals—on noble rivers and arms of the sea—which bind together the north and the south, the east and the west of our confederacy. Annihilate this trade, arrest its free progress by the geographical lines of jealous and hostile States, and you destroy the prosperity and onward march of the whole and every part, and involve all in one common ruin. But such considerations, important as they are in themselves, sink into insignificance when we reflect on the terrific evils which would result from disunion to every portion of the confederacy— to the north not more than to the south, to the east not more than to the west. These I shall not attempt to portray; because I feel an humble confidence that the kind Providence which inspired our fathers with wisdom to frame the most perfect form of Government and Union ever devised by man will not suffer it to perish until it shall have been peacefully instrumental, by its example, in the extension of civil and religious liberty throughout the world.

Next in importance to the maintenance of the Constitution and the Union is the duty of preserving the government free from the taint, or even the suspicion, of corruption. Public virtue is the vital spirit of republics; and history shows that when this has decayed, and the love of money has usurped its place, although the forms of free government may remain for a season, the substance has departed forever.

Our present financial condition is without a parallel in history. No nation has ever before been embarrassed from too large a surplus in its treasury. This almost necessarily gives birth to extravagant legislation. It produces wild schemes of expenditure, and begets a race of speculators and jobbers, whose ingenuity is exerted in contriving and promoting expedients to obtain public money. The purity of official agents, whether rightfully or wrongfully, is suspected, and the character of the government suffers in the estimation of the people. This is in itself a very great evil.

The natural mode of relief from this embarrassment is to appropriate the surplus in the treasury to great national objects, for which a clear warrant can be found in the Constitution. Among these I might mention the extinguishment of the public debt, a reasonable increase of the navy, which is at present inadequate to the protection of our vast tonnage afloat, now greater than that of any other nation, as well as to the defence of our extended seacoast.

It is beyond all question the true principle, that no more revenue ought to be collected from the people than the amount necessary to defray the expenses of a wise, economical, and efficient administration of the government. To reach this point, it was necessary to resort to a modification of the tariff; and this has, I trust, been accomplished in such a manner as to do as little injury as may have been practicable to our domestic manufactures, especially those necessary for the defence of the country. Any discrimination against a particular branch, for the purpose of benefiting favored corporations, individuals, or interests, would have been unjust to the rest of the community, and inconsistent with that spirit of fairness and equality which ought to govern in the adjustment of a revenue tariff.

But the squandering of the public money sinks into comparative insignificance as a temptation to corruption when compared with the squandering of the public lands.

No nation in the tide of time has ever been blessed with so rich and noble an inheritance as we enjoy in the public lands. In administering this important trust, whilst it may be wise to grant portions of them for the improvement of the remainder, yet we should never forget that it is our cardinal policy to reserve these lands, as much as may be, for actual settlers, and this at moderate prices. We shall thus not only best promote the prosperity of the new States and Territories by furnishing them a hardy and independent race of honest and industrious citizens, but shall secure homes for our children and our children's children, as well as for those exiles from foreign shores who may seek in this country to improve their condition, and to enjoy the blessings of civil and religious liberty. Such emigrants have done much to promote the growth and prosperity of the country. They have proved faithful both in peace and war. After becoming citizens, they are entitled, under the Constitution and laws, to be placed on a perfect equality with native-born citizens, and in this character they should ever be kindly recognized.

The Federal Constitution is a grant from the States to Congress of certain specific powers; and the question whether this grant should be liberally or strictly construed, has, more or less, divided political parties from the beginning. Without entering into the argument, I desire to state, at the commencement of my administration, that long experience and observation have convinced me that a strict construction of the powers of the Government is the only true, as well as the only safe, theory of the Constitution. Whenever, in our past history, doubtful powers have been exercised by Congress, these have never failed to produce injurious and unhappy consequences. Many such instances might be adduced, if this were the proper occasion. Neither is it necessary for the public service to strain the language of the Constitution; because all the great and useful powers required for a successful administration of the Government both in peace and in war, have been granted, either in express terms or by the plainest implication.

Whilst deeply convinced of these truths, I yet consider it

clear that, under the war-making power, Congress may appropriate money towards the construction of a military road, when this is absolutely necessary for the defence of any State or Territory of the Union against foreign invasion. Under the Constitution, Congress has power " to declare war," " to raise and support armies," " to provide and maintain a navy," and to call forth the militia to " repel invasions." Thus endowed, in an ample manner, with the war-making power, the corresponding duty is required that " the United States shall protect each of them [the States] against invasion." Now, how is it possible to afford this protection to California and our Pacific possessions, except by means of a military road through the Territories of the United States, over which men and munitions of war may be speedily transported from the Atlantic States to meet and to repel the invader? In the event of a war with a naval power much stronger than our own, we should then have no other available access to the Pacific coast, because such a power would instantly close the route across the isthmus of Central America. It is impossible to conceive that, whilst the Constitution has expressly required Congress to defend all the States, it should yet deny to them, by any fair construction, the only possible means by which one of these States can be defended. Besides, the Government, ever since its origin, has been in the constant practice of constructing military roads. It might also be wise to consider whether the love for the Union which now, animates our fellow-citizens on the Pacific coast may not be impaired by our neglect or refusal to provide for them, in their remote and isolated condition, the only means by which the power of the States, on this side of the Rocky Mountains, can reach them in sufficient time to " protect " them " against invasion." I forbear for the present from expressing an opinion as to the wisest and most economical mode in which the Government can lend its aid in accomplishing this great and necessary work. I believe that many of the difficulties in the way, which now appear formidable, will, in a great degree, vanish as soon as the nearest and best route shall have been satisfactorily ascertained.

It may be proper that, on this occasion, I should make some brief remarks in regard to our rights and duties as a member of the great family of nations. In our intercourse with them there are some plain principles, approved by our own experience, from which we should never depart. We ought to cultivate peace, commerce, and friendship with all nations; and this not merely as the best means of promoting our own material interests, but in a spirit of Christian benevolence towards our fellow-men, wherever their lot may be cast. Our diplomacy should be direct and frank, neither seeking to obtain more nor accepting less than is our due. We ought to cherish a sacred regard for the independence of all nations, and never attempt to interfere in the domestic concerns of any, unless this shall be imperatively required by the great laws of self-preservation. To avoid entangling alliances has been a maxim of our policy ever since the days of Washington, and its wisdom no one will attempt to dispute. In short, we ought to do justice, in a kindly spirit, to all nations, and require justice from them in return.

It is our glory that, whilst other nations have extended their dominions by the sword, we have never acquired any territory except by fair purchase, or, as in the case of Texas, by the voluntary determination of a brave, kindred, and independent people to blend their destinies with our own. Even our acquisitions from Mexico form no exception. Unwilling to take advantage of the fortune of war against a sister republic, we purchased these possessions, under the treaty of peace, for a sum which was considered at the time a fair equivalent. Our past history forbids that we shall in the future acquire territory, unless this be sanctioned by the laws of justice and honor. Acting on this principle, no nation will have a right to interfere or to complain if, in the progress of events, we shall still further extend our possessions. Hitherto, in all our acquisitions, the people, under the protection of the American flag, have enjoyed civil and religious liberty, as well as equal and just laws, and have been contented, prosperous, and happy. Their trade with the rest of the world has rapidly increased, and thus every commercial nation has shared largely in their successful progress.

I shall now proceed to take the oath prescribed by the Constitution, whilst humbly invoking the blessing of Divine Providence on this great people.

TO JUDGE BLACK.[1]

WASHINGTON 6th March 1857.

MY DEAR SIR,

I have this moment signed your commission as Attorney General of the United States, and I have done this with great pleasure. I hope you may find it agreeable to yourself to accept this important office; and I entertain no doubt that we shall get on harmoniously and happily together.

There were certainly great difficulties in the way of your appointment, and Mr. J. Glancy Jones has behaved very well in contributing to the result. I may also add that Governor Bigler is quite satisfied with it, and I venture to express the hope that any past difficulties between you and himself may pass away and be forgotten.

We must be a unit here if possible. I hope you will come to Washington immediately, and in the mean time believe me to be always very respectfully

Your friend,

JAMES BUCHANAN.

HON: J. S. BLACK.

FROM LORD CLARENDON.[1]

Private.   F. O., March 13/57.

MY DEAR MR. BUCHANAN,

I thank you for your letter & assure you it was a great satisfaction to me again to receive an autograph of yours. I hope it will not be the last.

I cordially join in hoping with you that " there's a better day a-coming," & that with it there will be an end of all those wrangles which for a long time past have done so much harm in both Countries. I need not tell you that the feeling here towards the United States is precisely that which I rejoice to hear from you animates your countrymen towards Great Britain, & this makes it all the more incumbent upon the two Govts., resting as they both do on public opinion, to cultivate the most friendly relations with each other.

---

[1] Buchanan Papers, Historical Society of Pennsylvania.

I shall deeply regret the non-ratification of the Treaty because I am convinced that, so far from proving "an entangling alliance," it would have put an end to the trifling difficulties which exist in that part of the world. However, whether it is ratified or not, pray bear in mind that beyond the point of honor respecting the Mosquito Indians we possess no interest in Central America, & that, so far from wishing to create one, we would not accept such a "damnosa possessio" as Central America if it could be offered to England as a gift.

I am glad to learn from you that the Anglophobia of General Cass no longer exists, & I am not disposed to believe the report of the Times Correspondent that I am the object of his special aversion, & for the simple reason that I am not aware of ever having said or done any thing which could justify such a feeling. He has, I believe, at different times spoken strongly against me in the Senate, for which I have never borne him any ill will, & I dare say we shall get on well together thro' Ld. Napier.

Lady Clarendon desires me to send you her kindest regards, & we both beg to be kindly remembered to Miss Lane.

Believe me always, my dear Mr. Buchanan,

Very faithfully yours,

CLARENDON.

FROM LORD CLARENDON.[1]

Private.   LONDON, April 22/57.

MY DEAR MR. BUCHANAN,

I thank you for the friendly letter of which Mr. Evans was the Bearer. I don't suppose there are many instances of the President of the United States & the English Foreign Secretary corresponding directly with each other, but if the practice is as agreeable to you as it is to me, I shall hope for its continuance.

We did not much like the amendments of the Treaty, particularly as to the Land Claims, for the Land Claimants are "Legion." They are very clamorous & will give a deal of trouble, as it cannot be denied that their prospects are now less *brilliant* than they were. However, we adopted this & all the other amendments except one to the Additional Article 2d. To that, unfortunately, we could not agree, because our Treaty with Honduras was not ratified, & we could not recognize the Bay Islands as forming part of that Republic unconditionally & without being sure that the British Settlers in those Islands would have the securities provided for them by the Treaty. If the Treaty had been ratified, as the Senate may have supposed it was, we would have had no difficulty in agreeing to the amendment,

---

[1] Buchanan Papers, Historical Society of Pennsylvania.

but under existing circumstances we were compelled to ask you to agree to an addition to your amendment. Your object is that those Islands should no longer be held as British Dependencies, & if we are willing to give them up, it cannot signify to the U. S. that we are careful not to hand over British Subjects to the tender mercies of such a Govt. as that of Honduras without at least procuring for them that amount of protection which a Treaty can afford.

Pray believe that we don't mean to extend our *Belize Farm,* & that we neither wish nor want to have any thing to do with Central America. The difficulty which has arisen about the Treaty will not make the slightest difference in our policy. We have, as you know, a point of honor with respect to the Mosquito Indians, & we want certain securities for the people of the Bay Islands. These two matters being settled, we shall take our leave of those *pleasant lands* & become like the rest of the world mere travellers from one ocean to the other.

It gave me great pleasure to learn your opinion of Ld. Napier. He is delighted with his reception & the kindness & cordiality he has met with.

Lady Clarendon desires her best regards to you & her love to Miss Lane, to whom I beg you will offer my respectful remembrance.

Believe me, my dear Mr. Buchanan, always

Very faithfully yours,

CLARENDON.

TO MR. WILLIAMS.[1]

WASHINGTON, April 29, 1857.

SIR: I have carefully perused your communication of this morning in relation to Messrs. Carmick & Ramsey, and in answer have to state that the 6th section of the act of August 18, 1856, refers the question to the First Comptroller of the Treasury, and to him alone for decision, and I shall not interfere with the duty which has thus been assigned to him. He will give such weight to the opinion of the Attorney General, as well as to the other evidence and documents before him, as in his judgment they may deserve.

Neither do I feel myself at liberty to prolong the period of office of the First Comptroller in reference to any particular case. When he expressed his desire and purpose to resign, he

---

[1] H. Ex. Doc. 30, 35 Cong. 2 Sess. 33.

informed me that he was then engaged in the investigation of several cases, and it would occasion much inconvenience and loss of time if he should leave the office before these cases were decided.   Cordially concurring in these views, I requested him to fix the day when his resignation should take effect, allowing himself ample time for the purpose he had in view.   This he accordingly did.   His successor was then appointed, whose commission will take effect from that day according to its terms.

Yours, very respectfully,

JAMES BUCHANAN.

JOSEPH L. WILLIAMS, ESQUIRE.[1]

REPLY TO A MEMORIAL

OF CITIZENS OF CONNECTICUT ON KANSAS [2]

WASHINGTON CITY, August 15, 1857.

GENTLEMEN: On my recent return to this city after a fortnight's absence, your memorial, without date, was placed in my hands, through the agency of Mr. Horatio King of the Post

---

[1] Joseph L. Williams was a representative in Congress, from Tennessee, from 1837 to 1843.   He was the attorney for Messrs. Carmick & Ramsey, the claimants in this case.   President Buchanan upon another letter of Mr. Williams made, May 5, 1858, the following endorsement: "Referred to the First Comptroller, with a declaration that I entertain the same opinion now which I did a year ago, and which is now on file in his office." (H. Ex. Doc. 30, 35 Cong. 2 Sess. 70.)

[2] S. Ex. Doc. 8, 35 Cong. 1 Sess. 71.   The memorial, which is printed in the same document, was signed by the following persons: Nathaniel W. Taylor, Theodore D. Woolsey, Henry Dutton, Charles L. English, J. H. Brockway, Eli W. Blake, Eli Ives, B. Silliman, Jr., Noah Porter, Thomas A. Thatcher, J. A. Davenport, Worthington Hooker, Philos Blake, E. K. Foster, C. S. Lyman, John A. Blake, Wm. H. Russell, A. N. Skinner, Horace Bushnell, John Boyd, Chas. Robinson, David Smith, J. Hawes, James F. Babcock, G. A. Calhoun, E. R. Gilbert, Leonard Bacon, H. C. Kingsley, B. Silliman, Edward C. Herrick, Charles Ives, Wm. P. Eustis, Jr., Alex. C. Twinning, Josiah W. Gibbs, Alfred Walker, James Brewster, Stephen G. Hubbard, Hawley Olmstead, Seagrove W. Magill, Amos Townsend, Timothy Dwight, David M. Smith, Henry Peck.

Office Department, to whom it has been entrusted. From the distinguished source whence it proceeds, as well as its peculiar character, I have deemed it proper to depart from my general rule in such cases, and to give it an answer.

You first assert that "the fundamental principle of the Constitution of the United States and of our political institutions is, that the people shall make their own laws and elect their own rulers." You then express your grief and astonishment that I should have violated this principle, and through Governor Walker have employed an army, "one purpose of which is *to force the people of Kansas to obey laws not their own, nor of the United States,* but laws which it is notorious, and established upon evidence, they never made, and rulers they never elected." And, as a corollary from the foregoing, you represent that I am "openly held up and proclaimed, to the great derogation of our national character, as violating in its most essential particulars the solemn *oath* which the President has taken *to support the Constitution of this Union.*"

These are heavy charges, proceeding from gentlemen of your high character, and, if well founded, ought to consign my name to infamy. But in proportion to their gravity, common justice, to say nothing of Christian charity, required that, before making them, you should have clearly ascertained that they were well founded. If not, they will rebound with withering condemnation upon their authors. Have you performed this preliminary duty towards the man who, however unworthy, is the Chief Magistrate of your country? If so, either you or I am laboring under a strange delusion. Should this prove to be your case, it will present a memorable example of the truth that political prejudice is blind even to the existence of the plainest and most palpable historical facts. To these facts let us refer.

When I entered upon the duties of the Presidential office, on the fourth of March last, what was the condition of Kansas? This Territory had been organized under the Act of Congress of 30th May, 1854, and the government in all its branches was in full operation. A governor, secretary of the Territory, chief justice, two associate justices, a marshal, and district attorney had been appointed by my predecessor, by and with the advice and consent of the Senate, and were all engaged in discharging their respective duties. A code of laws had been enacted by the Territorial legislature; and the judiciary were employed in expounding and carrying these laws into effect. It is quite true that a controversy had previously arisen respecting the validity of the election of members of the Territorial legislature and of the laws passed by them; but at the time I entered upon my official duties, Congress had recognized this legislature in different enactments. The delegate elected to the House of Representatives, under a Territorial law, had just completed his term of service on the day previous to my inauguration. In fact, I found the government of Kansas as well established as that of any other Territory. Under these circumstances, what was my duty? Was it not to sustain this government? to protect it from the violence of lawless men, who were determined either to rule or ruin? to prevent it from being overturned by force?—in the language of the Constitution, to " take care that the laws be faithfully executed? " It was for this purpose, and this alone, that I ordered a military force to Kansas, to act as a posse comitatus in aiding the civil magistrate to carry the laws into execution.

The condition of the Territory at the time, which I need not portray, rendered this precaution absolutely necessary. In this state of affairs, would I not have been justly condemned had I left the marshal and other officers of a like character impotent to execute the process and judgments of courts of justice established by Congress, or by the Territorial legislature under its express authority, and thus have suffered the government itself to become an object of contempt in the eyes of the people? And yet this is what you designate as forcing " the people of Kansas to obey laws not their own, nor of the United States; " and for doing which you have denounced me as having violated my solemn oath. I ask, what else could I have done, or ought I to have done? Would you have desired that I should abandon the Territorial government, sanctioned as it had been by Congress, to illegal violence, and thus renew the scenes of civil war and bloodshed which every patriot in the country had deplored? This would, indeed, have been to violate my oath of office, and to fix a damning blot on the character of my administration.

I most cheerfully admit that the necessity for sending a military force to Kansas to aid in the execution of the civil law, reflects no credit upon the character of our country. But let the blame fall upon the heads of the guilty. Whence did this necessity arise? A portion of the people of Kansas, unwilling to trust to the ballot-box—the certain American remedy for the redress of all grievances—undertook to create an independent government for themselves. Had this attempt proved successful, it would, of course, have subverted the existing government, prescribed and recognized by Congress, and substituted a revolutionary government in its stead. This was a usurpation of the same character as it would be for a portion of the people of Connecticut to undertake to establish a separate government within its chartered limits, for the purpose of redressing any grievance, real or imaginary, of which they might have complained against the legitimate State government. Such a principle, if carried into execution, would destroy all lawful authority and produce universal anarchy.

I ought to specify more particularly a condition of affairs, which I have embraced only in general terms, requiring the presence of a military force in Kansas. The Congress of the United States had most wisely declared it to be " the true intent and meaning of this act (the act organizing the Territory) not to legislate slavery into any Territory or State, nor to exclude it therefrom, but to leave the people thereof perfectly free to form and regulate their domestic institutions in their own way, subject only to the Constitution of the United States."

As a natural consequence, Congress has also prescribed, by the same act, that when the Territory of Kansas shall be admitted as a State, it " shall be received into the Union with or without slavery, as their constitution may prescribe at the time of their admission."

Slavery existed at that period and still exists in Kansas, under the Constitution of the United States. This point has at last been finally decided by the highest tribunal known to our laws. How it could ever have been seriously doubted is a mystery. If a confederation of sovereign States acquire a new territory at the expense of their common blood and treasure, surely one set of the partners can have no right to exclude the other from its enjoyment, by prohibiting them from taking into it whatsoever is recognized to be property by the common Constitution. But when the people, the *bona fide* residents of such territory, proceed to frame a State constitution, then it is their right to decide the important question for themselves whether they will continue, modify, or abolish slavery. To them, and to them alone, does this question belong, free from all foreign interference.

In the opinion of the territorial legislature of Kansas, the time had arrived for entering the Union, and they accordingly passed a law to elect delegates for the purpose of framing a State constitution. This law was fair and just in its provisions. It conferred the right of suffrage on " every *bona fide* inhabitant of the Territory; " and, for the purpose of preventing fraud, and the intrusion of citizens of near or distant States, most properly confined this right to those who had resided therein three months previous to the election. Here a fair opportunity was presented for all the qualified resident citizens of the Territory, to whatever organization they might have previously belonged, to participate in the election, and to express their opinions at the ballot box on the question of slavery. But numbers of lawless men still continued to resist the regular territorial government. They refused either to be registered or to vote; and the members of the convention were elected, legally and properly, without their intervention. The convention will soon assemble to perform the solemn duty of framing a constitution for themselves and their posterity; and in the state of incipient rebellion which still exists in Kansas, it is my imperative duty to employ the troops of the United States, should this become necessary, in defending the convention against violence whilst framing the constitution, and in protecting the " *bona fide* inhabitants " qualified to vote under the provisions of this instrument in the free exercise of the right of suffrage when it shall be submitted to them for their approbation or rejection.

I have entire confidence in Governor Walker that the troops will not be employed except to resist actual aggression or in the execution of the laws, and this not until the power of the civil magistrate shall prove unavailing. Following the wise example of Mr. Madison towards the Hartford convention, illegal and dangerous combinations, such as that of the Topeka convention, will not be disturbed, unless they shall attempt to perform some act which will bring them into actual collision with the Constitution and the laws. In that event they shall be resisted and put down by the whole power of the government. In performing this duty I shall have the approbation of my own conscience, and, as I humbly trust, of my God.

I thank you for the assurances that you will " not refrain from the prayer that Almighty God will make my administration an example of justice and beneficence." You can greatly assist me in arriving at this blessed consummation by exerting your influence in allaying the existing sectional excitement on the subject of slavery, which has been productive of much evil and no good, and which, if it could succeed in attaining its object, would ruin the slave as well as his master. This would be a work of genuine philanthropy. Every day of my life I feel how inadequate I am to perform the duties of my high station without the continued support of Divine Providence; yet, placing my trust in Him, and in Him alone, I entertain a good hope that He will enable me to do equal justice to all portions of the Union, and thus render me an humble instrument in restoring peace and harmony among the people of the several States.

Yours, very respectfully,

JAMES BUCHANAN.

REV. NATHANIEL W. TAYLOR, D. D., REV. THEODORE D. WOOLSEY, D. D., LL. D., HON. HENRY DUTTON, REV. DAVID SMITH, D. D., REV. J. HAWES, D. D., and others.

TO LORD CLARENDON.[1]

Private.   WASHINGTON CITY 9 September 1857.

MY DEAR LORD CLARENDON/

I have long been in your debt a letter. I should have written ere this, but for some time have been in weekly expectation of learning that the difficulties between the two Countries, in Central America, had been adjusted. I confess that I felt a warm desire to announce this fact in my first message to Con-

---

[1] Buchanan Papers, Historical Society of Pennsylvania.

gress as the harbinger of perpetual peace & friendship between the two nations.   But I must do the best I can without it.   That unfortunate Clayton & Bulwer Treaty must be put out of the way.   What else should be done with a Treaty on which directly opposite constructions have been placed by the two nations? What I have often told you is literal truth, that I do not believe it would have received a single vote in the Senate had it even been seriously suspected that the construction you place upon it was correct.   It will be a bone of contention & a root of bitterness between the two Governments as long as it exists.

I have been very much gratified at the tone of public sentiment in this Country on the East Indian Insurrection.   It was quite spontaneous everywhere.   We heartily wish you success in putting down this most cruel & barbarous insurrection, & entertain not a doubt but that your power, energy, & resources as a nation will speedily accomplish this object.   Whilst in England I often had but little else to do than examine & reflect upon British questions, & I formed my own conclusions as to your policy in India.   I think it might be improved; but your system is so ancient, so complicated, & so many vested rights are involved that I consider it would be presumption in me even to make suggestions.

I have seen but little of Lord Napier.   He has, however, made himself quite popular in this country,—more so, I think, than any preceding British minister, not even excepting Crampton.   Shortly after I came into the White House, Miss Lane lost an unmarried brother to whom she was devotedly attached, & I was sick until the season for gaiety in Washington was over. These are the reasons why I have seen so little of the members of the Diplomatic Corps; but these reasons no longer exist.

I think you ought to keep your protégés in Central America in better order.   I wish I could induce you to believe that the interest of the U. S. in that region is the very same with your own.   Your special favorite Costa Rica is now endeavoring to convert her patriotic assistance to her sister State against the filibusters into a war of conquest, & she modestly claims the right to sell the transit route to the highest bidder.   To this I shall not submit.   She has got hold of the greatest scamps as purchasers; but they have not been able to pay the first instalment. The truth is that these States on the Isthmus expect to make large profit by the transit of the persons & property of the world across their territory, & they are not scrupulous as to the means they may employ.   G. B. & the U. S., whilst treating them justly & even liberally, ought to let them know that *this transit shall be kept open & shall never again be interrupted by their miserable wars & jealousies;* & that they shall not exact any thing but what is reasonable from the commerce of the world for the right to cross their country.   I see from the papers that passengers on the Honduras Rail Road will each have to pay a capitation tax to the Govt. of one dollar for the privilege of riding across the country, in addition to what they may have to pay for their transportation.   If the Clayton & Bulwer Treaty had never existed, the British & American Governments, acting in concert, would long ere this have settled these questions for their own benefit & that of the world.

Wishing you all manner of prosperity, I remain, very respectfully

Your friend,

JAMES BUCHANAN.

MEMORANDUM

OF A CONVERSATION WITH LORD NAPIER.[1]

Monday, 19 October, 1857.   Lord Napier called upon me, as he said, to make an important communication.   This was that he had received a private letter from Lord Clarendon informing him that Sir William Gore Ouseley had been appointed Minister to Central America & his instructions would be to enter into arrangements with the different Central American States in conformity with the U. S.'s construction of the Central American Treaty.   That he himself had expressed the opinion to his Lordship that this would be the best mode of settling the difficulties between the two countries, & asked me if I would be satisfied with such an arrangement.   I told him that I certainly should—

[1] Buchanan Papers, Historical Society of Pennsylvania.

that provided our construction of the Treaty was carried into effect, the manner of doing it was immaterial.

He expressed some anxiety lest I might recommend to Congress the abrogation of the Clayton & Bulwer Treaty,—or if I even did not do that, that Congress might take up the subject & abrogate it themselves, & that he knew, unlike the British Government, I had no means of preventing it. I answered that I had already prepared that part of my message relating to this subject,—that it consisted of a historical statement, in mild but firm terms, stating the case exactly according to the facts as they existed,—that I had hoped something would occur to place the question in a more satisfactory light, which would enable me to say that all the difficulties between the two Governments had been settled, & to express my strong disposition to maintain & cultivate the most friendly relations between the two Governments. That their mutual interest was the same, & that the cause of civilisation & liberty required that they should be the best friends. That I could easily change the message if I had a positive official assurance from the British Government that they had sent a minister to Central America instructed to settle all the questions in dispute according to our construction of the Treaty.

He said he believed I was well acquainted with Sir William Gore Ouseley; that Lord Clarendon had informed him so, & he had no doubt Sir William would come to Washington on his way to Central America, if I desired it, & shew me his instructions. I told him I had first made the acquaintance of Sir William when he was attached to the mission of Sir Charles Vaughan, & that I had been very intimate with him & his lady during my residence in London. I entertained a very warm regard for both; but there was no necessity he should come by way of Washington,—all I wanted was a positive official assurance that the British Government would settle the Central American questions with these States agreeably to our construction of the Treaty. He said this I should have. I told him that this course was calculated to save the feelings of the British Government. He said it was,—it was the best & most satisfactory mode for them to arrange the matter. I conversed with him then about their Treaty with Honduras, & expressed myself dissatisfied with its terms,—it was ceding a nominal sovereignty whilst the British Government in fact retained a protectorate. We conversed at some length on this subject. He said the Treaty had not been ratified & Mr. ———, their minister there, thought the terms too severe. I told him they ought without limitation to restore the Bay Islands to Honduras,—that they would always be able to protect their own subjects now on the Islands,—that they consisted almost altogether of negroes & half breeds. He made no objection to this; but talked of the Slavery question on the Islands, &c. &c. &c.

The Panchita.

The Transit Route belonging to Nicaragua referred to in the Clayton & Bulwer Treaty.

What he had written to Mr. Canby, who informed him he had a grant from Costa Rica.

When His Lordship was about to depart, I said, that there may be no mistake, I shall repeat what I said. I shall be satisfied on condition that the British Government send a minister to Central America instructed to settle all the questions which have been controverted between the two Governments according to the American construction of the Treaty, & upon receiving an official assurance to this effect I shall change the character of my message. He expressed some apprehension for want of time. I told him there was time enough; I could make this change if I received the official information but a short time before the date of the message. He said this was his understanding, & he would go & write immediately to Lord Clarendon. He expressed the opinion that it was a great deal better to pursue this course than have any difficulties about the Dallas Treaty.

The Belize settlement & their encroachments beyond it.

TO GENERAL CASS.[1]

Private. WASHINGTON CITY 24 October 1857.

MY DEAR GENERAL/

I return Lord Napier's draft of our conversations on Monday last & last evening, which you left with me this morning.

In that portion of it which relates to the exclusion of slavery from the Bay Islands by the British Treaty with Honduras, His Lordship has certainly misunderstood me, or I may not have explained myself properly. You know well after what transpired in the Senate that it would be quite impossible for the Government of the United States to sanction & endorse a Treaty between Great Britain & any other Power for the exclusion of Domestic Slavery from its limits. Indeed the utter improbability, nay, I might say the impossibility, that our Southern planters would leave their own profitable plantations & carry their negroes with them to the little Island of Ruatan, where Slavery has been already prohibited, induced some Senators to believe, as I have been informed, that the provision was intended as a gratuitous censure on an Institution recognised & maintained by our Constitution & productive of advantages both to the Master and the Slave as well as necessary to the existence of the Cotton Manufactures of Great Britain & other Countries. Such was not my own belief.

With this exception, for which I am myself partly to blame, His Lordship's Statement, though not sufficiently full, is in the main correct, frank, & fair.

Two omissions I would remark. At the conclusion of our first interview, after his Lordship had risen to go away, according to my memorandum as well as my distinct recollection, I resumed the subject & said, " I shall be satisfied on condition that the British Government send a minister to Central America instructed to settle all the questions which have been controverted between the two Governments according to the American construction of the Treaty, & upon receiving an official assurance to this effect I shall change the character of my message."

The draft does not contain the very satisfactory communi-

---

[1] Buchanan Papers, Historical Society of Pennsylvania.

cation made to me by his Lordship concerning the Panchita & the right of search which I communicated to you; but this is not important.

In our second interview, in reply to His Lordship's remarks on the influence which that clause of the Dallas Clarendon Treaty ought to have, making the Sarstoon instead of the Sibun the limit of Belize,—I said that no person knew better than Lord Clarendon that I would not have entered into such a Treaty.   It yielded to Great Britain the territory in Central America between the Sibun and the Sarstoon, & it recognised in fact a British protectorate over the Bay Islands whilst nominally restoring the Sovereignty over them to Honduras.   Had I been President, I would not have negotiated such a Treaty; but it had been negotiated under the administration of my predecessor & transmitted by him to the Senate.   It was so distasteful to that Body that it had not been touched till after the 4th March;—that I had urged Senators to take it up & decide it one way or the other, this being due to the British Government, & after they had amended & passed it I did not feel myself at liberty under all the circumstances to refuse to ratify & send it to Great Britain;—that in fact I was so anxious to cultivate the most friendly relations with Great Britain that, though I did not like the Treaty as amended, I was greatly disappointed & sorry at their rejection of it.   As it stood originally, however, I think I would not have sent it to the Senate, had it arrived after my inauguration; & then I proceeded to observe according to the statement of his Lordship.

You may read this hasty letter to Lord Napier & give it to him if he desires it.

Yr. friend, very respectfully,

JAMES BUCHANAN.

GENERAL CASS.

FIRST ANNUAL MESSAGE,
DECEMBER 8, 1857.[1]

FELLOW-CITIZENS OF THE SENATE AND HOUSE OF REPRESEN-
TATIVES:

In obedience to the command of the Constitution, it has now become my duty " to give to Congress information of the state of the Union, and recommend to their consideration such measures " as I judge to be " necessary and expedient."

But first, and above all, our thanks are due to Almighty God for the numerous benefits which He has bestowed upon this people; and our united prayers ought to ascend to Him that He would continue to bless our great republic in time to come as He has blessed it in time past. Since the adjournment of the last Congress our constituents have enjoyed an unusual degree of health. The earth has yielded her fruits abundantly, and has bountifully rewarded the toil of the husbandman. Our great staples have commanded high prices, and, up till within a brief period, our manufacturing, mineral, and mechanical occu- pations have largely partaken of the general prosperity. We have possessed all the elements of material wealth in rich abun- dance, and yet, notwithstanding all these advantages, our country, in its monetary interests, is at the present moment in a deplorable condition. In the midst of unsurpassed plenty in all the produc- tions of agriculture, and in all the elements of national wealth, we find our manufactures suspended, our public works retarded, our private enterprises of different kinds abandoned, and thou- sands of useful laborers thrown out of employment and reduced to want. The revenue of the government, which is chiefly derived from duties on imports from abroad, has been greatly reduced, whilst the appropriations made by Congress at its last session for the current fiscal year are very large in amount.

Under these circumstances a loan may be required before the close of your present session; but this, although deeply to be regretted, would prove to be only a slight misfortune when com- pared with the suffering and distress prevailing among the people. With this the government cannot fail deeply to sympathize, though it may be without the power to extend relief.

---

[1] H. Ex. Doc. 2, 35 Cong. 1 Sess.

It is our duty to inquire what has produced such unfortunate results, and whether their recurrence can be prevented. In all former revulsions the blame might have been fairly attributed to a variety of co-operating causes; but not so upon the present occasion. It is apparent that our existing misfortunes have proceeded solely from our extravagant and vicious system of paper currency and bank credits, exciting the people to wild speculations and gambling in stocks. These revulsions must continue to recur at successive intervals so long as the amount of the paper currency and bank loans and discounts of the country shall be left to the discretion of fourteen hundred irresponsible banking institutions, which, from the very law of their nature, will consult the interest of their stockholders rather than the public welfare.

The framers of the Constitution, when they gave to Congress the power " to coin money and to regulate the value thereof," and prohibited the States from coining money, emitting bills of credit, or making anything but gold and silver coin a tender in payment of debts, supposed they had protected the people against the evils of an excessive and irredeemable paper currency. They are not responsible for the existing anomaly that a government endowed with the sovereign attribute of coining money and regulating the value thereof should have no power to prevent others from driving this coin out of the country and filling up the channels of circulation with paper which does not represent gold and silver.

It is one of the highest and most responsible duties of government to insure to the people a sound circulating medium, the amount of which ought to be adapted with the utmost possible wisdom and skill to the wants of internal trade and foreign exchanges. If this be either greatly above or greatly below the proper standard, the marketable value of every man's property is increased or diminished in the same proportion, and injustice to individuals as well as incalculable evils to the community are the consequence.

Unfortunately, under the construction of the Federal Constitution, which has now prevailed too long to be changed, this important and delicate duty has been dissevered from the coining power, and virtually transferred to more than fourteen hundred State banks, acting independently of each other, and regulating their paper issues almost exclusively by a regard to the present interest of their stockholders. Exercising the sovereign power of providing a paper currency instead of coin for the country, the first duty which these banks owe to the public is to keep in their vaults a sufficient amount of gold and silver to insure the convertibility of their notes into coin at all times and under all circumstances. No bank ought ever to be chartered without such restrictions on its business as to secure this result. All other restrictions are comparatively vain. This is the only true touchstone, the only efficient regulator of a paper currency—the only one which can guard the public against over issues and bank suspensions. As a collateral and eventual security it is doubtless wise, and in all cases ought to be required, that banks shall hold an amount of United States or State securities equal to their notes in circulation and pledged for their redemption. This, however, furnishes no adequate security against over issues. On the contrary, it may be perverted to inflate the currency. Indeed, it is possible by this means to convert all the debts of the United States and State governments into bank notes, without reference to the specie required to redeem them. However valuable these securities may be in themselves, they cannot be converted into gold and silver at the moment of pressure, as our experience teaches, in sufficient time to prevent bank suspensions and the depreciation of bank notes. In England, which is to a considerable extent a paper money country, though vastly behind our own in this respect, it was deemed advisable, anterior to the act of Parliament of 1844, which wisely separated the issue of notes from the banking department, for the bank of England always to keep on hand gold and silver equal to one-third of its combined circulation and deposits. If this proportion was no more than sufficient to secure the convertibility of its notes, with the whole of Great Britain, and to some extent the continent of Europe, as a field for its circulation, rendering it almost impossible that a sudden and immediate run to a dangerous amount should be made upon it, the same proportion would certainly be insufficient under our banking system. Each of our fourteen hundred banks has but a limited circumference for its circulation, and in the course of a very few days the depositors and noteholders might demand from such a bank a sufficient amount in specie to compel it to suspend, even although it had coin in its vaults equal to one-third of its immediate liabilities. And yet I am not aware, with the exception of the banks of Louisiana, that any State bank throughout the Union has been required by its charter to keep this or any other proportion of gold and silver compared with the amount of its combined circulation and deposits. What has been the consequence? In a recent report made by the Treasury Department on the condition of the banks throughout the different States, according to returns dated nearest to January, 1857, the aggregate amount of actual specie in their vaults is $58,349,838, of their circulation $214,778,822, and of their deposits $230,351,352. Thus it appears that these banks, in the aggregate, have considerably less than one dollar in seven of gold and silver compared with their circulation and deposits. It was palpable, therefore, that the very first pressure must drive them to suspension, and deprive the people of a convertible currency with all its disastrous consequences. It is truly wonderful that they should have so long continued to preserve their credit, when a demand for the payment of one-seventh of their immediate liabilities would have driven them into insolvency. And this is the condition of the banks, notwithstanding that four hundred millions of gold from California have flowed in upon us within the last eight years, and the tide still continues to flow. Indeed, such has been the extravagance of bank credits that the banks now hold a considerably less amount of specie, either in proportion to their capital or to their circulation and deposits combined, than they did before the discovery of gold in California. Whilst in the year 1848 their specie, in proportion to their capital, was more than equal to one dollar for four and a half, in 1857 it does not amount to one dollar for every six dollars and thirty-three cents of their capital. In the year 1848 the specie was equal within a very small fraction to one dollar in five of their circulation and deposits; in 1857 it is not equal to one dollar in seven and a half of their circulation and deposits.

From this statement it is easy to account for our financial history for the last forty years. It has been a history of extravagant expansions in the business of the country, followed by ruinous contractions. At successive intervals the best and most enterprising men have been tempted to their ruin by excessive bank loans of mere paper credit, exciting them to extravagant importations of foreign goods, wild speculations, and ruinous and demoralizing stock gambling. When the crisis arrives, as arrive it must, the banks can extend no relief to the people. In a vain struggle to redeem their liabilities in specie, they are compelled to contract their loans and their issues; and, at last, in the hour of distress, when their assistance is most needed, they and their debtors together sink into insolvency.

It is this paper system of extravagant expansion, raising the nominal price of every article far beyond its real value, when compared with the cost of similar articles in countries whose circulation is wisely regulated, which has prevented us from competing in our own markets with foreign manufacturers, has produced extravagant importations, and has counteracted the effect of the large incidental protection afforded to our domestic manufactures by the present revenue tariff. But for this, the branches of our manufactures composed of raw materials, the production of our own country—such as cotton, iron, and woolen fabrics—would not only have acquired almost exclusive possession of the home market, but would have created for themselves a foreign market throughout the world.

Deplorable, however, as may be our present financial condition, we may yet indulge in bright hopes for the future. No other nation has ever existed which could have endured such violent expansions and contractions of paper credits without lasting injury; yet the buoyancy of youth, the energies of our population, and the spirit which never quails before difficulties, will enable us soon to recover from our present financial embarrassment, and may even occasion us speedily to forget the lesson which they have taught.

In the mean time it is the duty of the government, by all proper means within its power, to aid in alleviating the sufferings of the people occasioned by the suspension of the banks, and to provide against a recurrence of the same calamity. Unfortunately, in either aspect of the case, it can do but little. Thanks to the independent treasury, the government has not suspended payment, as it was compelled to do by the failure of the banks in 1837. It will continue to discharge its liabilities to the people in gold and silver. Its disbursements in coin will pass into circulation, and materially assist in restoring a sound currency. From its high credit, should we be compelled to make a temporary loan, it can be effected on advantageous terms. This, however, shall, if possible, be avoided; but, if not, then the amount shall be limited to the lowest practicable sum.

I have therefore determined, that whilst no useful government works already in progress shall be suspended, new works, not already commenced, will be postponed, if this can be done without injury to the country. Those necessary for its defence shall proceed as though there had been no crisis in our monetary affairs.

But the federal government cannot do much to provide against a recurrence of existing evils. Even if insurmountable constitutional objections did not exist against the creation of a National Bank, this would furnish no adequate preventive security. The history of the last Bank of the United States abundantly proves the truth of this assertion. Such a bank could not, if it would, regulate the issues and credits of fourteen hundred State banks in such a manner as to prevent the ruinous expansions and contractions in our currency which afflicted the country throughout the existence of the late bank, or secure us against future suspensions. In 1825 an effort was made by the Bank of England to curtail the issues of the country banks, under the most favorable circumstances. The paper currency had been expanded to a ruinous extent, and the Bank put forth all its power to contract it in order to reduce prices and restore the equilibrium of the foreign exchanges. It accordingly commenced a system of curtailment of its loans and issues, in the vain hope that the joint-stock and private banks of the kingdom would be compelled to follow its example. It found, however, that as it contracted they expanded, and at the end of the process, to employ the language of a very high official authority, " whatever reduction of the paper circulation was effected by the Bank of England (in 1825) was more than made up by the issues of the country banks."

But a Bank of the United States would not, if it could, restrain the issues and loans of the State banks, because its duty as a regulator of the currency must often be in direct conflict with the immediate interest of its stockholders. If we expect ¬one agent to restrain or control another, their interests must, at least in some degree, be antagonistic. But the directors of a Bank of the United States would feel the same interest and the same inclination with the directors of the State banks to expand the currency, to accommodate their favorites and friends with loans, and to declare large dividends. Such has been our experience in regard to the last Bank.

After all, we must mainly rely upon the patriotism and wisdom of the States for the prevention and redress of the evil. If they will afford us a real specie basis for our paper circulation by increasing the denomination of bank notes, first to twenty, and afterwards to fifty dollars; if they will require that the banks shall at all times keep on hand at least one dollar of gold and silver for every three dollars of their circulation and deposits; and if they will provide by a self-executing enactment, which nothing can arrest, that the moment they suspend they shall go into liquidation, I believe that such provisions, with a weekly publication by each bank of a statement of its condition, would go far to secure us against future suspensions of specie payments.

Congress, in my opinion, possesses the power to pass a uniform bankrupt law applicable to all banking institutions throughout the United States, and I strongly recommend its exercise. This would make it the irreversible organic law of each bank's existence, that a suspension of specie payments shall produce its civil death. The instinct of self-preservation would then compel it to perform its duties in such a manner as to escape the penalty and preserve its life.

The existence of banks and the circulation of bank paper are so identified with the habits of our people, that they cannot, at this day, be suddenly abolished without much immediate injury to the country. If we could confine them to their appropriate sphere, and prevent them from administering to the spirit of wild and reckless speculation by extravagant loans and issues, they might be continued with advantage to the public.

But this I say, after long and much reflection: If experience shall prove it to be impossible to enjoy the facilities which well-regulated banks might afford, without at the same time suffering the calamities which the excesses of the banks have hitherto inflicted upon the country, it would then be far the lesser evil to deprive them altogether of the power to issue a paper currency, and confine them to the functions of banks of deposit and discount.

Our relations with foreign governments are, upon the whole, in a satisfactory condition.

The diplomatic difficulties which existed between the government of the United States and that of Great Britain at the adjournment of the last Congress have been happily terminated by the appointment of a British minister to this country, who has been cordially received.

Whilst it is greatly to the interest, as I am convinced it is the sincere desire, of the governments and people of the two countries to be on terms of intimate friendship with each other, it has been our misfortune almost always to have had some irritating, if not dangerous, outstanding question with Great Britain.

Since the origin of the government we have been employed in negotiating treaties with that power, and afterwards in discussing their true intent and meaning. In this respect, the convention of April 19, 1850, commonly called the Clayton and Bulwer treaty, has been the most unfortunate of all; because the two governments place directly opposite and contradictory constructions upon its first and most important article. Whilst, in the United States, we believed that this treaty would place both powers upon an exact equality by the stipulation that neither will ever " occupy, or fortify, or colonize, or assume or exercise any dominion " over, any part of Central America, it is contended by the British government that the true construction of this language has left them in the rightful possession of all that portion of Central America which was in their occupancy at the date of the treaty; in fact, that the treaty is a virtual recognition on the part of the United States of the right of Great Britain, either as owner or protector, to the whole extensive coast of Central America, sweeping round from the Rio Hondo to the port and harbor of San Juan de Nicaragua, together with the adjacent Bay Islands, except the comparatively small portion of this between the Sarstoon and Cape Honduras. According to their construction, the treaty does no more than simply prohibit them from extending their possessions in Central America beyond the present limits. It is not too much to assert, that if in the United States the treaty had been considered susceptible of such a construction, it never would have been negotiated under the authority of the President, nor would it have received the approbation of the Senate. The universal conviction in the United States was, that when our government consented to violate its traditional and time-honored policy, and to stipulate with a foreign government never to occupy or acquire territory in the Central American portion of our own continent, the consideration for this sacrifice was that Great Britain should, in this respect at least, be placed in the same position with ourselves. Whilst we have no right to doubt the sincerity of the British government in their construction of the treaty, it is at the same time my deliberate conviction that this construction is in opposition both to its letter and its spirit.

Under the late administration negotiations were instituted between the two governments for the purpose, if possible, of removing these difficulties; and a treaty having this laudable object in view was signed at London on the 17th October, 1856, and was submitted by the President to the Senate on the following 10th of December. Whether this treaty, either in its original or amended form, would have accomplished the object intended without giving birth to new and embarrassing complications between the two governments, may perhaps be well questioned. Certain it is, however, it was rendered much less objectionable by the different amendments made to it by the Senate. The treaty, as amended, was ratified by me on the 12th March, 1857, and was transmitted to London for ratification by the British government. That government expressed its willingness to concur in all the amendments made by the Senate with the single exception of the clause relating to Ruatan and the other islands in the Bay of Honduras. The article in the original treaty, as submitted to the Senate, after reciting that these islands and their inhabitants " having been, by a convention bearing date the 27th day of August, 1856, between her Britannic Majesty and the republic of Honduras, constituted and declared a free territory under the sovereignty of the said republic of Honduras," stipulated that " the two contracting parties do hereby mutually engage to recognize and respect in all future time the independence and rights of the said free territory as a part of the republic of Honduras."

Upon an examination of this convention between Great Britain and Honduras of the 27th August, 1856, it was found that, whilst declaring the Bay Islands to be " a free territory under the sovereignty of the republic of Honduras," it deprived that republic of rights without which its sovereignty over them could scarcely be said to exist. It divided them from the remainder of Honduras, and gave to their inhabitants a separate government of their own, with legislative, executive, and judicial officers, elected by themselves. It deprived the government of Honduras of the taxing power in every form, and exempted the people of the islands from the performance of military duty, except for their own exclusive defence. It also prohibited that republic from erecting fortifications upon them for their protection—thus leaving them open to invasion from any quarter; and, finally, it provided " that slavery shall not at any time hereafter be permitted to exist therein."

Had Honduras ratified this convention, she would have ratified the establishment of a State substantially independent within her own limits, and a State at all times subject to British influence and control. Moreover, had the United States ratified the treaty with Great Britain in its original form, we should have been bound " to recognize and respect in all future time " these stipulations to the prejudice of Honduras. Being in direct opposition to the spirit and meaning of the Clayton and Bulwer treaty as understood in the United States, the Senate rejected the entire clause, and substituted in its stead a simple recognition of the sovereign right of Honduras to these islands in the following language: " The two contracting parties do hereby mutually engage to recognize and respect the islands of Ruatan, Bonaco, Utila, Barbaretta, Helena, and Morat, situate in the Bay of Honduras, and off the coast of the republic of Honduras, as under the sovereignty and as part of the said republic of Honduras."

Great Britain rejected this amendment, assigning as the only reason that the ratifications of the convention of the 27th August, 1856, between her and Honduras, had not been " exchanged, owing to the hesitation of that government." Had this been done, it is stated that " her Majesty's government would have had little difficulty in agreeing to the modification proposed by the Senate, which then would have had in effect the same signification as the original wording." Whether this would have been the effect—whether the mere circumstance of the exchange of the ratifications of the British convention with Honduras prior in point of time to the ratification of our treaty with Great Britain would, " in effect," have had " the same signification as the original wording," and thus have nullified the amendment of the Senate, may well be doubted. It is, perhaps, fortunate that the question has never arisen.

The British government, immediately after rejecting the treaty as amended, proposed to enter into a new treaty with the United States, similar in all respects to the treaty which they had just refused to ratify, if the United States would consent to add to the Senate's clear and unqualified recognition of the sovereignty of Honduras over the Bay Islands the following conditional stipulation: "Whenever and so soon as the republic of Honduras shall have concluded and ratified a treaty with Great Britain, by which Great Britain shall have ceded, and the republic of Honduras shall have accepted, the said islands, subject to the provisions and conditions contained in such treaty."

This proposition was, of course, rejected. After the Senate had refused to recognize the British convention with Honduras of the 27th August, 1856, with full knowledge of its contents, it was impossible for me, necessarily ignorant of "the provisions and conditions" which might be contained in a future convention between the same parties, to sanction them in advance.

The fact is, that when two nations like Great Britain and the United States, mutually desirous as they are, and I trust ever may be, of maintaining the most friendly relations with each other, have unfortunately concluded a treaty which they understand in senses directly opposite, the wisest course is to abrogate such a treaty by mutual consent, and to commence anew. Had this been done promptly, all difficulties in Central America would most probably ere this have been adjusted to the satisfaction of both parties. The time spent in discussing the meaning of the Clayton and Bulwer treaty would have been devoted to this praiseworthy purpose, and the task would have been the more easily accomplished because the interest of the two countries in Central America is identical, being confined to securing safe transits over all the routes across the Isthmus.

Whilst entertaining these sentiments, I shall nevertheless not refuse to contribute to any reasonable adjustment of the Central American questions which is not practically inconsistent with the American interpretation of the treaty. Overtures for this purpose have been recently made by the British government in a friendly spirit, which I cordially reciprocate; but whether this renewed effort will result in success I am not yet prepared to express an opinion. A brief period will determine.

With France our ancient relations of friendship still continue to exist. The French government have in several recent instances, which need not be enumerated, evinced a spirit of good will and kindness towards our country which I heartily reciprocate. It is, notwithstanding, much to be regretted that two nations whose productions are of such a character as to invite the most extensive exchanges and freest commercial intercourse, should continue to enforce ancient and obsolete restrictions of trade against each other. Our commercial treaty with France is, in this respect, an exception from our treaties with all other commercial nations. It jealously levies discriminating duties both on tonnage and on articles, the growth, produce, or manufacture of the one country, when arriving in vessels belonging to the other.

More than forty years ago, on the 3d March, 1815, Congress passed an act offering to all nations to admit their vessels laden with their national productions into the ports of the United States upon the same terms with our own vessels, provided they would reciprocate to us similar advantages. This act confined the reciprocity to the productions of the respective foreign nations who might enter into the proposed arrangement with the United States. The act of May 24, 1828, removed this restriction, and offered a similar reciprocity to all such vessels, without reference to the origin of their cargoes. Upon these principles our commercial treaties and arrangements have been founded, except with France, and let us hope that this exception may not long exist.

Our relations with Russia remain, as they have ever been, on the most friendly footing. The present emperor, as well as his predecessors, have never failed, when the occasion offered, to manifest their good will to our country; and their friendship has always been highly appreciated by the government and people of the United States.

With all other European governments, except that of Spain, our relations are as peaceful as we could desire. I regret to say that no progress whatever has been made, since the adjournment of Congress, towards the settlement of any of the numerous claims of our citizens against the Spanish government. Besides, the outrage committed on our flag by the Spanish war-frigate Ferrolana on the high seas, off the coast of Cuba, in March, 1855, by firing into the American mail steamer El Dorado, and detaining and searching her, remains unacknowledged and unredressed. The general tone and temper of the Spanish government towards that of the United States are much to be regretted. Our present envoy extraordinary and minister plenipotentiary to Madrid has asked to be recalled; and it is my purpose to send out a new minister to Spain, with special instructions on all questions pending between the two governments, and with a determination to have them speedily and amicably adjusted, if this be possible. In the mean time, whenever our minister urges the just claims of our citizens on the notice of the Spanish government, he is met with the objection that Congress has never made the appropriation recommended by President Polk, in his annual message of December, 1847, " to be paid to the Spanish government for the purpose of distribution among the claimants in the Amistad case." A similar recommendation was made by my immediate predecessor, in his message of December, 1853; and entirely concurring with both in the opinion that this indemnity is justly due under the treaty with Spain of the 27th of October, 1795, I earnestly recommend such an appropriation to the favorable consideration of Congress.

A treaty of friendship and commerce was concluded at Constantinople on the 13th December, 1856, between the United States and Persia, the ratifications of which were exchanged at Constantinople on the 13th June, 1857, and the treaty was proclaimed by the President on the 18th August, 1857. This treaty, it is believed, will prove beneficial to American commerce. The Shah has manifested an earnest disposition to cultivate friendly relations with our country, and has expressed a strong wish that we should be represented at Teheran by a minister plenipotentiary; and I recommend that an appropriation be made for this purpose.

Recent occurrences in China have been unfavorable to a revision of the treaty with that empire of the 3d July, 1844, with a view to the security and extension of our commerce. The 24th article of this treaty stipulated for a revision of it, in case experience should prove this to be requisite; " in which case the two governments will, at the expiration of twelve years from the date of said convention, treat amicably concerning the same, by means of suitable persons appointed to conduct such negotiations." These twelve years expired on the 3d July, 1856; but long before that period it was ascertained that important changes in the treaty were necessary; and several fruitless attempts were made by the commissioner of the United States to effect these changes.   Another effort was about to be made for the same purpose by our commissioner, in conjunction with the ministers of England and France, but this was suspended by the occurrence of hostilities in the Canton river between Great Britain and the Chinese Empire.   These hostilities have necessarily interrupted the trade of all nations with Canton, which is now in a state of blockade, and have occasioned a serious loss of life and property.   Meanwhile the insurrection within the empire against the existing imperial dynasty still continues, and it is difficult to anticipate what will be the result.

Under these circumstances, I have deemed it advisable to appoint a distinguished citizen of Pennsylvania envoy extraordinary and minister plenipotentiary to proceed to China, and to avail himself of any opportunities which may offer to effect changes in the existing treaty favorable to American commerce. He left the United States for the place of his destination in July last, in the war steamer Minnesota.   Special ministers to China have also been appointed by the governments of Great Britain and France.

Whilst our minister has been instructed to occupy a neutral position in reference to the existing hostilities at Canton, he will cordially co-operate with the British and French ministers in all peaceful measures to secure by treaty stipulations those just concessions to commerce which the nations of the world have a right to expect, and which China cannot long be permitted to withhold.   From assurances received, I entertain no doubt that the three ministers will act in harmonious concert to obtain similar commercial treaties for each of the powers they represent.

We cannot fail to feel a deep interest in all that concerns the welfare of the independent republics on our own continent, as well as of the empire of Brazil.

Our difficulties with New Granada, which a short time since bore so threatening an aspect, are, it is to be hoped, in a fair train of settlement in a manner just and honorable to both parties.

The Isthmus of Central America, including that of Panama,

is the great highway between the Atlantic and Pacific, over which a large portion of the commerce of the world is destined to pass. The United States are more deeply interested than any other nation in preserving the freedom and security of all the communications across this isthmus. It is our duty, therefore, to take care that they shall not be interrupted either by invasions from our own country or by wars between the independent States of Central America. Under our treaty with New Granada of the 12th December, 1846, we are bound to guaranty the neutrality of the Isthmus of Panama, through which the Panama railroad passes, " as well as the rights of sovereignty and property which New Granada has and possesses over the said territory." This obligation is founded upon equivalents granted by the treaty to the government and people of the United States.

Under these circumstances, I recommend to Congress the passage of an act authorizing the President, in case of necessity, to employ the land and naval forces of the United States to carry into effect this guarantee of neutrality and protection. I also recommend similar legislation for the security of any other route across the isthmus in which we may acquire an interest by treaty.

With the independent republics on this continent it is both our duty and our interest to cultivate the most friendly relations. We can never feel indifferent to their fate, and must always rejoice in their prosperity. Unfortunately, both for them and for us, our example and advice have lost much of their influence in consequence of the lawless expeditions which have been fitted out against some of them within the limits of our country. Nothing is better calculated to retard our steady material progress, or impair our character as a nation, than the toleration of such enterprises in violation of the law of nations.

It is one of the first and highest duties of any independent State, in its relations with the members of the great family of nations, to restrain its people from acts of hostile aggression against their citizens or subjects. The most eminent writers on public law do not hesitate to denounce such hostile acts as robbery and murder.

Weak and feeble States, like those of Central America, may not feel themselves able to assert and vindicate their rights. The case would be far different if expeditions were set on foot within our own territories to make private war against a power-ful nation. If such expeditions were fitted out from abroad against any portion of our own country, to burn down our cities, murder and plunder our people, and usurp our govern-ment, we should call any power on earth to the strictest account for not preventing such enormities.

Ever since the administration of General Washington, acts of Congress have been in force to punish severely the crime of setting on foot a military expedition within the limits of the United States, to proceed from thence against a nation or State with whom we are at peace. The present neutrality act of April 20, 1818, is but little more than a collection of pre-existing laws. Under this act, the President is empowered to employ the land and naval forces and the militia " for the purpose of preventing the carrying on of any such expedition or enterprise from the territories and jurisdiction of the United States," and the col-lectors of customs are authorized and required to detain any vessel in port when there is reason to believe she is about to take part in such lawless enterprises.

When it was first rendered probable that an attempt would be made to get up another unlawful expedition against Nica-ragua, the Secretary of State issued instructions to the marshals and district attorneys, which were directed by the Secretaries of War and the Navy to the appropriate army and navy officers, requiring them to be vigilant and to use their best exertions in carrying into effect the provisions of the act of 1818. Notwith-standing these precautions, the expedition has escaped from our shores. Such enterprises can do no possible good to the coun-try, but have already inflicted much injury both on its interests and its character. They have prevented peaceful emigration from the United States to the States of Central America, which could not fail to prove highly beneficial to all the parties con-cerned. In a pecuniary point of view alone, our citizens have sustained heavy losses from the seizure and closing of the transit route by the San Juan between the two oceans.

The leader of the recent expedition was arrested at New Orleans, but was discharged on giving bail for his appearance in the insufficient sum of two thousand dollars.

I commend the whole subject to the serious attention of Congress, believing that our duty and our interest, as well as

our national character, require that we should adopt such measures as will be effectual in restraining our citizens from committing such outrages.

I regret to inform you that the President of Paraguay has
refused to ratify the treaty between the United States and that
State as amended by the Senate, the signature of which was
mentioned in the message of my predecessor to Congress at the
opening of its session in December, 1853. The reasons assigned
for this refusal will appear in the correspondence herewith submitted.

It being desirable to ascertain the fitness of the river La
Plata and its tributaries for navigation by steam, the United
States steamer Water Witch was sent thither for that purpose
in 1853. This enterprise was successfully carried on until February, 1855, when, whilst in the peaceful prosecution of her
voyage up the Parana river, the steamer was fired upon by a Paraguayan fort. The fire was returned; but as the Water Witch
was of small force, and not designed for offensive operations,
she retired from the conflict. The pretext upon which the attack
was made was a decree of the President of Paraguay of October,
1854, prohibiting foreign vessels-of-war from navigating the
rivers of that State. As Paraguay, however, was the owner of
but one bank of the river of that name, the other belonging to
Corientes, a State of the Argentine Confederation, the right of
its government to expect that such a decree would be obeyed
cannot be acknowledged. But the Water Witch was not, properly speaking, a vessel-of-war. She was a small steamer engaged
in a scientific enterprise intended for the advantage of commercial states generally. Under these circumstances, I am constrained to consider the attack upon her as unjustifiable, and as
calling for satisfaction from the Paraguayan government.

Citizens of the United States, also, who were established in
business in Paraguay, have had their property seized and taken
from them, and have otherwise been treated by the authorities
in an insulting and arbitrary manner, which requires redress.

A demand for these purposes will be made in a firm but
conciliatory spirit. This will the more probably be granted if
the Executive shall have authority to use other means in the
event of a refusal. This is accordingly recommended.

It is unnecessary to state in detail the alarming condition of the Territory of Kansas at the time of my inauguration. The opposing parties then stood in hostile array against each other, and any accident might have relighted the flames of civil war. Besides, at this critical moment, Kansas was left without a governor by the resignation of Governor Geary.

On the 19th of February previous, the territorial legislature had passed a law providing for the election of delegates on the third Monday of June, to a convention to meet on the first Monday of September, for the purpose of framing a constitution preparatory to admission into the Union. This law was in the main fair and just; and it is to be regretted that all the qualified electors had not registered themselves and voted under its provisions.

At the time of the election for delegates, an extensive organization existed in the Territory, whose avowed object it was, if need be, to put down the lawful government by force, and to establish a government of their own under the so-called Topeka constitution. The persons attached to this revolutionary organization abstained from taking any part in the election.

The act of the territorial legislature had omitted to provide for submitting to the people the constitution which might be framed by the convention; and in the excited state of public feeling throughout Kansas, an apprehension extensively prevailed that a design existed to force upon them a constitution, in relation to slavery, against their will. In this emergency it became my duty, as it was my unquestionable right, having in view the union of all good citizens in support of the territorial laws, to express an opinion on the true construction of the provisions concerning slavery contained in the organic act of Congress of the 30th May, 1854. Congress declared it to be " the true intent and meaning of this act, not to legislate slavery into any Territory or State, nor to exclude it therefrom, but to leave the people thereof perfectly free to form and regulate their domestic institutions in their own way." Under it Kansas, " when admitted as a State," was to " be received into the Union with or without slavery, as their constitution may prescribe at the time of their admission."

Did Congress mean by this language that the delegates elected to frame a constitution should have authority finally to decide the question of slavery, or did they intend by leaving it to the people that the people of Kansas themselves should decide this question by a direct vote? On this subject I confess I had never entertained a serious doubt, and, therefore, in my instructions to Governor Walker of the 28th March last, I merely said that when "a constitution shall be submitted to the people of the Territory, they must be protected in the exercise of their right of voting for or against that instrument, and the fair expression of the popular will must not be interrupted by fraud or violence."

In expressing this opinion it was far from my intention to interfere with the decision of the people of Kansas, either for or against slavery. From this I have always carefully abstained. Intrusted with the duty of taking "care that the laws be faithfully executed," my only desire was that the people of Kansas should furnish to Congress the evidence required by the organic act, whether for or against slavery; and in this manner smooth their passage into the Union. In emerging from the condition of territorial dependence into that of a sovereign State, it was their duty, in my opinion, to make known their will by the votes of the majority, on the direct question, whether this important domestic institution should or should not continue to exist. Indeed, this was the only possible mode in which their will could be authentically ascertained.

The election of delegates to a convention must necessarily take place in separate districts. From this cause it may readily happen, as has often been the case, that a majority of the people of a State or Territory are on one side of a question, whilst a majority of the representatives from the several districts into which it is divided may be upon the other side. This arises from the fact that in some districts delegates may be elected by small majorities, whilst in others those of different sentiments may receive majorities sufficiently great not only to overcome the votes given for the former, but to leave a large majority of the whole people in direct opposition to a majority of the delegates. Besides, our history proves, that influences may be brought to bear on the representative sufficiently powerful to induce him to disregard the will of his constituents. The truth is, that no other authentic and satisfactory mode exists of ascertaining the will of a majority of the people of any State or Territory on an important and exciting question like that of slavery in Kansas,

except by leaving it to a direct vote. How wise, then, was it
for Congress to pass over all subordinate and intermediate agencies, and proceed directly to the source of all legitimate power
under our institutions!

How vain would any other principle prove in practice!
This may be illustrated by the case of Kansas. Should she be
admitted into the Union with a constitution either maintaining
or abolishing slavery, against the sentiment of the people, this
could have no other effect than to continue and to exasperate the
existing agitation during the brief period required to make the
constitution conform to the irresistible will of the majority.

The friends and supporters of the Nebraska and Kansas act,
when struggling on a recent occasion to sustain its wise provisions before the great tribunal of the American people, never
differed about its true meaning on this subject. Everywhere
throughout the Union they publicly pledged their faith and their
honor that they would cheerfully submit the question of slavery
to the decision of the *bona fide* people of Kansas, without any
restriction or qualification whatever. All were cordially united
upon the great doctrine of popular sovereignty, which is the
vital principle of our free institutions. Had it, then, been insin-
uated from any quarter that it would be a sufficient compliance
with the requisitions of the organic law for the members of a
convention, thereafter to be elected, to withhold the question of
slavery from the people, and to substitute their own will for
that of a legally-ascertained majority of all their constituents,
this would have been instantly rejected. Everywhere they remained true to the resolution adopted on a celebrated occasion
recognizing " the right of the people of all the Territories—
including Kansas and Nebraska, acting through the legally and
fairly expressed will of a majority of actual residents, and whenever the number of their inhabitants justifies it—to form a constitution with or without slavery, and be admitted into the Union
upon terms of perfect equality with the other States."

The convention to frame a constitution for Kansas met on
the first Monday of September last. They were called together
by virtue of an act of the territorial legislature, whose lawful
existence had been recognized by Congress in different forms and
by different enactments. A large proportion of the citizens of
Kansas did not think proper to register their names and to vote

at the election for delegates; but an opportunity to do this having been fairly afforded, their refusal to avail themselves of their right could in no manner affect the legality of the convention.

This convention proceeded to frame a constitution for Kansas, and finally adjourned on the 7th day of November. But little difficulty occurred in the convention, except on the subject of slavery. The truth is, that the general provisions of our recent State constitutions are so similar, and, I may add, so excellent, that the difference between them is not essential. Under the earlier practice of the government, no constitution framed by the convention of a Territory preparatory to its admission into the Union as a State had been submitted to the people. I trust, however, the example set by the last Congress, requiring that the constitution of Minnesota " should be subject to the approval and ratification of the people of the proposed State," may be followed on future occasions. I took it for granted that the convention of Kansas would act in accordance with this example, founded, as it is, on correct principles; and hence my instructions to Governor Walker, in favor of submitting the constitution to the people, were expressed in general and unqualified terms.

In the Kansas-Nebraska act, however, this requirement, as applicable to the whole constitution, had not been inserted, and the convention were not bound by its terms to submit any other portion of the instrument to an election, except that which relates to the " domestic institution " of slavery. This will be rendered clear by a simple reference to its language. It was " not to legislate slavery into any Territory or State, nor to exclude it therefrom, but to leave the people thereof perfectly free to form and regulate their domestic institutions in their own way." According to the plain construction of the sentence, the words " domestic institutions " have a direct as they have an appropriate reference to slavery. " Domestic institutions " are limited to the family. The relation between master and slave and a few others are " domestic institutions," and are entirely distinct from institutions of a political character. Besides, there was no question then before Congress, nor indeed has there since been any serious question before the people of Kansas or the country, except that which relates to the " domestic institution " of slavery.

The convention, after an angry and excited debate, finally determined, by a majority of only two, to submit the question of slavery to the people, though at the last forty-three of the fifty delegates present affixed their signatures to the constitution.

A large majority of the convention were in favor of establishing slavery in Kansas. They accordingly inserted an article in the constitution for this purpose similar in form to those which had been adopted by other territorial conventions. In the schedule, however, providing for the transition from a territorial to a State government, the question has been fairly and explicitly referred to the people, whether they will have a constitution "with or without slavery." It declares that, before the constitution adopted by the convention "shall be sent to Congress for admission into the Union as a State," an election shall be held to decide this question, at which all the white male inhabitants of the Territory above the age of 21 are entitled to vote. They are to vote by ballot; and "the ballots cast at said election shall be endorsed 'constitution with slavery,' and 'constitution with no slavery.'" If there be a majority in favor of the "constitution with slavery," then it is to be transmitted to Congress by the president of the convention in its original form. If, on the contrary, there shall be a majority in favor of the "constitution with no slavery," "then the article providing for slavery shall be stricken from the constitution by the president of this convention;" and it is expressly declared that "no slavery shall exist in the State of Kansas, except that the right of property in slaves now in the Territory shall in no manner be interfered with;" and in that event it is made his duty to have the constitution thus ratified transmitted to the Congress of the United States for the admission of the State into the Union.

At this election every citizen will have an opportunity of expressing his opinion by his vote "whether Kansas shall be received into the Union with or without slavery," and thus this exciting question may be peacefully settled in the very mode required by the organic law. The election will be held under legitimate authority, and if any portion of the inhabitants shall refuse to vote, a fair opportunity to do so having been presented, this will be their own voluntary act, and they alone will be responsible for the consequences.

Whether Kansas shall be a free or a slave State, must eventually, under some authority, be decided by an election; and the question can never be more clearly or distinctly presented to the people than it is at the present moment. Should this opportunity be rejected, she may be involved for years in domestic discord, and possibly in civil war, before she can again make up the issue now so fortunately tendered, and again reach the point she has already attained.

Kansas has for some years occupied too much of the public attention. It is high time this should be directed to far more important objects. When once admitted into the Union, whether with or without slavery, the excitement beyond her own limits will speedily pass away, and she will then, for the first time, be left, as she ought to have been long since, to manage her own affairs in her own way. If her constitution on the subject of slavery, or on any other subject, be displeasing to a majority of the people, no human power can prevent them from changing it within a brief period. Under these circumstances it may well be questioned whether the peace and quiet of the whole country are not of greater importance than the mere temporary triumph of either of the political parties in Kansas.

Should the constitution without slavery be adopted by the votes of the majority, the rights of property in slaves now in the Territory are reserved. The number of these is very small; but if it were greater the provision would be equally just and reasonable. The slaves were brought into the Territory under the Constitution of the United States, and are now the property of their masters. This point has at length been finally decided by the highest judicial tribunal of the country—and this upon the plain principle that when a confederacy of sovereign States acquire a new territory at their joint expense, both equality and justice demand that the citizens of one and all of them shall have the right to take into it whatsoever is recognized as property by the common Constitution. To have summarily confiscated the property in slaves already in the Territory would have been an act of gross injustice, and contrary to the practice of the older States of the Union which have abolished slavery.

A territorial government was established for Utah by act of Congress approved the 9th September, 1850, and the Constitution and laws of the United States were thereby extended over it " so far as the same, or any provisions thereof, may be applicable." This act provided for the appointment by the President, by and with the advice and consent of the Senate, of a governor, who was to be ex-officio superintendent of Indian affairs, a secretary, three judges of the supreme court, a marshal, and a district attorney. Subsequent acts provided for the appointment of the officers necessary to extend our land and our Indian system over the Territory. Brigham Young was appointed the first governor on the 20th September, 1850, and has held the office ever since. Whilst Governor Young has been both governor and superintendent of Indian affairs throughout this period, he has been at the same time the head of the church called the Latter-Day Saints, and professes to govern its members and dispose of their property by direct inspiration and authority from the Almighty. His power has been, therefore, absolute over both church and State.

The people of Utah, almost exclusively, belong to this church, and believing with a fanatical spirit that he is governor of the Territory by divine appointment, they obey his commands as if these were direct revelations from Heaven. If, therefore, he chooses that his government shall come into collision with the government of the United States, the members of the Mormon church will yield implicit obedience to his will. Unfortunately, existing facts leave but little doubt that such is his determination. Without entering upon a minute history of occurrences, it is sufficient to say that all the officers of the United States, judicial and executive, with the single exception of two Indian agents, have found it necessary for their own personal safety to withdraw from the Territory, and there no longer remains any government in Utah but the despotism of Brigham Young. This being the condition of affairs in the Territory, I could not mistake the path of duty. As Chief Executive Magistrate, I was bound to restore the supremacy of the Constitution and laws within its limits. In order to effect this purpose, I appointed a new governor and other federal officers for Utah, and sent with them a military force for their protection, and to aid as a *posse comitatus,* in case of need, in the execution of the laws.

With the religious opinions of the Mormons, as long as they remained mere opinions, however deplorable in themselves and revolting to the moral and religious sentiments of all Christendom, I had no right to interfere. Actions alone, when in violation of the Constitution and laws of the United States, become the legitimate subjects for the jurisdiction of the civil magistrate.

My instructions to Governor Cumming have therefore been framed in strict accordance with these principles. At their date a hope was indulged that no necessity might exist for employing the military in restoring and maintaining the authority of the law; but this hope has now vanished. Governor Young has, by proclamation, declared his determination to maintain his power by force, and has already committed acts of hostility against the United States. Unless he should retrace his steps the Territory of Utah will be in a state of open rebellion. He has committed these acts of hostility notwithstanding Major Van Vliet, an officer of the army, sent to Utah by the commanding general to purchase provisions for the troops, had given him the strongest assurances of the peaceful intentions of the government, and that the troops would only be employed as a *posse comitatus* when called on by the civil authority to aid in the execution of the laws.

There is reason to believe that Governor Young has long contemplated this result. He knows that the continuance of his despotic power depends upon the exclusion of all settlers from the Territory, except those who will acknowledge his divine mission and implicitly obey his will; and that an enlightened public opinion there would soon prostrate institutions at war with the laws both of God and man. He has, therefore, for several years, in order to maintain his independence, been industriously employed in collecting and fabricating arms and munitions of war, and in disciplining the Mormons 'for military service. As superintendent of Indian Affairs he has had an opportunity of tampering with the Indian tribes, and exciting their hostile feelings against the United States. This, according to our information, he has accomplished in regard to some of these tribes, while others have remained true to their allegiance, and have communicated his intrigues to our Indian agents. He has laid in a store of provisions for three years, which, in case of necessity, as he informed Major Van Vliet, he will conceal, " and then take to the mountains, and bid defiance to all the powers of the government."

A great part of all this may be idle boasting; but yet no wise government will lightly estimate the efforts which may be inspired by such frenzied fanaticism as exists among the Mormons of Utah. This is the first rebellion which has existed in our Territories; and humanity itself requires that we should put it down in such a manner that it shall be the last. To trifle with it would be to encourage it and to render it formidable. We ought to go there with such an imposing force as to convince these deluded people that resistance would be vain, and thus spare the effusion of blood. We can in this manner best convince them that we are their friends, not their enemies. In order to accomplish this object, it will be necessary, according to the estimate of the War Department, to raise four additional regiments; and this I earnestly recommend to Congress. At the present moment of depression in the revenues of the country I am sorry to be obliged to recommend such a measure; but I feel confident of the support of Congress, cost what it may, in suppressing the insurrection and in restoring and maintaining the sovereignty of the Constitution and laws over the Territory of Utah.

I recommend to Congress the establishment of a territorial government over Arizona, incorporating with it such portions of New Mexico as they may deem expedient. I need scarcely adduce arguments in support of this recommendation. We are bound to protect the lives and the property of our citizens inhabiting Arizona, and these are now without any efficient protection. Their present number is already considerable, and is rapidly increasing, notwithstanding the disadvantages under which they labor. Besides, the proposed Territory is believed to be rich in mineral and agricultural resources, especially in silver and copper. The mails of the United States to California are now carried over it throughout its whole extent, and this route is known to be the nearest, and believed to be the best to the Pacific.

Long experience has deeply convinced me that a strict construction of the powers granted to Congress is the only true, as well as the only safe, theory of the Constitution. Whilst this principle shall guide my public conduct, I consider it clear that under the war-making power Congress may appropriate money for the construction of a military road through the territories of the United States, when this is absolutely necessary for the defence of any of the States against foreign invasion. The Constitution has conferred upon Congress power " to declare war," " to raise and support armies," " to provide and maintain a navy," and to call forth the militia to " repel invasions." These high sovereign powers necessarily involve important and responsible public duties, and among them there is none so sacred and so imperative as that of preserving our soil from the invasion of a foreign enemy. The Constitution has, therefore, left nothing on this point to construction, but expressly requires that "the United States shall protect each of them [the States] against invasion." Now, if a military road over our own territories be indispensably necessary to enable us to meet and repel the invader, it follows as a necessary consequence not only that we possess the power, but it is our imperative duty to construct such a road. It would be an absurdity to invest a government with the unlimited power to make and conduct war, and at the same time deny to it the only means of reaching and defeating the enemy at the frontier. Without such a road it is quite evident we cannot "protect" California and our Pacific possessions "against invasion." We cannot by any other means transport men and munitions of war from the Atlantic States in sufficient time successfully to defend these remote and distant portions of the republic.

Experience has proved that the routes across the isthmus of Central America are at best but a very uncertain and unreliable mode of communication. But even if this were not the case, they would at once be closed against us in the event of war with a naval power so much stronger than our own as to enable it to blockade the ports at either end of these routes. After all, therefore, we can only rely upon a military road through our own territories; and ever since the origin of the government Congress has been in the practice of appropriating money from the public treasury for the construction of such roads.

The difficulties and the expense of constructing a military railroad to connect our Atlantic and Pacific States have been greatly exaggerated. The distance on the Arizona route near the 32d parallel of north latitude, between the western boundary of Texas on the Rio Grande and the eastern boundary of California on the Colorado, from the best explorations now within our knowledge, does not exceed four hundred and seventy miles, and the face of the country is, in the main, favorable. For obvious reasons the government ought not to undertake the work itself by means of its own agents. This ought to be committed to other agencies, which Congress might assist, either by grants of land or money, or by both, upon such terms and conditions as they may deem most beneficial for the country. Provision might

thus be made not only for the safe, rapid, and economical transportation of troops and munitions of war, but also of the public
mails. The commercial interests of the whole country, both east
and west, would be greatly promoted by such a road; and, above
all, it would be a powerful additional bond of Union. And
although advantages of this kind, whether postal, commercial, or
political, cannot confer constitutional power, yet they may furnish auxiliary arguments in favor of expediting a work which,
in my judgment, is clearly embraced within the war-making
power.

For these reasons I commend to the friendly consideration
of Congress the subject of the Pacific railroad, without finally
committing myself to any particular route.

The report of the Secretary of the Treasury will furnish a
detailed statement of the condition of the public finances and
of the respective branches of the public service devolved upon
that department of the government. By this report it appears
that the amount of revenue received from all sources into the
treasury during the fiscal year ending the 30th June, 1857, was
sixty-eight million six hundred and thirty-one thousand five
hundred and thirteen dollars and sixty-seven cents, ($68,631,-
513.67,) which amount, with the balance of nineteen million nine
hundred and one thousand three hundred and twenty-five dollars
and forty-five cents, ($19,901,325.45,) remaining in the treas-
ury at the commencement of the year, made an aggregate for the
service of the year of eighty-eight million five hundred and thirty-
two thousand eight hundred and thirty-nine dollars and twelve
cents, ($88,532,839.12.)

The public expenditures for the fiscal year ending 30th June,
1857, amounted to seventy million eight hundred and twenty-two
thousand seven hundred and twenty-four dollars and eighty-five
cents, ($70,822,724.85,) of which five million nine hundred and
forty-three thousand eight hundred and ninety-six dollars and
ninety-one cents ($5,943,896.91) were applied to the redemption
of the public debt, including interest and premium, leaving in the
treasury at the commencement of the present fiscal year on the
1st July, 1857, seventeen million seven hundred and ten thousand
one hundred and fourteen dollars and twenty-seven cents,
($17,710,114.27.)

The receipts into the treasury for the first quarter of the

present fiscal year, commencing 1st July, 1857, were twenty million nine hundred and twenty-nine thousand eight hundred and nineteen dollars and eighty-one cents, ($20,929,819.81,) and the estimated receipts of the remaining three quarters to the 30th June, 1858, are thirty-six million seven hundred and fifty thousand dollars, ($36,750,000,) making, with the balance before stated, an aggregate of seventy-five million three hundred and eighty-nine thousand nine hundred and thirty-four dollars and eight cents ($75,389,934.08) for the service of the present fiscal year.

The actual expenditures during the first quarter of the present fiscal year were twenty-three million seven hundred and fourteen thousand five hundred and twenty-eight dollars and thirty-seven cents, ($23,714,528.37,) of which three million eight hundred and ninety-five thousand two hundred and thirty-two dollars and thirty-nine cents ($3,895,232.39) were applied to the redemption of the public debt, including interest and premium. The probable expenditures of the remaining three quarters, to 30th June, 1858, are fifty-one million two hundred and forty-eight thousand five hundred and thirty dollars and four cents, ($51,248,530.04,) including interest on the public debt, making an aggregate of seventy-four million nine hundred and sixty-three thousand fifty-eight dollars and forty-one cents, ($74,963,058.41,) leaving an estimated balance in the treasury at the close of the present fiscal year of four hundred and twenty-six thousand eight hundred and seventy-five dollars and sixty-seven cents, ($426,875.67.)

The amount of the public debt at the commencement of the present fiscal year was twenty-nine million sixty thousand three hundred and eighty-six dollars and ninety cents, ($29,060,386.90.)

The amount redeemed since the 1st July was three million eight hundred and ninety-five thousand two hundred and thirty-two dollars and thirty-nine cents, ($3,895,232.39,) leaving a balance unredeemed at this time of twenty-five million one hundred and sixty-five thousand one hundred and fifty-four dollars and fifty-one cents, ($25,165,154.51.)

The amount of estimated expenditures for the remaining three quarters of the present fiscal year will, in all probability, be increased from the causes set forth in the report of the Secretary. His suggestion, therefore, that authority should be given to supply any temporary deficiency by the issue of a limited amount of treasury notes, is approved, and I accordingly recommend the passage of such a law.

As stated in the report of the Secretary, the tariff of March 3, 1857, has been in operation for so short a period of time, and under circumstances so unfavorable to a just development of its results as a revenue measure, that I should regard it as inexpedient, at least for the present, to undertake its revision.

I transmit herewith the reports made to me by the Secretaries of War, of the Navy, and of the Interior, and the Postmaster General. They all contain valuable and important information and suggestions, which I commend to the favorable consideration of Congress.

I have already recommended the raising of four additional regiments, and the report of the Secretary of War presents strong reasons, proving this increase of the army, under existing circumstances, to be indispensable.

I would call the special attention of Congress to the recommendation of the Secretary of the Navy in favor of the construction of ten small war steamers of light draught. For some years the government has been obliged on many occasions to hire such steamers from individuals to supply its pressing wants. At the present moment we have no armed vessel in the navy which can penetrate the rivers of China. We have but few which can enter any of the harbors south of Norfolk, although many millions of foreign and domestic commerce annually pass in and out of these harbors. Some of our most valuable interests and most vulnerable points are thus left exposed. This class of vessels of light draught, great speed, and heavy guns would be formidable in coast defence. The cost of their construction will not be great, and they will require but a comparatively small expenditure to keep them in commission. In time of peace they will prove as effective as much larger vessels, and more useful. One of them should be at every station where we maintain a squadron, and three or four should be constantly employed on our Atlantic and Pacific coasts. Economy, utility, and efficiency combine to recommend them as almost indispensable. Ten of these small vessels would be of incalculable advantage to the naval service, and the whole cost of their construction would not exceed two million three hundred thousand dollars, or $230,000 each.

The report of the Secretary of the Interior is worthy of grave consideration. It treats of the numerous, important, and diversified branches of domestic administration intrusted to him by law. Among these the most prominent are the public lands and our relations with the Indians.

Our system for the disposal of the public lands, originating with the fathers of the republic, has been improved as experience pointed the way, and gradually adapted to the growth and settlement of our western States and Territories. It has worked well in practice. Already thirteen States and seven Territories have been carved out of these lands, and still more than a thousand millions of acres remain unsold. What a boundless prospect this presents to our country of future prosperity and power!

We have heretofore disposed of 363,862,464 acres of the public land.

Whilst the public lands, as a source of revenue, are of great importance, their importance is far greater as furnishing homes for a hardy and independent race of honest and industrious citizens, who desire to subdue and cultivate the soil. They ought to be administered mainly with a view of promoting this wise and benevolent policy. In appropriating them for any other purpose, we ought to use even greater economy than if they had been converted into money and the proceeds were already in the public treasury. To squander away this richest and noblest inheritance which any people have ever enjoyed upon objects of doubtful constitutionality or expediency, would be to violate one of the most important trusts ever committed to the people. Whilst I do not deny to Congress the power, when acting *bona fide* as a proprietor, to give away portions of them for the purpose of increasing the value of the remainder, yet, considering the great temptation to abuse this power, we cannot be too cautious in its exercise.

Actual settlers under existing laws are protected against other purchasers at the public sales, in their right of pre-emption, to the extent of a quarter-section, or 160 acres of land. The remainder may then be disposed of at public or entered at private sale in unlimited quantities.

Speculation has of late years prevailed to a great extent in the public lands. The consequence has been that large portions of them have become the property of individuals and companies, and thus the price is greatly enhanced to those who desire to purchase for actual settlement. In order to limit the area of speculation as much as possible, the extinction of the Indian title and the extension of the public surveys ought only to keep pace with the tide of emigration.

If Congress should hereafter grant alternate sections to States or companies, as they have done heretofore, I recommend that the intermediate sections retained by the government should be subject to pre-emption by actual settlers.

It ought ever to be our cardinal policy to reserve the public lands as much as may be for actual settlers, and this at moderate prices. We shall thus not only best promote the prosperity of the new States and Territories, and the power of the Union, but shall secure homes for our posterity for many generations.

The extension of our limits has brought within our jurisdiction many additional and populous tribes of Indians, a large proportion of which are wild, intractable, and difficult to control. Predatory and warlike in their disposition and habits, it is impossible altogether to restrain them from committing aggressions on each other, as well as upon our frontier citizens and those emigrating to our distant States and Territories. Hence expensive military expeditions are frequently necessary to overawe and chastise the more lawless and hostile.

The present system of making them valuable presents to influence them to remain at peace has proved ineffectual. It is believed to be the better policy to colonize them in suitable localities, where they can receive the rudiments of education and be gradually induced to adopt habits of industry. So far as the experiment has been tried it has worked well in practice, and it will doubtless prove to be less expensive than the present system.

The whole number of Indians within our territorial limits is believed to be, from the best data in the Interior Department, about 325,000.

The tribes of Cherokees, Choctaws, Chickasaws, and Creeks, settled in the territory set apart for them west of Arkansas, are rapidly advancing in education and in all the arts of civilization and self-government; and we may indulge the agreeable anticipation that at no very distant day they will be incorporated into the Union as one of the sovereign States.

It will be seen from the report of the Postmaster General

that the Post Office Department still continues to depend on the treasury, as it has been compelled to do for several years past, for an important portion of the means of sustaining and extending its operations. Their rapid growth and expansion are shown by a decennial statement of the number of post offices, and the length of post roads, commencing with the year 1827. In that year there were 7,000 post offices; in 1837, 11,177; in 1847, 15,146; and in 1857 they number 26,586. In this year 1,725 post offices have been established and 704 discontinued, leaving a net increase of 1,021. The postmasters of 368 offices are appointed by the President.

The length of post roads in 1827 was 105,336 miles; in 1837, 141,242 miles; in 1847, 153,818 miles; and in the year 1857 there are 242,601 miles of post road, including 22,530 miles of railroad, on which the mails are transported.

The expenditures of the department for the fiscal year ending on the 30th June, 1857, as adjusted by the Auditor, amounted to $11,507,670. To defray these expenditures there was to the credit of the department on the 1st July, 1856, the sum of $789,599; the gross revenue of the year, including the annual allowances for the transportation of free mail matter, produced $8,053,951; and the remainder was supplied by the appropriation from the treasury of $2,250,000, granted by the act of Congress approved August 18, 1856, and by the appropriation of $666,883 made by the act of March 3, 1857, leaving $252,763 to be carried to the credit of the department in the accounts of the current year. I commend to your consideration the report of the department in relation to the establishment of the overland mail route from the Mississippi river to San Francisco, California. The route was selected with my full concurrence, as the one, in my judgment, best calculated to attain the important objects contemplated by Congress.

The late disastrous monetary revulsion may have one good effect should it cause both the government and the people to return to the practice of a wise and judicious economy both in public and private expenditures.

An overflowing treasury has led to habits of prodigality and extravagance in our legislation. It has induced Congress to make large appropriations to objects for which they never would have provided had it been necessary to raise the amount of revenue required to meet them by increased taxation or by loans. We are now compelled to pause in our career, and to scrutinize our expenditures with the utmost vigilance; and in performing this duty, I pledge my co-operation to the extent of my constitutional competency.

It ought to be observed at the same time that true public economy does not consist in withholding the means necessary to accomplish important national objects intrusted to us by the Constitution, and especially such as may be necessary for the common defence. In the present crisis of the country it is our duty to confine our appropriations to objects of this character, unless in cases where justice to individuals may demand a different course. In all cases care ought to be taken that the money granted by Congress shall be faithfully and economically applied.

Under the Federal Constitution, " every bill which shall have passed the House of Representatives and the Senate shall, before it becomes a law," be approved and signed by the President; and, if not approved, " he shall return it with his objections to that house in which it originated." In order to perform this high and responsible duty, sufficient time must be allowed the President to read and examine every bill presented to him for approval. Unless this be afforded, the Constitution becomes a dead letter in this particular; and even worse, it becomes a means of deception. Our constituents, seeing the President's approval and signature attached to each act of Congress, are induced to believe that he has actually performed this duty, when, in truth, nothing is, in many cases, more unfounded.

From the practice of Congress, such an examination of each bill as the Constitution requires has been rendered impossible. The most important business of each session is generally crowded into its last hours, and the alternative presented to the President is either to violate the constitutional duty which he owes to the people, and approve bills which, for want of time, it is impossible he should have examined, or, by his refusal to do this, subject the country and individuals to great loss and inconvenience.

Besides, a practice has grown up of late years to legislate in appropriation bills, at the last hours of the session, on new and important subjects. This practice constrains the President either to suffer measures to become laws which he does not approve, or to incur the risk of stopping the wheels of the government by vetoing an appropriation bill. Formerly, such bills were confined to specific appropriations for carrying into effect existing laws and the well-established policy of the country, and little time was then required by the President for their examination.

For my own part, I have deliberately determined that I shall approve no bill which I have not examined, and it will be a case of extreme and most urgent necessity which shall ever induce me to depart from this rule. I therefore respectfully, but earnestly, recommend that the two Houses would allow the President at least two days previous to the adjournment of each session within which no new bill shall be presented to him for approval. Under the existing joint rule one day is allowed; but this rule has been hitherto so constantly suspended in practice, that important bills continue to be presented to him up till the very last moments of the session. In a large majority of cases no great public inconvenience can arise from the want of time to examine their provisions, because the Constitution has declared that if a bill be presented to the President within the last ten days of the session, he is not required to return it, either with an approval or with a veto, " in which case it shall not be a law." It may then lie over, and be taken up and passed at the next session. Great inconvenience would only be experienced in regard to appropriation bills; but fortunately, under the late excellent law allowing a salary, instead of a per diem, to members of Congress, the expense and inconvenience of a called session will be greatly reduced.

I cannot conclude without commending to your favorable consideration the interest of the people of this District. Without a representative on the floor of Congress, they have for this very reason peculiar claims upon our just regard. To this I know, from my long acquaintance with them, they are eminently entitled.

JAMES BUCHANAN.

WASHINGTON, December 8, 1857.

MESSAGE

ON A TREATY WITH DENMARK.[1]

To the Senate of the United States:

Herewith I transmit to the Senate, for its consideration with a view to ratification, a convention between the United States and His Majesty the King of Denmark for the discontinuance of the Sound dues, signed in this city on the 11th day of April last.

JAMES BUCHANAN.

WASHINGTON, December 8th, 1857.

MESSAGE

RELATING TO CHINA.[2]

To the Senate and House of Representatives:

I transmit a copy of a letter, of the 30th of May last, from the Commissioner of the United States in China, and of the decree and regulation which accompanied it, for such revision thereof as Congress may deem expedient, pursuant to the sixth section of the act approved the 11th of August, 1848.

JAMES BUCHANAN.

WASHINGTON, December 10, 1857.

---

[1] Senate Executive Journal, X. 262.
[2] S. Ex. Doc. 5, 35 Cong. 1 Sess. 1; H. Ex. Doc. 9, 35 Cong. 1 Sess. 1.

TO MR. FALLON.[1]

Private & Confidential.

WASHINGTON CITY 14 December 1857.

MY DEAR SIR/

In reference to our conversation of yesterday respecting Cuba, I desire to say that the Government of the United States is as willing now to obtain the Island by fair purchase as it was in 1848. You are well acquainted with the efforts made in that year to accomplish the object, & the cause of their failure. It is now, I think, manifest that a transfer of the Island to the United States for a reasonable & fair price would greatly promote the interest of both countries. You are, therefore, authorised to ascertain whether Spain is willing to sell, & upon what terms; & should your report be encouraging, you shall immediately receive more formal instructions. I shall be glad to hear from you on the subject as soon as you can furnish me with any reliable information as to the prospect of success. Both you & those with whom you converse may rely with confidence upon my silence & discretion.

From your friend, very respectfully,

JAMES BUCHANAN.

CHRISTOPHER FALLON, ESQUIRE.

MESSAGE

ON A TREATY WITH THE NETHERLANDS.[2]

[December 17, 1857.]

TO THE SENATE OF THE UNITED STATES:

I transmit to the Senate, for its consideration with a view to ratification, a convention for the mutual delivery of criminals, fugitives from justice in certain cases, and for other purposes,

------

[1] Buchanan Papers, Historical Society of Pennsylvania.
[2] Senate Executive Journal, X. 276–277.

concluded at The Hague on the 21st day of August last, between the United States and His Majesty the King of the Netherlands. The instrument in this form embodies the Senate's amendments of the 16th of February last to the convention between the same parties of the 29th of May, 1856, and is, in fact, a mere copy of that instrument as amended by the Senate. Pursuant to the usual course in such cases, the Senate's amendments were not included in the text of the United States exchange copy of the convention, but appeared in the act of ratification only. As the Dutch Government objected to this, it is now proposed to substitute the new convention herewith submitted.

JAMES BUCHANAN.

WASHINGTON, 17th Decr., 1857.

MESSAGE
ON AFFAIRS IN KANSAS.[1]

TO THE SENATE OF THE UNITED STATES:

In answer to resolutions of the Senate of the 16th and 18th instant, requesting correspondence and documents relative to the Territory of Kansas, I transmit a report from the Secretary of State. and the papers by which it was accompanied.

JAMES BUCHANAN.

WASHINGTON, December 22, 1857.

---

[1] S. Ex. Doc. 8, 35 Cong. 1 Sess. 1.

MESSAGE

ON THE GREYTOWN CLAIMS.[1]

WASHINGTON, December 23, 1857.

TO THE SENATE OF THE UNITED STATES:

I herewith transmit to the Senate a communication, dated on the 22d instant, with the accompanying papers, received from the Department of State, in compliance with a resolution adopted by the Senate on the 17th instant, requesting the President, if compatible with the public interest, to communicate to that body " copies of any correspondence which may have taken place between the Department of State and the British and French ministers on the subject of claims for losses alleged to have been sustained by subjects of Great Britain and France at the bombardment of Greytown."

JAMES BUCHANAN.

TO MR. KANE.[2]

WASHINGTON CITY, December 31, 1857.

MY DEAR SIR: You furnish the strongest evidence of your desire to serve the Mormons by abandoning the comforts of friends, family, and home, and voluntarily encountering the perils and dangers of a journey to Utah at the present inclement season of the year, at your own expense, and without official position. Your only reward must be a consciousness that you are doing your duty. Nothing but pure philanthropy and a strong desire to serve the Mormon people could have dictated a course so much at war with your private interests.

---

[1] S. Ex. Doc. 9, 35 Cong. 1 Sess. 1. December 29, 1857, President Buchanan transmitted to the Senate, in response to its resolution of December 18, with a purely formal message, a report of the Secretary of State and accompanying correspondence relating to the Greytown claims of subjects of the Hanse Towns. (S. Ex. Doc. 10, 35 Cong. 1 Sess. 1.)

[2] H. Ex. Doc. 2, 35 Cong. 2 Sess. II. 162.

You express a strong conviction, in which however I do not participate, that a large portion of the Mormons labor under a mistake as to the intentions of the federal government towards them. If this be so, my late message will disabuse their minds. My views therein expressed, as I have already informed you, have undergone no change. These sentiments were expressed in sincerity and truth, and I trust that your representations of them may meet with the success you anticipate. I hope that the people of Utah may be convinced, ere it is too late, that there exist no duties of higher obligation than those which they owe to their country. They cannot doubt your friendship, and the services which you have rendered to them in times past will conciliate their regard.

At the same time I deem it my duty to say that, whilst reposing entire confidence in the purity and patriotism of your motives, and entertaining a warm personal regard for yourself, I would not at the present moment, in view of the hostile attitude they have assumed against the United States, send any agent to visit them on behalf of the government. If the case were otherwise, however, I know no person to whom I should more cheerfully confide such a mission than yourself.

With every sentiment of personal regard, I remain truly your friend,

JAMES BUCHANAN.

COLONEL THOMAS L. KANE.

TO MR. KANE.[1]

WASHINGTON CITY, December 31, 1857.

MY DEAR SIR: As you have been impelled by your own sense of duty to visit Utah, and having informed me that nothing can divert you from this purpose, it affords me pleasure to commend you to the favorable regard of all officers of the United States whom you may meet in the course of your travels. Pos-

[1] H. Ex. Doc. 2, 35 Cong. 2 Sess. II. 163.

sessed as you are of my confidence, and being well informed as to passing events, you may have it in your power to impart to them useful information from this side of the continent.   I do not doubt that they will, in the exercise of whatever discretion their instructions may permit, render you all the aid and facilities in their power in expediting you on your journey, undertaken of your own accord, to accomplish the pacific and philanthropic objects you have in view.

Heartily wishing you success, I remain, very respectfully, your friend,

JAMES BUCHANAN.

COLONEL THOMAS L. KANE.

1858.

MESSAGE

ON A TREATY WITH THE PAWNEE INDIANS.[1]

WASHINGTON, January 5, 1858.

TO THE SENATE:

I transmit herewith, for the constitutional action of the Senate, a treaty recently concluded with the Pawnee Indians, with accompanying papers.

JAMES BUCHANAN.

MESSAGE

ON KANSAS AFFAIRS.[2]

TO THE SENATE OF THE UNITED STATES:

In compliance with the resolution of the Senate of the 28th of February last, requesting a communication of all the correspondence of John W. Geary, late governor of the Territory of

---

[1] Senate Executive Journal, X. 281.
[2] S. Ex. Doc. 17, 35 Cong. 1 Sess. 1.

Kansas, not heretofore communicated to Congress, I transmit a report from the Secretary of State and the documents by which it was accompanied.

JAMES BUCHANAN.

WASHINGTON, January 6, 1858.

MESSAGE

ON KANSAS AFFAIRS.[1]

TO THE SENATE OF THE UNITED STATES:

In answer to the resolution of the Senate of the 18th of last month, requesting certain information relative to the territory of Kansas, I transmit a report from the Secretary of State, and the documents by which it was accompanied.

JAMES BUCHANAN.

WASHINGTON, January 6, 1858.

MESSAGE

ON THE ARREST OF WILLIAM WALKER IN NICARAGUA.[2]

TO THE HOUSE OF REPRESENTATIVES:

I transmit a report from the Secretary of State, in answer to the resolution of the House of Representatives of the 4th instant, requesting to be informed if any complaint had been made against our government by the government of Nicaragua, on account of the recent arrest of William Walker and his followers, by Captain Paulding, within the territory of that republic.

JAMES BUCHANAN.

WASHINGTON, January 7, 1858.

---

[1] S. Ex. Doc. 12, 35 Cong. 1 Sess. 1.   The information related to the election held in Kansas in October, 1856.

[2] H. Ex. Doc. 26, 35 Cong. 1 Sess. 1.   The report of the Secretary of State said that no such complaint had reached his department.

MESSAGE

ON THE ARREST OF WILLIAM WALKER IN NICARAGUA.[1]

[January 7, 1858.]

TO THE SENATE OF THE UNITED STATES:

I herewith transmit to the Senate a report from the Secretary of the Navy, with the accompanying documents, containing the information called for by the resolution of the Senate of the 4th instant, requesting me " to communicate to the Senate the correspondence, instructions, and orders to the United States naval forces on the coast of Central America, connected with the arrest of William Walker and his associates," &c. &c. &c.

In submitting to the Senate the papers for which they have called, I deem it proper to make a few observations.

In capturing General Walker and his command after they had landed on the soil of Nicaragua, Commodore Paulding has, in my opinion, committed a grave error. It is quite evident, however, from the communications herewith transmitted, that this was done from pure and patriotic motives, and in the sincere conviction that he was promoting the interests and vindicating the honor of his country. In regard to Nicaragua, she has sustained no injury by the act of Commodore Paulding. This has inured to her benefit, and relieved her from a dreaded invasion. She alone would have any right to complain of the violation of her territory; and it is quite certain she will never exercise this right. It unquestionably does not lie in the mouth of her invaders to complain in her name that she has been rescued by Commodore Paulding from their assaults. The error of this gallant officer consists in exceeding his instructions, and landing his sailors and marines in Nicaragua, whether with or without her consent, for the purpose of making war upon any military force whatever which he might find in the country, no matter from whence they came. This power certainly did not belong to him. Obedience to law and conformity to instructions are the best and safest guides for all officers, civil and military, and when they transcend these limits, and act upon their own personal responsibility, evil consequences almost inevitably follow.

---

[1] S. Doc. 13, 35 Cong. 1 Sess.

Under these circumstances, when Marshal Rynders presented himself at the State Department on the 29th ultimo, with General Walker in custody, the Secretary informed him "that the Executive department of the Government did not recognize General Walker as a prisoner; that it had no directions to give concerning him, and that it is only through the action of the judiciary that he could be lawfully held in custody to answer any charges that might be brought against him."

In thus far disapproving the conduct of Commodore Paulding, no inference must be drawn that I am less determined than I have ever been to execute the neutrality laws of the United States. This is my imperative duty, and I shall continue to perform it by all the means which the Constitution and the laws have placed in my power.

My opinion of the value and importance of these laws corresponds entirely with that expressed by Mr. Monroe in his message to Congress of December 7, 1819. That wise, prudent, and patriotic statesman says: "It is of the highest importance to our national character, and indispensable to the morality of our citizens, that all violations of our neutrality should be prevented. No door should be left open for the evasion of our laws, no opportunity afforded to any who may be disposed to take advantage of it, to compromit the interests or the honor of the nation."

The crime of setting on foot or providing the means for a military expedition within the United States to make war against a foreign State with which we are at peace is one of an aggravated and dangerous character, and early engaged the attention of Congress. Whether the Executive Government possesses any or what power under the Constitution, independently of Congress, to prevent or punish this and similar offences against the law of nations, was a subject which engaged the attention of our most eminent statesmen in the time of the administration of General Washington, and on the occasion of the French Revolution. The act of Congress of the 5th of June, 1794, fortunately removed all the difficulties on this question which had theretofore existed. The fifth and seventh sections of this act, which relate to the present question, are the same in substance with the sixth and eighth sections of the act of April 20, 1818, and have now been in force for a period of more than sixty years.

The military expedition rendered criminal by the act, must have its origin, must " begin," or be " set on foot," in the United States; but the great object of the law was to save foreign States with whom we were at peace from the ravages of these lawless expeditions proceeding from our shores. The seventh section alone, therefore, which simply defines the crime and its punishment, would have been inadequate to accomplish this purpose and enforce our international duties. In order to render the law effectual, it was necessary to prevent " the carrying on " of such expeditions to their consummation after they had succeeded in leaving our shores.

This has been done effectually, and in clear and explicit language, by the authority given to the President under the eighth section of the act to employ the land and naval forces of the United States " for the purpose of preventing the carrying on of any such expedition or enterprise from the territories or jurisdiction of the United States against the territories or domain of any foreign prince or State, or of any colony, district, or people with whom the United States are at peace."

For these reasons, had Commodore Paulding intercepted the steamer " Fashion," with General Walker and his command on board, at any period before they entered the port of San Juan de Nicaragua, and conducted them back to Mobile, this would have prevented them from " carrying on " the expedition, and have been not only a justifiable but a praiseworthy act.

The crime well deserves the punishment inflicted upon it by our laws. It violates the principles of Christianity, morality, and humanity, held sacred by all civilized nations, and by none more than by the people of the United States. Disguise it as we may, such a military expedition is an invitation to reckless and lawless men to enlist under the banner of any adventurer to rob, plunder, and murder the unoffending citizens of neighboring States who have never done them harm. It is a usurpation of the war-making power, which belongs alone to Congress; and the Government itself, at least in the estimation of the world, becomes an accomplice in the commission of this crime, unless it adopts all the means necessary to prevent and to punish it.

It would be far better, and more in accordance with the bold and manly character of our countrymen, for the Government itself to get up such expeditions, than to allow them to proceed under the command of irresponsible adventurers. We could then, at least, exercise some control over our own agents, and prevent them from burning down cities, and committing other acts of enormity of which we have read.

The avowed principle which lies at the foundation of the law of nations is contained in the Divine command that " All things whatsoever ye would that men should do to you, do ye even so to them." Tried by this unerring rule, we should be severely condemned if we shall not use our best exertions to arrest such expeditions against our feeble sister Republic of Nicaragua. One thing is very certain, that people never existed who would call any other nation to a stricter account than we should ourselves for tolerating lawless expeditions from their shores to make war upon any portion of our territories.

By tolerating such expeditions, we shall soon lose the high character which we have enjoyed ever since the days of Washington for the faithful performance of our international obligations and duties, and inspire distrust against us among the members of the great family of civilized nations.

But if motives of duty were not sufficient to restrain us from engaging in such lawless enterprises, our evident interest ought to dictate this policy. These expeditions are the most effectual mode of retarding American progress; although to promote this is the avowed object of the leaders and contributors in such undertakings.

It is, beyond question, the destiny of our race to spread themselves over the Continent of North America, and this at no distant day, should events be permitted to take their natural course. The tide of emigrants will flow to the South, and nothing can eventually arrest its progress. If permitted to go there, peacefully, Central America will soon contain an American population which will confer blessings and benefits as well upon the natives as their respective Governments. Liberty under the restraint of law will preserve domestic peace, whilst the different transit routes across the Isthmus, in which we are so deeply interested, will have assured protection.

Nothing has retarded this happy condition of affairs so much as the unlawful expeditions which have been fitted out in the United States to make war upon the Central American States. Had one half of the number of American citizens who have miserably perished in the first disastrous expedition of General Walker settled in Nicaragua as peaceful emigrants, the object which we all desire would ere this have been in a great degree accomplished. These expeditions have caused the people of the Central American States to regard us with dread and suspicion. It is our true policy to remove this apprehension, and to convince them that we intend to do them good, and not evil. We desire, as the leading Power on this continent, to open and, if need be, to protect every transit route across the Isthmus, not only for our own benefit, but that of the world, and thus open a free access to Central America, and through it to our Pacific possessions. This policy was commenced under favorable auspices, when the expedition, under the command of General Walker, escaped from our territories and proceeded to Punta Arenas. Should another expedition of a similar character again evade the vigilance of our officers, and proceed to Nicaragua, this would be fatal, at least for a season, to the peaceful settlement of these countries, and to the policy of American progress. The truth is, that no Administration can successfully conduct the foreign affairs of the country in Central America, or anywhere else, if it is to be interfered with at every step by lawless military expeditions " set on foot " in the United States.

JAMES BUCHANAN.

WASHINGTON, January 7, 1858.

MESSAGE

ON THE CONSTITUTION OF MINNESOTA.[1]

To THE SENATE AND HOUSE OF REPRESENTATIVES OF THE UNITED STATES:

I have received from Samuel Medary, governor of the Territory of Minnesota, a copy of the constitution of Minnesota, " together with an abstract of the votes polled for and against said constitution," at the election held in that Territory on the second Tuesday of October last, certified by the governor in due

---

[1] S. Ex. Doc. 14, 35 Cong. 1 Sess. 1 ; H. Ex. Doc. 25, 35 Cong. 1 Sess. 1.

form, which I now lay before Congress in the manner prescribed by that instrument.

Having received but a single copy of the constitution, I transmit this to the Senate.

JAMES BUCHANAN.

WASHINGTON, January 11, 1858.

MESSAGE

ON THE ARREST OF WILLIAM WALKER IN NICARAGUA.[1]

TO THE HOUSE OF REPRESENTATIVES:

I herewith transmit to the House of Representatives the reports of the Secretaries of State, the Treasury, and the Navy, and of the Attorney General, with the accompanying documents, containing the information called for by the resolution of the House of the 4th instant concerning " the late seizure of General William Walker and his followers in Nicaragua," &c., &c.

JAMES BUCHANAN.

WASHINGTON, January 11, 1858.

TO MR. BAKER.[2]

WASHINGTON 11 January 1858.

MY DEAR SIR/

I saw Mr. Florence to-day, who has behaved very well in the matter of Severns & in all other matters since my inauguration. I hope to have that matter satisfactorily adjusted without your aid, though I do not yet know.

---

[1] H. Ex. Doc. 24, 35 Cong. 1 Sess. 1.

[2] Buchanan Papers, Historical Society of Pennsylvania. Joseph B. Baker, often called Colonel Baker, was a man of large political influence in Pennsylvania, and during Buchanan's administration was collector of the port of Philadelphia. He was a warm personal friend of Mr. Buchanan, who reposed entire confidence in his integrity and personal fidelity. His brother, Lafayette C. Baker, married Mary Lane, sister of Harriet Lane, Mr. Buchanan's niece.

The Kansas question, from present appearances, will not be one of much difficulty; & *all is not yet told*. If what we have heard be true, there will be an end of it speedily. In any event it will, I think, terminate favorably. Kansas must be brought into the Union at the present session, or many of the Democratic members who now hesitate will be certain to lose their seats at the next election. Their safety consists in their firmness & fidelity.

Douglas has alienated the South on the Kansas question & the North upon the Filibuster question.

I mourn over Forney. I fear he can never return to us, & yet he must feel awkward in his new associations. They will, I trust, at least make the fortune of his paper. I have not the slightest wish that you should remove Sheridan. In this do what you deem best in your own judgment.

I do not read the Press, simply because it distresses me to witness its course. I would, however, do nothing harsh towards Forney. Should he finally leave us, he is a man of too much spirit to desire the continuance of Sheridan. I repeat, I mourn over Forney.

Always yr. friend

JAMES BUCHANAN.

J. B. BAKER ESQ.

MESSAGE

ON A TREATY WITH PERU.[1]

TO THE SENATE OF THE UNITED STATES:

I transmit to the Senate, for its consideration with a view to ratification, a convention between the United States and the Republic of Peru, signed on the 4th July last, at Lima, by the plenipotentiaries of the contracting parties, with regard to the interpretation to be given to article 12 of the treaty of the 26th July, 1851.

JAMES BUCHANAN.

January 12, 1858.

---

[1] Senate Executive Journal, X. 289.

MESSAGE

ON A CONVENTION WITH DENMARK.[1]

To the Senate and House of Representatives:

I transmit to Congress a copy of a convention between the United States and his Majesty the King of Denmark for the discontinuance of the Sound dues, the ratifications of which were exchanged in this city on the 12th instant, and recommend that an appropriation be made to enable the Executive seasonably to carry into effect the stipulations in regard to the sums payable to his Danish Majesty's government.

JAMES BUCHANAN.

WASHINGTON, January 14, 1858.

MESSAGE

ON EMIGRANT TICKETS.[2]

To the Senate of the United States:

In answer to the resolution of the Senate of the 7th instant, requesting information on the subject of contracts made in Europe for inland passage tickets for intending emigrants to the United States, I transmit a report from the Secretary of State, and the documents by which it was accompanied.

JAMES BUCHANAN.

WASHINGTON, January 27, 1858.

---

[1] S. Ex. Doc. 28, 35 Cong. 1 Sess. 1; H. Ex. Doc. 31, 35 Cong. 1 Sess. 1.
[2] S. Ex. Doc. 26, 35 Cong. 1 Sess. 1.

MESSAGE

ON THE CENSUS OF MINNESOTA TERRITORY.[1]

[January 28, 1858.]

To the House of Representatives:

I herewith transmit to the House of Representatives a report from the Secretary of the Interior, under date of the 27th instant, with the accompanying papers, in compliance with a resolution adopted by the House on the 18th instant, requesting the President to communicate to that body "whether the census of the Territory of Minnesota has been taken, in accordance with the provisions of the fourth section of the act of Congress providing for the admission of Minnesota as a State, approved February 26, 1857; and if said census has been taken and returned to him, or any department of the government, to communicate the same to this House, and if the said census has not been so taken and returned, to state the reasons, if any exist, to his knowledge, why it has not been done."

JAMES BUCHANAN.

Washington, January 28, 1858.

MESSAGE

ON THE CONSTITUTION OF KANSAS.[2]

[February 2, 1858.]

To the Senate and House of Representatives of the United States:

I have received from J. Calhoun, Esq., president of the late constitutional convention of Kansas, a copy, duly certified by himself, of the constitution framed by that body, with the expres-

---

[1] H. Ex. Doc. 49, 35 Cong. 1 Sess. 1.
[2] S. Ex. Doc. 21, 35 Cong. 1 Sess.

sion of a hope that I would submit the same to the consideration of Congress, " with the view of the admission of Kansas into the Union as an independent State." In compliance with this request, I herewith transmit to Congress, for their action, the constitution of Kansas, with the ordinance respecting the public lands, as well as the letter of Mr. Calhoun, dated at Lecompton on the 14th ultimo, by which they were accompanied. Having received but a single copy of the constitution and ordinance, I send this to the Senate.

A great delusion seems to pervade the public mind in relation to the condition of parties in Kansas. This arises from the difficulty of inducing the American people to realize the fact that any portion of them should be in a state of rebellion against the government under which they live. When we speak of the affairs of Kansas, we are apt to refer merely to the existence of two violent political parties in that Territory, divided on the question of slavery, just as we speak of such parties in the States. This presents no adequate idea of the true state of the case. The dividing line there is not between two political parties, both acknowledging the lawful existence of the government, but between those who are loyal to this government and those who have endeavored to destroy its existence by force and by usurpation— between those who sustain and those who have done all in their power to overthrow the territorial government established by Congress. This government they would long since have subverted had it not been protected from their assaults by the troops of the United States. Such has been the condition of affairs since my inauguration. Ever since that period a large portion of the people of Kansas have been in a state of rebellion against the government, with a military leader at their head of a most turbulent and dangerous character. They have never acknowledged, but have constantly renounced and defied the government to which they owe allegiance, and have been all the time in a state of resistance against its authority. They have all the time been endeavoring to subvert it and to establish a revolutionary government, under the so-called Topeka constitution, in its stead. Even at this very moment the Topeka legislature are in session. Whoever has read the correspondence of Governor Walker with the State Department, recently communicated to the Senate, will be convinced that this picture is not overdrawn. He always protested against the withdrawal of any portion of the military force of the United States from the Territory, deeming its presence absolutely necessary for the preservation of the regular government and the execution of the laws. In his very first despatch to the Secretary of State, dated June 2, 1857, he says: "The most alarming movement, however, proceeds from the assembling on the 9th June of the so-called Topeka legislature, with a view to the enactment of an entire code of laws. Of course it will be my endeavor to prevent such a result, as it would lead to inevitable and disastrous collision, and, in fact, renew the civil war in Kansas." This was with difficulty prevented by the efforts of Governor Walker; but soon thereafter, on the 14th of July, we find him requesting General Harney to furnish him a regiment of dragoons to proceed to the city of Lawrence—and this for the reason that he had received authentic intelligence, verified by his own actual observation, that a dangerous rebellion had occurred, "involving an open defiance of the laws and the establishment of an insurgent government in that city."

In the governor's despatch of July 15, he informs the Secretary of State "that this movement at Lawrence was the beginning of a plan, originating in that city, to organize insurrection throughout the Territory; and especially in all towns, cities, or counties where the republican party have a majority. Lawrence is the hot bed of all the abolition movements in this Territory. It is the town established by the abolition societies of the east, and whilst there are respectable people there, it is filled by a considerable number of mercenaries who are paid by abolition societies to perpetuate and diffuse agitation throughout Kansas, and prevent a peaceful settlement of this question. Having failed in inducing their own so-called Topeka State legislature to organize this insurrection, Lawrence has commenced it herself, and, if not arrested, the rebellion will extend throughout the Territory."

And again: "In order to send this communication immediately by mail, I must close by assuring you that the spirit of rebellion pervades the great mass of the republican party of this Territory, instigated, as I entertain no doubt they are, by eastern societies, having in view results most disastrous to the government and to the Union; and that the continued presence of General Harney here is indispensable, as originally stipulated by me, with a large body of dragoons and several batteries."

On the 20th July, 1857, General Lane, under the authority of the Topeka convention, undertook, as Governor Walker informs us, " to organize the whole so-called free State party into volunteers, and to take the names of all who refuse enrolment. The professed object is to protect the polls, at the election in August, of the new insurgent Topeka State legislature."

" The object of taking the names of all who refuse enrolment is to terrify the free State conservatives into submission. This is proved by recent atrocities committed on such men by Topekaites. The speedy location of large bodies of regular troops here, with two batteries, is necessary. The Lawrence insurgents await the development of this new revolutionary military organization," &c., &c.

In the governor's despatch of July 27th, he says that " General Lane and his staff everywhere deny the authority of the territorial laws, and counsel a total disregard of these enactments."

Without making further quotations of a similar character from other despatches of Governor Walker, it appears by a reference to Mr. Stanton's communication to General Cass, of the 9th of December last, that the " important step of calling the legislature together was taken after I [he] had become satisfied that the election ordered by the convention on the 21st instant could not be conducted without collision and bloodshed." So intense was the disloyal feeling among the enemies of the government established by Congress, that an election which afforded them an opportunity, if in the majority, of making Kansas a free State, according to their own professed desire, could not be conducted without collision and bloodshed!

The truth is, that, up till the present moment, the enemies of the existing government still adhere to their Topeka revolutionary constitution and government. The very first paragraph of the message of Governor Robinson, dated on the 7th of December, to the Topeka legislature, now assembled at Lawrence, contains an open defiance of the Constitution and laws of the United States. The governor says: " The convention which framed the constitution at Topeka originated with the people of Kansas Territory. They have adopted and ratified the same twice by a direct vote, and also indirectly through two elections of State officers and members of the

State legislature. Yet it has pleased the administration to regard the whole proceeding as revolutionary."

This Topeka government, adhered to with such treasonable pertinacity, is a government in direct opposition to the existing government prescribed and recognized by Congress. It is a usurpation of the same character as it would be for a portion of the people of any State of the Union to undertake to establish a separate government, within its limits, for the purpose of redressing any grievance, real or imaginary, of which they might complain, against the legitimate State government. Such a principle, if carried into execution, would destroy all lawful authority and produce universal anarchy.

From this statement of facts, the reason becomes palpable why the enemies of the government authorized by Congress have refused to vote for delegates to the Kansas constitutional convention, and also afterwards on the question of slavery submitted by it to the people. It is because they have ever refused to sanction or recognize any other constitution than that framed at Topeka.

Had the whole Lecompton constitution been submitted to the people, the adherents of this organization would doubtless have voted against it, because, if successful, they would thus have removed an obstacle out of the way of their own revolutionary constitution. They would have done this, not upon a consideration of the merits of the whole or any part of the Lecompton constitution, but simply because they have ever resisted the authority of the government authorized by Congress, from which it emanated.

Such being the unfortunate condition of affairs in the Territory, what was the right, as well as the duty, of the law abiding people? Were they silently and patiently to submit to the Topeka usurpation, or adopt the necessary measures to establish a constitution under the authority of the organic law of Congress?

That this law recognized the right of the people of the Territory, without any enabling act from Congress, to form a State constitution, is too clear for argument. For Congress " to leave the people of the Territory perfectly free," in framing their constitution, "to form and regulate their domestic institutions in their own way, subject only to the Constitution of the

United States," and then to say that they shall not be permitted to proceed and frame a constitution in their own way, without an express authority from Congress, appears to be almost a contradiction in terms.   It would be much more plausible to contend that Congress had no power to pass such an enabling act, than to argue that the people of a Territory might be kept out of the Union for an indefinite period, and until it might please Congress to permit them to exercise the right of self-government. This would be to adopt not "their own way," but the way which Congress might prescribe.

It is impossible that any people could have proceeded with more regularity in the formation of a constitution than the people of Kansas have done.   It was necessary, first, to ascertain whether it was the desire of the people to be relieved from their territorial dependence and establish a State government. For this purpose, the territorial legislature, in 1855, passed a law " for taking the sense of the people of this Territory upon the expediency of calling a convention to form a State constitution " at the general election to be held in October, 1856.   The " sense of the people " was accordingly taken, and they decided in favor of a convention.   It is true that at this election the enemies of the territorial government did not vote, because they were then engaged at Topeka, without the slightest pretext of lawful authority, in framing a constitution of their own for the purpose of subverting the territorial government.

In pursuance of this decision of the people in favor of a convention, the territorial legislature, on the 27th day of February, 1857, passed an act for the election of delegates on the third Monday of June, 1857, to frame a State constitution. This law is as fair in its provisions as any that ever passed a legislative body for a similar purpose.   The right of suffrage at this election is clearly and justly defined.   " Every *bona fide* inhabitant of the Territory of Kansas " on the third Monday of June, the day of the election, who was a citizen of the United States above the age of twenty-one, and had resided therein for three months previous to that date, was entitled to vote.   In order to avoid all interference from neighboring States or Territories with the freedom and fairness of the election, provision was made for the registry of the qualified voters; and, in pursuance thereof, nine thousand two hundred and fifty-one voters

were registered.   Governor Walker did his whole duty in urging
all the qualified citizens of Kansas to vote at this election.   In
his inaugural address, on the 27th May last, he informed them
that "under our practice the preliminary act of framing a State
constitution is uniformly performed through the instrumentality
of a convention of delegates chosen by the people themselves.
That convention is now about to be elected by you under the
call of the territorial legislature, created and still recognized by
the authority of Congress, and clothed by it, in the comprehensive
language of the organic law, with full power to make such an
enactment.   The territorial legislature, then, in assembling this
convention, were fully sustained by the act of Congress, and the
authority of the convention is distinctly recognized in my instructions from the President of the United States."

The governor also clearly and distinctly warns them what
would be the consequences if they should not participate in
the election.   "The people of Kansas, then, (he says) are
invited by the highest authority known to the Constitution, to
participate, freely and fairly, in the election of delegates to
frame a constitution and State government.   The law has
performed its entire appropriate function when it extends to
the people the right of suffrage, but it cannot compel the performance of that duty.   Throughout our whole Union, however,
and wherever free government prevails, those who abstain from
the exercise of the right of suffrage authorize those who do vote
to act for them in that contingency; and the absentees are as
much bound, under the law and Constitution, where there is no
fraud or violence, by the act of the majority of those who do
vote, as if all had participated in the election.   Otherwise, as
voting must be voluntary, self-government would be impracticable, and monarchy or despotism would remain as the only
alternative."

It may also be observed, that at this period any hope, if
such had existed, that the Topeka constitution would ever be
recognized by Congress, must have been abandoned.   Congress
had adjourned on the 3d March previous, having recognized the
legal existence of the territorial legislature in a variety of forms,
which I need not enumerate.   Indeed, the delegate elected to
the House of Representatives, under a territorial law, had been
admitted to his seat, and had just completed his term of service
on the day previous to my inauguration.

This was the propitious moment for settling all difficulties in Kansas. This was the time for abandoning the revolutionary Topeka organization, and for the enemies of the existing government to conform to the laws, and to unite with its friends in framing a State constitution. But this they refused to do, and the consequences of their refusal to submit to lawful authority and vote at the election of delegates may yet prove to be of a most deplorable character. Would that the respect for the laws of the land which so eminently distinguished the men of the past generation could be revived! It is a disregard and violation of law which have for years kept the Territory of Kansas in a state of almost open rebellion against its government. It is the same spirit which has produced actual rebellion in Utah. Our only safety consists in obedience and conformity to law. Should a general spirit against its enforcement prevail, this will prove fatal to us as a nation. We acknowledge no master but the law; and should we cut loose from its restraints, and every one do what seemeth good in his own eyes, our case will indeed be hopeless.

The enemies of the territorial government determined still to resist the authority of Congress. They refused to vote for delegates to the convention, not because, from circumstances which I need not detail, there was an omission to register the comparatively few voters who were inhabitants of certain counties of Kansas in the early spring of 1857, but because they had predetermined, at all hazards, to adhere to their revolutionary organization, and defeat the establishment of any other constitution than that which they had framed at Topeka. The election was, therefore, suffered to pass by default; but of this result the qualified electors who refused to vote can never justly complain.

From this review, it is manifest that the Lecompton convention, according to every principle of constitutional law, was legally constituted and was invested with power to frame a constitution.

The sacred principle of popular sovereignty has been invoked in favor of the enemies of law and order in Kansas. But in what manner is popular sovereignty to be exercised in this country, if not through the instrumentality of established law? In certain small republics of ancient times the people did assemble in primary meetings, passed laws, and directed public affairs. In our country this is manifestly impossible. Popular sovereignty can be exercised here only through the ballot-box; and if the people will refuse to exercise it in this manner, as they have done in Kansas at the election of delegates, it is not for them to complain that their rights have been violated.

The Kansas convention, thus lawfully constituted, proceeded to frame a constitution, and, having completed their work, finally adjourned on the 7th day of November last. They did not think proper to submit the whole of this constitution to a popular vote, but they did submit the question whether Kansas should be a free or a slave State to the people. This was the question which had convulsed the Union and shaken it to its very centre. This was the question which had lighted up the flames of civil war in Kansas, and had produced dangerous sectional parties throughout the confederacy. It was of a character so paramount in respect to the condition of Kansas as to rivet the anxious attention of the people of the whole country upon it, and it alone. No person thought of any other question. For my own part, when I instructed Governor Walker, in general terms, in favor of submitting the constitution to the people, I had no object in view except the all-absorbing question of slavery. In what manner the people of Kansas might regulate their other concerns was not a subject which attracted any attention. In fact, the general provisions of our recent State constitutions, after an experience of eighty years, are so similar and so excellent that it would be difficult to go far wrong at the present day in framing a new constitution.

I then believed, and still believe, that, under the organic act, the Kansas convention were bound to submit this all-important question of slavery to the people. It was never, however, my opinion that, independently of this act, they would have been bound to submit any portion of the constitution to a popular vote, in order to give it validity. Had I entertained such an opinion, this would have been in opposition to many precedents in our history, commencing in the very best age of the republic. It would have been in opposition to the principle which pervades our institutions, and which is every day carried out into practice, that the people have the right to delegate to representatives, chosen by themselves, their sovereign power to frame constitutions, enact laws, and perform many other important acts, without requiring that these should be subjected to their subsequent approbation.   It would be a most inconvenient limitation of their own power, imposed by the people upon themselves, to exclude them from exercising their sovereignty in any lawful manner they think proper.   It is true that the people of Kansas might, if they had pleased, have required the convention to submit the constitution to a popular vote; but this they have not done.   The only remedy, therefore, in this case, is that which exists in all other similar cases.   If the delegates who framed the Kansas constitution have in any manner violated the will of their constituents, the people always possess the power to change their constitution or their laws, according to their own pleasure.

The question of slavery was submitted to an election of the people of Kansas on the 21st December last, in obedience to the mandate of the Constitution.   Here, again, a fair opportunity was presented to the adherents of the Topeka constitution, if they were the majority, to decide this exciting question " in their own way," and thus restore peace to the distracted Territory; but they again refused to exercise their right of popular sovereignty, and again suffered the election to pass by default.

I heartily rejoice that a wiser and better spirit prevailed among a large majority of these people on the first Monday of January; and that they did, on that day, vote under the Lecompton constitution for a governor and other State officers, a member of Congress, and for members of the legislature. This election was warmly contested by the parties, and a larger vote was polled than at any previous election in the Territory.   We may now reasonably hope that the revolutionary Topeka organization will be speedily and finally abandoned, and this will go far towards the final settlement of the unhappy differences in Kansas.   If frauds have been committed at this election, either by one or both parties, the legislature and the people of Kansas, under their constitution, will know how to redress themselves and punish these detestable but too common crimes without any outside interference.

The people of Kansas have, then, " in their own way," and in strict accordance with the organic act, framed a constitution and State government; have submitted the all-important question of slavery to the people, and have elected a governor, a member to represent them in Congress, members of the State legislature.

and other State officers. They now ask admission into the Union
under this constitution, which is republican in its form. It is
for Congress to decide whether they will admit or reject the
State which has thus been created. For my own part, I am
decidedly in favor of its admission, and thus terminating the
Kansas question. This will carry out the great principle of
non-intervention recognized and sanctioned by the organic act,
which declares in express language in favor of " non-intervention
by Congress with slavery in the States or Territories," leaving
" the people thereof perfectly free to form and regulate their
domestic institutions in their own way, subject only to the
Constitution of the United States." In this manner, by localiz-
ing the question of slavery, and confining it to the people whom
it immediately concerned, every patriot anxiously expected that
this question would be banished from the halls of Congress,
where it has always exerted a baneful influence throughout the
whole country.

It is proper that I should briefly refer to the election held
under an act of the territorial legislature, on the first Monday
of January last, on the Lecompton constitution. This election
was held after the Territory had been prepared for admission
into the Union as a sovereign State, and when no authority
existed in the territorial legislature which could possibly destroy
its existence or change its character. The election, which was
peaceably conducted under my instructions, involved a strange
inconsistency. A large majority of the persons who voted
against the Lecompton constitution were at the very same time
and place recognizing its valid existence in the most solemn and
authentic manner, by voting under its provisions. I have yet
received no official information of the result of this election.

As a question of expediency, after the right has been maintained, it may be wise to reflect upon the benefits to Kansas
and to the whole country which would result from its immediate
admission into the Union, as well as the disasters which may
follow its rejection. Domestic peace will be the happy consequence of its admission, and that fine Territory, which has
hitherto been torn by dissensions, will rapidly increase in population and wealth, and speedily realize the blessings and the
comforts which follow in the train of agricultural and mechanical industry. The people will then be sovereign, and can
regulate their own affairs in their own way. If a majority of

them desire to abolish domestic slavery within the State, there is no other possible mode by which this can be effected so speedily as by prompt admission. The will of the majority is supreme and irresistible when expressed in an orderly and lawful manner. They can make and unmake constitutions at pleasure. It would be absurd to say that they can impose fetters upon their own power which they cannot afterwards remove. If they could do this, they might tie their own hands for a hundred as well as for ten years. These are fundamental principles of American freedom, and are recognized, I believe, in some form or other, by every State constitution; and if Congress, in the act of admission, should think proper to recognize them, I can perceive no objection to such a course. This has been done emphatically in the constitution of Kansas. It declares in the bill of rights that " all political power is inherent in the people, and all free governments are founded on their authority and instituted for their benefit, and therefore they have at all times an inalienable and indefeasible right to alter, reform, or abolish their form of government in such manner as they may think proper." The great State of New York is at this moment governed under a constitution framed and established in direct opposition to the mode prescribed by the previous constitution. If, therefore, the provision changing the Kansas constitution, after the year one thousand eight hundred and sixty-four, could by possibility be construed into a prohibition to make such a change previous to that period, this prohibition would be wholly unavailing. The legislature already elected may, at its very first session, submit the question to a vote of the people whether they will or will not have a convention to amend their constitution and adopt all necessary means for giving effect to the popular will.

It has been solemnly adjudged by the highest judicial tribunal known to our laws, that slavery exists in Kansas by virtue of the Constitution of the United States. Kansas is, therefore, at this moment as much a slave State as Georgia or South Carolina. Without this the equality of the sovereign States composing the Union would be violated, and the use and enjoyment of a Territory acquired by the common treasure of all the States would be closed against the people and the property of nearly half the members of the confederacy. Slavery can therefore never be prohibited in Kansas except by means of a constitutional provision, and in no other manner can this be obtained so promptly, if a majority of the people desire it, as by admitting it into the Union under its present constitution.

On the other hand, should Congress reject the constitution, under the idea of affording the disaffected in Kansas a third opportunity of prohibiting slavery in the State, which they might have done twice before if in the majority, no man can foretell the consequences.

If Congress, for the sake of those men who refused to vote for delegates to the convention when they might have excluded slavery from the constitution, and who afterwards refused to vote on the 21st December last, when they might, as they claim, have stricken slavery from the constitution, should now reject the State because slavery remains in the constitution, it is manifest that the agitation upon this dangerous subject will be renewed in a more alarming form than it has ever yet assumed.

Every patriot in the country had indulged the hope that the Kansas and Nebraska act would put a final end to the slavery agitation, at least in Congress, which had for more than twenty years convulsed the country and endangered the Union. This act involved great and fundamental principles, and if fairly carried into effect will settle the question. Should the agitation be again revived, should the people of the sister States be again estranged from each other with more than their former bitterness, this will arise from a cause, so far as the interests of Kansas are concerned, more trifling and insignificant than has ever stirred the elements of a great people into commotion. To the people of Kansas, the only practical difference between admission or rejection depends simply upon the fact whether they can themselves more speedily change the present constitution if it does not accord with the will of the majority, or frame a second constitution to be submitted to Congress hereafter. Even if this were a question of mere expediency, and not of right, the small difference of time, one way or the other, is of not the least importance, when contrasted with the evils which must necessarily result to the whole country from a revival of the slavery agitation.

In considering this question, it should never be forgotten that, in proportion to its insignificance, let the decision be what it may, so far as it may affect the few thousand inhabitants of Kansas, who have from the beginning resisted the constitution and the laws, for this very reason the rejection of the constitution will be so much the more keenly felt by the people of fourteen of the States of this Union, where slavery is recognized under the Constitution of the United States.

Again: The speedy admission of Kansas into the Union would restore peace and quiet to the whole country. Already the affairs of this Territory have engrossed an undue proportion of public attention. They have sadly affected the friendly relations of the people of the States with each other, and alarmed the fears of patriots for the safety of the Union. Kansas once admitted into the Union, the excitement becomes localized, and will soon die away for want of outside aliment. Then every difficulty will be settled at the ballot-box.

Besides—and this is no trifling consideration—I shall then be enabled to withdraw the troops of the United States from Kansas, and employ them on branches of service where they are much needed. They have been kept there, on the earnest importunity of Governor Walker, to maintain the existence of the territorial government and secure the execution of the laws. He considered that at least two thousand regular troops, under the command of General Harney, were necessary for this purpose. Acting upon his reliable information, I have been obliged, in some degree, to interfere with the expedition to Utah, in order to keep down rebellion in Kansas. This has involved a very heavy expense to the government. Kansas once admitted, it is believed there will no longer be any occasion there for troops of the United States.

I have thus performed my duty on this important question, under a deep sense of responsibility to God and my country. My public life will terminate within a brief period; and I have no other object of earthly ambition than to leave my country in a peaceful and prosperous condition, and to live in the affections and respect of my countrymen. The dark and ominous clouds which now appear to be impending over the Union, I conscientiously believe may be dissipated with honor to every portion of it by the admission of Kansas during the present session of Congress; whereas, if she should be rejected, I greatly fear these clouds will become darker and more ominous than any which have ever yet threatened the Constitution and the Union.

JAMES BUCHANAN.

WASHINGTON, February 2, 1858.

MESSAGE

ON A TREATY WITH JAPAN.[1]

To the Senate of the United States:

I transmit to the Senate, for its consideration with a view to ratification, a convention for the purpose of further regulating the intercourse of American citizens within the Empire of Japan, signed at Simoda on the 17th day of June last, by Townsend Harris, consul-general of the United States, and by the governors of Simoda, empowered for that purpose by their respective Governments.

JAMES BUCHANAN.

February 10, 1858.

MESSAGE

ON A TREATY WITH FRANCE.[2]

To the Senate of the United States:

I transmit to the Senate for its consideration, with a view to ratification, an additional article to the extradition convention between the United States and France, of the 9th of November, 1843, and the additional article thereto of the 24th February, 1845, signed in this city yesterday by the Secretary of State and the minister of His Imperial Majesty the Emperor of the French.

JAMES BUCHANAN.

Washington, February 11, 1858.

---

[1] Senate Executive Journal, X. 303.
[2] Senate Executive Journal, X. 320.

MESSAGE

ON THE EXECUTION OF COLONEL CRABB.[1]

To the House of Representatives:

I herewith transmit a report from the Secretary of State, with the accompanying documents, in reply to the resolution of the House of Representatives of the 18th ultimo, requesting to be furnished with official information and correspondence in relation to the execution of Colonel Crabb and his associates within or near the limits of the republic of Mexico.

JAMES BUCHANAN.

WASHINGTON, February 12, 1858.

PROCLAMATION

ABOLISHING DISCRIMINATING DUTIES IN THE CASE
OF THE PAPAL STATES.[2]

[February 25, 1858.]

By the President of the United States of America.

A Proclamation.

Whereas by an act of Congress of the United States, of the 24th of May, 1828, entitled " An act in addition to an act entitled ' An act concerning discriminating duties of tonnage and impost,' and to equalize the duties on Prussian vessels and their cargoes," it is provided that upon satisfactory evidence being given to the President of the United States, by the government of any foreign nation, that no discriminating duties of tonnage or impost are imposed or levied in the ports of the said nation upon vessels wholly belonging to citizens of the United States, or upon the produce, manufactures, or merchandise imported in the same from the United States, or from any foreign country, the President is thereby authorized to issue his proclamation declaring that the foreign discriminating duties of tonnage and impost

[1] H. Ex. Doc. 64, 35 Cong. 1 Sess. 1.
[2] United States Statutes at Large, XI. 795.

within the United States are, and shall be, suspended and discontinued, so far as respects the vessels of the said foreign nation, and the produce, manufactures, or merchandise imported into the United States in the same from the said foreign nation, or from any other foreign country, the said suspension to take effect from the time of such notification being given to the President of the United States, and to continue so long as the reciprocal exemption of vessels belonging to citizens of the United States, and their cargoes, as aforesaid, shall be continued, and no longer; and

Whereas satisfactory evidence has lately been received from the Government of His Holiness the Pope, through an official communication addressed by Cardinal Antonelli, his secretary of state, to the minister resident of the United States at Rome, under date of the 7th day of December, one thousand eight hundred and fifty-seven, that no discriminating duties of tonnage or impost are imposed or levied in the ports of the Pontifical States upon vessels wholly belonging to citizens of the United States, or upon the produce, manufactures, or merchandise imported in the. same from the United States, or from any foreign country:

Now, therefore, I, James Buchanan, President of the United States of America, do hereby declare and proclaim that the foreign discriminating duties of tonnage and impost within the United States are, and shall be, suspended and discontinued so far as respects the vessels of the subjects of His Holiness the Pope, and the produce, manufactures, or merchandise imported into the United States in the same from the Pontifical States, or from any other foreign country; the said suspension to take effect from the 7th day of December, one thousand eight hundred and fifty-seven, above mentioned, and to continue so long as the reciprocal exemption of vessels belonging to citizens of the United States and their cargoes, as aforesaid, shall be continued, and no longer.

Given under my hand, at the city of Washington, the 25th day of February, in the year of our Lord one thousand (Seal.) eight hundred and fifty-eight, and of the Independence of the United States the eighty-second.

JAMES BUCHANAN.

By the President:
LEWIS CASS, Secretary of State.

MESSAGE

ON THE UTAH EXPEDITION.[1]

[February 26, 1858.]

To the House of Representatives:

I herewith transmit to the House of Representatives the reports of the Secretaries of State, of War, and of the Interior, and of the Attorney General, containing the information called for by a resolution of the House, of the 27th ultimo, requesting "the President, if not incompatible with the public interest, to communicate to the House of Representatives the information which gave rise to the military expeditions ordered to Utah Territory, the instructions to the army officers in connexion with the same, and all correspondence which has taken place with said army officers, with Brigham Young and his followers, or with others, throwing light upon the question as to how far said Brigham Young and his followers are in a state of rebellion or resistance to the government of the United States."

JAMES BUCHANAN.

WASHINGTON CITY, February 26, 1858.

MESSAGE

ON NOMINEES FOR THE MARINE CORPS.[2]

To the Senate of the United States:

I herewith transmit to the Senate a report from the Secretary of the Navy, dated on the 24th instant [ultimo], furnishing the information called for by a resolution of the Senate adopted on the 16th instant [ultimo], requesting me "to inform the Senate, in executive session, on what evidence the nominees for

[1] H. Ex. Doc. 71, 35 Cong. 1 Sess. 1.
[2] Senate Executive Journal, X. 327.

the Marine Corps are stated to be taken from the States as designated in his message communicating the nominations, of January 13."

JAMES BUCHANAN.

WASHINGTON, March 2nd, 1858.

MESSAGE

ON THE NUMBER OF TROOPS IN THE WAR OF 1812.[1]

TO THE HOUSE OF REPRESENTATIVES:

I herewith transmit to the House of Representatives communications from the Secretary of War and Secretary of the Interior, in answer to the resolution adopted by the House on the 5th ultimo, requesting the President to furnish certain information in relation to the number of troops, whether regulars, volunteers, drafted men, or militia, who were engaged in the service of the United States in the last war with Great Britain, &c., &c.

JAMES BUCHANAN.

WASHINGTON CITY, March 4, 1858.

MESSAGE

ON THE LAWS OF THE DISTRICT OF COLUMBIA.[2]

TO THE SENATE AND HOUSE OF REPRESENTATIVES:

I transmit herewith a report of the Attorney General, with accompanying papers, dated March 1, 1858, detailing proceedings, under the act approved March 3, 1855, entitled " An act to improve the laws of the District of Columbia, and to codify the same."

JAMES BUCHANAN.

WASHINGTON, March 9, 1858.

[1] H. Ex. Doc. 72, 35 Cong. 1 Sess. 1.
[2] H. Ex. Doc. 74, 35 Cong. 1 Sess. 1.

TO PRINCE ALBERT.[1]

WASHINGTON CITY, March 13, 1858.

SIR:—

I have had the honor to receive from Lord Napier your very kind note of the 16th ultimo, with the medal struck in commemoration of the marriage of the Princess Royal with Prince Frederick William. Whilst in England I had upon one or two occasions the privilege of meeting and conversing with the Princess Royal, which caused me to form a very high estimate of the excellence of her character, and to feel a deep interest in her prosperity and happiness. May her destiny prove fortunate, and her married life be crowned by a kind Providence with all the blessings which it is the lot of humanity to enjoy.

With my most respectful regards to the queen, I remain truly yours,

JAMES BUCHANAN.

MESSAGE

ON THE CORRESPONDENCE BETWEEN THE LATE SECRETARY OF WAR AND GENERAL WOOL.[2]

TO THE HOUSE OF REPRESENTATIVES:

In compliance with a resolution of the House of Representatives, of the 26th of January, requesting the President to com-

---

[1] Curtis's Buchanan, II. 229. The letter, to which this was a reply, was as follows:

BUCKINGHAM PALACE, Feb. 16, 1858.

MY DEAR MR. BUCHANAN:—

The belief that your recollection of the time passed by you in England will have made you feel an interest in the late happy marriage of our eldest daughter, induces me to send for your acceptance a medal struck in commemoration of that event. You will, I think, be able easily to recognize the Princess Royal's features; the likeness of Prince Frederick William is also very good.

Trusting that your health continues unimpaired, notwithstanding the manifold duties of your high and responsible office, in which hope the queen joins with me, I remain, ever, my dear Mr. Buchanan, yours truly,

ALBERT.

[2] H. Ex. Doc. 88, 35 Cong. 1 Sess. 1.

municate to the House " so much of the correspondence between the late Secretary of War and Major General John E. Wool, late commander of the Pacific department, relative to the affairs of such department, as has not heretofore been published under a call of this House," I herewith transmit all the correspondence called for so far as is afforded by the files of the War Department.

JAMES BUCHANAN.

WASHINGTON, March 23, 1858.

TO LORD CLARENDON.[1]

Private. WASHINGTON 27 March 1858.

MY DEAR LORD CLARENDON,

I had determined to address you a line, immediately after the late ministerial change; but my numerous and pressing engagements have hitherto rendered this almost impossible. I have now scarcely time to say my prayers. In the earlier history of our Government, the President was able to give his personal attention to almost every subject of the least importance. The practice has continued whilst the business has increased ten, I may say twenty fold, & is now so onerous that no man can very long bear the burden. There must be some change; but innovation is the difficulty.

Facts are sometimes stranger than fiction, & the change in your ministry is an illustration of this truth. If I believed this would do you a serious injury, either personally or politically, it would be a cause of deep regret to me. I shall always gratefully remember your kindness & courtesy whilst I was in England. I know, if Providence should spare your life, you must rise again; & I am happy to entertain this conviction. I believe that you participate with me in the desire to promote peace and friendship between the two countries. The material interests of both are essentially involved in the welfare of each other; & according to the old Scotch proverb, " blood is thicker than water." This will shew itself some day.

[1] Buchanan Papers, Historical Society of Pennsylvania.

I have been anxiously awaiting developments from Sir William Ouseley's mission. I have never yet learned specifically the terms which he intended to propose to the Central American States. From the beginning I always supposed that this might prove the most acceptable mode of settling the vexed questions arising out of the Clayton & Bulwer Treaty. It is stated somewhere in the correspondence that you were under the impression I did not receive the overtures made by Lord N. kindly. This was an entire mistake, & I think it is impossible His Lordship could have left me under this impression. I know not what course Lord Derby's administration may pursue; but it will find me always ready & willing to settle all difficulties with England in the most conciliatory spirit.

I suppose it is almost certain we shall never meet again in this world. This is certain, unless some happy contingency might bring you on a visit to this country. Whether we shall ever meet again or not, my best wishes for the long life, prosperity, & happiness of Lady Clarendon & yourself shall never cease. Miss Lane most cordially unites with me in this sentiment.

From your friend, very respectfully,

JAMES BUCHANAN.

TO MR. DENVER.[1]

Private & Confidential.

WASHINGTON CITY 27 March 1858.

MY DEAR SIR/

It gratifies me to learn from different sources that you stand so well with the people of Kansas of all parties. Had you been sent there at first instead of Walker, the territory would have been in a much more quiet condition than it is at present.

---

[1] Buchanan Papers, Historical Society of Pennsylvania. General James Wilson Denver, after whom Denver, Colorado, was named, was successively an editor, a captain in the Mexican War, a public official in California, a member of Congress, commissioner of Indian affairs, governor of Kansas (1858), again commissioner of Indian affairs, a brigadier general of volunteers in the Civil War, and afterwards a lawyer in Washington, D. C. He died at Denver in 1892.

In the House, the question of the admission of Kansas, under the Lecompton constitution, will probably be decided next week. Both parties hope for success; but fear defeat. My own opinion is that it will pass; but I do not speak with confidence. The Public is tired even ad nauseam with the Kansas agitation. The defeat of the Bill would alarm the fears of the country for the Union, reduce the value of property, & injuriously interfere with our reviving trade. You are doubtless aware of the fact that, upon the defeat of the Bill, the Governors of Georgia & Alabama are required by existing Legislation to cause an election of Delegates to a State Convention to be held for the purpose of determining what course they shall pursue, " in case Kansas should be refused admission into the Union," under " the Lecompton Constitution." I quote from the Resolutions of Alabama.

The Southern people say,—the Free State men have now got every thing in Kansas their own way,—they have a large majority of the Legislature,—the right of the people is recognised to change & reform their Constitution at pleasure,—if they desire to abolish Slavery, which now exists there under the Constitution of the United States and the Dred Scott decision, the admission of the State is the speediest mode by which it can be accomplished. If, say they, Congress will not admit a State whose Constitution contains Slavery under all these favorable circumstances, it is vain for them to expect that they will ever admit a bona fide Slave State.

I have no doubt you will do your best to inaugurate the new Government, should the Bill pass, in peace and in a manner satisfactory to the people. There will be several important offices to bestow; and in the selection of officers I shall be very much guided by your advice. The best and most influential men ought to be selected. A great trust has been confided to you; & should you prove successful in executing it, which I pray Heaven you may, you will deserve the gratitude of your Country and make for yourself a historical name. I shall send Mr. Walsh's nomination to the Senate as Secretary of the Territory on Monday next.

Kansas cannot be admitted into the Union for a long time to come if this be not done under the Lecompton Constitution. The proceedings there to frame a second constitution whilst the first is pending will not be regarded. Should Mr. Crittenden's amendment prevail, which is highly improbable, what will be the result?

1. An Election on the Lecompton Constitution.

2. Should this be rejected by the people, then the Territorial Legislature will not meet till January, 1859; & it is not possible, I presume, that a Constitution could be framed & the State admitted before 3 March '59. This could not be accomplished until some time in the year 1860; & in the mean time what will become of the material interests of Kansas? They will be the sport & the capital of the Black Republicans in the Presidential Election of 1860.

California has come out nobly in support of the Kansas policy of the administration, as you will see by the enclosed. The Resolutions doubtless passed the Senate by an equally large proportionate majority on the day the Steamer left.

With sentiments of warm regard, I remain very respectfully
Your friend
JAMES BUCHANAN.

HON. J. W. DENVER.

PROCLAMATION
ON THE REBELLION IN UTAH.[1]

[April 6, 1858.]

By JAMES BUCHANAN, PRESIDENT OF THE UNITED STATES OF AMERICA.

A PROCLAMATION.

Whereas, the Territory of Utah was settled by certain emigrants from the States, and from foreign countries, who have for several years past manifested a spirit of insubordination to the Constitution and laws of the United States. The great mass of

---

[1] H. Ex. Doc. 2, 35 Cong. 2 Sess. I. 69–72; United States Statutes at Large, XI. 796.

those settlers, acting under the influence of leaders to whom they
seem to have surrendered their judgment, refuse to be controlled
by any other authority. They have been often advised to obedience, and these friendly counsels have been answered with defiance. Officers of the federal government have been driven from
the Territory for no offence but an effort to do their sworn duty.
Others have been prevented from going there by threats of
assassination. Judges have been violently interrupted in the
performance of their functions, and the records of the courts
have been seized and either destroyed or concealed. Many other
acts of unlawful violence have been perpetrated, and the right to
repeat them has been openly claimed by the leading inhabitants,
with at least the silent acquiescence of nearly all the others.
Their hostility to the lawful government of the country has at
length become so violent that no officer bearing a commission
from the Chief Magistrate of the Union can enter the Territory
or remain there with safety; and all the officers recently appointed
have been unable to go to Salt Lake or anywhere else in Utah
beyond the immediate power of the army. Indeed, such is believed to be the condition to which a strange system of terrorism
has brought the inhabitants of that region, that no one among
them could express an opinion favorable to this government, or
even propose to obey its laws, without exposing his life and
property to peril.

After carefully considering this state of affairs, and ma-
turely weighing the obligation I was under to see the laws faithfully executed, it seemed to me right and proper that I should
make such use of the military force at my disposal as might be
necessary to protect the federal officers in going into the Territory of Utah, and in performing their duties after arriving there.
I accordingly ordered a detachment of the army to march for
the City of Salt Lake, or within reach of that place, and to act,
in case of need, as a posse for the enforcement of the laws. But,
in the meantime, the hatred of that misguided people for the just
and legal authority of the government had become so intense that
they resolved to measure their military strength with that of the
Union. They have organized an armed force far from contemptible in point of numbers, and trained it, if not with skill, at
least with great assiduity and perseverance. While the troops
of the United States were on their march, a train of baggage

wagons, which happened to be unprotected, was attacked and destroyed by a portion of the Mormon forces, and the provisions and stores with which the train was laden were wantonly burnt. In short, their present attitude is one of decided and unreserved enmity to the United States and to all their loyal citizens. Their determination to oppose the authority of the government by military force has not only been expressed in words, but manifested in overt acts of the most unequivocal character.

Fellow-citizens of Utah! this is rebellion against the government to which you owe allegiance. It is levying war against the United States, and involves you in the guilt of treason. Persistence in it will bring you to condign punishment, to ruin, and to shame; for it is mere madness to suppose that, with your limited resources, you can successfully resist the force of this great and powerful nation.

If you have calculated upon the forbearance of the United States—if you have permitted yourselves to suppose that this government will fail to put forth its strength and bring you to submission—you have fallen into a grave mistake. You have settled upon territory which lies geographically in the heart of the Union. The land you live upon was purchased by the United States and paid for out of their treasury; the proprietary right and title to it is in them, and not in you. Utah is bounded on every side by States and Territories whose people are true to the Union. It is absurd to believe that they will or can permit you to erect in their very midst a government of your own, not only independent of the authority which they all acknowledge, but hostile to them and their interests.

Do not deceive yourselves nor try to mislead others by propagating the idea that this is a crusade against your religion. The Constitution and laws of this country can take no notice of your creed, whether it be true or false. That is a question between your God and yourselves, in which I disclaim all right to interfere. If you obey the laws, keep the peace, and respect the just rights of others, you will be perfectly secure, and may live on in your present faith or change it for another at your pleasure. Every intelligent man among you knows very well that this government has never, directly or indirectly, sought to molest you in your worship, to control you in your ecclesiastical affairs, or even to influence you in your religious opinions.

This rebellion is not merely a violation of your legal duty; it is without just cause, without reason, without excuse. You never made a complaint that was not listened to with patience. You never exhibited a real grievance that was not redressed as promptly as it could be. The laws and regulations enacted for your government by Congress have been equal and just, and their enforcement was manifestly necessary for your own welfare and happiness. You have never asked their repeal. They are similar in every material respect to the laws which have been passed for the other Territories of the Union, and which everywhere else (with one partial exception) have been cheerfully obeyed. No people ever lived who were freer from unnecessary legal restraints than you. Human wisdom never devised a political system which bestowed more blessings or imposed lighter burdens than the government of the United States in its operation upon the Territories.

But being anxious to save the effusion of blood, and to avoid the indiscriminate punishment of a whole people for crimes of which it is not probable that all are equally guilty, I offer now a free and full pardon to all who will submit themselves to the authority of the federal government. If you refuse to accept it, let the consequences fall upon your own heads. But I conjure you to pause deliberately, and reflect well, before you reject this tender of peace and good will.

Now, therefore, I, James Buchanan, *President of the United States,* have thought proper to issue this, my Proclamation, enjoining upon all public officers in the Territory of Utah to be diligent and faithful, to the full extent of their power, in the execution of the laws; commanding all citizens of the United States in said Territory to aid and assist the officers in the performance of their duties; offering to the inhabitants of Utah, who shall submit to the laws, a free pardon for the seditions and treasons heretofore by them committed; warning those who shall persist, after notice of this proclamation, in the present rebellion against the United States, that they must expect no further lenity, but look to be rigorously dealt with according to their deserts; and declaring that the military forces now in Utah, and hereafter to be sent there, will not be withdrawn until the inhabitants of that Territory shall manifest a proper sense of the duty which they owe to this government.

In testimony whereof, I have hereunto set my hand, and caused the seal of the United States to be affixed to these presents.

Done at the city of Washington, the sixth day of April, one (L. S.) thousand eight hundred and fifty-eight, and of the independence of the United States the eighty-second.

JAMES BUCHANAN.

By the President:
LEWIS CASS, Secretary of State.

MESSAGE

ON A TREATY WITH THE TONAWANDA INDIANS.[1]

TO THE SENATE OF THE UNITED STATES:

I submit to the Senate, for its consideration and constitutional action, a treaty made with the Tonawanda Indians, of New York, on the 5th of November, 1857, with the accompanying papers from the Department of the Interior.

JAMES BUCHANAN.

WASHINGTON, 7 April, 1858.

MESSAGE

ON AFFAIRS IN UTAH.[2]

TO THE HOUSE OF REPRESENTATIVES:

I transmit to the House of Representatives a memorial addressed to myself by a committee appointed by the citizens of that portion of the Territory of Utah which is situated west of

---

[1] Senate Executive Journal, X. 358.
[2] H. Ex. Doc. 102, 35 Cong. 1 Sess. 1.

the Goose Creek range of mountains, commonly known as " Carson's Valley," in favor of the establishment of a territorial government over them, and containing the request that I should communicate it to Congress. I have received but one copy of this memorial, which I transmit to the House upon the suggestion of James M. Crane, Esq., the delegate elect of the people ot the proposed new Territory, for the reason, as he alleges, that the subject is now under consideration before the Committee on the Territories of that body.

JAMES BUCHANAN.

WASHINGTON, April 9, 1858.

FROM LORD CLARENDON.[1]

Private. LONDON April 15/58.

MY DEAR MR. BUCHANAN,

I cordially thank you for your letter of the 27th. It gave me great pleasure to receive such a friendly remembrance written in the midst of affairs which I have no doubt must be overwhelming, for the daily increasing facilities of communication generate business; but as they do not increase the strength of man nor add to the number of hours in the day, the life of a public man has become a sad scramble.

I was nearly worn out by 5 years at the F. O., but am now getting a new lease of life from the strange accident which overthrew the Palmerston administration. In the present state of parties here, every Government must be exposed to defeat by claptrap motions which for a night bring together the "*discerpta membra*" of faction, but we have, in consequence, a Government of a small minority existing upon the sufferance which it owes to the dissensions among the liberal party. Personal animosities contribute largely to this state of things, which is injurious to the public interests & not very creditable to the representative system.

Be the Government of England, however, Tory, Whig, or Radical, & be its blunders & shortcomings ever so great at home, it is sure to be animated by friendly feelings towards the United States. Public opinion will take care of that. The material interests concerned will not suffer themselves to be made the sport of party, & I have no doubt that the present administration will be found as desirous as I know the late one was to promote peace & amity between the two Countries.

Sir Wm. Ouseley's instructions were communicated to you, & my object in sending him to Washington was that those instructions should receive

---

[1] Buchanan Papers, Historical Society of Pennsylvania.

any development there which might seem necessary. We at the same time proposed arbitration upon the points on which the two Governments were at issue, leaving it entirely to you to select the arbitrator, & I was in hopes that if this proposal did not prove acceptable, you would have suggested some other course to which we might have agreed, as the British interests concerned are in reality trifling & our only wish was to wind up the whole affair in a manner honorable to both countries & which should not give rise to future differences.

I have not the means now of referring to official correspondence, but I have no recollection of Ld. Napier having reported that you had received his overtures unkindly, tho' of course he could not say that they had been successful.

It has always been a matter of regret to me not to have visited your great & glorious Country, & if I live long enough, I will take care that my son shall not have the same cause for regret, as he will learn more of what will be useful to him in the United States than by any amount of travel in Europe; but as regards myself, I have let the opportunity slip past, & the locomotive powers of a man with a wife & 6 children are reduced to nil. I fear then that we shall not meet again, but I shall always retain the most agreeable recollection of the relations we had together & I shall continue to watch your proceedings in your present exalted position with all the interest of friendship & with an ardent desire for your welfare & success.

Lady Clarendon sends you her kindest regards & her love to Miss Lane, to whom also I beg to be respectfully remembered.

Believe me always, my dear Mr. Buchanan,
Your sincere & faithful friend

CLARENDON.

MESSAGE

ON AFFAIRS IN CHINA.[1]

To the Senate of the United States:

I transmit a report from the Secretary of State, with accompanying papers, in answer to the resolution of the Senate of the 5th instant.[2]

JAMES BUCHANAN.

WASHINGTON, April 20, 1858.

---

[1] S. Ex. Doc. 47, 35 Cong. 1 Sess.

[2] This resolution requested the President, if not incompatible with the public interest, to communicate to the Senate "a copy of the instructions which have been given William B. Reed, the commissioner of the United States to China."

MESSAGE

ON THE AFRICAN SLAVE TRADE.[1]

To the Senate of the United States:

I herewith transmit the reports of the Secretary of State and the Secretary of the Navy, with accompanying papers, in answer to the resolution of the Senate of the 19th of January last.[2]

JAMES BUCHANAN.

WASHINGTON, April 21, 1858.

MESSAGE

ON THE SEIZURE OF AMERICAN PROPERTY IN PERU BY CHILEAN AUTHORITIES.[3]

To the Senate of the United States:

I transmit a report from the Secretary of State, in answer to the resolution of the Senate of the 24th ultimo, requesting information relative to the seizure, in the valley of Sitana, in Peru, by authorities of Chile, of a sum of money belonging to citizens of the United States.

JAMES BUCHANAN.

WASHINGTON, April 28, 1858.

---

[1] S. Ex. Doc. 49, 35 Cong. 1 Sess.

[2] This resolution requested the President, if not incompatible with the public interest, to communicate to the Senate "any information in his possession, derived from the officers connected with the American squadron on the coast of Africa, or from the British government, or the French government, or other official sources, concerning the condition of the African slave trade, and concerning the movements of the French government to establish a colonization in the possessions of that government from the coast of Africa."

[3] S. Ex. Doc. 58, 35 Cong. 1 Sess. 1. For a history of the case of the Brig Macedonia, which is the subject of this message, see Moore, International Arbitrations, II. 1449-1468.

MESSAGE

ON OUTRAGES ON AMERICAN CITIZENS IN PALESTINE.[1]

To THE SENATE OF THE UNITED STATES:

In compliance with the resolution of the Senate of the 24th ultimo,[2] I herewith transmit a report of the Secretary of State, with accompanying documents.

JAMES BUCHANAN.

WASHINGTON, May 1, 1858.

MESSAGE

ON INDIAN AFFAIRS IN OREGON AND WASHINGTON.[3]

WASHINGTON, May 3, 1858.

To THE HOUSE OF REPRESENTATIVES:

In compliance with the resolutions of the House of Representatives of the 19th January, 1857, and 3d February, 1858, I herewith transmit the report of the Secretary of the Interior, with accompanying documents.[4]

JAMES BUCHANAN.

---

[1] S. Ex. Doc. 54, 35 Cong. 1 Sess.

[2] This resolution requested the President "to transmit to the Senate, if not incompatible with the public interest, copies of any correspondence in the Department of State concerning the outrages lately committed against the family of Mr. Dickson, an American citizen residing at Jaffa, in Palestine."

[3] Richardson's Messages and Papers of the Presidents, V. 484.

[4] The papers here referred to relate to Indian affairs in the Territories of Oregon and Washington and to the official conduct of Anson Dart, late superintendent of Indian affairs in Oregon.

MESSAGE

ON INDIAN AFFAIRS IN OREGON AND WASHINGTON.[1]

To the House of Representatives:

In compliance with the resolution of the House of Representatives of the 3d of February, 1858, I transmit herewith a report from the Secretary of War, with all papers and correspondence, so far as the same is afforded by the files of the department.[2]

JAMES BUCHANAN.

WASHINGTON, May 6, 1858.

MESSAGE

ON THE PROTECTION OF AMERICAN TRADE IN MEXICAN PORTS.[3]

To the Senate of the United States:

I transmit to the Senate a report dated 13th instant, with the accompanying papers, received from the Secretary of State, in answer to the resolution of the Senate of the 5th instant, requesting information in regard to measures which may have been adopted for the protection of American commerce in the ports of Mexico.

JAMES BUCHANAN.

WASHINGTON, May [13], 1858.

---

[1] H. Ex. Doc. 112, 35 Cong. 1 Sess.
[2] The papers related to Indian affairs in Oregon and Washington Territories and to the official conduct of Anson Dart.
[3] S. Ex. Doc. 56, 35 Cong. 1 Sess.

LETTER

ON THE GEOLOGICAL SURVEY OF OREGON AND WASHINGTON.[1]

WASHINGTON CITY, May 13, 1858.

HON. JAMES L. ORR,

Speaker of the House of Representatives.

SIR: I herewith transmit, to be laid before the House of Representatives, the letter of the Secretary of the Interior, dated the 12th instant, covering the report, maps, etc., of the geological survey of Oregon and Washington Territories, which has been made by John Evans, Esq., United States geologist, under appropriations made by Congress for that purpose.

Respectfully,

JAMES BUCHANAN.

MESSAGE

ON A TREATY WITH THE PONCA INDIANS.[2]

WASHINGTON, May, 1858.

TO THE SENATE OF THE UNITED STATES:

I transmit herewith, for the constitutional action of the Senate, a treaty negotiated with the Ponca tribe of Indians on the 12th of March, 1858, with the accompanying documents from the Department of the Interior.

JAMES BUCHANAN.

---

[1] Richardson's Messages and Papers of the Presidents, V. 485.
[2] Senate Executive Journal, X. 411.

MESSAGE

ON A TREATY WITH THE SIOUX INDIANS.[1]

WASHINGTON, May 13, 1858.

TO THE SENATE OF THE UNITED STATES:

I transmit herewith, for the constitutional action of the Senate, a treaty negotiated on the 19th April, 1858, with the Yancton tribe of Sioux or Dacotah Indians, with accompanying papers from the Department of the Interior.

JAMES BUCHANAN.

LETTER

ON INDIAN AFFAIRS IN CALIFORNIA.[2]

WASHINGTON CITY, May 18, 1858.

HON. J. C. BRECKINRIDGE,
    Vice-President of the United States.

SIR: In reply to the resolutions of the Senate of the United States of the 20th February and 14th March, 1857, I herewith transmit, to be laid before that body, copies of all correspondence, vouchers, and other papers having reference to the accounts of Edward F. Beale, Esq., late superintendent of Indian affairs in California, which are on file or record in the Departments of the Treasury and Interior.

JAMES BUCHANAN.

---

[1] Senate Executive Journal, X. 411.
[2] Richardson's Messages and Papers of the Presidents, V. 485.

MESSAGE

ON INTERFERENCE WITH VESSELS IN THE GULF OF MEXICO.[1]

TO THE SENATE OF THE UNITED STATES:

In answer to the resolution of the Senate of the 14th instant, requesting information concerning the recent search or seizure of American vessels by foreign armed cruisers in the Gulf of Mexico, I transmit reports from the Secretaries of State and of the Navy.

JAMES BUCHANAN.

WASHINGTON, May 19, 1858.

TO MISS LANE.[2]

[WASHINGTON, May 20, 1858.]

My dear Harriet/

Learning that you were about to purchase furniture in New York [for the White House] I requested Dr. Blake to furnish me a statement of the balance of the appropriation unexpended. This balance is $8,369.02. In making your purchases, therefore, I wish you to consider that this sum must answer our purpose until the end of my term. I wish you therefore not to expend the whole of it; but to leave enough to meet all contingencies up till 4 March, 1861. Any sum which may be expended above the appropriation I shall most certainly pay out of my own pocket. I shall never ask Congress for the Deficiency.

Who should make his appearance this morning but Mr. Keitt. After talking about other matters for some time he said he was married. I expressed strong doubts upon the subject, when he insisted that he was actually & bona fide married. The lady is Miss Sparks, whom he has been so long addressing.

With my kind regards to Mr. and Mrs. R., I remain

Yours affectionately

JAMES BUCHANAN.

---

[1] S. Ex. Doc. 59, 35 Cong. 1 Sess. 1.
[2] Buchanan Papers, private collection; Curtis's Buchanan, II. 240.

MESSAGE

ON THE ARREST OF WILLIAM WALKER IN NICARAGUA.[1]

To the Senate of the United States:

I transmit herewith, in compliance with the resolution of the Senate of the 19th of May,[2] a communication from the Secretary of the Navy, with copies of the correspondence, &c., as afforded by the files of the department.

JAMES BUCHANAN.

WASHINGTON, May 27, 1858.

MESSAGE

ON THE SEIZURE OF THE PANCHITA.[3]

To the Senate of the United States:

I transmit a report from the Secretary of State, with accompanying papers, in answer to the resolution of the Senate of the 22nd instant,[4] requesting information in regard to the seizure of the American vessel Panchita on the coast of Africa.

JAMES BUCHANAN.

WASHINGTON, May 29, 1858.

----

[1] S. Ex. Doc. 63, 35 Cong. 1 Sess.

[2] This resolution called for correspondence, instructions, and orders connected with the arrest of William Walker and his associates in Nicaragua, by the naval forces under the command of Commodore Paulding.

[3] S. Ex. Doc. 61, 35 Cong. 1 Sess.

[4] This resolution called for "any correspondence that may have been held between this government and the government of England concerning the seizure on the coast of Africa, by the naval forces of the latter power, of the American vessel 'Panchita,' sent in charge of a British naval officer, after said seizure, to the port of New York; and if there be any further correspondence or documents received by the Executive concerning the visitation or search of American vessels in the Gulf of Mexico, or elsewhere, by foreign armed cruisers, since the message of the President, of the 19th of May instant, that he communicate the same to the Senate."

MESSAGE

ON ATTACKS ON AMERICAN VESSELS.[1]

To THE HOUSE OF REPRESENTATIVES:

In answer to the resolution of the House of Representatives of the 17th instant, requesting information relative to attacks upon United States vessels in the Gulf of Mexico and on the coast of Cuba, I transmit a report from the Secretary of State, with the papers by which it was accompanied.[2]

JAMES BUCHANAN.

WASHINGTON, May 31, 1858.

MESSAGE

ON GUANO DISCOVERIES.[3]

WASHINGTON, June 1, 1858.

To THE SENATE OF THE UNITED STATES:

I transmit herewith a report from the Secretaries of State and the Navy, with the accompanying papers, in compliance with the resolution of the Senate of the 11th of March, 1858, requesting the President " to communicate to the Senate any information in possession of any of the Executive Departments in relation to alleged discoveries of guano in the year 1855, and the measures taken to ascertain the correctness of the same; and also any report made to the Navy Department in relation to the discovery of guano in Jarvis and Baker's islands, with the charts, soundings, and sailing directions for those islands."

JAMES BUCHANAN.

----

[1] H. Ex. Doc. 132, 35 Cong. 1 Sess.

[2] The resolution requested information " in relation to firing into, boarding, and searching vessels belonging to the United States, in the Gulf of Mexico and on the coast of Cuba, by British ships-of-war."

[3] Richardson's Messages and Papers of the Presidents, V. 486.

MESSAGE

ON THE PROTECTION OF GUANO PURCHASES IN PERU.[1]

To the Senate of the United States:

I transmit, herewith, a report from the Secretary of State, together with the documents by which it is accompanied, as embracing all the information which it is practicable or expedient to communicate in reply to the resolution of the Senate of the 31st ultimo on the subject of guano.[2]

JAMES BUCHANAN.

WASHINGTON, June 4, 1858.

MESSAGE

ON AFFAIRS IN UTAH.[3]

To the Senate and House of Representatives:

I transmit the copy of a despatch from Governor Cumming to the Secretary of State, dated at Great Salt Lake City, on the 2d of May, and received at the Department of State on yesterday. From this there is reason to believe that our difficulties with the Territory of Utah have terminated, and the reign of the Constitution and the laws has been restored. I congratulate you on this auspicious event.

I lose no time in communicating this information, and in expressing the opinion that there will now be no occasion to make any appropriation for the purpose of calling into service the two

---

[1] S. Ex. Doc. 69, 35 Cong. 1 Sess.

[2] The resolution requested information as to whether the government of the United States had, in its correspondence with the Peruvian minister, recognized the existence of a state of civil war in Peru during the late struggle between Vivanco and Castillo, and whether any and what measures had been taken to protect American interests in cargoes of guano purchased from Vivanco, or his officers or agents, during his occupation of any of the guano islands within the territory of Peru. For an elucidation of this subject, see the cases of the Georgiana and Lizzie Thompson (Moore, International Arbitrations, II. 1593 et seq.).

[3] S. Ex. Doc. 67, 35 Cong. 1 Sess.; H. Ex. Doc. 138, 35 Cong. 1 Sess.

regiments of volunteers authorized by the act of Congress approved on the 7th April last, " For the purpose of quelling disturbances in the Territory of Utah, for the protection of supply and emigrant trains, and the suppression of Indian hostilities on the frontiers."

I am the more gratified at this satisfactory intelligence from Utah, because it will afford some relief to the Treasury at a time demanding from us the strictest economy, and when the question which now arises upon every new appropriation is, whether it be of a character so important and urgent as to brook no delay, and to justify and require a loan, and most probably a tax upon the people to raise the money necessary for its payment.

In regard to the regiment of volunteers authorized by the same act of Congress to be called into service for the defence of the frontiers of Texas against Indian hostilities, I desire to leave this question to Congress, observing at the same time that, in my opinion, this State can be defended for the present by the regular troops, which have not yet been withdrawn from its limits.

JAMES BUCHANAN.

WASHINGTON CITY, June 10, 1858.

MESSAGE

ON THE ISTHMUS OF TEHUANTEPEC.[1]

To THE SENATE OF THE UNITED STATES:

In answer to the resolution of the Senate of the 19th ultimo, respecting the Isthmus of Tehuantepec,[2] I transmit herewith a report from the Secretary of State, with the documents by which

---

[1] S. Ex. Doc. 72, 35 Cong. 1 Sess.

[2] This resolution requested information as to " whether any efforts have been made or authorized by the executive department, or any officer thereof, to induce the government of Mexico to annul or impair the grant of February 5, 1853, for the construction of a plank road and railroad across the isthmus of Tehuantepec, as recognized in the treaty published at Washington, on the 30th of June, 1854, and to obtain a new grant of the same, or like character, for other parties; and, if so," as to " the names of those parties, together with the terms, conditions, and considerations of the grant."

it is accompanied, together with the copy of a letter from the Postmaster General of the 24th ultimo to the Department of State.

JAMES BUCHANAN.

WASHINGTON, June 11, 1858.

MESSAGE

ON MISSISSIPPI RIVER IMPROVEMENTS.[1]

To THE HOUSE OF REPRESENTATIVES:

I transmit herewith a report from the Secretary of War, with the accompanying papers, in obedience to the resolution of the House of Representatives of the 2d of June, 1858.[2]

JAMES BUCHANAN.

WASHINGTON CITY, June 11, 1858.

MESSAGE

ON THE CONDITION OF THE TREASURY.[3]

[June 12, 1858.]

To THE SENATE AND HOUSE OF REPRESENTATIVES:

I feel it to be an indispensable duty to call your attention to the condition of the Treasury. On the 19th day of May last, the Secretary of the Treasury submitted a report to Congress

---

[1] H. Ex. Doc. 139, 35 Cong. 1 Sess.

[2] This resolution called for " copies of the contracts entered into between the United States and Messrs. Craig and Rightor for deepening the channels of the Southwest Pass and Pass à l'Outre, at the mouth of the Mississippi river, together with the report of the board of engineers appointed to examine the several proposals made therefor, and the reports of the officer superintending the work, with other correspondence relative to its progress under said contract."

[3] S. Ex. Doc. 68, 35 Cong. 1 Sess.; H. Ex. Doc. 140, 35 Cong. 1 Sess.

" on the present condition of the finances of the Government."
In this report he states that, after a call upon the heads of Departments, he had received official information that the sum of
$37,000,000 would probably be required during the first two
quarters of the next fiscal year, from the 1st of July to the 1st
of January. " This sum," the Secretary says, " does not include
such amounts as may be appropriated by Congress over and above
the estimates submitted to them by the Departments, and I have
no data on which to estimate for such expenditures. Upon this
point Congress is better able to form a correct opinion than
I am."

The Secretary then estimates that the receipts into the
Treasury from all sources, between the 1st of July and the 1st
of January, would amount to $25,000,000, leaving a deficit of
$15,000,000, inclusive of the sum of about three million dollars,
the least amount required to be in the Treasury at all times to
secure its successful operation. For this amount he recommends
a loan. This loan, it will be observed, was required, after a
close calculation, to meet the estimates from the different Departments, and not such appropriations as might be made by Congress
over and above these estimates.

There were embraced in this sum of $15,000,000 estimates
to the amount of about one million seven hundred and fifty
thousand dollars for the three volunteer regiments authorized
by the act of Congress approved April 7, 1858, for two of which,
if not for the third, no appropriation will now be required. To
this extent a portion of the loan of $15,000,000 may be applied
to pay the appropriations made by Congress beyond the estimates
from the different Departments, referred to in the report of the
Secretary of the Treasury.

To what extent a probable deficiency may exist in the
Treasury between the 1st July and the 1st January next, cannot
be ascertained until the appropriation bills, as well as the private
bills containing appropriations, shall have finally passed.

Adversity teaches useful lessons to nations as well as to individuals. The habit of extravagant expenditures fostered by
a large surplus in the Treasury must now be corrected, or the
country will be involved in serious financial difficulties.

Under any form of government, extravagance in expenditure must be the natural consequence, when those who authorize the expenditure feel no responsibility in providing the means of payment. Such had been for a number of years our condition previous to the late monetary revulsion in the country. Fortunately, at least for the cause of public economy, the case is now reversed; and to the extent of the appropriations, whatever these may be, engrafted on the different appropriation bills, as well as those made by private bills, over and above the estimates of the different Departments, it will be necessary for Congress to provide the means of payment before their adjournment. Without this, the Treasury will be exhausted before the 1st January, and the public credit will be seriously impaired. This disgrace must not fall upon the country.

It is impossible for me, however, now to ascertain this amount; nor does there at present seem to be the least probability that this can be done, and the necessary means provided by Congress to meet any deficiency which may exist in the Treasury before Monday next at twelve o'clock, the hour fixed for adjournment, it being now Saturday morning at half-past eleven o'clock. To accomplish this object, the appropriation bills, as they shall have finally passed Congress, must be before me, and time must be allowed to ascertain the amount of the moneys appropriated, and to enable Congress to provide the necessary means. At this writing it is understood that several of these bills are yet before the committees of conference, and the amendments to some of them have not even been printed.

Foreseeing that such a state of things might exist at the close of the session, I stated, in the annual message to Congress, of December last, that " from the practice of Congress such an examination of each bill as the Constitution requires has been rendered impossible. The most important business of each session is generally crowded into its last hours, and the alternative presented to the President is either to violate the constitutional duty which he owes to the people and approve bills which, for want of time, it is impossible he should have examined, or by his refusal to do this, subject the country and individuals to great loss and inconvenience." . . .

" For my own part, I have deliberately determined that I shall approve no bills which I have not examined; and it will be a case of extreme and most urgent necessity which shall ever induce me to depart from this rule."

The present condition of the Treasury absolutely requires that I should adhere to this resolution on the present occasion for the reasons which I have heretofore presented.

In former times it was believed to be the true character of an appropriation bill simply to carry into effect existing laws, and the established policy of the country. A practice has, however, grown up of late years to ingraft on such bills, at the last hours of the session, large appropriations for new and important objects not provided for by preëxisting laws, and when no time is left to the Executive for their examination and investigation. No alternative is thus left to the President but either to approve measures without examination, or, by vetoing an appropriation bill, seriously to embarrass the operations of the Government. This practice could never have prevailed without a surplus in the Treasury sufficiently large to cover an indefinite amount of appropriations. Necessity now compels us to arrest it, at least so far as to afford time to ascertain the amount appropriated, and to provide the means of its payment.

For all these reasons, I recommend to Congress to postpone the day of adjournment for a brief period. I promise that not an hour shall be lost in ascertaining the amount of appropriations made by them for which it will be necessary to provide. I know it will be inconvenient for the members to attend a called session, and this, above all things, I desire to avoid.

JAMES BUCHANAN.

WASHINGTON CITY, June 12, 1858.

PROCLAMATION

FOR A SPECIAL SESSION OF THE SENATE.[1]

[June 14, 1858.]

BY THE PRESIDENT OF THE UNITED STATES OF AMERICA.

A PROCLAMATION.

Whereas an extraordinary occasion has occurred, rendering it necessary and proper that the Senate of the United States shall be convened to receive and act upon such communications as have been or may be made to it on the part of the Executive:

---

[1] United States Statutes at Large, XI. 798.

Now, therefore, I, James Buchanan, President of the United States, do issue this my proclamation, declaring that an extraordinary occasion requires the Senate of the United States to convene for the transaction of business at the Capitol, in the city of Washington, on the 15th day of this month, at 12 o'clock at noon of that day, of which all who shall at that time be entitled to act as members of that body are hereby required to take notice.

Given under my hand and the seal of the United States, at Washington, this fourteenth day of June, A. D. (Seal.)   1858, and of the Independence of the United States the eighty-second.

JAMES BUCHANAN.

By the President:
LEWIS CASS, Secretary of State.

TO MR. HOLT.[1]

WASHINGTON 27th July 1858.

MY DEAR SIR,

I intend to leave for the Bedford Springs this afternoon, and I would thank you to call and see Secretary Toucey, who will give you a number of the Naval cases for examination. You will greatly oblige me by examining them and making a report to me on my return. Please to call upon Mr. Toucey and converse with him on the subject.

From your friend very respectfully

JAMES BUCHANAN.

JOSEPH HOLT ESQ.

---

[1] Holt Papers, Library of Congress.

TO MR. REED.[1]

BEDFORD SPRINGS 31 July 1858.

MY DEAR SIR

I would reproach myself for not having written to you heretofore, had it been possible for me to do more than address very brief notes to my friends. Besides, long ere this can reach you, you will have learned that I had attended to the request contained in your favor of the 22d February last.

Should you conclude a Treaty, there will be no difficulty in the way of your immediate return. Should a Treaty not be concluded before 1 January, 1859, & at that moment a fair prospect shall exist that a Treaty may be concluded within a reasonable time thereafter, you will doubtless remain. The interest of the Country, as well as your own fame, will require this sacrifice at your hands. I can readily appreciate the privations which you suffer in being absent from your family; but you have gone upon a great mission, & should you succeed, your name will be honorably identified with the history of your Country. Should you leave, & the object be accomplished within a reasonable time by another, you would never forgive yourself. If you make the Treaty, come home at once;—if there be no hope of making a Treaty, come home on the 1 January next;— but if there be a reasonable hope, I would advise you to " see it out."

You will naturally expect from me some political information; but this you will receive in detail from the Newspapers. The administration has hitherto been successful in its measures both of foreign & domestic policy. It does not follow from this, however, that it will be sustained by the election of a majority of Representatives to the next Congress. I can now feel the reason which caused General Jackson & several of his successors to lose their own States immediately after their election. The number of applicants for office from Pennsylvania has been very great, & most of these have been worthy & excellent men to whom I am under political obligations. Under these circumstances, the appointment of one is the disappointment of many; & although I have nominated such a number of Pennsylvanians to the Senate as to have produced at last a titter throughout the Body when such nominations were read, yet this perhaps has

---

[1] Buchanan Papers, Historical Society of Pennsylvania.

only increased the number of disappointed. Of one thing, however, I feel confident, that whether we have a majority or not in the next House of Representatives, all will be well in 1860. Things look rather " blue " in your good City of Philadelphia; but this arises rather from divisions among our friends than from the apostasy of Forney & Packer. I entertain but little hope of the election of William A. Porter, though I ardently desire it. He is an excellent man, & from all I can learn would make an excellent Judge; but the equivocal position which he holds upon the Kansas question will lose him many votes. Some say he is on one side, & some say he is on the other, & for my own part I am strongly inclined to believe he is with us; but the people of this Country will forgive a man for almost any political offence except a want of firmness, frankness, & candor in expressing his political opinions.

I shall ever thank Heaven that my administration has been so successful in pacifying the Country on the Kansas question. Had Mr. Douglas been successful in defeating Legislation on the subject, the Country would have been in a terrible condition at the present moment. The exasperation between the North & the South would have been more terrible & dangerous than ever, & the Union would have been shaken to its centre. Georgia & Alabama, in this contingency, had provided by law for the call of State Conventions with a view to secession. Throughout the South all or nearly all are now satisfied; & General Davis of Mississippi & other gentlemen of high character who had been hitherto considered extreme have been making speeches in the North in favor of the Union. General D. is " a marvellous proper man."

I greatly preferred the Senate Bill. This would have more certainly & effectually pacified Kansas than any other measure; but how Douglas, Packer, Forney, or any other person who had ever been a Democrat could have preferred the do-nothing policy, with all its inevitable consequences, to the English Bill, which leaves to the people of Kansas to decide their own destiny, I am utterly at a loss to imagine. Whether these people shall accept or reject the Lecompton Constitution, the Kansas question as a national question is at an end.

With very warm regard, I remain,
   Sincerely & respectfully your friend
        JAMES BUCHANAN.

HON: WM. B. REED.
 VOL. X—15

TO MR. TOUCEY.[1]

BEDFORD SPRINGS 5 August '58.

My DEAR SIR/

I have had a long conversation with Sir Wm. Ouseley this morning, introduced by himself, concerning our Paraguay Expedition. He is beyond all question friendly, & having had much to do with Paraguay & those Countries & his son having lived & died at Assumption, what he says is entitled to great respect. He informs me that Lopez is an artful & unscrupulous & insincere man of considerable abilities. He made professions & promises to the British Government on condition that they would recognise the independence of Paraguay; all of which he has violated.

He says that from their experience & that of the French, propellers are not the proper vessels to ascend those rivers. From the shallowness of the water & from the reefs of Rocks, the machinery is liable to be injured or destroyed. He says that side wheel steamers are much better for the purpose of navigating these rivers; & on this we may depend. The quantity of weeds which grow to a great height in certain portions of the river is an impediment. The machinery of propellers is entangled in them & arrests their progress.

Lopez has been busily & quietly at work for some years in erecting fortifications at the bends of the rivers & in the most favorable positions under the direction of French & Hungarian officers, & these are formidable, especially the water batteries.

He thinks it would be all-important to us to secure the friendship of the Argentine Confederacy, who are all the time almost at war with Lopez, whom they detest. He speaks especially of General Urquiza, of whom he entertains a good opinion.

Lopez, he thinks, is evidently following in the footsteps of his predecessor, Dr. Francia, in his exclusive policy. He is a tyrant & a despot, & many Paraguayans have fled to Buenos Ayres, from whom we may obtain much valuable information & probably co-operation.

These are hints that ought not to be disregarded & you might shew this hasty letter to General Cass.

---

[1] Buchanan Papers, Historical Society of Pennsylvania.

Sir William says that there is a powerful & warlike tribe of Indians on the River opposite to Paraguay, called " Chaco Indians," which Lopez has never been able to subdue. They are always the enemies of Lopez, & might easily by a few presents be excited to war.

It is his opinion that if our expedition be of such a character as to render our victory certain, that Lopez will yield without a fight; but not otherwise.

I have deemed it best to write you this hasty letter. *We must not fail.* Better take time than to run any risk.

We intend to leave for Washington on Wednesday or at latest on Thursday next, & hope to reach there the next day. In haste

From your friend, very respectfully,

JAMES BUCHANAN.

MR. TOUCEY.[1]

P. S. Of course I consider these suggestions only as hints for inquiry. You might talk to Captain Page about them.

TO MR. McLAIN.[2]

WASHINGTON CITY, September 7, 1858.

SIR: After our conversations on the subject, I understand you to propose that the Colonization Society, for and in consideration of the sum of forty-five thousand dollars, to be paid by the government of the United States, shall receive in Liberia, from the agent of the United States, the three hundred and odd African negroes now at Fort Sumter, near Charleston, and furnish them comfortable shelter, clothing, provisions, and

---

[1] Mr. Isaac Toucey was Secretary of the Navy under Buchanan. For a history of the expedition to Paraguay, see Moore, International Arbitrations, II. 1485 et seq.

[2] H. Ex. Doc. 2, 35 Cong. 2 Sess. I. 67.

medical attendance for the period of one year from the time of their landing. The society shall also during this period cause the children to receive schooling; and they engage that all of these Africans, whether children or adults, shall be instructed in the arts of civilized life suitable to their condition. It is distinctly understood that under no circumstances will the government of the United States be called upon for any additional expenses above the sum of forty-five thousand dollars.

I hereby accept this proposition, so far as my constitutional competency extends, and shall recommend to Congress to make the appropriation necessary to carry it into effect. In the meantime I can advance no money to the Society, as none has been appropriated by law for this purpose.

When you signify explicitly in writing, on behalf of the society, that they will in good faith carry all these engagements into effect, the contract will then be completed, and held valid and binding.

Yours, very respectfully,

JAMES BUCHANAN.

REV. WILLIAM MCLAIN,
    Financial Agent of the Colonization Society.

TO MISS LANE.[1]

WHEATLAND 18 September 1858.

MY DEAR HARRIET/

God willing, I shall leave here on Tuesday morning early in a carriage, & go to Wrightsville in time to take the train from that place to Baltimore at 7.30 A.M., & arrive in Washington by the train which leaves Baltimore at 3.30 P.M.

Enclosed I send a letter to you which I opened by mistake; but finding it addressed to " My dear Miss Lane," I read no

---

[1] Buchanan Papers, private collection.

further. It is evidently from Lady Ouseley, & I desired much to learn the condition of Sir William; but my principles forbade.

As I shall so soon be with you I need not tell you the news. In haste I remain

Yours affectionately

JAMES BUCHANAN.

TO MISS LANE.[1]

WASHINGTON 15 October 1858.

MY DEAR HARRIET/

We have not yet heard from you since you left us. I hope you arrived safely in Philadelphia & did not contract a hoarseness in talking to Mr. Schell on the way. We get along very nicely since your absence & will give a big dinner on Thursday next. I have not seen any of your lady friends since your departure & can therefore give you no news.

Well! we have met the enemy in Pennsylvania & we are theirs. This I have anticipated for three months & was not taken by surprise except as to the extent of our defeat. I am astonished at myself for bearing it with so much philosophy.

The conspirators against poor Jones have at length succeeded in hunting him down. Ever since my election the hounds have been in pursuit of him. I now deeply regret;—but I shall say no more. With the blessing of Providence I shall endeavor to raise him up & place him in some position where they cannot reach him.

Judge Black, General Anderson of Tennessee, Mr. Brenner, & Mr. Van Dyke dined with me yesterday, & we had a merry time of it, laughing among other things over our crushing defeat. It is so great that it is almost absurd.

We will present a record of success at the meeting of Congress which has rarely been equalled. We have hitherto succeeded in all our undertakings. Poor bleeding Kansas is quiet & is behaving herself in an orderly manner; but her wrongs have

---

[1] Buchanan Papers, private collection; Curtis's Buchanan, II. 241.

melted the hearts of the sympathetic Pennsylvanians or rather Philadelphians. In the interior of the State the Tariff was the damaging question, & in defeating Jones the iron interest have prostrated a man who could render them more service than all the black Republican Representatives from Pennsylvania. He will be a loss to the whole Country in the House of Representatives.

I have heard nothing of the good & excellent Robert since you left us. He is a man among a thousand. I wish I could say so much for his brother.

It is growing late & I must retire. I sleep much better now but not near so well as at the Soldiers' Home.

With kind remembrances to Mr. & Mrs. Plitt I bid you good night.

Yours affectionately,

JAMES BUCHANAN.

MISS HARRIET REBECCA LANE.

P. S.   Give my love to Lilly.

PROCLAMATION

CONCERNING AN EXPEDITION AGAINST NICARAGUA.[1]

[October 30, 1858.]

BY JAMES BUCHANAN, PRESIDENT OF THE UNITED STATES OF AMERICA.

A PROCLAMATION.

Whereas, information has reached me from sources which I can not disregard that certain persons, in violation of the neutrality laws of the United States, are making a third attempt to set on foot a military expedition within their territory against

---

[1] United States Statutes at Large, XI. 798–799.

Nicaragua, a foreign State, with which they are at peace. In order to raise money for equipping and maintaining this expedition, persons connected therewith, as I have reason to believe, have issued and sold bonds and other contracts pledging the public lands of Nicaragua and the transit route through its territory as a security for their redemption and fulfilment.

The hostile design of this expedition is rendered manifest by the fact that these bonds and contracts can be of no possible value to their holders, unless the present Government of Nicaragua shall be overthrown by force. Besides, the envoy extraordinary and minister plenipotentiary of that Government in the United States has issued a notice, in pursuance of his instructions, dated on the 27th instant, forbidding the citizens or subjects of any nation, except passengers intending to proceed through Nicaragua over the transit route from ocean to ocean, to enter its territory without a regular passport, signed by the proper minister or consul-general of the Republic resident in the country from whence they shall have departed. Such persons, with this exception, " will be stopped and compelled to return by the same conveyance that took them to the country." From these circumstances, the inference is irresistible that persons engaged in this expedition will leave the United States with hostile purposes against Nicaragua. They can not, under the guise which they have assumed, that they are peaceful emigrants, conceal their real intentions, and especially when they know, in advance, that their landing will be resisted and can only be accomplished by an overpowering force. This expedient was successfully resorted to previous to the last expedition, and the vessel in which those composing it were conveyed to Nicaragua obtained a clearance from the collector of the port of Mobile. Although, after a careful examination, no arms or munitions of war were discovered on board, yet, when they arrived in Nicaragua, they were found to be armed and equipped and immediately commenced hostilities.

The leaders of former illegal expeditions of the same character have openly expressed their intention to renew hostilities against Nicaragua. One of them, who has already been twice expelled from Nicaragua, has invited, through the public newspapers, American citizens to emigrate to that Republic, and has designated Mobile as the place of rendezvous and departure, and

San Juan del Norte as the port to which they are bound. This person, who has renounced his allegiance to the United States, and claims to be President of Nicaragua, has given notice to the collector of the port of Mobile that two or three hundred of these emigrants will be prepared to embark from that port about the middle of November.

For these and other good reasons, and for the purpose of saving American citizens who may have been honestly deluded into the belief that they are about to proceed to Nicaragua as peaceful emigrants, if any such there be, from the disastrous consequences to which they will be exposed, I, James Buchanan, President of the United States, have thought it fit to issue this my proclamation, enjoining upon all officers of the Government, civil and military, in their respective spheres, to be vigilant, active, and faithful in suppressing these illegal enterprises, and in carrying out their standing instructions to that effect; exhorting all good citizens, by their respect for the laws and their regard for the peace and welfare of the country, to aid the efforts of the public authorities in the discharge of their duties.

In testimony whereof, I have hereunto set my hand and caused the seal of the United States to be affixed to these presents.

Done at the city of Washington, the thirtieth day of October one thousand eight hundred and fifty-eight, and of (Seal.)   the Independence of the United States the eighty-third.

JAMES BUCHANAN.

By the President:
    LEWIS CASS, Secretary of State.

TO THE COMMITTEE

ON THE CENTENNIAL ANNIVERSARY OF FORT DUQUESNE.[1]

WASHINGTON, 22d November, 1858.

GENTLEMEN:

I have had the honor to receive your invitation to be present, on the 25th instant, at the Centennial Anniversary of the capture of Fort Duquesne; and I regret that the pressure of public affairs, at a period so near the meeting of Congress, renders it impossible that I should enjoy this privilege.

Every patriot must rejoice whilst reflecting upon the unparalleled progress of our country within the last century. What was, at its commencement, an obscure Fort, far beyond the western frontier of civilization, has now become the centre of a populous commercial and manufacturing city, sending its productions to large and prosperous sovereign States still further west, whose territories were then a vast, unexplored, and silent wilderness.

From the standpoint at which we have arrived, the anxious patriot cannot fail, whilst reviewing the past, to cast a glance into the future, and to speculate upon what may be the condition of our country when your posterity shall assemble to celebrate the second Centennial Anniversary of the capture of Fort Duquesne. Shall our *whole* country then compose one united nation, more populous, powerful, and free than any other which has ever existed? Or will the confederacy have been rent asunder, and divided into groups of hostile and jealous States? Or may it not be possible that ere the next celebration all the fragments, exhausted by intermediate conflicts with each other, may have finally reunited and sought refuge under the shelter of one great and overshadowing Despotism?

These questions will, I firmly believe, under the Providence of God, be virtually decided by the present generation. We have reached a crisis when upon their action depends the preservation of the Union, according to the letter and spirit of the Constitution; and this once gone, all is lost.

I regret to say that the present omens are far from propitious. In the last age of the Republic it was considered almost

---

[1] Buchanan Papers, Historical Society of Pennsylvania.

treasonable to pronounce the word *Disunion*. Times have since sadly changed, and now Disunion is freely prescribed as the remedy for evanescent evils, real or imaginary, which, if left to themselves, would speedily vanish away in the progress of events.

Our revolutionary fathers have passed away, and the generation next after them, who were inspired by their personal counsel and example, have nearly all disappeared. The present generation, deprived of these lights, must, whether they will or not, decide the fate of their posterity. Let them cherish the Union in their heart of hearts; let them resist every measure which may tend to relax or dissolve its bonds; let the citizens of the different States cultivate feelings of kindness and forbearance towards each other; and let all resolve to transmit it to their descendants in the form and spirit they have inherited it from their forefathers; and all will then be well for our country in future times.

I shall assume the privilege of advancing years in referring to another growing and dangerous evil. In the last age, although our fathers, like ourselves, were divided into political parties which often had severe conflicts with each other, yet we never heard, until within a recent period, of the employment of money to carry elections. Should this practice increase until the voters and their Representatives in the State and National Legislatures shall become infected, the fountain of free Government will then be poisoned at its source, and we must end, as history proves, in a military despotism. A Democratic Republic, all agree, cannot long survive unless sustained by public virtue. When this is corrupted and the people become venal, there is a canker at the root of the tree of Liberty, which must cause it to wither and die.

Praying Almighty God that your remote posterity may continue, century after century, for ages yet to come, to celebrate the anniversary of the capture of Fort Duquesne in peace and prosperity, under the banner of the Constitution and the Union, I remain,

Very respectfully, your friend,

JAMES BUCHANAN.

To RUSSELL ERRETT, J. HERON FOSTER, JAMES P. BARR, CHARLES MCKNIGHT, J. G. BACKOFEN, WILLIAM M. DARLINGTON, & T. J. BIGHAM, Committee on Invitation.

SECOND ANNUAL MESSAGE,
DECEMBER 6, 1858.[1]

FELLOW-CITIZENS OF THE SENATE AND HOUSE OF REPRESEN-
TATIVES:

When we compare the condition of the country at the present day with what it was one year ago, at the meeting of Congress, we have much reason for gratitude to that Almighty
Providence which has never failed to interpose for our relief
at the most critical periods of our history. One year ago the
sectional strife between the North and the South on the dangerous subject of slavery had again become so intense as to
threaten the peace and perpetuity of the confederacy. The
application for the admission of Kansas as a State into the
Union fostered this unhappy agitation, and brought the whole
subject once more before Congress. It was the desire of every
patriot that such measures of legislation might be adopted as
would remove the excitement from the States and confine it
to the Territory where it legitimately belonged. Much has been
done, I am happy to say, towards the accomplishment of this
object during the last session of Congress.

The Supreme Court of the United States had previously decided that all American citizens have an equal right to take
into the Territories whatever is held as property under the
laws of any of the States, and to hold such property there under
the guardianship of the Federal Constitution, so long as the
territorial condition shall remain.

This is now a well established position, and the proceedings
of the last session were alone wanting to give it practical effect.
The principle has been recognized, in some form or other, by
an almost unanimous vote of both houses of Congress, that a
Territory has a right to come into the Union either as a free
or a slave State, according to the will of a majority of its people.
The just equality of all the States has thus been vindicated, and
a fruitful source of dangerous dissension among them has been
removed.

Whilst such has been the beneficial tendency of your legislative proceedings outside of Kansas, their influence has nowhere

[1] H. Ex. Doc. 2, 35 Cong. 2 Sess. I. 3–33.

been so happy as within that Territory itself. Left to manage and control its own affairs in its own way, without the pressure of external influence, the revolutionary Topeka organization and all resistance to the territorial government established by Congress have been finally abandoned. As a natural consequence, that fine Territory now appears to be tranquil and prosperous, and is attracting increasing thousands of immigrants to make it their happy home.

The past unfortunate experience of Kansas has enforced the lesson, so often already taught, that resistance to lawful authority, under our form of government, cannot fail in the end to prove disastrous to its authors. Had the people of the Territory yielded obedience to the laws enacted by their legislature, it would at the present moment have contained a large additional population of industrious and enterprising citizens, who have been deterred from entering its borders by the existence of civil strife and organized rebellion.

It was the resistance to rightful authority and the persevering attempts to establish a revolutionary government under the Topeka constitution which caused the people of Kansas to commit the grave error of refusing to vote for delegates to the convention to frame a constitution under a law not denied to be fair and just in its provisions. This refusal to vote has been the prolific source of all the evils which have followed. In their hostility to the territorial government they disregarded the principle, absolutely essential to the working of our form of government, that a majority of those who vote—not the majority who may remain at home, from whatever cause—must decide the result of an election. For this reason, seeking to take advantage of their own error, they denied the authority of the convention thus elected to frame a constitution.

The convention, notwithstanding, proceeded to adopt a constitution unexceptionable in its general features, and providing for the submission of the slavery question to a vote of the people, which, in my opinion, they were bound to do under the Kansas and Nebraska act. This was the all-important question which had alone convulsed the Territory; and yet the opponents of the lawful government, persisting in their first error, refrained from exercising their right to vote, and preferred that slavery should continue, rather than surrender their revolutionary Topeka organization.

A wiser and better spirit seemed to prevail before the first Monday of January last, when an election was held under the constitution. A majority of the people then voted for a governor and other State officers, for a member of Congress, and members of the State legislature. This election was warmly contested by the two political parties in Kansas, and a greater vote was polled than at any previous election. A large majority of the members of the legislature elect belonged to that party which had previously refused to vote. The anti-slavery party were thus placed in the ascendant, and the political power of the State was in their own hands. Had Congress admitted Kansas into the Union under the Lecompton constitution, the legislature might, at its very first session, have submitted the question to a vote of the people, whether they would or would not have a convention to amend their constitution, either on the slavery or any other question, and have adopted all necessary means for giving speedy effect to the will of the majority. Thus the Kansas question would have been immediately and finally settled.

Under these circumstances, I submitted to Congress the constitution thus framed, with all the officers already elected necessary to put the State government into operation, accompanied by a strong recommendation in favor of the admission of Kansas as a State. In the course of my long public life I have never performed any official act which, in the retrospect, has afforded me more heartfelt satisfaction. Its admission could have inflicted no possible injury on any human being, whilst it would, within a brief period, have restored peace to Kansas and harmony to the Union. In that event, the slavery question would ere this have been finally settled, according to the legally expressed will of a majority of the voters, and popular sovereignty would thus have been vindicated in a constitutional manner.

With my deep convictions of duty, I could have pursued no other course. It is true, that, as an individual, I had expressed an opinion, both before and during the session of the convention, in favor of submitting the remaining clauses of the constitution, as well as that concerning slavery, to the people. But, acting in an official character, neither myself nor any human authority had the power to rejudge the proceedings of the convention, and declare the constitution which it had framed to be a nullity. To have done this would have been a violation of the

Kansas and Nebraska act, which left the people of the Territory " perfectly free to form and regulate their domestic institutions in their own way, subject only to the Constitution of the United States." It would equally have violated the great principle of popular sovereignty, at the foundation of our institutions, to deprive the people of the power, if they thought proper to exercise it, of confiding to delegates elected by themselves the trust of framing a constitution, without requiring them to subject their constituents to the trouble, expense, and delay of a second election. It would have been in opposition to many precedents in our history, commencing in the very best age of the republic, of the admission of Territories as States into the Union, without a previous vote of the people approving their constitution.

It is to be lamented that a question so insignificant, when viewed in its practical effects on the people of Kansas, whether decided one way or the other, should have kindled such a flame of excitement throughout the country. This reflection may prove to be a lesson of wisdom and of warning for our future guidance. Practically considered, the question is simply whether the people of that Territory should first come into the Union and then change any provision in their constitution not agreeable to themselves, or accomplish the very same object by remaining out of the Union and framing another constitution in accordance with their will? In either case, the result would be precisely the same. The only difference in point of fact is, that the object would have been much sooner attained, and the pacification of Kansas more speedily effected, had it been admitted as a State during the last session of Congress.

My recommendation, however, for the immediate admission of Kansas, failed to meet the approbation of Congress. They deemed it wiser to adopt a different measure for the settlement of the question. For my own part, I should have been willing to yield my assent to almost any constitutional measure to accomplish this object. I therefore cordially acquiesced in what has been called the English Compromise, and approved the " Act for the admission of the State of Kansas into the Union " upon the terms therein prescribed.

Under the ordinance which accompanied the Lecompton constitution the people of Kansas had claimed double the quantity of public lands for the support of common schools which had ever been previously granted to any State upon entering the Union; and also the alternate sections of land for twelve miles on each side of two railroads, proposed to be constructed from the northern to the southern boundary, and from the eastern to the western boundary of the State. Congress, deeming these claims unreasonable, provided, by the act of May 4, 1858, to which I have just referred, for the admission of the State on an equal footing with the original States, but " upon the fundamental condition precedent " that a majority of the people thereof, at an election to be held for that purpose, should, in place of the very large grants of public lands which they had demanded under the ordinance, accept such grants as had been made to Minnesota and other new States. Under this act, should a majority reject the proposition offered them, " it shall be deemed and held that the people of Kansas do not desire admission into the Union with said constitution under the conditions set forth in said proposition." In that event, the act authorizes the people of the Territory to elect delegates to form a constitution and State government for themselves "whenever, and not before, it is ascertained by a census, duly and legally taken, that the population of said Territory equals or exceeds the ratio of representation required for a member of the House of Representatives of the Congress of the United States." The delegates thus assembled " shall first determine by a vote whether it is the wish of the people of the proposed State to be admitted into the Union at that time, and if so, shall proceed to form a constitution, and take all necessary steps for the establishment of a State government in conformity with the Federal Constitution." After this constitution shall have been formed, Congress, carrying out the principles of popular sovereignty and non-intervention, have left " the mode and manner of its approval or ratification by the people of the proposed State " to be " prescribed by law," and they " shall then be admitted into the Union as a State under such constitution thus fairly and legally made, with or without slavery, as said constitution may prescribe."

An election was held throughout Kansas, in pursuance of the provisions of this act, on the second day of August last, and it resulted in the rejection, by a large majority, of the proposition submitted to the people by Congress. This being the case, they are now authorized to form another constitution, preparatory to admission into the Union, but not until their number, as ascertained by a census, shall equal or exceed the ratio required to elect a member to the House of Representatives.

It is not probable, in the present state of the case, that a third constitution can be lawfully framed and presented to Congress by Kansas before its population shall have reached the designated number. Nor is it to be presumed that, after their sad experience in resisting the territorial laws, they will attempt to adopt a constitution in express violation of the provisions of an act of Congress. During the session of 1856 much of the time of Congress was occupied on the question of admitting Kansas under the Topeka constitution. Again, nearly the whole of the last session was devoted to the question of its admission under the Lecompton constitution. Surely it is not unreasonable to require the people of Kansas to wait, before making a third attempt, until the number of their inhabitants shall amount to ninety-three thousand four hundred and twenty. During this brief period the harmony of the States, as well as the great business interests of the country, demands that the people of the Union shall not for a third time be convulsed by another agitation on the Kansas question. By waiting for a short time, and acting in obedience to law, Kansas will glide into the Union without the slightest impediment.

This excellent provision, which Congress has applied to Kansas, ought to be extended and rendered applicable to all Territories which may hereafter seek admission into the Union.

Whilst Congress possesses the undoubted power of admitting a new State into the Union, however small may be the number of its inhabitants, yet this power ought not, in my opinion, to be exercised before the population shall amount to the ratio required by the act for the admission of Kansas. Had this been previously the rule, the country would have escaped all the evils and misfortunes to which it has been exposed by the Kansas question.

Of course, it would be unjust to give this rule a retrospective application, and exclude a State which, acting upon the past practice of the government, has already formed its constitution, elected its legislature and other officers, and is now prepared to enter the Union.

The rule ought to be adopted, whether we consider its bearing on the people of the Territories or upon the people of the existing States. Many of the serious dissensions which have prevailed in Congress and throughout the country would have been avoided had this rule been established at an earlier period of the government.

Immediately upon the formation of a new Territory, people from different States and from foreign countries rush into it, for the laudable purpose of improving their condition. Their first duty to themselves is to open and cultivate farms, to construct roads, to establish schools, to erect places of religious worship, and to devote their energies generally to reclaim the wilderness, and to lay the foundations of a flourishing and prosperous commonwealth. If, in this incipient condition, with a population of a few thousand, they should prematurely enter the Union, they are oppressed by the burden of State taxation, and the means necessary for the improvement of the Territory and the advancement of their own interests are thus diverted to very different purposes.

The federal government has ever been a liberal parent to the Territories, and a generous contributor to the useful enterprises of the early settlers. It has paid the expenses of their governments and legislative assemblies out of the common treasury, and thus relieved them from a heavy charge. Under these circumstances, nothing can be better calculated to retard their material progress than to divert them from their useful employments, by prematurely exciting angry political contests among themselves, for the benefit of aspiring leaders. It is surely no hardship for embryo governors, senators, and members of Congress, to wait until the number of inhabitants shall equal those of a single congressional district. They surely ought not to be permitted to rush into the Union with a population less than one-half of several of the large counties in the interior of some of the States. This was the condition of Kansas when it made application to be admitted under the Topeka constitution. Besides, it requires some time to render the mass of a population collected in a new Territory at all homogeneous, and to unite them on anything like a fixed policy. Establish the rule, and all will look forward to it and govern themselves accordingly.

But justice to the people of the several States requires that this rule should be established by Congress. Each State is entitled to two senators and at least one representative in Congress. Should the people of the States fail to elect a Vice President, the power devolves upon the Senate to select this officer from the two highest candidates on the list. In case of the death of the President, the Vice President, thus elected by the Senate, becomes President of the United States. On all questions of legislation the senators from the smallest States of the Union have an equal vote with those from the largest. The same may be said in regard to the ratification of treaties and of Executive appointments. All this has worked admirably in practice, whilst it conforms in principle with the character of a government instituted by sovereign States. I presume no American citizen would desire the slightest change in the arrangement. Still, is it not unjust and unequal to the existing States to invest some forty or fifty thousand people collected in a Territory with the attributes of sovereignty, and place them on an equal footing with Virginia and New York in the Senate of the United States?

For these reasons, I earnestly recommend the passage of a general act, which shall provide that, upon the application of a territorial legislature, declaring their belief that the Territory contains a number of inhabitants which, if in a State, would entitle them to elect a member of Congress, it shall be the duty of the President to cause a census of the inhabitants to be taken, and if found sufficient, then by the terms of this act to authorize them to proceed "in their own way" to frame a State constitution preparatory to admission into the Union. I also recommend that an appropriation may be made, to enable the President to take a census of the people of Kansas.

The present condition of the Territory of Utah, when contrasted with what it was one year ago, is a subject for congratulation. It was then in a state of open rebellion, and, cost what it might, the character of the government required that this rebellion should be suppressed and the Mormons compelled to yield obedience to the Constitution and the laws. In order to accomplish this object, as I informed you in my last annual message, I appointed a new governor instead of Brigham Young, and other federal officers to take the place of those who, consulting their personal safety, had found it necessary to withdraw from the Territory. To protect these civil officers, and to aid them, as a *posse comitatus,* in the execution of the laws in case of need, I ordered a detachment of the army to accompany them to Utah. The necessity for adopting these measures is now demonstrated.

On the 15th of September, 1857, Governor Young issued his proclamation, in the style of an independent sovereign, announcing his purpose to resist by force of arms the entry of the United States troops into our own Territory of Utah. By this he required all the forces in the Territory to "hold themselves in readiness to march at a moment's notice to repel any and all such invasion," and established martial law from its date throughout the Territory. These proved to be no idle threats. Forts Bridger and Supply were vacated and burnt down by the Mormons, to deprive our troops of a shelter after their long and fatiguing march. Orders were issued by Daniel H. Wells, styling himself "Lieutenant-General, Nauvoo Legion," to stampede the animals of the United States troops on their march, to set fire to their trains, to burn the grass and the whole country before them and on their flanks, to keep them from sleeping by night surprises, and to blockade the road by felling trees, and destroying the fords of rivers, &c., &c., &c.

These orders were promptly and effectually obeyed. On the 4th of October, 1857, the Mormons captured and burned, on Green river, three of our supply trains, consisting of seventy-five wagons loaded with provisions and tents for the army, and carried away several hundred animals. This diminished the supply of provisions so materially that General Johnston was obliged to reduce the ration, and even with this precaution there was only sufficient left to subsist the troops until the first of June.

Our little army behaved admirably in their encampment at Fort Bridger under these trying privations. In the midst of the mountains, in a dreary, unsettled, and inhospitable region, more than a thousand miles from home, they passed the severe and inclement winter without a murmur. They looked forward with confidence for relief from their country in due season, and in this they were not disappointed.

The Secretary of War employed all his energies to forward them the necessary supplies, and to muster and send such a military force to Utah as would render resistance on the part of the Mormons hopeless, and thus terminate the war without the effusion of blood. In his efforts he was efficiently sustained by Congress. They granted appropriations sufficient to cover the deficiency thus necessarily created, and also provided for raising two regiments of volunteers " for the purpose of quelling disturbances in the Territory of Utah, for the protection of supply and emigrant trains, and the suppression of Indian hostilities on the frontiers." Happily, there was no occasion to call these regiments into service. If there had been, I should have felt serious embarrassment in selecting them, so great was the number of our brave and patriotic citizens anxious to serve their country in this distant and apparently dangerous expedition. Thus it has ever been, and thus may it ever be!

The wisdom and economy of sending sufficient reinforcements to Utah are established not only by the event, but in the opinion of those who, from their position and opportunities, are the most capable of forming a correct judgment. General Johnston, the commander of the forces, in addressing the Secretary of War from Fort Bridger, under date of October 18, 1857, expresses the opinion that " unless a large force is sent here, from the nature of the country, a protracted war on their [the Mormons'] part is inevitable." This he considered necessary, to terminate the war " speedily and more economically than if attempted by insufficient means."

In the mean time it was my anxious desire that the Mormons should yield obedience to the Constitution and the laws, without rendering it necessary to resort to military force. To aid in accomplishing this object I deemed it advisable, in April last, to despatch two distinguished citizens of the United States, Messrs. Powell and McCulloch, to Utah. They bore with them a proclamation addressed by myself to the inhabitants of Utah, dated on the 6th day of that month, warning them of their true condition, and how hopeless it was on their part to persist in rebellion against the United States, and offering all those who should submit to the laws a full pardon for their past seditions and treasons. At the same time I assured those who should persist in rebellion against the United States that they must expect no further lenity, but look to be rigorously dealt with, according to their deserts. The instructions to these agents, as well as a copy of the proclamation and their reports, are herewith submitted. It will be seen by their report of the 3d of July last that they have fully confirmed the opinion expressed by General Johnston in the previous October as to the necessity of sending reinforcements to Utah. In this they state that they "are firmly impressed with the belief that the presence of the army here, and the large additional force that had been ordered to this Territory, were the chief inducements that caused the Mormons to abandon the idea of resisting the authority of the United States. A less decisive policy would probably have resulted in a long, bloody, and expensive war."

These gentlemen conducted themselves to my entire satisfaction, and rendered useful services in executing the humane intentions of the government.

It also affords me great satisfaction to state that Governor Cumming has performed his duty in an able and conciliatory manner, and with the happiest effect. I cannot, in this connection, refrain from mentioning the valuable services of Colonel Thomas L. Kane, who, from motives of pure benevolence, and without any official character or pecuniary compensation, visited Utah during the last inclement winter for the purpose of contributing to the pacification of the Territory.

I am happy to inform you that the governor and other civil officers of Utah are now performing their appropriate functions without resistance. The authority of the Constitution and the laws has been fully restored, and peace prevails throughout the Territory.

A portion of the troops sent to Utah are now encamped in Cedar valley, forty-four miles southwest of Salt Lake city, and the remainder have been ordered to Oregon to suppress Indian hostilities.

The march of the army to Salt Lake city, through the Indian Territory, has had a powerful effect in restraining the hostile feelings against the United States which existed among the Indians in that region, and in securing emigrants to the Far West against their depredations. This will also be the means of establishing military posts and promoting settlements along the route.

I recommend that the benefits of our land laws and preemption system be extended to the people of Utah, by the establishment of a land office in that Territory.

I have occasion, also, to congratulate you on the result of our negotiations with China.

You were informed by my last annual message that our minister had been instructed to occupy a neutral position in the hostilities conducted by Great Britain and France against Canton. He was, however, at the same time, directed to co-operate cordially with the British and French ministers in all peaceful measures to secure by treaty those just concessions to foreign commerce which the nations of the world had a right to demand. It was impossible for me to proceed further than this on my own authority, without usurping the war-making power, which, under the Constitution, belongs exclusively to Congress.

Besides, after a careful examination of the nature and extent of our grievances, I did not believe they were of such a pressing and aggravated character as would have justified Congress in declaring war against the Chinese empire, without first making another earnest attempt to adjust them by peaceful negotiation. I was the more inclined to this opinion, because of the severe chastisement which had then but recently been inflicted upon the Chinese by our squadron in the capture and destruction of the Barrier forts to avenge an alleged insult to our flag.

The event has proved the wisdom of our neutrality. Our minister has executed his instructions with eminent skill and ability. In conjunction with the Russian plenipotentiary, he has peacefully, but effectually, co-operated with the English and French plenipotentiaries; and each of the four powers has concluded a separate treaty with China, of a highly satisfactory character. The treaty concluded by our own plenipotentiary will immediately be submitted to the Senate.

I am happy to announce that, through the energetic yet conciliatory efforts of our consul general in Japan, a new treaty has been concluded with that empire, which may be expected materially to augment our trade and intercourse in that quarter, and remove from our countrymen the disabilities which have heretofore been imposed upon the exercise of their religion. The treaty shall be submitted to the Senate for approval without delay.

It is my earnest desire that every misunderstanding with the government of Great Britain should be amicably and speedily adjusted. It has been the misfortune of both countries, almost ever since the period of the revolution, to have been annoyed by a succession of irritating and dangerous questions, threatening their friendly relations. This has partially prevented the full development of those feelings of mutual friendship between the people of the two countries, so natural in themselves and so conducive to their common interest. Any serious interruption of the commerce between the United States and Great Britain would be equally injurious to both. In fact, no two nations have ever existed on the face of the earth which could do each other so much good or so much harm.

Entertaining these sentiments, I am gratified to inform you that the long-pending controversy between the two governments, in relation to the question of visitation and search, has been amicably adjusted. The claim, on the part of Great Britain, forcibly to visit American vessels on the high seas in time of peace could not be sustained under the law of nations, and it had been overruled by her own most eminent jurists. This question was recently brought to an issue by the repeated acts of British cruisers, in boarding and searching our merchant vessels in the Gulf of Mexico and the adjacent seas. These acts were the more injurious and annoying, as these waters are traversed by a large portion of the commerce and navigation of the United States, and their free and unrestricted use is essential to the security of the coastwise trade between the different States of the Union. Such vexatious interruptions could not fail to excite the feelings of the country, and to require the interposition of the Government. Remonstrances were addressed to the British government against these violations of our rights of sovereignty, and a naval force was at the same time ordered to the Cuban waters, with directions "to protect all vessels of the United States on the high seas from search or detention by the vessels-of-war of any other nation." These measures received the unqualified and even enthusiastic approbation of the American people. Most fortunately, however, no collision took place, and the British government promptly avowed its recognition of the principles of international law upon this subject as laid down by the government of the United States in the note of the Secretary of State to the British minister at Washington, of April 10, 1858, which secure the vessels of the United States upon the high seas from visitation or search in time of peace, under any circumstances whatever. The claim has been abandoned in a manner reflecting honor on the British government.

and evincing a just regard for the law of nations, and cannot fail to strengthen the amicable relations between the two countries.

The British government, at the same time, proposed to the United States that some mode should be adopted, by mutual arrangement between the two countries, of a character which may be found effective without being offensive, for verifying the nationality of vessels suspected on good grounds of carrying false colors. They have also invited the United States to take the initiative, and propose measures for this purpose. Whilst declining to assume so grave a responsibility, the Secretary of State has informed the British government that we are ready to receive any proposals which they may feel disposed to offer, having this object in view, and to consider them in an amicable spirit. A strong opinion is, however, expressed, that the occasional abuse of the flag of any nation is an evil far less to be deprecated than would be the establishment of any regulations which might be incompatible with the freedom of the seas. This government has yet received no communication specifying the manner in which the British government would propose to carry out their suggestion and I am inclined to believe that no plan which can be devised will be free from grave embarrassments. Still, I shall form no decided opinion on the subject until I shall have carefully and in the best spirit examined any proposals which they may think proper to make.

I am truly sorry I cannot also inform you that the complications between Great Britain and the United States arising out of the Clayton and Bulwer treaty of April, 1850, have been finally adjusted.

At the commencement of your last session I had reason to hope that, emancipating themselves from further unavailing discussions, the two governments would proceed to settle the Central American questions in a practical manner, alike honorable and satisfactory to both; and this hope I have not yet abandoned. In my last annual message I stated that overtures had been made by the British government for this purpose in a friendly spirit, which I cordially reciprocated. Their proposal was, to withdraw these questions from direct negotiation between the two governments; but to accomplish the same object by a negotiation between the British government and each of the Central American republics whose territorial interests are immediately involved.

The settlement was to be made in accordance with the general tenor of the interpretation placed upon the Clayton and Bulwer treaty by the United States, with certain modifications. As negotiations are still pending upon this basis, it would not be proper for me now to communicate their present condition. A final settlement of these questions is greatly to be desired, as this would wipe out the last remaining subject of dispute between the two countries.

Our relations with the great empires of France and Russia, as well as with all other governments on the continent of Europe, except that of Spain, continue to be of the most friendly character.

With Spain our relations remain in an unsatisfactory condition. In my message of December last I informed you that our envoy extraordinary and minister plenipotentiary to Madrid had asked for his recall; and it was my purpose to send out a new minister to that court, with special instructions on all questions pending between the two governments, and with a determination to have them speedily and amicably adjusted, if that were possible. This purpose has been hitherto defeated by causes which I need not enumerate.

The mission to Spain has been intrusted to a distinguished citizen of Kentucky, who will proceed to Madrid without delay, and make another and a final attempt to obtain justice from that government.

Spanish officials, under the direct control of the captain general of Cuba, have insulted our national flag, and in repeated instances have, from time to time, inflicted injuries on the persons and property of our citizens. These have given birth to numerous claims against the Spanish government, the merits of which have been ably discussed for a series of years by our successive diplomatic representatives. Notwithstanding this, we have not arrived at a practical result in any single instance, unless we may except the case of the Black Warrior, under the late administration; and that presented an outrage of such a character as would have justified an immediate resort to war. All our attempts to obtain redress have been baffled and defeated. The frequent and oft-recurring changes in the Spanish ministry have been employed as reasons for delay. We have been compelled to wait, again and again, until the new minister shall have had time to investigate the justice of our demands.

Even what have been denominated " the Cuban claims," in which more than a hundred of our citizens are directly interested, have furnished no exception.   These claims were for the refunding of duties unjustly exacted from American vessels at different custom-houses in Cuba so long ago as the year 1844. The principles upon which they rest are so manifestly equitable and just, that, after a period of nearly ten years, in 1854 they were recognized by the Spanish government.   Proceedings were afterwards instituted to ascertain their amount, and this was finally fixed according to their own statement (with which we were satisfied) at the sum of one hundred and twenty-eight thousand six hundred and thirty-five dollars and fifty-four cents. Just at the moment, after a delay of fourteen years, when we had reason to expect that this sum would be repaid with interest, we have received a proposal offering to refund one-third of that amount, (forty-two thousand eight hundred and seventy-eight dollars and forty-one cents,) but without interest, if we would accept this in full satisfaction.   The offer is also accompanied by a declaration that this indemnification is not founded on any reason of strict justice, but is made as a special favor.

One alleged cause for procrastination in the examination and adjustment of our claims arises from an obstacle which it is the duty of the Spanish government to remove.   Whilst the captain general of Cuba is invested with general despotic authority in the government of that island, the power is withheld from him to examine and redress wrongs committed by officials under his control on citizens of the United States.   Instead of making our complaints directly to him at Havana, we are obliged to present them through our minister at Madrid.   These are then referred back to the captain general for information, and much time is thus consumed in preliminary investigations and correspondence between Madrid and Cuba before the Spanish government will consent to proceed to negotiation.   Many of the difficulties between the two governments would be obviated, and a long train of negotiation avoided, if the captain general were invested with authority to settle questions of easy solution on the spot, where all the facts are fresh, and could be promptly and satisfactorily ascertained.   We have hitherto in vain urged upon the Spanish government to confer this power upon the captain general, and our minister to Spain will again be instructed to urge this subject on their notice.   In this respect we occupy a different position from the powers of Europe.   Cuba is almost within sight of our shores; our commerce with it is far greater than that of any other nation, including Spain itself, and our citizens are in habits of daily and extended personal intercourse with every part of the island.   It is, therefore, a great grievance that when any difficulty occurs, no matter how unimportant, which might be readily settled at the moment, we should be obliged to resort to Madrid, especially when the very first step to be taken there is to refer it back to Cuba.

The truth is, that Cuba, in its existing colonial condition, is a constant source of injury and annoyance to the American people.   It is the only spot in the civilized world where the African slave trade is tolerated; and we are bound by treaty with Great Britain to maintain a naval force on the coast of Africa, at much expense both of life and treasure, solely for the purpose of arresting slavers bound to that island.   The late serious difficulties between the United States and Great Britain respecting the right of search, now so happily terminated, could never have arisen if Cuba had not afforded a market for slaves.   As long as this market 'shall remain open, there can be no hope for the civilization of benighted Africa.   Whilst the demand for slaves continues in Cuba, wars will be waged among the petty and barbarous chiefs in Africa for the purpose of seizing subjects to supply this trade.   In such a condition of affairs, it is impossible that the light of civilization and religion can ever penetrate these dark abodes.

It has been made known to the world by my predecessors that the United States have, on several occasions, endeavored to acquire Cuba from Spain by honorable negotiation.   If this were accomplished, the last relic of the African slave trade would instantly disappear.   We would not, if we could, acquire Cuba in any other manner.   This is due to our national character. All the territory which we have acquired since the origin of the government has been by fair purchase from France, Spain, and Mexico, or by the free and voluntary act of the independent State of Texas in blending her destinies with our own.   This course we shall ever pursue, unless circumstances should occur.

which we do not now anticipate, rendering a departure from it clearly justifiable, under the imperative and overruling law of self-preservation.

The island of Cuba, from its geographical position, commands the mouth of the Mississippi, and the immense and annually increasing trade, foreign and coastwise, from the valley of that noble river, now embracing half the sovereign States of the Union. With that island under the dominion of a distant foreign power, this trade, of vital importance to these States, is exposed to the danger of being destroyed in time of war, and it has hitherto been subjected to perpetual injury and annoyance in time of peace. Our relations with Spain, which ought to be of the most friendly character, must always be placed in jeopardy, whilst the existing colonial government over the island shall remain in its present condition.

Whilst the possession of the island would be of vast importance to the United States, its value to Spain is, comparatively, unimportant. Such was the relative situation of the parties when the great Napoleon transferred Louisiana to the United States. Jealous, as he ever was, of the national honor and interests of France, no person throughout the world has imputed blame to him for accepting a pecuniary equivalent for this cession.

The publicity which has been given to our former negotiations upon this subject, and the large appropriation which may be required to effect the purpose, render it expedient, before making another attempt to renew the negotiation, that I should lay the whole subject before Congress. This is especially necessary, as it may become indispensable to success, that I should be intrusted with the means of making an advance to the Spanish government immediately after the signing of the treaty, without awaiting the ratification of it by the Senate. I am encouraged to make this suggestion by the example of Mr. Jefferson, previous to the purchase of Louisiana from France, and by that of Mr. Polk, in view of the acquisition of territory from Mexico. I refer the whole subject to Congress, and commend it to their careful consideration.

I repeat the recommendation made in my message of December last in favor of an appropriation " to be paid to the Spanish government for the purpose of distribution among the claimants in the Amistad case." President Polk first made a similar recommendation in December, 1847, and it was repeated by my immediate predecessor in December, 1853. I entertain no doubt that indemnity is fairly due to these claimants under our treaty with Spain of October 27, 1795; and whilst demanding justice we ought to do justice. An appropriation promptly made for this purpose could not fail to exert a favorable influence on our negotiations with Spain.

Our position in relation to the independent States south of us on this continent, and especially those within the limits of North America, is of a peculiar character. The northern boundary of Mexico is coincident with our own southern boundary from ocean to ocean, and we must necessarily feel a deep interest in all that concerns the well being and the fate of so near a neighbor. We have always cherished the kindest wishes for the success of that republic, and have indulged the hope that it might at last, after all its trials, enjoy peace and prosperity under a free and stable government. We have never hitherto interfered, directly or indirectly, with its internal affairs, and it is a duty which we owe to ourselves to protect the integrity of its territory against the hostile interference of any other power. Our geographical position, our direct interest in all that concerns Mexico, and our well-settled policy in regard to the North American continent, render this an indispensable duty.

Mexico has been in a state of constant revolution almost ever since it achieved its independence. One military leader after another has usurped the government in rapid succession; and the various constitutions from time to time adopted have been set at naught almost as soon as they were proclaimed. The successive governments have afforded no adequate protection, either to Mexican citizens or foreign residents, against lawless violence. Heretofore, a seizure of the capital by a military chieftain has been generally followed by at least the nominal submission of the country to his rule for a brief period; but not so at the present crisis of Mexican affairs. A civil war has been raging for some time throughout the republic between the central government at the city of Mexico, which has endeavored to subvert the constitution last framed by military power, and those who maintain the authority of that constitution. The antagonist parties each hold possession of different States of the republic, and the fortunes of the war are constantly changing. Meanwhile the most reprehensible means have been employed by both parties to extort money from foreigners, as well as natives, to carry on this ruinous contest. The truth is, that this fine country, blessed with a productive soil and a benign climate, has been reduced by civil dissension to a condition of almost hopeless anarchy and imbecility. It would be vain for this government to attempt to enforce payment in money of the claims of American citizens, now amounting to more than ten million dollars, against Mexico, because she is destitute of all pecuniary means to satisfy these demands.

Our late minister was furnished with ample powers and instructions for the adjustment of all pending questions with the central government of Mexico, and he performed his duty with zeal and ability. The claims of our citizens, some of them arising out of the violation of an express provision of the treaty of Guadalupe Hidalgo, and others from gross injuries to persons as well as property, have remained unredressed, and even unnoticed. Remonstrances against these grievances have been addressed, without effect, to that government. Meantime, in various parts of the republic, instances have been numerous of the murder, imprisonment, and plunder of our citizens by different parties claiming and exercising a local jurisdiction; but the central government, although repeatedly urged thereto, have made no effort either to punish the authors of these outrages or to prevent their recurrence. No American citizen can now visit Mexico on lawful business without imminent danger to his person and property. There is no adequate protection to either; and in this respect our treaty with that republic is almost a dead letter.

This state of affairs was brought to a crisis in May last by the promulgation of a decree levying a contribution *pro rata* upon all the capital in the republic, between certain specified amounts, whether held by Mexicans or foreigners. Mr. Forsyth, regarding this decree in the light of a " forced loan," formally protested against its application to his countrymen, and advised them not to pay the contribution, but to suffer it to be forcibly exacted. Acting upon this advice an American citizen refused to pay the contribution and his property was seized by armed men to satisfy the amount. Not content with this, the government proceeded still further and issued a decree banishing him from the country.   Our minister immediately notified them that, if this decree should be carried into execution, he would feel it to be his duty to adopt " the most decided measures that belong to the powers and obligations of the representative office."   Notwithstanding this warning, the banishment was enforced, and Mr. Forsyth promptly announced to the government the suspension of the political relations of his legation with them, until the pleasure of his own government should be ascertained.

This government did not regard the contribution imposed by the decree of the 15th May last to be in strictness a " forced loan," and as such prohibited by the 10th article of the treaty of 1826 between Great Britain and Mexico, to the benefits of which American citizens are entitled by treaty; yet the imposition of the contribution upon foreigners was considered an unjust and oppressive measure.   Besides, internal factions in other parts of the republic were at the same time levying similar exactions upon the property of our citizens and interrupting their commerce.   There had been an entire failure on the part of our minister to secure redress for the wrongs which our citizens had endured, notwithstanding his persevering efforts.   And from the temper manifested by the Mexican government he had repeatedly assured us that no favorable change could be expected until the United States should "give striking evidence of their will and power to protect their citizens," and that " severe chastening is the only earthly remedy for our grievances."   From this statement of facts, it would have been worse than idle to direct Mr. Forsyth to retrace his steps and resume diplomatic relations with that government; and it was therefore deemed proper to sanction his withdrawal of the legation from the city of Mexico.

Abundant cause now undoubtedly exists for a resort to hostilities against the government still holding possession of the capital.   Should they succeed in subduing the constitutional forces all reasonable hope will then have expired of a peaceful settlement of our difficulties.

On the other hand, should the constitutional party prevail and their authority be established over the republic, there is reason to hope that they will be animated by a less unfriendly spirit, and may grant that redress to American citizens which justice requires, so far as they may possess the means.   But for this expectation I should at once have recommended to Congress to grant the necessary power to the President to take possession of a sufficient portion of the remote and unsettled territory of Mexico, to be held in pledge until our injuries shall be redressed and our just demands be satisfied. We have already exhausted every milder means of obtaining justice. In such a case this remedy of reprisals is recognized by the law of nations, not only as just in itself, but as a means of preventing actual war.

But there is another view of our relations with Mexico, arising from the unhappy condition of affairs along our southwestern frontier, which demands immediate action. In that remote region, where there are but few white inhabitants, large bands of hostile and predatory Indians roam promiscuously over the Mexican States of Chihuahua and Sonora, and our adjoining Territories. The local governments of these States are perfectly helpless, and are kept in a state of constant alarm by the Indians. They have not the power, if they possessed the will, even to restrain lawless Mexicans from passing the border and committing depredations on our remote settlers. A state of anarchy and violence prevails throughout that distant frontier. The laws are a dead letter, and life and property wholly insecure. For this reason the settlement of Arizona is arrested, whilst it is of great importance that a chain of inhabitants should extend all along its southern border, sufficient for their own protection and that of the United States mail passing to and from California. Well-founded apprehensions are now entertained, that the Indians, and wandering Mexicans equally lawless, may break up the important stage and postal communication recently established between our Atlantic and Pacific possessions. This passes very near to the Mexican boundary throughout the whole length of Arizona. I can imagine no possible remedy for these evils, and no mode of restoring law and order on that remote and unsettled frontier, but for the government of the United States to assume a temporary protectorate over the northern portions of Chihuahua and Sonora, and to establish military posts within the same—and this I earnestly recommend to Congress. This protection may be withdrawn as soon as local governments shall be established in these Mexican States, capable of performing their duties to the United States, restraining the lawless, and preserving peace along the border.

I do not doubt that this measure will be viewed in a friendly spirit by the governments and people of Chihuahua and Sonora, as it will prove equally effectual for the protection of their citizens on that remote and lawless frontier, as for citizens of the United States.

And, in this connection, permit me to recall your attention to the condition of Arizona. The population of that Territory, numbering, as is alleged, more than ten thousand souls, are practically without a government, without laws, and without any regular administration of justice. Murder and other crimes are committed with impunity. This state of things calls loudly for redress, and I therefore repeat my recommendation for the establishment of a territorial government over Arizona.

The political condition of the narrow isthmus of Central America, through which transit routes pass between the Atlantic and Pacific oceans, presents a subject of deep interest to all commercial nations. It is over these transits that a large proportion of the trade and travel between the European and Asiatic continents is destined to pass. To the United States these routes are of incalculable importance as a means of communication between their Atlantic and Pacific possessions. The latter now extend throughout seventeen degrees of latitude on the Pacific coast, embracing the important State of California and the flourishing Territories of Oregon and Washington. All commercial nations, therefore, have a deep and direct interest that these communications shall be rendered secure from interruption. If an arm of the sea connecting the two oceans penetrated through Nicaragua and Costa Rica, it could not be pretended that these States would have the right to arrest or retard its navigation, to the injury of other nations. The transit by land over this narrow isthmus occupies nearly the same position. It is a highway in which they themselves have little interest when compared with the vast interests of the rest of the world. Whilst their rights of sovereignty ought to be respected, it is the duty of other nations to require that this important passage shall not be interrupted by the civil wars and revolutionary outbreaks which have so frequently occurred in that region. The stake is too important to be left at the mercy of rival companies claiming to hold conflicting contracts with Nicaragua. The commerce of other nations is not to stand still and await the adjust-

ment of such petty controversies. The government of the
United States expect no more than this, and they will not be
satisfied with less. They would not, if they could, derive any
advantage from the Nicaragua transit not common to the rest
of the world. Its neutrality and protection for the common use
of all nations is their only object. They have no objection that
Nicaragua shall demand and receive a fair compensation from
the companies and individuals who may traverse the route; but
they insist that it shall never hereafter be closed by an arbitrary
decree of that government. If disputes arise between it and
those with whom they may have entered into contracts, these
must be adjusted by some fair tribunal provided for the purpose,
and the route must not be closed pending the controversy. This
is our whole policy, and it cannot fail to be acceptable to other
nations.

All these difficulties might be avoided, if, consistently with
the good faith of Nicaragua, the use of this transit could be
thrown open to general competition; providing at the same time
for the payment of a reasonable rate to the Nicaraguan government on passengers and freight.

In August, 1852, the Accessory Transit Company made its
first interoceanic trip over the Nicaraguan route, and continued
in successful operation with great advantage to the public, until
the 18th February, 1856, when it was closed, and the grant to
this company, as well as its charter, was summarily and arbi-
trarily revoked by the government of President Rivas. Previous
to this date, however, in 1854, serious disputes concerning the
settlement of their accounts had arisen between the company and
the government, threatening the interruption of the route at any
moment. These the United States in vain endeavored to compose. It would be useless to narrate the various proceedings
which took place between the parties up till the time when the
transit was discontinued. Suffice it to say that, since February,
1856, it has remained closed, greatly to the prejudice of citizens
of the United States. Since that time the competition has ceased
between the rival routes of Panama and Nicaragua, and in
consequence thereof, an unjust and unreasonable amount
has been exacted from our citizens for their passage to and from
California.

A treaty was signed on the 16th day of November, 1857,
by the Secretary of State and minister of Nicaragua, under the

stipulations of which the use and protection of the transit route would have been secured not only to the United States, but equally to all other nations. How, and on what pretext this treaty has failed to receive the ratification of the Nicaraguan government, will appear by the papers herewith communicated from the State Department. The principal objection seems to have been to the provision authorizing the United States to employ force to keep the route open, in case Nicaragua should fail to perform her duty in this respect. From the feebleness of that republic, its frequent changes of government, and its constant internal dissensions this had become a most important stipulation, and one essentially necessary not only for the security of the route, but for the safety of American citizens passing and repassing to and from our Pacific possessions. Were such a stipulation embraced in a treaty between the United States and Nicaragua, the knowledge of this fact would of itself most probably prevent hostile parties from committing aggressions on the route, and render our actual interference for its protection unnecessary.

The Executive government of this country, in its intercourse with foreign nations, is limited to the employment of diplomacy alone. When this fails it can proceed no further. It cannot legitimately resort to force without the direct authority of Congress, except in resisting and repelling hostile attacks. It would have no authority to enter the territories of Nicaragua, even to prevent the destruction of the transit, and protect the lives and property of our own citizens on their passage. It is true, that on a sudden emergency of this character, the President would direct any armed force in the vicinity to march to their relief; but in doing this he would act upon his own responsibility.

Under these circumstances, I earnestly recommend to Congress the passage of an act authorizing the President, under such restrictions as they may deem proper, to employ the land and naval forces of the United States in preventing the transit from being obstructed or closed by lawless violence, and in protecting the lives and property of American citizens travelling thereupon, requiring at the same time that these forces shall be withdrawn the moment the danger shall have passed away. Without such a provision our citizens will be constantly exposed to interruption in their progress, and to lawless violence,

A similar necessity exists for the passage of such an act for the protection of the Panama and Tehuantepec routes.

In reference to the Panama route, the United States, by their existing treaty with New Granada, expressly guaranty the neutrality of the isthmus, " with the view that the free transit from the one to the other sea may not be interrupted or embarrassed in any future time while this treaty exists."

In regard to the Tehuantepec route, which has been recently opened under the most favorable auspices, our treaty with Mexico of the 30th December, 1853, secures to the citizens of the United States a right of transit over it for their persons and merchandise, and stipulates that neither government shall " interpose any obstacle " thereto.   It also concedes to the United States the " right to transport across the isthmus, in closed bags, the mails of the United States not intended for distribution along the line of the communication; also, the effects of the United States government and its citizens which may be intended for transit, and not for distribution on the isthmus, free of custom-house or other charges by the Mexican government."

These treaty stipulations with New Granada and Mexico, in addition to the considerations applicable to the Nicaragua route, seem to require legislation for the purpose of carrying them into effect.

The injuries which have been inflicted upon our citizens in Costa Rica and Nicaragua, during the last two or three years, have received the prompt attention of this government.   Some of these injuries were of the most aggravated character.   The transaction at Virgin Bay, in April, 1856, when a company of unarmed Americans, who were in no way connected with any belligerent conduct or party, were fired upon by the troops of Costa Rica, and numbers of them killed and wounded, was brought to the knowledge of Congress by my predecessor soon after its occurrence, and was also presented to the government of Costa Rica for that immediate investigation and redress which the nature of the case demanded.   A similar course was pursued with reference to other outrages in these countries, some of which were hardly less aggravated in their character than the transaction at Virgin Bay.   At the time, however, when our present minister to Nicaragua was appointed, in December, 1857, no redress had been obtained for any of these wrongs, and no reply even had been received to the demands which had been made by this government upon that of Costa Rica more than a year before. Our minister was instructed, therefore, to lose no time in expressing to those governments the deep regret with which the President had witnessed this inattention to the just claims of the United States, and in demanding their prompt and satisfactory adjustment. Unless this demand shall be complied with at an early day, it will only remain for this government to adopt such other measures as may be necessary, in order to obtain for itself that justice which it has in vain attempted to secure by peaceful means from the governments of Nicaragua and Costa Rica. While it has shown, and will continue to show, the most sincere regard for the rights and honor of these republics, it cannot permit this regard to be met by an utter neglect on their part, of what is due to the government and citizens of the United States.

Against New Granada we have long standing causes of complaint arising out of the unsatisfied claims of our citizens upon that republic; and to these have been more recently added the outrages committed upon our citizens at Panama in April, 1856. A treaty for the adjustment of these difficulties was concluded by the Secretary of State and the minister of New Granada, in September, 1857, which contained just and acceptable provisions for that purpose. This treaty was transmitted to Bogota, and was ratified by the government of New Granada, but with certain amendments. It was not, however, returned to this city until after the close of the last session of the Senate. It will be immediately transmitted to that body for their advice and consent; and should this be obtained, it will remove all our existing causes of complaint against New Granada on the subject of claims.

Questions have arisen between the two governments, as to the right of New Granada to levy a tonnage duty upon the vessels of the United States in its ports of the isthmus, and to levy a passenger tax upon our citizens arriving in that country, whether with a design to remain there or to pass from ocean to ocean by the transit route; and also a tax upon the mail of the United States transported over the Panama railroad. The government of New Granada has been informed, that the United States would consider the collection of either of these taxes as an act in violation of the treaty between the two countries, and as such would be resisted by the United States. At the same time, we are prepared to discuss these questions in a spirit of amity and justice, and with a sincere desire to adjust them in a satisfactory manner. A negotiation for that purpose has already been commenced. No effort has recently been made to collect these taxes, nor is any anticipated under present circumstances.

With the empire of Brazil our relations are of the most friendly character. The productions of the two countries, and especially those of an agricultural nature, are such as to invite extensive mutual exchanges. A large quantity of American flour is consumed in Brazil, whilst more than treble the amount in value of Brazilian coffee is consumed in the United States. Whilst this is the case, a heavy duty has been levied, until very recently, upon the importation of American flour into Brazil. I am gratified, however, to be able to inform you that in September last this has been reduced from $1.32 to about forty-nine cents per barrel, and the duties on other articles of our production have been diminished in nearly the same proportion.

I regret to state that the government of Brazil still continues to levy an export duty of about 11 per cent. on coffee, notwithstanding this article is admitted free from duty in the United States. This is a heavy charge upon the consumers of coffee in our country, as we purchase half of the entire surplus crop of that article raised in Brazil. Our minister, under instructions, will reiterate his efforts to have this export duty removed; and it is hoped that the enlightened government of the Emperor will adopt this wise, just, and equal policy. In that event, there is good reason to believe that the commerce between the two countries will greatly increase, much to the advantage of both.

The claims of our citizens against the government of Brazil are not, in the aggregate, of very large amount; but some of these rest upon plain principles of justice, and their settlement ought not to be longer delayed. A renewed and earnest, and I trust a successful effort will be made by our minister to procure their final adjustment.

On the 2d of June last, Congress passed a joint resolution authorizing the President " to adopt such measures and use such force as, in his judgment, may be necessary and advisable " " for the purpose of adjusting the differences between the United States and the republic of Paraguay, in connection with the attack on the United States steamer Water Witch, and with other measures referred to " in his annual message. And on the 12th of July following, they made an appropriation to defray the expenses and compensation of a commissioner to that republic, should the President deem it proper to make such an appointment.

In compliance with these enactments, I have appointed a commissioner, who has proceeded to Paraguay, with full powers and instructions to settle these differences in an amicable and peaceful manner, if this be practicable. His experience and discretion justify the hope that he may prove successful in convincing the Paraguayan government that it is due both to honor and justice, that they should voluntarily and promptly make atonement for the wrongs which they have committed against the United States, and indemnify our injured citizens whom they have forcibly despoiled of their property.

Should our commissioner prove unsuccessful, after a sincere and earnest effort to accomplish the object of his mission, then no alternative will remain but the employment of force to obtain " just satisfaction " from Paraguay. In view of this contingency, the Secretary of the Navy, under my direction, has fitted out and despatched a naval force to rendezvous near Buenos Ayres, which, it is believed, will prove sufficient for the occasion. It is my earnest desire, however, that it may not be found necessary to resort to this last alternative.

When Congress met in December last, the business of the country had just been crushed by one of those periodical revulsions which are the inevitable consequence of our unsound and extravagant system of bank credits and inflated currency. With all the elements of national wealth in abundance, our manufactures were suspended, our useful public and private enterprises were arrested, and thousands of laborers were deprived of employment and reduced to want. Universal distress prevailed among the commercial, manufacturing, and mechanical classes. This revulsion was felt the more severely in the United States, because similar causes had produced the like deplorable effects throughout the commercial nations of Europe. All were experiencing sad reverses at the same moment. Our manufacturers everywhere suffered severely, not because of the recent reduction in the tariff of duties on imports, but because there was no demand at any price for their productions. The people were obliged to restrict themselves in their purchases, to articles of prime necessity. In the general prostration of business the iron manufacturers in different States probably suffered more than any other class, and much destitution was the inevitable consequence among the great number of workmen who had been employed in this useful branch of industry. There could be no supply where there was no demand. To present an example, there could be no demand for railroad iron, after our magnificent system of railroads, extending its benefits to every portion of the Union, had been brought to a dead pause. The same consequences have resulted from similar causes to many other branches of useful manufactures. It is self-evident that where there is no ability to purchase manufactured articles, these cannot be sold, and consequently must cease to be produced.

No government, and especially a government of such limited powers as that of the United States, could have prevented the late revulsion. The whole commercial world seemed for years to have been rushing to this catastrophe. The same ruinous consequences would have followed in the United States, whether the duties upon foreign imports had remained as they were under the tariff of 1846, or had been raised to a much higher standard. The tariff of 1857 had no agency in the result. The general causes existing throughout the world, could not have been controlled by the legislation of any particular country.

The periodical revulsions which have existed in our past history, must continue to return at intervals, so long as our present unbounded system of bank credits shall prevail. They will, however, probably be the less severe in future; because it is not to be expected, at least for many years to come, that the commercial nations of Europe, with whose interests our own are so materially involved, will expose themselves to similar calamities. But this subject was treated so much at large in my last annual message that I shall not now pursue it further. Still, I respectfully renew the recommendation in favor of the passage of a uniform bankrupt law, applicable to banking institutions. This is all the direct power over the subject, which, I believe, the federal government possesses. Such a law would mitigate, though it might not prevent the evil. The instinct of self-preservation might produce a wholesome restraint upon their banking business, if they knew in advance that a suspension of specie payments would inevitably produce their civil death.

But the effects of the revulsion are now slowly but surely passing away. The energy and enterprise of our citizens, with our unbounded resources, will, within the period of another year, restore a state of wholesome industry and trade. Capital has again accumulated in our large cities. The rate of interest is there very low. Confidence is gradually reviving, and so soon as it is discovered that this capital can be profitably employed in commercial and manufacturing enterprises, and in the construction of railroads and other works of public and private improvement, prosperity will again smile throughout the land. It is vain, however, to disguise the fact from ourselves, that a speculative inflation of our currency, without a corresponding inflation in other countries whose manufactures come into competition with our own, must ever produce disastrous results to our domestic manufactures. No tariff short of absolute prohibition can prevent these evil consequences.

In connection with this subject, it is proper to refer to our financial condition. The same causes which have produced pecuniary distress throughout the country, have so reduced the amount of imports from foreign countries, that the revenue has proved inadequate to meet the necessary expenses of the government. To supply the deficiency, Congress by the act of December 23, 1857, authorized the issue of $20,000,000 of Treasury notes; and this proving inadequate, they authorized, by the act of June 14, 1858, a loan of $20,000,000 "to be applied to the payment of appropriations made by law."

No statesman would advise that we should go on increasing the national debt to meet the ordinary expenses of the government. This would be a most ruinous policy. In case of war our credit must be our chief resource, at least for the first year, and this would be greatly impaired by having contracted a large debt in time of peace. It is our true policy to increase our revenue so as to equal our expenditures. It would be ruinous to continue to borrow. Besides it may be proper to observe that the incidental protection thus afforded by a revenue tariff would at the present moment, to some extent, increase the confidence of the manufacturing interests, and give a fresh impulse to our reviving business. To this surely no person will object.

In regard to the mode of assessing and collecting duties under a strictly revenue tariff, I have long entertained and often expressed the opinion that sound policy requires this should be done by specific duties, in cases to which these can be properly applied. They are well adapted to commodities which are usually sold by weight or by measure, and which from their nature are of equal or of nearly equal value. Such, for example, are the articles of iron of different classes, raw sugar, and foreign wines and spirits.

In my deliberate judgment, specific duties are the best; if not the only means of securing the revenue against false and fraudulent invoices, and such has been the practice adopted for this purpose by other commercial nations. Besides, specific duties would afford to the American manufacturer the incidental advantages to which he is fairly entitled under a revenue tariff. The present system is a sliding scale to his disadvantage. Under it, when prices are high and business prosperous, the duties rise in amount when he least requires their aid. On the contrary, when prices fall and he is struggling against adversity, the duties are diminished in the same proportion, greatly to his injury.

Neither would there be danger that a higher rate of duty than that intended by Congress, could be levied in the form of specific duties. It would be easy to ascertain the average value of any imported article for a series of years; and, instead of subjecting it to an *ad valorem* duty at a certain rate per centum, to substitute in its place an equivalent specific duty.

By such an arrangement the consumer would not be injured. It is true, he might have to pay a little more duty on a given article in one year; but if so, he would pay a little less in another, and in a series of years these would counterbalance each other, and amount to the same thing so far as his interest is concerned. This inconvenience would be trifling when contrasted with the additional security thus afforded against frauds upon the revenue, in which every consumer is directly interested.

I have thrown out these suggestions as the fruit of my own observation, to which Congress, in their better judgment, will give such weight as they may justly deserve.

The report of the Secretary of the Treasury will explain in detail the operations of that department of the government. The receipts into the treasury from all sources during the fiscal year ending June 30, 1858, including the treasury notes authorized by the act of December 23, 1857, were seventy million two hundred and seventy-three thousand eight hundred and sixty-nine dollars and fifty-nine cents, ($70,273,869.59,) which amount, with the balance of seventeen million seven hundred and ten thousand one hundred and fourteen dollars and twenty-seven cents ($17,710,-114.27) remaining in the treasury at the commencement of the year, made an aggregate for the service of the year of eighty-seven million nine hundred and eighty-three thousand nine hundred and eighty-three dollars and eighty-six cents, ($87,983,983.86.)

The public expenditures during the fiscal year ending June 30, 1858, amounted to eighty-one million five hundred and eighty-five thousand six hundred and sixty-seven dollars and seventy-six cents, ($81,585,667.76,) of which nine million six hundred and eighty-four thousand five hundred and thirty-seven dollars and ninety-nine cents ($9,684,537.99) were applied to the payment of the public debt, and the redemption of treasury notes with the interest thereon, leaving in the treasury on July 1, 1858, being the commencement of the present fiscal year, six million three hundred and ninety-eight thousand three hundred and sixteen dollars and ten cents, ($6,398,316.10.)

The receipts into the treasury, during the first quarter of the present fiscal year, commencing the 1st of July, 1858, including one-half of the loan of twenty million dollars, with the premium upon it, authorized by the act of June 14, 1858, were twenty-five million two hundred and thirty thousand eight hundred and seventy-nine dollars and forty-six cents, ($25,230,-879.46,) and the estimated receipts for the remaining three quarters to the 30th of June, 1859, from ordinary sources, are thirty-eight million five hundred thousand dollars, ($38,500,000,) making with the balance before stated an aggregate of seventy million one hundred and twenty-nine thousand one hundred and ninety-five dollars and fifty-six cents, ($70,129,195.56.)

The expenditures, during the first quarter of the present fiscal year, were twenty-one million seven hundred and eight thousand one hundred and ninety-eight dollars and fifty-one cents, ($21,708,198.51;) of which one million and ten thousand one hundred and forty-two dollars and thirty-seven cents ($1,010,142.37) were applied to the payment of the public debt and the redemption of treasury notes and the interest thereon. The estimated expenditures, during the remaining three quarters to June 30, 1859, are fifty-two million three hundred and fifty-seven thousand six hundred and ninety-eight dollars and forty-eight cents, ($52,357,698.48,) making an aggregate of seventy-four million sixty-five thousand eight hundred and ninety-six dollars and ninety-nine cents, ($74,065,896.99,) being an excess of expenditure, beyond the estimated receipts into the treasury from ordinary sources, during the fiscal year to the 30th of June, 1859, of three million nine hundred and thirty-six thousand seven hundred and one dollars and forty-three cents, ($3,936,701.43.) Extraordinary means are placed by law within the command of the Secretary of the Treasury, by the reissue of treasury notes redeemed, and by negotiating the balance of the loan authorized by the act of June 14, 1858, to the extent of eleven millions of dollars, which, if realized during the present fiscal year, will leave a balance in the treasury, on the first day of July, 1859, of seven million sixty-three thousand two hundred and ninety-eight dollars and fifty-seven cents, ($7,063,298.57.)

The estimated receipts during the next fiscal year ending June 30, 1860, are sixty-two millions of dollars, ($62,000,000) which, with the above estimated balance of seven million sixty-three thousand two hundred and ninety-eight dollars and fifty-seven cents, ($7,063,298.57,) make an aggregate for the service of the next fiscal year of sixty-nine million sixty-three thousand two hundred and ninety-eight dollars and fifty-seven cents, ($69,063,298.57.) The estimated expenditures during the next fiscal year ending June 30, 1860, are seventy-three million one hundred and thirty-nine thousand one hundred and forty-seven dollars and forty-six cents, ($73,139,147.46,) which leave a deficit of estimated means, compared with the estimated expenditures for that year, commencing on July 1, 1859, of four million seventy-five thousand eight hundred and forty-eight dollars and eighty-nine cents, ($4,075,848.89.)

In addition to this sum, the Postmaster General will require from the treasury, for the service of the Post Office Department, three million eight hundred and thirty-eight thousand seven hundred and twenty-eight dollars, ($3,838,728,) as explained in the report of the Secretary of the Treasury, which will increase the estimated deficit on June 30, 1860, to seven million nine hundred and fourteen thousand five hundred and seventy-six dollars and eighty-nine cents, ($7,914,576.89.) To provide for the payment of this estimated deficiency, which will be increased by such appropriations as may be made by Congress, not estimated for in the report of the Treasury Department, as well as to provide for the gradual redemption, from year to year, of the out-standing treasury notes, the Secretary of the Treasury recommends such a revision of the present tariff as will raise the required amount. After what I have already said, I need scarcely add that I concur in the opinion expressed in his report—that the public debt should not be increased by an additional loan—and would therefore strongly urge upon Congress the duty of making, at their present session, the necessary provision for meeting these liabilities.

The public debt on July 1, 1858, the commencement of the present fiscal year, was $25,155,977.66.

During the first quarter of the present year the sum of $10,000,000 has been negotiated of the loan authorized by the act of June 14, 1858—making the present outstanding public debt, exclusive of treasury notes, $35,155,977.66. There was, on the 1st of July, 1858, of treasury notes issued by authority of the act of December 23, 1857, unredeemed, the sum of $19,754,-800, making the amount of actual indebtedness at that date $54,910,777.66. To this will be added $10,000,000 during the present fiscal year—this being the remaining half of the loan of $20,000,000 not yet negotiated.

The rapid increase of the public debt, and the necessity which exists for a modification of the tariff, to meet even the ordinary expenses of the government, ought to admonish us all, in our respective spheres of duty, to the practice of rigid economy. The objects of expenditure should be limited in number, as far as this may be practicable, and the appropriations necessary to carry them into effect ought to be disbursed under the strictest accountability. Enlightened economy does not consist in the refusal to appropriate money for constitutional purposes essential to the defence, progress, and prosperity of the republic, but in taking care that none of this money shall be wasted by mismanagement in its application to the objects designated by law.

Comparisons between the annual expenditure at the present time and what it was ten or twenty years ago are altogether fallacious. The rapid increase of our country in extent and population renders a corresponding increase of expenditure, to some extent, unavoidable. This is constantly creating new objects of expenditure and augmenting the amount required for the old. The true questions, then, are, have these objects been unnecessarily multiplied? or has the amount expended upon any or all of them been larger than comports with due economy? In accordance with these principles, the heads of the different Executive departments of the government have been instructed to reduce their estimates for the next fiscal year to the lowest standard consistent with the efficiency of the service, and this duty they have performed in a spirit of just economy. The estimates of the Treasury, War, Navy, and Interior Departments, have each been in some degree reduced; and unless a sudden and unforeseen emergency should arise, it is not anticipated that a deficiency will exist in either within the present or the next fiscal year. The Post Office Department is placed in a peculiar position, different from the other departments, and to this I shall hereafter refer.

I invite Congress to institute a rigid scrutiny to ascertain whether the expenses in all the departments cannot be still further reduced; and I promise them all the aid in my power in pursuing the investigation.

I transmit herewith the reports made to me by the Secretaries of War, of the Navy, of the Interior, and by the Postmaster General. They each contain valuable information and important recommendations, to which I invite the attention of Congress.

In my last annual message, I took occasion to recommend the immediate construction of ten small steamers, of light draught, for the purpose of increasing the efficiency of the navy. Congress responded to the recommendation by authorizing the construction of eight of them. The progress which has been made in executing this authority is stated in the report of the Secretary of the Navy. I concur with him in the opinion that a greater number of this class of vessels is necessary, for the purpose of protecting in a more efficient manner the persons and property of American citizens on the high seas and in foreign countries, as well as in guarding more effectually our own coasts. I accordingly recommend the passage of an act for this purpose.

The suggestions contained in the report of the Secretary of the Interior, especially those in regard to the disposition of the public domain, the pension and bounty land system, the policy towards the Indians, and the amendment of our patent laws, are worthy of the serious consideration of Congress.

The Post Office Department occupies a position very different from that of the other departments. For many years it was the policy of the government to render this a self-sustaining department; and if this cannot now be accomplished, in the present condition of the country, we ought to make as near an approach to it as may be practicable.

The Postmaster General is placed in a most embarrassing position by the existing laws. He is obliged to carry these into effect. He has no other alternative. He finds, however, that this cannot be done without heavy demands upon the treasury over and above what is received for postage; and these have been progressively increasing from year to year until they amounted for the last fiscal year, ending on the 30th of June, 1858, to more than four millions and a half of dollars; whilst it is estimated that for the present fiscal year they will amount to $6,290,000. These sums are exclusive of the annual appropriation of $700,000 for "compensation for the mail service performed for the two houses of Congress and the other departments and officers of the government in the transmission of free matter."

The cause of these large deficits is mainly attributable to the increased expense of transporting the mails. In 1852 the sum paid for this service was but a fraction above four millions and a quarter. Since that year it has annually increased until in 1858 it has reached more than eight millions and a quarter; and for the service of 1859 it is estimated that it will amount to more than ten millions of dollars.

The receipts of the Post Office Department can be made to approach or to equal its expenditure only by means of the legislation of Congress. In applying any remedy care should be taken that the people shall not be deprived of the advantages which they are fairly entitled to enjoy from the Post Office Department. The principal remedies recommended to the consideration of Congress by the Postmaster General, are to restore the former rate of postage upon single letters to five cents; to substitute for the franking privilege the delivery, to those now entitled to enjoy it, of post office stamps for their correspondence, and to direct the department in making contracts for the transportation of the mail, to confine itself to the payment of the sum necessary for this single purpose, without requiring it to be transported in post coaches or carriages of any particular description. Under the present system the expense to the Government is greatly increased, by requiring that the mail shall be carried in such vehicles as will accommodate passengers. This will be done, without pay from the department, over all roads where the travel will remunerate the contractors.

These recommendations deserve the grave consideration of Congress.

I would again call your attention to the construction of a Pacific railroad. Time and reflection have but served to confirm me in the truth and justice of the observations which I made on this subject in my last annual message, to which I beg leave respectfully to refer.

It is freely admitted that it would be inexpedient for this government to exercise the power of constructing the Pacific railroad by its own immediate agents. Such a policy would increase the patronage of the Executive to a dangerous extent, and introduce a system of jobbing and corruption which no vigilance on the part of federal officials could either prevent or detect. This can only be done by the keen eye and active and careful supervision of individual and private interest. The construction of this road ought, therefore, to be committed to companies incorporated by the States, or other agencies whose pecuniary interests would be directly involved. Congress might then assist them in the work by grants of land or of money, or both, under such conditions and restrictions as would secure the transportation of troops and munitions of war free from any charge, and that of the United States mail at a fair and reasonable price.

The progress of events since the commencement of your last session has shown how soon difficulties disappear before a firm and determined resolution. At that time such a road was deemed by wise and patriotic men to be a visionary project. The great distance to be overcome, and the intervening mountains and deserts in the way, were obstacles which, in the opinion of many, could not be surmounted. Now, after the lapse of but a single year, these obstacles, it has been discovered, are far less formidable than they were supposed to be; and mail stages with passengers now pass and repass regularly twice in each week, by a common wagon road, between San Francisco and St. Louis and Memphis, in less than twenty-five days. The service has been as regularly performed as it was in former years, between New York and this city.

Whilst disclaiming all authority to appropriate money for the construction of this road, except that derived from the war-making power of the Constitution, there are important collateral considerations urging us to undertake the work as speedily as possible.

The first and most momentous of these is that such a road would be a powerful bond of union between the States east and west of the Rocky mountains. This is so self-evident as to require no illustration.

But again, in a commercial point of view, I consider this the great question of the day. With the eastern front of our republic stretching along the Atlantic, and its western front along the Pacific, if all the parts should be united by a safe, easy, and rapid intercommunication, we must necessarily command a very large proportion of the trade both of Europe and Asia. Our recent treaties with China and Japan will open these rich and populous empires to our commerce; and the history of the world proves that the nation which has gained possession of the trade with Eastern Asia, has always become wealthy and powerful. The peculiar geographical position of California and our Pacific possessions, invites American capital and enterprise into this fruitful field. To reap the rich harvest, however, it is an indispensable prerequisite, that we shall first have a railroad to convey and circulate its products throughout every portion of the Union. Besides, such a railroad through our temperate latitude, which would not be impeded by the frosts and snows of winter, nor by the tropical heats of summer, would attract to itself much of the travel and the trade of all nations passing between Europe and Asia.

On the 21st of August last, Lieutenant J. N. Maffit, of the United States brig Dolphin, captured the slaver "Echo," (formerly the Putnam, of New Orleans,) near Kay Verde, on the coast of Cuba, with more than three hundred African negroes on board. The prize, under the command of Lieutenant Bradford of the United States navy, arrived at Charleston on the 27th August; when the negroes, three hundred and six in number, were delivered into the custody of the United States marshal for the district of South Carolina. They were first placed in Castle Pinckney, and afterwards in Fort Sumter, for safe-keeping, and were detained there until the 19th September, when the survivors, two hundred and seventy-one in number, were delivered on board the United States steamer Niagara, to be transported to the coast of Africa, under the charge of the agent of the United States, pursuant to the provisions of the act of the 3d March, 1819, " in addition to the acts prohibiting the slave trade."   Under the 2d section of this act, the President is " authorized to make such regulations and arrangements as he may deem expedient, for the safe-keeping, support, and removal beyond the limits of the United States, of all such negroes, mulattoes, or persons of color," captured by vessels of the United States, as may be delivered to the marshal of the district into which they are brought; " and to appoint a proper person or persons residing upon the coast of Africa, as agent or agents for receiving the negroes, mulattoes, or persons of color, delivered from on board vessels seized in the prosecution of the slave trade by commanders of the United States armed vessels."

A doubt immediately arose as to the true construction of this act. It is quite clear from its terms that the President was authorized to provide " for the safe-keeping, support, and removal " of these negroes up till the time of their delivery to the agent on the coast of Africa; but no express provision was made for their protection and support after they had reached the place of their destination. Still, an agent was to be appointed to receive them in Africa, and it could not have been supposed that Congress intended he should desert them at the moment they were received, and turn them loose on that inhospitable coast to perish for want of food or to become again the victims of the slave trade. Had this been the intention of Congress, the employment of an agent to receive them, who is required to reside on the coast, was unnecessary, and they might have been landed by our vessels anywhere in Africa and left exposed to the sufferings and the fate which would certainly await them.

Mr. Monroe, in his special message of December 17, 1819,

at the first session after the act was passed, announced to Congress what, in his opinion, was its true construction. He believed it to be his duty under it to follow these unfortunates into Africa, and make provision for them there until they should be able to provide for themselves. In communicating this interpretation of the act to Congress he stated that some doubt had been entertained as to its true intent and meaning, and he submitted the question to them, so that they might, " should it be deemed advisable, amend the same before further proceedings are had under it." Nothing was done by Congress to explain the act, and Mr. Monroe proceeded to carry it into execution according to his own interpretation. This, then, became the practical construction. When the Africans from on board the Echo were delivered to the marshal at Charleston it became my duty to consider what disposition ought to be made of them under the law. For many reasons it was expedient to remove them from that locality as speedily as possible. Although the conduct of the authorities and citizens of Charleston in giving countenance to the execution of the law was just what might have been expected from their high character, yet a prolonged continuance of three hundred Africans in the immediate vicinity of that city could not have failed to become a source of inconvenience and anxiety to its inhabitants. Where to send them, was the question. There was no portion of the coast of Africa, to which they could be removed with any regard to humanity, except to Liberia. Under these circumstances, an agreement was entered into with the Colonization Society on the 7th of September last, a copy of which is herewith transmitted, under which the Society engaged, for the consideration of forty-five thousand dollars, to receive these Africans in Liberia from the agent of the United States, and furnish them during the period of one year thereafter, with comfortable shelter, clothing, provisions, and medical attendance, causing the children to receive schooling; and all, whether children or adults, to be instructed in the arts of civilized life suitable to their condition. This aggregate of forty-five thousand dollars was based upon an allowance of one hundred and fifty dollars for each individual, and as there has been considerable mortality among them, and may be more before they reach Africa, the society have agreed, in an equitable spirit, to make such a deduction from the amount, as under the circumstances may appear just and reasonable. This cannot be fixed until we shall ascertain the actual number which may become a charge to the society.

It was also distinctly agreed, that under no circumstances shall this government be called upon for any additional expenses.

The agents of the society manifested a laudable desire to conform to the wishes of the government, throughout the transaction. They assured me that, after a careful calculation, they would be required to expend the sum of one hundred and fifty dollars on each individual in complying with the agreement, and they would have nothing left to remunerate them for their care, trouble, and responsibility. At all events, I could make no better arrangement, and there was no other alternative. During the period when the government itself, through its own agents, undertook the task of providing for captured negroes in Africa, the cost per head was very much greater.

There having been no outstanding appropriation applicable to this purpose, I could not advance any money on the agreement. I therefore recommend that an appropriation may be made of the amount necessary to carry it into effect.

Other captures of a similar character may, and probably will be made by our naval forces; and I earnestly recommend that Congress may amend the second section of the act of March 3, 1819, so as to free its construction from the ambiguity which has so long existed, and render the duty of the President plain in executing its provisions.

I recommend to your favorable regard the local interests of the District of Columbia. As the residence of Congress and the Executive departments of the government, we cannot fail to feel a deep concern in its welfare. This is heightened by the high character and the peaceful and orderly conduct of its resident inhabitants.

I cannot conclude without performing the agreeable duty of expressing my gratification that Congress so kindly responded to the recommendation of my last annual message, by affording me sufficient time before the close of their late session for the examination of all the bills presented to me for approval. This change in the practice of Congress has proved to be a wholesome reform. It exerted a beneficial influence on the transaction of legislative business, and elicited the general approbation of the country. It enabled Congress to adjourn with that dignity and deliberation so becoming to the representatives of this great republic, without having crowded into general appropriation bills provisions foreign to their nature, and doubtful constitutionality and expediency. Let me warmly and strongly commend this precedent, established by themselves, as a guide to their proceedings during the present session.

JAMES BUCHANAN.

WASHINGTON CITY, December 6, 1858.

MESSAGE

ON A TREATY WITH JAPAN.[1]

WASHINGTON, December 7, 1858.

TO THE SENATE OF THE UNITED STATES:

I transmit to the Senate, for its consideration with a view to ratification, a treaty of amity and commerce between the United States and Japan, concluded at the city of Yeddo on the 29th of July last.

JAMES BUCHANAN.

MESSAGE

ON A TREATY WITH CHINA.[1]

WASHINGTON, December 7, 1858.

TO THE SENATE OF THE UNITED STATES:

I transmit to the Senate, for its consideration with a view to ratification, a treaty between the United States and China, signed at Tientsin, by the plenipotentiaries of the parties, on the 18th day of June last.

JAMES BUCHANAN.

---

[1] Senate Executive Journal, XI. 1.

LETTER

ON GOVERNMENT PENSIONS.[1]

EXECUTIVE MANSION, December 10, 1858.

SIR: In compliance with the resolution of the Senate of June 12, 1858, I herewith communicate a report from the Secretary of the Interior, showing the "amount of money paid for pensions in each of the States and Territories since the commencement of the present government."

JAMES BUCHANAN.

THE PRESIDENT OF THE SENATE.

MESSAGE

ON A TREATY WITH SIAM.[2]

[December 10, 1858.]

TO THE SENATE AND HOUSE OF REPRESENTATIVES:

I transmit to Congress a copy of the treaty between the United States and the kingdom of Siam, concluded on the 29th May, 1856, and proclaimed on the 16th August last, and call the attention of that body to the necessity of an act for carrying into effect the provisions of article II. of the said treaty, conferring certain judicial powers upon the consul of the United States who may be appointed to reside at Bangkok. I would also suggest that the extension to the kingdom of Siam of the provisions of the act approved August 11, 1848, entitled "An act to carry into effect certain provisions in the treaties between the United States and China and the Ottoman Porte, giving certain judicial powers to ministers and consuls of the United States in those countries," might obviate the necessity of any other legislation upon the subject.

JAMES BUCHANAN.

WASHINGTON, December 10, 1858.

---

[1] S. Ex. Doc. 4, 35 Cong. 2 Sess. 1.
[2] H. Ex. Doc. 8, 35 Cong. 2 Sess. 1.

MESSAGE

ON THE VISITATION OF AMERICAN VESSELS.[1]

EXECUTIVE OFFICE,
WASHINGTON, December 15, 1858.

SIR: In compliance with a resolution of the House of Representatives of the 13th instant, requesting the President of the United States (if not inconsistent with the public interest) " to communicate all information in his possession, or which may shortly come into his possession, respecting the reported recent acts of visitation by officers of the British navy of American vessels in the waters of the Gulf of Mexico," I transmit the accompanying reports from the Secretaries of State and of the Navy. The report from the Secretary of State is not, in strictness, embraced by the terms of the resolution, but I deem it advisable to communicate to the House the information therein contained.

JAMES BUCHANAN.

HON. JAMES L. ORR,
Speaker of the House of Representatives.

MESSAGE

ON CHINESE AFFAIRS.[2]

TO THE SENATE OF THE UNITED STATES:

I transmit a report from the Secretary of State with accompanying documents in answer to the resolution of the Senate of the 7th of January last, calling for all the official despatches and correspondence of the Hon. Robert M. McLane, and of the Hon. Peter Parker, late commissioners of the United States in China, with the Department of State.

JAMES BUCHANAN.

WASHINGTON, December 20, 1858.

[1] H. Ex. Doc. 11, 35 Cong. 2 Sess.
[2] S. Ex. Doc. 22, 35 Cong. 2 Sess. 1.

MESSAGE

ON NAVAL OFFICERS.[1]

WASHINGTON, December 20, 1858.

To THE SENATE OF THE UNITED STATES:

The Senate will learn from the thirty-five naval nominations herewith submitted the result of my investigations under the resolutions of Congress of March 10 and May 11, 1858. In compliance with these resolutions, I have carefully examined the records of the courts of inquiry in fifty-eight cases, and have arrived at the conclusion that twenty-three of the officers ought to remain in the positions where they have been fixed by the courts of inquiry.

The records are very voluminous and the labor of examination, in which I have been materially assisted by the Secretary of the Navy, the Attorney-General, and the Commissioner of Patents, has consumed much time.

Under the act of January 17, 1857, the courts of inquiry were directed to investigate " the physical, mental, professional, and moral fitness " of each officer who applied to them for relief. These investigations it was my duty to review. They have been very extensive and searching, as the Senate will perceive from an examination of the records, embracing in many instances almost the entire professional life of the individual from his first entrance into the service.

In the performance of my duty I have found the greatest difficulty in deciding what should be considered as " moral fitness " for the Navy. Physical, mental, and professional fitness may be decided with a considerable degree of accuracy by a naval court of inquiry, but the question of moral fitness is of a very different character. There has been but one perfect standard of morality on earth, and how far a departure from His precepts and example must proceed in order to disqualify an officer for the naval service is a question on which a great difference of honest opinions must always exist. On this question I have differed in several instances from the courts of inquiry.

There is one nomination which I regret that I have not the

---

[1] Senate Executive Journal, XI. 24.

power to present to the Senate, and this is in the case of Commodore Stewart. His name stood on the Register at the head of the list of captains in the Navy until it was removed from this well-earned position by the retiring board and placed on the list of retired officers. The deeply wounded feelings of this veteran officer, who had contributed so much to the efficiency and glory of the Navy from its infancy, prevented him from applying for restoration to his rank and submitting to a court of inquiry, composed of his junior officers, the question of his " physical, mental, professional, and moral fitness " for the naval service. I would ere this have recommended to Congress the passage of a joint resolution to restore him to his former rank, had I not believed this would more appropriately emanate from the legislative branch of Government.

I transmit herewith to the Senate the original records in the fifty-eight cases to which I have referred. After they shall have been examined by the Senate, I would respectfully request that they might be returned to the Navy Department.

JAMES BUCHANAN.

MESSAGE

ON A TREATY WITH BELGIUM.[1]

WASHINGTON, December 22, 1858.

To THE SENATE OF THE UNITED STATES:

I transmit to the Senate for its consideration, with a view to ratification, a convention between the United States and Belgium for regulating the commerce and navigation between the two countries, signed in this city on the 17th of July last.

JAMES BUCHANAN.

---

[1] Senate Executive Journal, XI. 28.

MESSAGE

ON A TREATY WITH NEW GRANADA.[1]

WASHINGTON, December 23, 1858.

To THE SENATE OF THE UNITED STATES:

I transmit for the consideration of the Senate a convention with New Granada, signed on the 10th day of September, 1857, and a translation of the decree of the President of that Republic ratifying and confirming the same with certain modifications and explanations.

JAMES BUCHANAN.

MESSAGE

ON CONSULAR POWERS IN CHINA.[2]

To THE SENATE AND HOUSE OF REPRESENTATIVES:

I transmit a copy of a letter of the 8th of April last, from the minister of the United States in China, and of the decree and regulation which accompanied it, for such revision thercof as Congress may deem expedient, pursuant to the sixth section of the act approved August 11, 1848.[3]

JAMES BUCHANAN.

WASHINGTON, December 27, 1858.

---

[1] Senate Executive Journal, XI. 33.

[2] S. Ex. Doc. 11, 35 Cong. 2 Sess. 1; H. Ex. Doc. 21, 35 Cong. 2 Sess.

[3] This act is entitled: "An act to carry into effect certain provisions in the treaties between the United States and China and the Ottoman Porte, giving certain legislative and judicial powers to ministers and consuls of the United States in those countries."

1859.

MESSAGE

ON THE CLEARANCE OF VESSELS AT MOBILE.[1]

To the House of Representatives:

I herewith transmit to the House of Representatives the report of the Secretary of the Treasury, with the accompanying documents, containing the information called for by the resolution of the House of the 23d of December, 1858, concerning the correspondence in reference to the clearance of vessels at the port of Mobile.

JAMES BUCHANAN.

WASHINGTON, January 4, 1859.

TO MR. HART.[2]

WASHINGTON CITY, Jan. 4, 1859.

MR. BENJAMIN W. HART,
    48 Pine St., New York.

SIR:

I have had the honor of receiving your favor of the 30th ultimo, with the resolutions recently adopted by the " Representatives of the United Congregations of the Israelites of the City of New York," on the subject of the abduction and detention of Edgar Mortara from his parents, under the authority of the Papal government.

The letters addressed to me on the 20th November and the 10th ultimo, to which you recall my attention, were referred in regular course to the State Department and have been substantially answered in the letters addressed by the Secretary of

---

[1] H. Ex. Doc. 25, 35 Cong. 2 Sess. 1. A company had been incorporated in Alabama, and had purchased a steamer, ostensibly for the purpose of engaging in trade between Mobile and ports in Texas. The collector of customs at Mobile suspected that this transaction was connected with a plan of Walker for a filibustering expedition to Nicaragua, and that the steamer, after one or two trips, would be sent with such an expedition to some Central American port.

[2] MSS. Department of State, 49 Domestic Letters, 474.

State on the 21st of November and on the 8th of December, last, to Mr. A. Hart, President of the Congregation of " Mickve Israel," Philadelphia.   These letters have been extensively published throughout the country, and it is evident from their face that the opinions therein expressed had received my approbation.

I have long been convinced that it is neither the right nor the duty of this Government to exercise a moral censorship over the conduct of other independent governments and to rebuke them for acts which we may deem arbitrary and unjust towards their own citizens or subjects.   Such a practice would tend to embroil us with all nations.   We ourselves would not permit any foreign power thus to interfere with our domestic concerns and enter protests against the legislation or the action of our Government towards our own citizens.   If such an attempt were made, we should promptly advise such a government in return to confine themselves to their own affairs and not intermeddle with our concerns.

It is perhaps fortunate that the assertion of the principle of non-intervention on the part of the United States between foreign sovereigns and their own subjects has arisen in a case so well calculated to enlist our sympathies as that of the Mortara family. For this reason the precedent will be so much the stronger and be entitled to the more binding force.

It is enough for us to defend the rights of our own citizens under treaties and the law of nations whenever and wherever these may be assailed by the Government of any foreign country.   Had Monola Mortara been a citizen of the United States, the case would have been very different.   The Israelitish citizens of the United States have had occasion to know that I have not been regardless of their just rights in foreign countries; and they may rest assured that they shall receive the same protection, when domiciled abroad, during my administration, which is extended to all other citizens of our common country.   They would ask no more and shall receive nothing less.

Yours very respectfully,

JAMES BUCHANAN.[1]

---

[1] In Moore's International Law Digest, §924, there is the following note on this case: " This singular case of the ' Mortara boy' attracted at the time great attention and produced much excitement in the United States as well as in Europe.   Edgar Mortara was born at Bologna, then in the Papal dominions, in 1851, of Jewish parents.   When less than a year old, being ill and apparently in danger of death, he was baptised by a Christian servant.

MESSAGE
ON A TREATY WITH THE SIOUX INDIANS.[1]

WASHINGTON, January 5, 1859.

To THE SENATE OF THE UNITED STATES:

I transmit herewith, for the constitutional action of the Senate, the articles of agreement and convention made and concluded on the 19th day of June last with the Mendawakanton and Wapakoota bands of the Dakota or Sioux Indians.

JAMES BUCHANAN.

MESSAGE
ON A TREATY WITH THE SIOUX INDIANS.[1]

WASHINGTON, January 5, 1859.

To THE SENATE OF THE UNITED STATES:

I transmit herewith, for the constitutional action of the Senate, the articles of agreement and convention made and concluded on the 19th day of June last, 1858, with the Sisseton and Wahpaton bands of the Dakota or Sioux Indians, with accompanying papers from the Department of the Interior.

JAMES BUCHANAN.

On June 23, 1858, at ten o'clock in the evening, he was seized by a functionary of the Holy See, accompanied by a squad of Papal police, and taken to Rome, where he was placed with an order of Monks to be brought up in the Catholic faith. This was done by order of Pope Pius IX. It was subsequently reported that Edgar's parents, after his baptism, refused to receive him, and left him to be reared by the servant who had baptised him. It was also affirmed that his mother eventually died in the Christian faith. In a letter written at Rome, April 18, 1900, more than forty years after his abduction, Edgar Mortara himself, subscribing his name as an apostolic missionary of the Roman Catholic Church, denied both these reports. He declared that after his baptism he remained quietly with his parents till he was taken from them by order of the Pope, and that his mother never gave any indication of conversion to the Catholic faith. It appears that his parents, after he was taken from them, continued to petition for his return, but without success. He himself became and remained a devout ecclesiastic, expressing, in the letter above mentioned, the wish that his relations might become partakers of the Catholic faith. (Journal de Genève, April 26, 1900.)"

[1] Senate Executive Journal, XI. 35.

MESSAGE

ON A TREATY WITH CHILE.[1]

WASHINGTON, January 5, 1859.

To THE SENATE OF THE UNITED STATES:

I transmit herewith to the Senate, for its consideration with a view to ratification, a convention between the United States and the Republic of Chile, signed by the plenipotentiaries of the parties on the 10th day of November last, providing for the reference to an arbiter of the questions which have long been in controversy between the two Governments, relative to a sum of money, the proceeds of the cargo of the brig Macedonia, alleged to have belonged to citizens of the United States, which was seized in the Valley of Sitana, in Peru, by orders of an officer in the service of the Republic of Chile.

JAMES BUCHANAN.

MESSAGE

ON INSTRUCTIONS TO NAVAL COMMANDERS.[2]

To THE HOUSE OF REPRESENTATIVES:

I herewith transmit to the House of Representatives a report from the Secretary of the Navy, with accompanying papers, in compliance with a resolution adopted December 23, 1858, requesting the President of the United States " to communicate to the House, if not deemed by him incompatible with the public interest, the instructions which have been given to our naval commanders in the Gulf of Mexico."

JAMES BUCHANAN.

WASHINGTON CITY, January 6, 1859.

---

[1] Senate Executive Journal, XI. 35.
[2] H. Ex. Doc. 24, 35 Cong. 2 Sess. 1.

MESSAGE

ON THE CASE OF CARMICK AND RAMSEY.[1]

TO THE HOUSE OF REPRESENTATIVES:

I herewith transmit reports from the Secretary of the Treasury and Postmaster General, with the accompanying papers, in compliance with the resolution of the House adopted December 23, 1858, requesting the President of the United States to report "what action, if any, has been taken under the sixth section of the Post Office appropriation act, approved August 18, 1856, for the adjustment of the damages due Carmick & Ramsey; and if the said section of said law yet remains unexecuted, that the President report the reasons therefor."

JAMES BUCHANAN.

WASHINGTON, January 7, 1859.

VETO MESSAGE, JANUARY 7, 1859.[2]

TO THE HOUSE OF REPRESENTATIVES:

On the last day of the last session of Congress, as appears by the Journal of the House of Representatives, "a joint resolution in regard to the carrying the United States mails from Saint Joseph, Missouri, to Placerville, California," was presented to me for my approval. This resolution authorized and directed the Postmaster General "to order an increase of speed upon said route, requiring the mails to be carried through in thirty days (instead of thirty-eight days, according to the existing contract) *Provided* the same can be done upon a *pro rata* increase of compensation to the contractors."

I did not approve this joint resolution: First, because it

---

[1] H. Ex. Doc. 30, 35 Cong. 2 Sess. 1.

[2] H. Ex. Doc. 28, 35 Cong. 2 Sess. 1–2. The Senate ordered the message to be laid on the table. (Veto Messages: S. Misc. Doc. 53, 49 Cong. 2 Sess. 258.)

was presented to me at so late a period that I had not the time necessary, on the day of the adjournment of the last session, for an investigation of the subject. Besides, no injury could result to the public, as the Postmaster General already possessed the discretionary power under existing laws to increase the speed upon this as well as all other mail routes.

Second, because the Postmaster-General, at the moment in the Capitol, informed me that the contractors themselves had offered to increase the speed on this route to thirty instead of thirty-eight days, at a less cost than that authorized by the joint resolution. Upon subsequent examination it has been ascertained at the Post Office Department that their bid, which is still pending, proposes to perform this service for a sum less by $49,000 than that authorized by the resolution.

JAMES BUCHANAN.

January 7, 1859.

MESSAGE

ON THE LANDING OF AFRICANS ON THE GEORGIA COAST.[1]

[January 11, 1859.]

To THE SENATE OF THE UNITED STATES:

In reply to the resolution of the Senate passed on the 16th ultimo, requesting me " to communicate, if, in my opinion, not incompatible with the public interest, any information in my possession in relation to the landing of the barque Wanderer on the coast of Georgia with a cargo of slaves," I herewith communicate the report made to me by the Attorney General, to whom the resolution was referred. From that report it will appear that the offence referred to in the resolution has been committed, and that effective measures have been taken to see the laws faithfully executed. I concur with the Attorney General in the opinion that it would be incompatible with the public interest at this time to communicate the correspondence with the officers of the government at Savannah, or the instructions

---

[1] S. Ex. Doc. 8, 35 Cong. 2 Sess. 11.

which they have received. In the meantime every practicable effort has been made and will be continued to discover all the guilty parties and to bring them to justice.

JAMES BUCHANAN.

WASHINGTON, January 11, 1859.

MESSAGE

ON THE CASE OF CARMICK AND RAMSEY.[1]

TO THE HOUSE OF REPRESENTATIVES:

I herewith transmit a report from the Comptroller, with a copy of the letter of Messrs. Johnson and Williams in relation to the decision upon the Carmick & Ramsey claim. This should have accompanied the papers which have already been transmitted to the House, but was omitted by mistake.

JAMES BUCHANAN.

WASHINGTON CITY, January 13, 1859.

MESSAGE ON CUBA.[2]

TO THE HOUSE OF REPRESENTATIVES:

I transmit a report from the Secretary of State, in answer to the resolution of the House of Representatives of the 10th instant, requesting a communication of the correspondence between this government and France and England respecting the acquisition of Cuba by the United States.

JAMES BUCHANAN.

WASHINGTON, January 15, 1859.

---

[1] H. Ex. Doc. 43, 35 Cong. 2 Sess. 1.

[2] H. Ex. Doc. 57, 35 Cong. 2 Sess. The report of the Secretary of State says: "The only correspondence between this government and those of France and England relative to the Island of Cuba, is that which occurred between Mr. Everett, Secretary of State, and the Count de Sartiges and Mr. Crampton, the French and British ministers, which was communicated to the Senate with the President's message of the 4th of January, 1853."

MESSAGE

ON CLAIMS AGAINST FOREIGN GOVERNMENTS.[1]

To the Senate of the United States:

In compliance with the resolution of the Senate of the 14th June last, requesting a list of claims of citizens of the United States on foreign governments, I transmit a report from the Secretary of State, with the documents which accompanied it.

JAMES BUCHANAN.

WASHINGTON, January 19, 1859.

MESSAGE ON CUBA.[2]

[January 21, 1859.]

To the Senate of the United States:

I transmit herewith a report from the Secretary of State, in answer to the resolution of the Senate of the 18th instant, requesting the President, if not incompatible with the public interest, " to communicate to the Senate any and all correspondence between the government of the United States and the government of her Catholic Majesty relating to any proposition for the purchase of the island of Cuba, which correspondence has not been furnished to either House of Congress." From this it appears that no such correspondence has taken place which has not already been communicated to Congress. In my late annual message I stated, in reference to the purchase of Cuba, that " the publicity which has been given to our former negotiation on this subject, and the large appropriation which may be required to effect the purpose, render it expedient, before making another attempt to renew the negotiation, that I should lay the whole subject before Congress." I still entertain the same opinion; deeming it highly

---

[1] S. Ex. Doc. 18, 35 Cong. 2 Sess. 1.
[2] S. Ex. Doc. 16, 35 Cong. 2 Sess. 1.

important if not indispensable to the success of any negotiation which I might institute for the purpose, that the measure should receive the previous sanction of Congress.

JAMES BUCHANAN.

WASHINGTON CITY, January 21, 1859.

MESSAGE

ON STATISTICS OF MANUFACTURES.[1]

TO THE SENATE OF THE UNITED STATES:

I herewith transmit to the Senate a Digest of the Statistics of Manufactures according to the returns of the Seventh Census, prepared under the direction of the Secretary of the Interior, in accordance with the provision in the first section of an act of Congress approved June 12, 1858, entitled "An act making appropriations for sundry civil expenses of the government for the year ending the thirtieth of June, eighteen hundred and fifty-nine."

JAMES BUCHANAN.

WASHINGTON, January 21, 1859.

MESSAGE

ON STATISTICS OF MANUFACTURES.[2]

TO THE HOUSE OF REPRESENTATIVES:

I have this day transmitted to the Senate a digest of the statistics of manufactures, according to the returns of the seventh census, prepared under the direction of the Secretary of the Interior, in accordance with a provision contained in the first section of an act of Congress approved June 12, 1858, entitled

---

[1] S. Ex. Doc. 39, 35 Cong. 2 Sess. 1.
[2] H. Ex. Doc. 61, 35 Cong. 2 Sess. 1.

" An act making appropriations for sundry civil expenses of the government for the year ending the thirtieth of June, eighteen hundred and fifty-nine." The magnitude of the work has prevented the preparation of another copy.

JAMES BUCHANAN.

WASHINGTON, January 21, 1859.

MESSAGE

ON CONSULAR FEES.[1]

TO THE SENATE AND HOUSE OF REPRESENTATIVES:

I transmit to Congress a report, dated the 25th instant, with the accompanying papers, received from the Secretary of State, in compliance with the requirement of the 18th section of the act entitled " An act to regulate the diplomatic and consular systems of the United States," approved August 18, 1856.

JAMES BUCHANAN.

WASHINGTON, January 25, 1859.

MESSAGE

ON CLAIMS AGAINST FOREIGN GOVERNMENTS.[2]

TO THE SENATE OF THE UNITED STATES:

I transmit another report from the Secretary of State, in answer to the resolution of the Senate of the 14th of June last, requesting information on the subject of claims of citizens of the United States against foreign governments.

JAMES BUCHANAN.

WASHINGTON, January 26, 1859.

---

[1] S. Ex. Doc. 20, 35 Cong. 2 Sess. 1; H. Ex. Doc. 67, 35 Cong. 2 Sess. 1.
[2] S. Ex. Doc. 18, 35 Cong. 2 Sess. 123.

MESSAGE

ON THE CLAIM OF GOVERNOR DOUGLAS.[1]

To the Senate and House of Representatives:

I transmit a report from the Secretary of War, with the accompanying documents, recommending the repayment to Governor Douglas, of Vancouver's Island, of the sum of $7,000 advanced by him to Governor Stevens, of Washington Territory, which was applied to the purchase of ammunition and subsistence stores for the forces of the United States in time of need and at a critical period of the late Indian war in that Territory. As this advance was made by Governor Douglas out of his own private means, and from friendly motives towards the United States, I recommend that an appropriation may be made for its immediate payment, with interest.

James Buchanan.

Washington, January 29, 1859.

MESSAGE

ON VANCOUVER'S ISLAND.[2]

To the Senate of the United States:

In compliance with the resolution of the Senate of the 25th instant, I transmit a copy of the report of the special agent of the United States recently sent to Vancouver's Island and British Columbia.

James Buchanan.

Washington, January 29, 1859.

---

[1] H. Ex. Doc. 72, 35 Cong. 2 Sess. 1.
[2] S. Ex. Doc. 29, 35 Cong. 2 Sess. 1.

MESSAGE

ON THE GUANO TRADE WITH PERU.[1]

To the Senate of the United States:

In reply to the resolution of the Senate of the 4th ultimo,[2] I transmit a report from the Secretary of State, together with the papers therein referred to.

JAMES BUCHANAN.

Washington, February 5, 1859.

MESSAGE

ON WILKES' EXPLORING EXPEDITION.[3]

To the House of Representatives:

I transmit herewith a report from the Secretary of the Navy, in compliance with the resolution of the House of Representatives adopted on the 24th of.January, requesting the President of the United States to communicate to the House " the aggregate expenditure of whatsoever nature, including all salaries, whether special, or by virtue of official position in the army or navy, or otherwise, on account of the preparation and publication of the work known as Wilkes' Exploring Expedition; also, what number of copies of the said work have been ordered; how they

---

[1] S. Ex. Doc. 25, 35 Cong. 2 Sess.

[2] The resolution called for correspondence with the government of Peru, or its agents, on the subject of trade in guano, and all information which might tend to explain the manner in which the trade was regulated, and whether such regulations had not the effect unduly to enhance the price of guano to the consumer, or to deprive vessels navigating under the flag of the United States of the fair and equal competition with those of other nations guaranteed by the treaty with Peru of July 19, 1852, and if so, whether any and what legislation was expedient to counteract the effect of such regulations.

[3] H. Ex. Doc. 84, 35 Cong. 2 Sess. 1.

have been distributed; what number of persons are now employed thereon; how long they have been employed, respectively; and the amount of the appropriation now remaining undrawn."

JAMES BUCHANAN.

WASHINGTON CITY, February 8, 1859.

MESSAGE

ON CONSULAR OFFICERS' ENGAGING IN BUSINESS.[1]

TO THE HOUSE OF REPRESENTATIVES:

I transmit herewith a report from the Secretary of State, with accompanying papers, in answer to the resolution of the House of Representatives of the 14th of June last requesting the communication of all information and correspondence which may have been received in regard to any consular officer engaged in business in violation of law.

JAMES BUCHANAN.

WASHINGTON, February 12, 1859.

MESSAGE

ON THE IMPORTATION OF AFRICANS.[2]

TO THE HOUSE OF REPRESENTATIVES:

I transmit herewith a report from the Attorney General, in reply to the resolution of the House of Representatives adopted on the 22d ultimo, requesting the President of the United States to ." report" " what information has been received by him, if

---

[1] H. Ex. Doc. 90, 35 Cong. 2 Sess. 1.
[2] H. Ex. Doc. 89, 35 Cong. 2 Sess. 1.

any, in regard to the recent importation of Africans into the State of Georgia, or any other State of this Union; and what steps have been taken to bring to trial and punishment the persons engaged in this inhuman violation of the laws of the United States, and to prevent similar violations hereafter." [1]

JAMES BUCHANAN.

WASHINGTON CITY, February 15, 1859.

MESSAGE

ON THE PROTECTION OF ISTHMIAN ROUTES. [2]

[February 18, 1859.]

TO THE SENATE AND HOUSE OF REPRESENTATIVES:

The brief period which remains of your present session, and the great urgency and importance of legislative action, before its termination, for the protection of American citizens and their

------

[1] The report of the Attorney General was as follows: "Agreeably to the resolution of the House of Representatives passed on the 22d ultimo, inquiring what measures have been taken with reference to the Africans imported contrary to law into the State of Georgia, which resolution was referred by you to this office, I have the honor to report that the local officers of the government at Savannah have been strictly and specially enjoined to perform the duties imposed upon them by the several acts of Congress relating to this subject; that special counsel has been employed to aid the district attorney in prosecuting the offenders, and that the advices received at this office satisfactorily show the diligence and activity of all persons engaged in the public service. To find the negroes who were clandestinely landed, to identify the parties engaged in the crime, and to ascertain other important facts connected with the transaction—all this has been attended with many difficulties, but there is good reason to hope that they will be overcome, and justice, according to the law of the land, executed upon the offenders. But the present condition of the affair is such as to make it absolutely impossible that the proceedings already instituted, or those in contemplation, should be given in detail without very great prejudice to the public interest."

[2] S. Ex. Doc. 33, 35 Cong. 2 Sess.; H. Ex. Doc. 100, 35 Cong. 2 Sess.

property whilst in transit across the Isthmus routes between our Atlantic and Pacific possessions, render it my duty again to recall this subject to your notice.   I have heretofore presented it in my annual messages, both of December, 1857 and 1858, to which I beg leave to refer.   In the latter, I stated that " The Executive Government of this country, in its intercourse with foreign nations, is limited to the employment of diplomacy alone. When this fails it can proceed no further.   It cannot legitimately resort to force, without the direct authority of Congress, except in resisting and repelling hostile attacks.   It would have no authority to enter the territories of Nicaragua, even to prevent the destruction of the transit and protect the lives and property of our own citizens on their passage.   It is true that, on a sudden emergency of this character, the President would direct any armed force in the vicinity to march to their relief; but, in doing this, he would act upon his own responsibility.

" Under these circumstances, I earnestly recommend to Congress the passage of an act authorizing the President, under such restrictions as they may deem proper, to employ the land and naval forces of the United States in preventing the transit from being obstructed or closed by lawless violence, and in protecting the lives and property of American citizens travelling thereupon, requiring, at the same time, that these forces shall be withdrawn the moment the danger shall have passed away.   Without such a provision, our citizens would be constantly exposed to interruption in their progress, and to lawless violence.

" A similar necessity exists for the passage of such an act for the protection of the Panama and Tehuantepec routes."

Another subject, equally important, commanded the attention of the Senate at the last session of Congress.

The republics south of the United States on this continent have, unfortunately, been frequently in a state of revolution and civil war ever since they achieved their independence.   As one or the other party has prevailed, and obtained possession of the ports open to foreign commerce, they have seized and confiscated American vessels and their cargoes in an arbitrary and lawless manner, and exacted money from American citizens by forced loans, and other violent proceedings, to enable them to carry on hostilities.   The Executive Governments of Great Britain, France, and other countries, possessing the war-making power, can promptly employ the necessary means to enforce immediate redress for similar outrages upon their subjects. Not so the Executive Government of the United States.

If the President orders a vessel of war to any of these ports to demand prompt redress for outrages committed, the offending parties are well aware that in case of refusal the commander can do no more than remonstrate. He can resort to no hostile act. The question must then be referred to diplomacy, and in many cases adequate redress can never be obtained. Thus, American citizens are deprived of the same protection under the flag of their country which the subjects of other nations enjoy. The remedy for this state of things can only be supplied by Congress, since the Constitution has confided to that body alone the power to make war. Without the authority of Congress, the Executive cannot lawfully direct any force, however near it may be to the scene of difficulty, to enter the territory of Mexico, Nicaragua or New Granada, for the purpose of defending the persons and property of American citizens, even though they may be violently assailed whilst passing in peaceful transit over the Tehuantepec, Nicaragua or Panama routes. He cannot, without transcending his constitutional power, direct a gun to be fired into a port, or land a seaman or marine to protect the lives of our countrymen on shore, or to obtain redress for a recent outrage on their property. The banditti which infest our neighboring Republic of Mexico, always claiming to belong to one or other of the hostile parties, might make a sudden descent on Vera Cruz, or on the Tehuantepec route, and he would have no power to employ the force on shipboard in the vicinity for their relief, either to prevent the plunder of our merchants or the destruction of the transit.

In reference to countries where the local authorities are strong enough to enforce the laws, the difficulty here indicated can seldom happen; but where this is not the case, and the local authorities do not possess the physical power, even if they possess the will, to protect our citizens within their limits, recent experience has shown that the American Executive should itself be authorized to render this protection. Such a grant of authority, thus limited in its extent, could in no just sense be regarded as a transfer of the war-making power to the Executive, but only as an appropriate exercise of that power by the body to whom it exclusively belongs. The riot at Panama, in 1856, in which a great number of our citizens lost their lives, furnishes a pointed illustration of the necessity which may arise for the exertion of this authority.

I therefore earnestly recommend to Congress, on whom the responsibility exclusively rests, to pass a law before their adjournment, conferring on the President the power to protect the lives and property of American citizens in the cases which I have indicated, under such restrictions and conditions as they may deem advisable. The knowledge that such a law exists would of itself go far to prevent the outrages which it is intended to redress, and to render the employment of force unnecessary.

Without this the President may be placed in a painful position before the meeting of the next Congress. In the present disturbed condition of Mexico, and one or more of the other Republics south of us, no person can foresee what occurrences may take place before that period. In case of emergency, our citizens, seeing that they do not enjoy the same protection with subjects of European Governments, will have just cause to complain. On the other hand, should the Executive interpose, and especially should the result prove disastrous, and valuable lives be lost, he might subject himself to severe censure for having assumed a power not confided to him by the Constitution. It is to guard against this contingency that I now appeal to Congress.

Having thus recommended to Congress a measure which I deem necessary and expedient for the interest and honor of the country, I leave the whole subject to their wisdom and discretion.

JAMES BUCHANAN.

WASHINGTON, February 18, 1859.

MESSAGE

ON TREATIES WITH CHINA.[1]

WASHINGTON, February 18, 1859.

TO THE SENATE OF THE UNITED STATES:

I transmit to the Senate, for its consideration with a view to ratification, two conventions between the United States and China, one providing for the adjustment of claims of citizens of the United States on the Government of that Empire, the other for the regulation of trade, both signed at Shanghai on the 8th of November last. A copy of the despatches of Mr. Reed to the Department of State on the subject is also herewith transmitted.

JAMES BUCHANAN.

VETO MESSAGE

ON A BILL DONATING PUBLIC LANDS.[2]

[February 24, 1859.]

TO THE HOUSE OF REPRESENTATIVES OF THE UNITED STATES:

I return, with my objections, to the House of Representatives, in which it originated, the bill entitled " An act donating public lands to the several States and Territories which may provide colleges for the benefit of agriculture and the mechanic arts," presented to me on the 18th instant.

This bill makes a donation to the several States of twenty thousand acres of the public lands for each Senator and Representative in the present Congress, and also an additional donation of twenty thousand acres for each additional Representative to which any State may be entitled under the census of 1860.

According to a report from the Interior Department, based upon the present number of Senators and Representatives, the

---

[1] Senate Executive Journal, XI. 58.
[2] S. Misc. Doc. 53, 49 Cong. 2 Sess. 259.

lands given to the States amount to six million and sixty thousand acres, and their value, at the minimum Government price of $1.25 per acre, to $7,575,000.

The object of this gift, as stated by the bill, is " the endowment, support, and maintenance of at least one college [in each State] where the leading object shall be, without excluding other scientific or classical studies, to teach such branches of learning as are related to agriculture and the mechanic arts, as the legislatures of the States may respectively prescribe, in order to promote the liberal and practical education of the industrial classes in the several pursuits and professions in life."

As there does not appear from the bill to be any beneficiaries in existence to which this endowment can be applied, each State is required " to provide, within five years at least, not less than one college, or the grant to said State shall cease."   In that event the " said State shall be bound to pay the United States the amount received of any lands previously sold, and that the title to purchasers under the State shall be valid."

The grant in land itself is confined to such States as have public lands within their limits worth $1.25 per acre, in the opinion of the governor.   For the remaining States the Secretary of the Interior is directed to issue " land scrip to the amount of their distributive shares in acres under the provisions of this act, said scrip to be sold by said States, and the proceeds thereof applied to the uses and purposes prescribed in this act, and for no other use or purpose whatsoever."   The lands are granted and the scrip is to be issued " in sections or subdivisions of sections of not less than one-quarter of a section."

According to an estimate from the Interior Department, the number of acres which will probably be accepted by States having public lands within their own limits will not exceed five hundred and eighty thousand acres, and it may be much less, leaving a balance of five million four hundred and eighty thousand acres to be provided for by scrip.   These grants of land and land scrip to each of the thirty-three States are made upon certain conditions, the principal of which is that if the fund shall be lost or diminished on account of unfortunate investments, or otherwise, the deficiency shall be replaced and made good by the respective States.

I shall now proceed to state my objections to this bill.   I deem it to be both inexpedient and unconstitutional.

1. This bill has been passed at a period when we can with great difficulty raise sufficient revenue to sustain the expenses of the Government. Should it become a law the Treasury will be deprived of the whole, or nearly the whole, of our income from the sale of public lands, which, for the next fiscal year, has been estimated at $5,000,000.

A bare statement of the case will make this evident. The minimum price at which we dispose of our lands is $1.25 per acre. At the present moment, however, the price has been reduced to those who purchase the bounty-land warrants of the old soldiers to eighty-five cents per acre, and of these warrants there are still outstanding and unlocated, as appears by a report (February 12, 1859) from the General Land Office, the amount of eleven million nine hundred and ninety thousand three hundred and ninety-one acres. This has already greatly reduced the current sales by the Government and diminished the revenue from this source. If, in addition, thirty-three States shall enter the market with their land scrip, the price must be greatly reduced below even eighty-five cents per acre, as much to the prejudice of the old soldiers who have not already parted with their land warrants as to the Government. It is easy to perceive that with this glut of the market the Government can sell little or no lands at $1.25 per acre, when the price of bounty-land warrants and scrip shall be reduced to half this sum. This source of revenue will be almost entirely dried up. Under the bill the States may sell their land scrip at any price it may bring. There is no limitation whatever in this respect. Indeed, they must sell for what the scrip will bring, for without this fund they cannot proceed to establish their colleges within the five years to which they are limited. It is manifest, therefore, that to the extent to which this bill will prevent the sale of public lands at $1.25 per acre, to that amount it will have precisely the same effect upon the Treasury as if we should impose a tax to create a loan to endow these State colleges.

Surely the present is the most unpropitious moment which could have been selected for the passage of this bill.

2. Waiving for the present the question of constitutional power, what effect will this bill have on the relations established between the Federal and State governments? The Constitution is a grant to Congress of a few enumerated but most important

powers, relating chiefly to war, peace, foreign and domestic commerce, negotiation, and other subjects which can be best or alone exercised beneficially by the common Government. All other powers are reserved to the States and to the people. For the efficient and harmonious working of both, it is necessary that their several spheres of action should be kept distinct from each other. This alone can prevent conflict and mutual injury. Should the time ever arrive when the State governments shall look to the Federal Treasury for the means of supporting themselves and maintaining their systems of education and internal policy, the character of both governments will be greatly deteriorated. The representatives of the States and of the people, feeling a more immediate interest in obtaining money to lighten the burdens of their constituents than for the promotion of the more distant objects intrusted to the Federal Government, will naturally incline to obtain means from the Federal Government for State purposes. If a question shall arise between an appropriation of land or money, to carry into effect the objects of the Federal Government and those of the States, their feelings will be enlisted in favor of the latter. This is human nature; and hence the necessity of keeping the two governments entirely distinct. The preponderance of this home feeling has been manifested by the passage of the present bill. The establishment of these colleges has prevailed over the pressing wants of the common treasury. No nation ever had such an inheritance as we possess in the public lands. These ought to be managed with the utmost care, but, at the same time, with a liberal spirit toward actual settlers.

In the first year of a war with a powerful naval nation the revenue from customs must, in a great degree, cease. A resort to loans will then become necessary, and these can always be obtained, as our fathers obtained them, on advantageous terms, by pledging the public lands as security. In this view of the subject, it would be wiser to grant money to the States for domestic purposes than to squander away the public lands, and transfer them in large bodies into the hands of speculators.

A successful struggle on the part of the State governments with the General Government for the public lands would deprive the latter of the means of performing its high duties, especially at critical and dangerous periods. Besides, it would operate with equal detriment to the best interests of the States. It would remove the most wholesome of all restraints on legislative bodies —that of being obliged to raise money by taxation from their constituents—and would lead to extravagance, if not to corruption.   What is obtained easily and without responsibility will be lavishly expended.

3. This bill, should it become a law, will operate greatly to the injury of the new States.   The progress of settlements and the increase of an industrious population, owning an interest in the soil they cultivate, are the causes which will build them up into great and flourishing commonwealths.   Nothing could be more prejudicial to their interests than for wealthy individuals to acquire large tracts of the public land and hold them for speculative purposes.   The low price to which this land scrip will probably be reduced will tempt speculators to buy it in large amounts, and locate it on the best lands belonging to the Government.   The eventual consequence must be, that the men who desire to cultivate the soil will be compelled to purchase these very lands at rates much higher than the price at which they could be obtained from the Government.

4. It is extremely doubtful, to say the least, whether this bill would contribute to the advancement of agriculture and the mechanic arts—objects the dignity and value of which cannot be too highly appreciated.

The Federal Government which makes the donation has confessedly no constitutional power to follow it into the States and enforce the application of the fund to the intended objects. As donors, we shall possess no control over our own gift after it shall have passed from our hands.   It is true that the State legislatures are required to stipulate that they will faithfully execute the trust in the manner prescribed by the bill.   But should they fail to do this, what would be the consequence? The Federal Government has no power, and ought to have no power, to compel the execution of the trust.   It would be in as helpless a condition as if even in this, the time of great need, we were to demand any portion of the many millions of surplus revenue deposited with the States for safe-keeping under the act of 1836.

5. This bill will injuriously interfere with existing colleges in the different States, in many of which agriculture is taught as a science, and in all of which it ought to be so taught.   These institutions of learning have grown up with the growth of the

country under the fostering care of the States and the munificence of individuals to meet the advancing demands for education. They have proved great blessings to the people. Many, indeed most of them, are poor, and sustain themselves with difficulty. What the effect will be on these institutions of creating an indefinite number of rival colleges, sustained by the endowment of the Federal Government, it is not difficult to determine.

Under this bill it is provided that scientific and classical studies shall not be excluded from them. Indeed, it would be almost impossible to sustain them without such a provision, for no father would incur the expense of sending a son to one of these institutions for the sole purpose of making him a scientific farmer or mechanic. The bill itself negatives this idea, and declares that their object is " to promote the liberal and practical education of the industrial classes in the several pursuits and professions of life." This certainly ought to be the case. In this view of the subject it would be far better, if such an appropriation of lands must be made to institutions of learning in the several States, to apply it directly to the establishment of professorships of agriculture and the mechanic arts in existing colleges without the intervention of the State legislatures. It would be difficult to foresee how these legislatures will manage this fund. Each Representative in Congress for whose district the proportion of twenty thousand acres has been granted will probably insist that the proceeds shall be expended within its limits. There will undoubtedly be a struggle between different localities in each State concerning the division of the gift, which may end in disappointing the hopes of true friends of agriculture. For this state of things we are without remedy. Not so in regard to State colleges. We might grant land to these corporations to establish agricultural and mechanical professorships; and, should they fail to comply with the conditions on which they accepted the grant, we might enforce specific performance of these before the ordinary courts of justice.

6. But does Congress possess the power, under the Constitution, to make a donation of public lands to the different States of the Union, to provide colleges for the purpose of educating their own people?

I presume the general proposition is undeniable, that Congress does not possess the power to appropriate money in the Treasury, raised by taxes on the people of the United States, for the purpose of educating the people of the respective States. It will not be pretended that any such power is to be found among the specific powers granted to Congress, nor that " it is necessary and proper for carrying into execution " any one of these powers. Should Congress exercise such a power, this would be to break down the barriers which have been so carefully constructed in the Constitution to separate Federal from State authority. We should then not only " lay and collect taxes, duties, imposts, and excises," for Federal purposes, but for every State purpose which Congress might deem expedient or useful. This would be an actual consolidation of the Federal and State governments, so far as the great taxing and money power is concerned, and constitute a sort of partnership between the two in the Treasury of the United States, equally ruinous to both.

But it is contended that the public lands are placed upon a different footing from money raised by taxation, and that the proceeds arising from their sale are not subject to the limitations of the Constitution, but may be appropriated or given away by Congress, at its own discretion, to States, corporations, or individuals, for any purpose they may deem expedient.

The advocates of this bill attempt to sustain their position upon the language of the second clause of the third section of the fourth article of the Constitution, which declares that " the Congress shall have power to dispose of, and make all needful rules and regulations respecting, the territory, or other property belonging to the United States." They contend that by a fair interpretation of the words " dispose of " in this clause, Congress possesses the power to make this gift of public lands to the States for purposes of education.

It would require clear and strong evidence to induce the belief that the framers of the Constitution, after having limited the powers of Congress to certain, precise, and specific objects intended by employing the words " dispose of," to give that body unlimited power over the vast public domain. It would be a strange anomaly, indeed, to have created two funds—the one by taxation, confined to the execution of the enumerated powers delegated to Congress, and the other from the public lands, applicable to all subjects, foreign and domestic, which Congress might designate. That this fund should be " disposed of," not to pay the debts of the United States, nor " to raise and support armies," nor " to provide and maintain a navy," nor to accomplish any one of the other great objects enumerated in the Constitution; but be diverted from them to pay the debts of the States, to educate their people, and to carry into effect any other measure of their domestic policy. This would be to confer upon Congress a vast and irresponsible authority, utterly at war with the well-known jealousy of Federal power which prevailed at the formation of the Constitution. The natural intendment would be, that as the Constitution confined Congress to well-defined specific powers, the funds placed at their command, whether in land or money, should be appropriated to the performance of the duties corresponding with these powers. If not, a Government has been created with all its other powers carefully limited, but without any limitation in respect to the public lands.

But I cannot so read the words " dispose of " as to make them embrace the idea of " giving away." The true meaning of words is always to be ascertained by the subject to which they are applied, and the known general intent of the law-giver. Congress is a trustee under the Constitution for the people of the United States to " dispose of " their public lands, and I think I may venture to assert with confidence, that no case can be found in which a trustee in the position of Congress has been authorized to " dispose of " property by its owner, where it has been held that these words authorized such trustee to give away the fund intrusted to his care. No trustee, when called upon to account for the disposition of the property placed under his management before any judicial tribunal, would venture to present such a plea in his defence. The true meaning of these words is clearly stated by Chief Justice Taney, in delivering the opinion of the court (19 Howard, page 436). He says, in reference to this clause of the Constitution, " it begins its enumeration of powers by that of disposing; in other words, making sale of the lands, or raising money from them, which, as we have already said, was the main object of the cession (from the States), and which is the first thing provided for in the article." It is unnecessary to refer to the history of the times to establish the known fact that this statement of the Chief Justice is perfectly well founded. That it never was intended by the framers of the Constitution that these lands should be given away by Congress is manifest from the concluding portion of the same clause. By it Congress has power not only " to dispose of " the territory, but of the " other property of the United States." In the language of the

Chief Justice (page 437): "And the same power of making needful rules respecting the territory is in precisely the same language applied to the other property of the United States, associating the power over the territory in this respect with the power over movable or personal property; that is, the ships, arms, or munitions of war which then belonged in common to the State sovereignties."

The question is still clearer in regard to the public lands in the States and Territories within the Louisiana and Florida purchases. These lands were paid for out of the public Treasury, from money raised by taxation. Now, if Congress had no power to appropriate the money with which these lands were purchased, is it not clear that the power over the lands is equally limited? The mere conversion of this money into land could not confer upon Congress new power over the disposition of land which they had not possessed over money. If it could, then a trustee, by changing the character of the fund intrusted to his care for special objects, from money into land, might give the land away, or devote it to any purpose he thought proper, however foreign from the trust. The inference is irresistible, that this land partakes of the very same character with the money paid for it, and can be devoted to no objects different from those to which the money could have been devoted. If this were not the case, then, by the purchase of a new territory from a foreign Government, out of the public Treasury, Congress could enlarge their own powers and appropriate the proceeds of the sales of the land thus purchased, at their own discretion, to other and far different objects from what they could have applied the purchase money which had been raised by taxation.

It has been asserted truly that Congress, in numerous instances, have granted lands for the purposes of education. These grants have been chiefly, if not exclusively, made to the new States as they successively entered the Union, and consisted at the first of one section, and afterwards of two sections of the public land in each township for the use of schools, as well as of additional sections for a State university. Such grants are not, in my opinion, a violation of the Constitution. The United States is a great landed proprietor, and from the very nature of this relation it is both the right and the duty of Congress, as their trustee, to manage these lands as any other prudent proprietor would manage them for his own best advantage. Now, no consideration could be presented of a stronger character to induce the American people to brave the difficulties and hardships of frontier life, and to settle upon these lands, and to purchase them at a fair price, than to give to them and to their children an assurance of the means of education. If any prudent individual had held these lands he could not have adopted a wiser course to bring them into market and enhance their value than to give a portion of them for purposes of education. As a mere speculation, he would pursue this course. No person will contend that donations of land to all the States of the Union for the erection of colleges within the limits of each can be embraced by this principle. It cannot be pretended that an agricultural college in New York or Virginia would aid the settlement or facilitate the sale of public lands in Minnesota or California. This cannot possibly be embraced within the authority which a prudent proprietor of land would exercise over his own possessions. I purposely avoid any attempt to define what portions of land may be granted, and for what purposes, to improve the value and promote the settlement and sale of the remainder without violating the Constitution. In this case I adopt the rule that "sufficient unto the day is the evil thereof."

JAMES BUCHANAN.

February 24, 1859.[1]

MESSAGE

ON INSTRUCTIONS TO THE AFRICAN SQUADRON.[2]

TO THE HOUSE OF REPRESENTATIVES:

I transmit herewith a report from the Secretary of the Navy with the accompanying documents, in obedience to the resolution of the House of Representatives adopted on the 28th of January, requesting the President of the United States "to communicate to this House a copy of all instructions given to the commanders

---

[1] This message was considered by the House immediately after its reception. After debate, the question "Will the House, on reconsideration, pass the said bill?" was decided in the negative by 105 yeas against 96 nays. (Veto Messages: S. Misc. Doc. 53, 49 Cong. 2 Sess. 266.)

[2] H. Ex. Doc. 104, 35 Cong. 2 Sess. 1.

of our African squadron since the ratification of the treaty of 1842, called the Washington treaty, with a copy or statement of whatever regulations were entered into by the commanders of the two squadrons for more fully accomplishing the object of the eighth article of said treaty," &c.

JAMES BUCHANAN.

WASHINGTON CITY, February 25, 1859.

MESSAGE

ON A COMMERCIAL TREATY WITH SPAIN.[1]

TO THE SENATE OF THE UNITED STATES:

In answer to the resolution of the Senate of the 23rd instant, requesting a copy of certain letters of Horatio J. Perry, late secretary to the legation of the United States at Madrid, I transmit a report from the Secretary of State, with the documents which accompanied it.

JAMES BUCHANAN.

WASHINGTON. February 26, 1859.

PROCLAMATION, FEBRUARY 26, 1859.[2]

BY THE PRESIDENT OF THE UNITED STATES OF AMERICA.

A PROCLAMATION.

Whereas an extraordinary occasion has occurred rendering it necessary and proper that the Senate of the United States shall be convened to receive and act upon such communications as have been or may be made to it on the part of the Executive:

Now, therefore, I, James Buchanan, President of the United States, do issue this my proclamation, declaring that an extraordinary occasion requires the Senate of the United States to

---

[1] S. Ex. Doc. 43, 35 Cong. 2 Sess. 1.
[2] United States Statutes at Large, XI. 799.

convene for the transaction of business at the Capitol, in the city of Washington, on the 4th day of next month, at 12 o'clock at noon of that day, of which all who shall then be entitled to act as members of that body are hereby required to take notice.

Given under my hand and the seal of the United States, at Washington, this twenty-sixth day of February, (Seal.) A. D. 1859, and of the Independence of the United States the eighty-third.

JAMES BUCHANAN.

By the President:
LEWIS CASS, Secretary of State.

MESSAGE

ON VANCOUVER'S ISLAND AND BRITISH COLUMBIA.[1]

TO THE HOUSE OF REPRESENTATIVES:

In compliance with the resolution of the House of Representatives of the 25th ultimo, I transmit a copy of the report of the special agent of the United States recently sent to Vancouver's Island and British Columbia.

JAMES BUCHANAN.

WASHINGTON, February 28, 1859.

MESSAGE

ON THE GREAT FALLS LAND CONDEMNATION CASE.[2]

TO THE SENATE OF THE UNITED STATES:

I transmit herewith a report from the Secretary of War, with accompanying paper, in obedience to the resolution of the Senate adopted 23d February, requesting the President of the

---

[1] H. Ex. Doc. 111, 35 Cong. 2 Sess. 1. Richardson, in his Messages and Papers of the Presidents, V. 541, gives March 3, 1859, as the date of this message.

[2] S. Ex. Doc. 42, 35 Cong. 2 Sess. 1.

United States "to communicate to the Senate a copy of the opinion of Judge Brewer in the Great Falls land condemnation case, involving a claim for damages to be paid by the United States."

JAMES BUCHANAN.

WASHINGTON CITY, March 1, 1859.

***

MESSAGE

ON OUTRAGES ON AMERICAN CITIZENS ON THE ISTHMUS OF PANAMA.[1]

WASHINGTON, March 2, 1859.

TO THE SENATE OF THE UNITED STATES:

I transmit to the Senate, in executive session, the report of the Secretary of State, with the accompanying documents, in reply to the resolution of the Senate, adopted in open session on the 11th January last, relating to outrages committed on citizens of the United States on the Isthmus of Panama.

JAMES BUCHANAN.

***

MESSAGE

ON PRESERVING THE PUBLIC CREDIT.[2]

[March 3, 1859.]

TO THE SENATE AND HOUSE OF REPRESENTATIVES:

An imperative sense of duty compels me to make an appeal to Congress to preserve the credit of the country. This is the last day of the present Congress, and no provision has yet been

---

[1] Senate Executive Journal, XI. 67.
[2] S. Ex. Doc. 44, 35 Cong. 2 Sess.; H. Ex. Doc. 110, 35 Cong. 2 Sess.

made for the payment of appropriations and to meet the outstanding Treasury notes issued under the authority of law. From the information which has already been communicated to Congress by the Secretary of the Treasury, it is manifest that the ordinary receipts into the Treasury, even under the most favorable circumstances, will scarcely meet the ordinary expenses of the Government during the remainder of the present fiscal year, ending the 30th of June. At that time nearly eighteen millions of Treasury notes will have become due, and many of those, not yet due, are daily paid for duties at the different ports, and there will be no means in the Treasury to meet them. Thus the country, which is full of resources, will be dishonored before the world, and the American people, who are a debt-paying people, will be disgraced by the omission on our part to do our duty. It is impossible to avoid this catastrophe, unless we make provision this very day to meet the lawful demands on the public Treasury. If this were the first instead of the last session of a Congress, the case would be different. You might then be convened by proclamation for to-morrow morning. But there are now thirteen States of the Union, entitled to seventy-eight Representatives, in which none have been elected. It will therefore be impracticable for a large majority of these States to elect their members before the Treasury shall be compelled to stop payment.

Under these circumstances, I earnestly recommend to Congress to make provision, within the few remaining hours of the session, for the preservation of the public credit. The urgency of the case not only justifies but demands that, if necessary, this shall be done by a separate bill. We ought to incur no risk when the good faith of the country is at stake.

JAMES BUCHANAN.

WASHINGTON, March 3, 1859.

MESSAGE

ON THE DEATH OF THE POSTMASTER-GENERAL.[1]

WASHINGTON, March 9, 1859.

TO THE SENATE OF THE UNITED STATES:

It has become my sad duty to announce to the Senate the death of Aaron V. Brown, late Postmaster-General, at his residence in this city on yesterday morning at twenty minutes past 9 o'clock.

The death of this distinguished public officer, especially at the present moment, when his eminent services are so much needed, is a great loss to his country. He was able, honest, and indefatigable in the discharge of his high and responsible duties, whilst his benevolent heart and his kind deportment endeared him to all who approached him.

Submitting, as I do, with humble resignation to the will of Divine Providence in this calamitous dispensation, I shall ever cherish his memory with affectionate regard.

JAMES BUCHANAN.

TO MR. HOLLINS.[2]

WASHINGTON, 24 March, 1859.

DEAR SIR:

I return the free ticket which Mr. Gittings has directed to be forwarded to me for the Northern Central Railroad with as many thanks for his kindness as though I had accepted it. It has

------

[1] Richardson's Messages and Papers of the Presidents, V. 551.

[2] The original of the foregoing letter is in the possession of Mrs. A. J. Cassatt, daughter of the late Rev. Edward Y. Buchanan and niece of President Buchanan. It is an holographic letter, and the envelope is addressed and franked in President Buchanan's own handwriting. A copy of the letter was taken by Mr. W. A. Patton, assistant to the president of the Pennsylvania Railroad Company. I am indebted for the copy here printed to the J. B. Lippincott Company, to whom Mr. Patton kindly furnished it. Mr. Hollins, to whom the letter was addressed, was secretary of the Northern Central Railroad at Baltimore.

been the practice of my life not to travel free on any Railroad, being opposed to the whole system of granting such privileges to individuals not connected with these Roads.

Yours very respectfully,

JAMES BUCHANAN.

ROBERT S. HOLLINS, ESQ., Secretary.

TO MR. HOLT.[1]

24 March 1859.

MY DEAR SIR,

Mr. Capen is under the impression you have already decided the P. O. Case at Boston. I know this cannot be so. I have not yet seen the Atty. General's opinion, and would thank you to bring the papers with you to the Cabinet to-morrow.

Your friend very respectfully

JAMES BUCHANAN.

HON. MR. HOLT.

TO LORD CLARENDON.[2]

Confidential.   WASHINGTON 8 April 1859.

MY DEAR LORD CLARENDON/

I owe you a letter, & should long since have paid the debt but for my incessant engagements. I can never forget our agreeable social intercourse, & shall always feel a deep interest in the prosperity of you & yours.

[1] Holt Papers, Library of Congress.
[2] Buchanan Papers, Historical Society of Pennsylvania.

No President of the United States has ever entered upon his office beset by so many difficulties as myself. I have been gradually & hitherto successfully working through them; & I trust in Providence that at the end of my term, which, thank Heaven, will be reached in less than two years, I shall leave the Country in a much better condition than I found it. I am soundly abused North & South, East & West, just as in the exercise of an equal & impartial policy I happen to run foul of their interests or prejudices. They have never yet said of me in this Country that I am not an honest man. The father of the magnificent Envoy to England from Paraguay, in his official Paper, accuses me of making war upon him to obtain payment of a claim in which I am interested & to put money in my own pocket! They must believe me to be a very bad fellow, in that enlightened Country.

I had hoped and believed that during my term I should bring to an end all difficulties between our two countries. For me this was a labor of love, though you never believed it. Just as I thought the work was on the eve of being completed, Sir William Ouseley goes to Central America to give it the last finish, & although sufficiently dull & pacific in his nature, he has succeeded in raising the very D—l. He was sent there to end, on just & fair terms, with our consent, the everlasting imbroglio arising out of the Clayton & Bulwer Treaty; but this most important duty he has hitherto wholly neglected. He has gone off upon another scent. When we made the Cass-Irisarri Treaty, the only object of which was to secure a transit across the Isthmus for ourselves & the rest of the world, we communicated it or the substance of it to the British Government so that they might go and do likewise. We desired & would have accepted no advantage. To act in concert with Great Britain was the spirit of the Clayton & Bulwer Treaty. But Sir William doubtless thought he would accomplish a great thing if he could get ahead of us & have our Treaty rejected & his own ratified. This he has done & left the Seat of Government of Nicaragua, leaving undone the great objects of his mission. He has also inserted an article in his Treaty, well knowing that we would never agree to insert a similar article in any Treaty. The Queen is bound to the great & mighty Republic of Nicaragua that she will execute her own laws against filibustering. Parliament cannot hereafter change them. In my day, at least, I will not enter into the insulting stipulation with any foreign nation that I shall faithfully execute the laws of the United States. Such a stipulation would not get half a dozen of votes in the Senate, although I think filibustering is at a low ebb in this country.

Sir William & Monsieur Belly are now the great actors in Central America. I know not whether there is any " Entente Cordiale " between them; but the little Frenchman, although repudiated by his Government, has made these silly people believe that he is going to dig a Ship Canal for them between ocean & ocean, a work which all the money in Paris would not accomplish. His plan is a subject of ridicule among capitalists both in England & this country; but the Nicaraguans venerate him as a perfect prodigy. I am writing currente calamo, upon a matter in which of course I feel a much greater interest than you do, & you must pardon me.

Lord Lyons, I understand, has arrived in this City, though I have not yet seen him. We have heard very little of him; but hope he may do well. Perhaps I attribute too much importance to the cultivation of friendly relations between the two countries; but I think you do not estimate this as highly as it deserves. Your mission here ought always to be filled by a first rate man whose character is known in this country & whose acts & opinions will command respect & influence in England. Above all things, he ought to be instructed not to interfere on one side or the other in our party politics.

Lord Napier is personally a very agreeable & well informed gentleman; & Lady Napier is charming. No lady ever made, or in my opinion deserved to make, a more favorable impression on the society of this City than she has done.

You once told me that Louis Napoleon was a fatalist & expressed the conviction that if he would pass 1858 in safety all would be well with him thereafter. Pity he had not said 1859. He must now either go to war or lose his prestige. All the congresses in the world cannot relieve him from this dilemma. They cannot cover his retreat with honor or even with safety before the bristling bayonets & open defiance of Austria. The sympathy for poor down-trodden Italy is very strong in this country, & our people would hail her deliverer with enthusiastic applause.

I would thank you to keep your Mormons at home.   The English Mormon is a strange article.   Although the glories of Brigham have faded, yet he believes him still, with unfaltering fidelity, to be a prophet sent from God to reform & regulate the affairs of all mankind in this lower world.   The American Mormons are fast losing their faith.

Miss Lane is thoroughly English, much more so than I am. We talk a great deal of the " ould country ; " & we never fail to remember, in the kindest spirit, our obligations to Lady Clarendon & yourself.   Please to present her Ladyship my very kindest regards, & believe me to be always

Very respectfully your friend

JAMES BUCHANAN.

LORD CLARENDON.

TO MISS LANE.[1]

WASHINGTON 13 May 1859.

MY DEAR HARRIET/

I send you an oration received from Hon: William Porcher Miles,[2] & franked by him to yourself.   A precious recognition!

I wrote a long letter to Mrs. Roosevelt ten days ago & left it on my table open.   It marvellously disappeared & I had neither courage nor time to copy it from memory.   I know not what has become of it but it contains nothing which might not be published in the New York Herald.   My respect & admiration for Mrs. R., to be sure, appear in the letter; but this is well known & does me honor.   It is possible that in clearing my own table I may have by mistake torn this letter up with other manuscripts; but I can not believe it.

I have but little news.   Mr. Magraw came to us on Saturday last & still remains, much to my gratification.   We get along

---

[1] Buchanan Papers, private collection; Curtis's Buchanan, II. 242.   A passage relating to a purely personal matter is omitted from this letter.

[2] Of South Carolina.

very comfortably & quietly. Miss Hetty is very busy. Washington, they say, is extremely dull. I called yesterday at Mr. Thompson's just before dinner. The lady was not at home. She had gone to a travelling circus & show in company with Mrs. Gwin, her sister, & Miss Lucy. I made no remark to Mr. Thompson on receiving the information except that you would certainly have been of the party had you been in Washington.

I met Mrs. Conrad & her daughters on the street the other day & walked with them some distance. She does not appear to have seen much of Lord Lyons. I think he keeps himself very much to himself. Count Sartiges has been here several times. I shall miss him more than I would any of the foreign ministers.

With my very kindest regards to the Judge & Mrs. Roosevelt I remain

Yours affectionately

JAMES BUCHANAN.

MISS LANE.

TO MISS LANE.[1]

WASHINGTON 14 May 1859.

MY DEAR HARRIET/

I send you the enclosed letter from Mr. John C. Schweizes of New York. It speaks for itself. He seems to be a warm hearted German, & I would advise you to address him a few lines. In acknowledging the compliment I have said I would send his letter to you at Judge Roosevelt's. You have been hailed as " the great Mother of the Indians," & it must gratify you to learn that your adopted countrymen desire to perpetuate your name by giving it to their children.

Two of the Secretaries & myself were to have visited Baltimore to-day to select a site for the Federal Courts; but we agreed to postpone our visit until Monday to enable them to attend a dinner given by Lord Lyons to-day to the members of

---

[1] Buchanan Papers, private collection; Curtis's Buchanan, II. 242.

the Cabinet.   It is quite probable we shall be accompanied on Monday by Mrs. Thompson, Mrs. Gwin, & other ladies.

What means the ominous conjunction between Mr. Van Buren & Mr. Douglas at the N. Y. Hotel?   I do not however consider it ominous at all, though others do.

Sir William ought to have been very careful in obeying his instructions especially after his former experience in S. America. The British Government are not all pleased with him.   We know this from Lord Lyons.

Here I was called away after ten at night to hear the music of the Knights Templars.   It was, I think, excellent though I am as you know no great Judge.   Good night!   My affectionate regards to Mrs. R. & my respectful compliments to the Judge.

Yours affectionately,

JAMES BUCHANAN.

MISS HARRIET LANE.

P. S.   Mr. Thompson & myself intend to set out for Chapel Hill on Monday, 30th Instant.   I think Mr. Magraw will accompany us.   They are making great preparations to receive us.   I hope you are enjoying yourself.   Stay as long as it affords you pleasure.   We are getting along very well.   Miss Hetty is very busy in having things put in order for the summer.

TO MISS LANE.[1]

18 May 1859.

MY DEAR HARRIET/

I return Lady Ouseley's letter.   When you write please to remember me to her in the very kindest terms.   I should be sorry, indeed, to think I should never meet her again.

The conduct of Sir William has been most decidedly disapproved by Lord Malmesbury.   Of this we have the official

---

[1] Buchanan Papers, private collection.   Imperfectly printed in Curtis's Buchanan, II. 243.

evidence. I am truly sorry he did not obey his instructions. But of this say nothing to Mrs. Roosevelt.

Our two successful Diplomatists Messrs. Reed & Bowlen with their ladies are to dine with me to-day en famille. Mr. Cobb now dines here regularly.

I know not from what source you could have learned that Mr. Walker had dined with me on Sunday. I determined for good reason to let the information reach the world through a channel different from myself. To Mr. Cobb alone I communicated it, to prevent him from coming to dinner. Miss Hetty, however, informs me that she had told Mr. & Mrs. Thompson of it when they called, in my absence on Sunday evening.

I am very, very glad that Mr. Walker & myself are again on good personal terms.

I think I never laughed as much on any one day as on Monday last at Baltimore & on the way.

Remember me always most affectionately to Mrs. Roosevelt & very kindly to the Judge.   In haste

Yours affectionately

JAMES BUCHANAN.

MISS LANE.

TO MR. HOLT.[1]

WASHINGTON 28 May, 1859.

MY DEAR SIR

Has Mr. Johnston given Bail? Mr. Jerez, the Minister from Nicaragua, will return to his Country on Monday, and in conversing with him I desire to know whether we may calculate on the Johnston Contract. Please answer by the Messenger.

Yr. friend very respectfully

JAMES BUCHANAN.

HON: MR. HOLT.

----

[1] Holt Papers, Library of Congress.

FROM SIR W. G. OUSELEY.[1]

Private & Confidential.

S. José (Costa Rica) 31 May '59.

My dear Mr. Buchanan,

I am sincerely obliged by your causing to be forwarded to me a copy of the despatch to Genl. Lamar (No. 22 of the 1st of April) only recd. a day or two since by me. It shews, as well as some Articles in late U. S. Journals, that reports from hence, utterly at variance, as usual, with the truth, have been credited, & have even served as texts for personal attacks upon myself.

I write to Lord Lyons by this opportunity, who will doubtless communicate my remarks. There are, however, points not suitable for an official despatch, a reference to which will remind you that the grounds for my proceedings in these negotiations were precisely such as we had, in general terms, agreed upon confidentially. You will recollect that on more than one occasion when conversing on our cessions of positions & possessions in or near Central America, the question arose, (when referring to conferences between yourself & Lord Clarendon,) of the mode of carrying them into effect with due regard to the dignity & honour of the Queen's Govt. I even asked you what you, if you represented the U. S., would yourself do, if, *mutatis mutandis,* similar demands were made on U. S. You replied "that if the present demands were made on England directly by U. S., it might be embarrassing, but that there could be no such feeling when dealing with these petty States, as concession to their claims could never be misunderstood in a way derogatory to England." These were possibly not the exact words, but their sense. It is true that the first conversation of this tenour took place when the late administration were in office; but subsequently, when Lord Derby became Minister, you reverted to the same topic, putting it in the same light. Acting then on this principle, in which I concurred, as it was far from conflicting with any of my instructions, I treated the concessions contemplated in the interpretation latterly admitted of the Bulwer Clayton Treaty, as being yielded, *de jure,* to the claims of the Central American governments.

I therefore preferred that the initiative on the Mosquito question should take the form of a request from the Nicaraguan Govt. rather than that of a proposal or offer on my part. This caused no appreciable delay, & throughout the negotiation I have sought to maintain the same line, but at the same time have been obliged to prevent the Nicaraguan Minister from making the Mosquito Treaty a pretext for indefinitely delaying all other negotiations. The Mosquito Convention necessarily required some time for reference to distant places (distant in *time* not *space*) (Greytown, Matagalpa, &c.) which was not the case with the others. I might in fact have remained in Nicaragua until now, without advancing a step in any negotiation, had I not, while pressing the Mosquito arrangement, continued at the same time to urge the general & postal Treaties.

---

[1] Buchanan Papers, Historical Society of Pennsylvania.

The late threatening movements of the Filibusters have certainly much impeded the settlement of the Mosquito Protectorate. But I also suspect that there is little disposition to fulfil the conditions favorable to the Indians;—the terms of which are known to you.

However, I hope soon to effect a satisfactory arrangement. There is something to me as yet unaccountable in the rejection of this Mosquito Convention. Genl. Lamar may perhaps be more in the secrets of the Nicaragua Congress than I am, from longer residence, and be better able to explain their conduct than I am. I neither wished for nor enjoined secrecy on the position of the Mosquito question, especially as to Genl. Lamar. Our course was very clear. The reference to the Mosquito Treaty being in progress—which the Nicaraguan Govt. proposed to add in the Treaty of Commerce &c.—was sufficient to shew that it had not been neglected by me. The delay is theirs.

I have thought it due to you, & to the kindness & confidence I have experienced at your hands, to make this explanation.

I will not dwell on the accusations in the American papers, of my hostility to U. S. &c. &c. I came resolved to do all I could to settle matters in a manner consistent with the wishes of U. S. & with the honor & dignity of both Govts.

I may not be as communicative and unreserved or make as many professions as others; but I may be allowed to say that my wish is to cultivate the most cordial and friendly feelings with U. S.—irrespective of the personal & amicable relations I have had the honor & pleasure of sustaining with yourself. My whole conduct public & private, for years, has proved this. I regard but little the attacks in the press, but I should much deplore that you should misunderstand me.

I am, my dear Mr. Buchanan, ever most truly yours

W. G. Ouseley.

TO MISS LANE.[1]

Washington 10 June 1859.

My dear Harriet/

I have received your favor of yesterday. We returned to this place on Tuesday morning last from our visit to North Carolina. On Wednesday morning Miss Hetty left for Wheatland with my full & entire approbation; & I wish to say to you emphatically that you need not return home on my account. I shall be rejoiced to see you whenever you may think proper to return; but I get along comfortably & happily in the absence both of Miss Hetty & yourself.

---

[1] Buchanan Papers, private collection; Curtis's Buchanan, II. 243.

I am sorry to find that your excursion to West Point on the Harriet Lane has been made the subject of Newspaper Criticism on yourself. This is most ungallant & ungentlemanly. The practice, however, of employing national vessels on pleasure excursions to gratify any class of people is a fair subject of public criticism. You know how much I condemned your former trip on the same vessel & I did not expect you would fall into a second error. The thing however is past & gone; & let it pass. After a fair time shall have elapsed, it is my purpose to cause general orders to be issued by the Treasury & Navy Departments to put a stop to the practice.

I am truly rejoiced to learn that James Henry is succeeding in his practice.

I have not the least idea of paying the price you mention for a cane. Let it pass for the present. I will get Mr. Baker to attend to it.

Washington has been very quiet but very agreeable since you left. I dined yesterday with Mrs. Thompson. Mrs. Gwin & her sister & Mr. Cobb were the only persons present out of the family. We had a merry time of it. The same party are to dine with Mrs. Gwin on Tuesday next.

It was with the utmost reluctance I removed Mr. Westcott, though his removal was inevitable. His brother, James D. Westcott, has done him much injury. I have known him long, and can say with truth that I know not a more unprincipled man in the United States. I wished to avoid the publication of Mr. Holt's report; but Mr. Westcott and his brother made this impossible. The trio are now all together in happy communion;— I mean Forney, Westcott, & Martin, the last the most contemptible of the set.

I have just had long & interesting letters from Jones & Preston. They are both pleased & both get along well. The former evidently stands well with the Austrian Government, & gives us valuable information.

With my kind regards to Mr. & Mrs. Plitt, with whom I infer you are staying though you do not mention their names, I remain

Yours affectionately

JAMES BUCHANAN.

MISS LANE.

TO MR. TYLER.[1]

Private.   WASHINGTON 27 June 1859.

MY DEAR SIR/

I presume your Committee intend to issue an address at their approaching meeting. In my humble judgment you ought to present clearly & strongly the broad & marked line of difference between Squatter Sovereignty & popular Sovereignty, between the revolutionary attempts of the first squatters in a new Territory to abolish Slavery or prevent its introduction into the Territory through the agency of a Territorial Legislature, & the Constitutional & quiet exercise of the rights of Sovereignty by the people of a Territory in the formation of a State Constitution, with or without domestic Slavery as they may determine. In the mean time slave holders take their property to the Territory, & whilst in a territorial condition it is protected by the Constitution and the Dred Scott decision. The Democratic party by adopting this course is placed on the sure foundation of the Constitution & the law against the arbitrary power of one set of settlers to confiscate the property of another set. The doctrine of Squatter Sovereignty, in my opinion, is equivalent to a declaration that no other Slave State shall ever be admitted into the Union, because the first ten or twenty thousand people who rush into a new territory are never slave holders. But if mistaken in this belief, then the contest between Slavery & Anti-Slavery Settlers would keep the people in a constant state of commotion throughout their entire territorial existence, much to the prejudice of their best interests & of the peace & harmony of the States of the Union. Let all look forward to the time when, in the language of the Cincinnati platform, the people of the territory have the right, " acting through the legally & fairly expressed will of a majority of actual residents, & whenever the number of their inhabitants justifies it, to form a constitution with or without domestic Slavery & be admitted into the Union upon terms of perfect equality with the other States."

The design attributed by Mr. Douglas to the Democratic party to reopen the Slave Trade or to establish a Congressional

---

[1] Buchanan Papers, Historical Society of Pennsylvania.

Slave Code is truly ridiculous. Non-intervention on the part of Congress with the question of Slavery is the true as it is the actual policy of the party. Neither is intervention necessary, because without it the Federal Judiciary is capable of maintaining the rights to Slave property in the Territories. The great Shibboleth of Mr. Douglas now is Squatter Sovereignty. By this he expects to conciliate the Anti-Slavery feeling in the North and thus to divide the Democratic party. This ought to be the point of our main attack. He will graciously condescend to become the Candidate of the Democratic party at Charleston if they will stultify themselves & adopt this plank. I write in haste. I have no doubt you have thought of all these things before; but I know you will not object to my crude suggestions.

Ever your friend

JAMES BUCHANAN.

ROBERT TYLER ESQ.

TO MR. HOLT.[1]

Private.   6th July '59.

MY DEAR SIR,

Have you asked Johnston, your contractor on the Nicaragua route, to come here? We have a right to know who are the parties interested in the contract to carry the Mail. We ought to give all necessary information to the Nicaraguan Government on this subject, and afford them every assurance that there will be no filibustering in the concern. This for the purpose of preventing all difficulties. Have you seen Gen. Cass or Mr. Appleton on the matter?

Yr. friend very respectfully

JAMES BUCHANAN.

HON: MR. HOLT.

---

[1] Holt Papers, Library of Congress.

TO MR. HOLT.[1]

16 July 1859.

My dear Sir,

I forgot to ask you yesterday if Johnston had made his appearance. I presume not. I fear there is something wrong in this matter. Please drop me a line by the bearer. Might you not ride out this evening or to-morrow morning to the Soldiers' Home?

Yr. friend very respectfully

JAMES BUCHANAN.

Hon: Mr. Holt.

TO MR. BAKER.[2]

BEDFORD SPRINGS, 25 July 1859.

My dear Sir/

I am so much employed here in business & pleasure, & withal feel so lazy, that I have not answered your favor of the 21st Instant. The matter of the selection of an individual to inspect coal must be delayed until Mr. Toucey & myself meet in Washington. In the mean time, please to say nothing about it.

Should Mr. Figueira come here during my visit to the Springs, I shall be happy to converse with him on the subject to which you refer. Still, I should not like to give him a formal invitation to meet me at this place. It is our purpose to leave for Washington on Tuesday morning, the 2d of August.

I was very much mortified with the article in the Pittsburg Post. From the hour when in accepting the Cincinnati nomination I avowed the resolution not to become a candidate for a second term, I have never, in thought, word, or deed, deviated from it. I shall not, under any circumstances, change my fixed purpose. To impute such an intention to me is to charge me with gross inconsistency & hypocrisy. Besides, the imputation

---

[1] Holt Papers, Library of Congress.
[2] Buchanan Papers, Historical Society of Pennsylvania.

is calculated to impair my influence in carrying out the remaining measures of the administration.   The Pennsylvanian may say as much as it pleases in contradiction of any speculations to the contrary.

The Springs are now very much crowded; but I meet but few of the old set here.   The water has always operated upon me like a charm, & it does so now.

From your friend very respectfully

JAMES BUCHANAN.

J. L. BAKER, ESQ.

TO MR. HOLT.[1]

BEDFORD SPRINGS 27 July 1859.

MY DEAR SIR,

I have received your favor of the 23d Instant;—but not until yesterday.

I think you are mistaken in supposing that the Van Dyke Company is the one against which the Nicaraguan Government entertain suspicions of filibustering.   The contract with the Company was, I believe, entered into with Jerez, the late Minister from Nicaragua; and it is my impression he earnestly desires its success.   I think the State Department can give you some information on the subject.   As Johnston cannot transfer his interest without the consent of the Department, would it not be well to call upon the Van Dyke Company for a Copy of their charter—of their contract with Jerez or the Nicaraguan Govt.— and all other information necessary to enable you to form a correct decision?

I wish Vanderbilt was the contractor, because he would accomplish the objects, "but we must be off with the old love honorably before we are on with the new."

It seems that Johnston is to make a good speculation out of his contract, which I do not like.

In view of the instructions which we must send to our

[1] Holt Papers, Library of Congress.

Minister to Mexico, immediately, and this Nicaraguan affair, I think I shall leave Bedford on Friday Morning and reach Washington, Deo volente, on Saturday evening. In haste

Yr. friend very respectfully

JAMES BUCHANAN.

HON: MR. HOLT.

P. S. I enclose a letter from Isaac Cook, which you will please to return after reading. I really had hoped this affair was at an end. It would be most unfortunate if any real cause existed for the removal of Cook. If it did, he certainly should be removed, but it would be extremely mortifying to myself and the true friends of the administration. I am sorry I do not entertain a very favorable opinion of Mr. Shalcross. My unfavorable impression is derived altogether from the course he pursued at Chicago during the last investigation.

TO MR. HOLT.[1]

Private & Confidential.

WASHINGTON 4 Aug: '59.

MY DEAR SIR,

I send you the enclosed three letters from Senator Bright, Mr. Pine, and Mr. Cook, and other letters, which you will please to return. I confess I have formed an unfavorable opinion of Mr. Shalcross and would pay very little attention to testimony elicited by him as the prosecutor of Mr. Cook. I have no doubt that there are people behind the scenes—the most bitter enemies of myself and my administration, actively stimulating this prosecution. It would indeed be an extreme case which would cause me to remove Mr. Cook. My political enemies know this and desire to place me in a false position by retaining him.

Yr. friend very respectfully

JAMES BUCHANAN.

HON: MR. HOLT.

---

[1] Holt Papers, Library of Congress.

TO MR. BERRET.[1]

WASHINGTON, August 17, 1859.

SIR: I have received your favor of the 2d instant, communicating, for my approval, an ordinance of the corporation entitled " An act authorizing the erection of a market-house in the Seventh Ward," passed on the 30th of July last.

The first section of this act of " the board of aldermen and common council of the city of Washington " appropriates the sum of $8,000 " for the purpose of erecting a market-house at the intersection of Virginia avenue and D street south, between Four-and-a-half and Sixth streets west: *Provided that the assent of the President of the United States be first obtained thereto.*"

After a careful examination of the act of Congress of May 15, 1820, " to incorporate the inhabitants of the city of Washington," I do not believe that the corporation, with or without the assent of the President, possess the power to erect a market-house in any public street of this city. The seventh section of the act confers upon the corporation the power " to open and keep in repair streets, avenues, lanes, alleys, drains, and sewers, agreeably to the plan of the city." This does not confer upon them any authority partially to close and obstruct any street by the erection of a market-house thereon. Nor is this much to be regretted. The experience of other cities has proved that such erections in the public streets are very inconvenient, and they have, in several instances, been removed. But no matter what may be the true construction of the city charter in this respect, it is quite clear that the power granted over the streets, whatever this may be, is vested in the corporation, without any, even the slightest, reference to the President. The case is different in regard to " the open spaces and squares of the city." These are entirely distinct from the streets. They were wisely reserved, in the original plan of the city, for the purposes of health, ventilation, ornament, and recreation. The charter has, therefore, properly provided that the assent of the President shall be obtained to any plan which may be devised for their occupation and improvement. To this extent the power of the corporation over them is limited.

---

[1] S. Ex. Doc. 18, 36 Cong. 1 Sess. 3.

The language of the charter is very clear. The corporation are invested with the power "to occupy and improve, for public purposes, *by and with the consent of the President of the United States*, any part of the public and open spaces and squares in said city, not interfering with any private rights." This is not a case in which it is proposed to erect a market-house on any of these "public and open spaces or squares," and therefore the President has no authority in the matter.

I regret very much to differ in any case from the corporation of Washington, for whom I entertain a very high regard. I regret this the less upon the present occasion because I believe that my opinion is in accordance with the true interests of the city, in whose welfare I shall never cease to feel the deepest concern.

Very respectfully,

JAMES BUCHANAN.

JAMES G. BERRET, ESQ.,
　　Mayor of the City of Washington.

TO MRS. POLK.[1]

WASHINGTON 19 September 1859.

MY DEAR MADAM/

I am truly sorry to give you trouble, but public duty would seem to require it, & I know, in your opinion, will justify it. You will doubtless recollect the Oregon negotiation. Mr. McLane, in a Despatch addressed to the State Department dated on the 18 May, 1846, in speaking of a proposition about to be made to the Government of the United States by Lord Aberdeen, says:—" The proposition most probably will offer, substantially, First, to divide the Territory by the extension of the line on the parallel of forty-nine to the Sea; that is to say, to the arm of the Sea called Birch's bay; thence *by the Canal de Aro* & Straits of Fuca to the Ocean," &c. &c.

---

[1] Buchanan Papers, Historical Society of Pennsylvania.

The Treaty itself in describing the Boundary has omitted to mention the *Canal de Aro,* whereupon the British Government insist that the Canal de Aro is not the true Treaty line, but the Straits of Rosario, which are considerably nearer to the American continent.   Under this construction they claim the Island of San Juan & several other Islands between the Canal de Aro & the Straits of Rosario; I think without any sufficient foundation.

Mr. McLane was in the habit of writing numerous private letters to President Polk & myself containing matters which he desired should not be placed on file.   Now you will oblige me very much by examining your deceased husband's papers for a letter from Mr. McLane dated on or about the 18 May, 1846, giving an account of a conversation between him & Lord Aberdeen on this subject.   They held a conference on the 15th May, 1846, relative to the proposition about to be submitted by Lord Aberdeen.   I should be gratified to hear from you in relation to this matter as soon as it may be quite convenient.

I recollect with peculiar pleasure our agreeable & friendly social intercourse " in the auld lang syne."   I have ever cherished for you the most respectful & friendly regard.   Why can we not meet again?   Why will you not visit Washington during the present autumn or the next Session of Congress?   Miss Lane & myself would give you a most cordial welcome to the White House, where you could pass a few months.   In common with your numerous friends, we should be delighted with such a visit. I am now in my 69th year & am heartily tired of my position as President.   I shall leave it in the beginning of March, 1861, should a kind Providence prolong my days until that period, with much greater satisfaction than when entering on the duties of the office.   *Pray do come.*   I should not ask this great favor, were I not thoroughly convinced that there would not be the least shadow of impropriety in your compliance with this my earnest request.

Ardently wishing you the enjoyment of long life, prosperity, & happiness, I remain always

Very respectfully your friend

JAMES BUCHANAN.

MRS. SARAH POLK.

FROM LORD CLARENDON.[1]

Confidential.   THE GROVE, Oct. 13/59.

MY DEAR MR. BUCHANAN

I ought long since to have thanked you for your kind & friendly letter, altho' you said it was only in payment of a debt to me. Pray excuse my procrastination & believe that I was very sensible of the spirit in which that letter was written, but *don't believe* that I ever doubted your sincerity in bringing our respective Countries into harmonious relation with each other, or that your efforts for that object were ever otherwise than a labor of love. You have proved this during your Presidential career, which I have watched with the interest of a friend who wished you well, & of an Englishman who is convinced that nothing but mismanagement can ever breed a quarrel between two great nations bound together by so many ties, & whose interests, rightly understood, need never clash. Each may have its peculiar merits & failings, but they are of a kindred character, & on either side should produce those feelings of admiration or forbearance which members of the same family ought to exercise towards each other.

You have had many & great difficulties to contend against, but you seem to have overcome them all, & I think you will always reflect with satisfaction upon the cordiality of the relations which have hitherto under your Presidency subsisted between the U. S. & G. Britain.

The vagaries of Sir Wm. Ouseley to which you alluded in your letter rather promoted than interrupted that cordiality, as I must do Lord Malmesbury the justice to say that he spoke of them to me as they deserved, & he had done what was right & called for in the matter before Mr. Dallas had time to act upon the instructions of his Govt.

This affair at San Juan, tho' more serious than the one at Nicaragua, is of a similar character. The over-zeal (which Talleyrand so much deprecated) & the over-slowness, & the over-desire to make political capital without reflecting on the consequences, of Employés, have caused difficulties which put the firmness & good faith of both Govts. to the test.

I am much mistaken if you did not learn the proceedings of Genl. Harney with as much regret as Ld. Malmesbury did those of Sir W. Ouseley. Ld. M. disowned his Plenipotentiary, & you seem to have taken the best course open to you under the circumstances by sending Genl. Scott to supersede Genl. Harney—at least I hope I am not wrong in so interpreting the object of the mission with which he is charged. I have carefully studied the question of right to the Island & have not the shadow of a doubt about it in my own mind, but I won't enter upon that which must be decided in a regular way. The one thing needful now is to prevent collision & the state of things which will render a calm judgment upon the question impossible. John Bull's usual habit is to take things quietly, but his dander has been roused by the high-handed proceedings of Genl. Harney more than I ever remember upon occasions of the kind, & this miserable business might be productive of the most

---

[1] Buchanan Papers, Historical Society of Pennsylvania.

disastrous consequences. May God of His infinite mercy avert from us all the responsibility & guilt of such disasters!

You treat lightly & with becoming contempt the abuse to which men in your high position are always exposed, but when your term expires I think you will have had enough of what are facetiously called "the sweets of office." For my own part, I am very glad not to be enjoying them. I had agreed reluctantly to return to the Foreign Office, but Ld. John Russell preferred to take that Department, & I was not only rejoiced to make way for him, but thought him quite right in selecting it. The Foreign Office is next in importance to that of First Minister, & it would have been improper that Ld. John, with his talents, experience, & position in the H. of Commons, should have occupied only the 3d place in the govt. Lord Palmerston wished me to take any other office, but I saw no necessity for that, as there were many others as desirous of being in office as I was to keep out of it.

The Italian question is at a deadlock. The Emperor of the French is tired of it. The Emperor of Austria holds to the fulfilment of the Villafranca Bond, which has become an impossibility. The King of Sardinia wants to aggrandize himself more than is agreeable to either of his powerful neighbours. The deposed Dukes want to be restored, but their late subjects won't have them at any price, & the complications arising out of all this increase daily. In the mean while the Italian people are behaving admirably under circumstances most trying, & their patience & national dignity, their moderation & love of order & respect for persons & property prove that they are fit to be free, & if they persevere & keep united they *will* be free & their liberties will be placed on a solid foundation.

I rejoice, & so does my wife, to hear that Miss Lane is "thoroughly English," but she would be rather ungrateful if she had not some affection for the "ould Country" where every body, man, woman, & child, who had the pleasure of her acquaintance thought her *perfectly charming,* & if she will but visit us again, she will find that the impression she made is ineffaceable. Pray have the goodness to present to her Lady C.'s & my kindest regards. Lady C. desires to be particularly remembered to you. She says, "Nobody ever said such kind & agreeable things to me as Mr. Buchanan."

Believe me always

Most truly yours

CLARENDON.

TO MR. DIMITRY.[1]

WASHINGTON, 1 November, 1859.

MY DEAR SIR,

This letter will be delivered to you by Commodore Vanderbilt. He is about to proceed to San Juan for the purpose of making arrangements to open the Nicaragua route. Under his contract to carry the mail to San Francisco, he is bound to convey it by that route as soon as this may be practicable; and I know no man in the United States who is so able and so willing to open it speedily as he is himself. This is an object the accomplishment of which I have much at heart.

Mr. Vanderbilt wants no exclusive privileges. He desires only to put the route in order and to be permitted to pass over it upon terms which may be granted to all. He is willing to pay a reasonable toll upon each passenger or a fixed sum annually. This in my opinion is the wisest and most advantageous course which the Government of Nicaragua can pursue. I have stated this opinion in my last message to Congress, as you will perceive in its 19th page. I send you herewith a copy of the Message.

It is my desire, therefore, that you should, as a private individual, exert yourself to obtain this permission for Mr. Vanderbilt. Should his effort fail, the route may not be opened for an indefinite period, much to the prejudice of the interests of Nicaragua as well as those of the people of the United States.

I need not repeat what I have so often said, that this Government do not desire and would not accept any exclusive privileges on the Nicaragua route. All they want is to make it a thoroughfare for the whole world.

From your friend, very respectfully,

JAMES BUCHANAN.

ALEXANDER DIMITRY, ESQUIRE.
&c. &c. &c.

----

[1] Buchanan Papers, Historical Society of Pennsylvania.

TO LORD CLARENDON.[1]

WASHINGTON, 3 November, 1859.

MY DEAR LORD CLARENDON/

I have received your favor of the 13th ultimo. Although I have but little time at present, engaged as I am in collecting and arranging materials for my message, I must snatch a moment to answer you. You appear to be satisfied to live in retirement. I hope you are happy in that condition and enjoy a tranquil spirit. Still I am truly sorry you are not in the Foreign Office. You will not be long out of public employment.

I had earnestly hoped to settle all the dangerous questions between our two countries during my Presidential term. This was one of the prime objects of my ambition; but I now find it impossible. For any thing I know, the Clayton and Bulwer affair still hangs fire. I have no knowledge of the character of the instructions given to Mr. Wyck in regard to Nicaragua or Honduras, though you have already obtained all you wanted from Guatemala. But in a friendly letter I will not advert to causes of former difference between us further than to say I am quite as confident that we are entitled to the Island of San Juan as you can be that it belongs to Great Britain. Indeed I had never thought about it until Lord John's note was presented to me by General Cass. My historical recollection was that we had with the greatest reluctance surrendered the portion of Vancouver's Island south of 49° to Great Britain; but that we had surrendered nothing more. It had never struck me that we had yielded any territory except this south of that parallel. I find upon examination that such was my opinion at the time, as well as that of Mr. McLane, Mr. Marcy, Col. Benton, and the Senate of the United States. We all believed that the line ran through the Canal de Arro. Under this impression you may judge of our astonishment when we found that Lord John, in his first diplomatic note, gives us fair notice that Great Britain never will surrender the subject in dispute. He waits not to hear what can be said on this side of the water in support of our title; but informs us in effect that he had prejudged the case.

---

[1] Buchanan Papers, Historical Society of Pennsylvania.

Should he act upon this principle, and take possession by force, I say with you, " May God of his infinite mercy avert from us all the responsibility and guilt of such disasters! " I have done my duty promptly by sending and instructing General Scott. Lord John himself must be satisfied with my course of action so far as this is concerned. It is now the duty of every friend to both countries to do what he can to preserve the peace and to avert the greatest calamity to which either could be subjected. Had the question of title been treated diplomatically, there could have been no danger; but the pride of the American people will revolt at the course which has been pursued on the part of Great Britain.

It will take us a long time to settle the claims of the Hudson's Bay Company, and I fear that the influence of their leaders has been and will be exerted, not in favor of peace but of war. But too much of this. We must submit to our fate, whatever this may be, with Christian patience. Still it worries me to think that after a two years' successful trial to unite the people of the two countries in the bonds of kindred and intimate friendship, all my labor may prove to have been in vain.

Miss Lane has been absent at home since the receipt of your letter; and I have not sent it to her. On her return she will be delighted with the kind messages from Lady Clarendon and yourself.

Lord Lyons is well spoken of by all his acquaintances. He is considered an able and discreet diplomatist both by General Cass and Mr. Appleton. I cannot say I am well acquainted with him. He is very reserved; and perhaps this is all for the best.

With my kindest and most respectful regards to Lady Clarendon and my most ardent wishes for the prosperity and happiness of you both, I remain always, very respectfully,

Your friend,

JAMES BUCHANAN.

P. S. I am sorry to perceive from the dates that Lord John's letter preceded any knowledge he could have had of Gen: Harney's conduct.

MESSAGE

ON RELATIONS WITH MEXICO.[1]

WASHINGTON, December 7, 1859.

TO THE SENATE OF THE UNITED STATES:

I transmit to the Senate a report from the Secretary of State and the papers referred to therein, in answer to the resolution of the Senate of the 21st of December last, in relation to the suspension of diplomatic relations with Mexico by the United States legation in that country.

JAMES BUCHANAN.

MESSAGE

ON A TREATY WITH CHINA.[2]

TO THE SENATE OF THE UNITED STATES:

Having ratified the treaty between the United States and the Empire of China, pursuant to the advice and consent of the Senate, as expressed in their resolution of the 15th of December last, I lost no time in forwarding my ratification thither, in the hope that it might reach that country in season to be exchanged for the ratification of the Emperor within the time limited for that purpose. Unforeseen circumstances, however, retarded the exchange until the 16th of August last. I consequently submit the instrument anew to the Senate, in order that they may declare their assent to the postponement of the exchange of the ratifications in such way as they may deem most expedient.

JAMES BUCHANAN.

WASHINGTON, 16th Decr., 1859.

---

[1] Richardson's Messages and Papers of the Presidents, V. 576.
[2] Senate Executive Journal, XI. 110.

THIRD ANNUAL MESSAGE,
DECEMBER 19, 1859.[1]

FELLOW-CITIZENS OF THE SENATE AND HOUSE OF REPRESEN-
TATIVES:

Our deep and heartfelt gratitude is due to that Almighty
Power which has bestowed upon us such varied and numerous
blessings throughout the past year. The general health of the
country has been excellent: our harvests have been unusually
plentiful, and prosperity smiles throughout the land. Indeed,
notwithstanding our demerits, we have much reason to believe,
from the past events in our history, that we have enjoyed the
special protection of Divine Providence ever since our origin as
a nation. We have been exposed to many threatening and alarming difficulties in our progress, but on each successive occasion the
impending cloud has been dissipated at the moment it appeared
ready to burst upon our head, and the danger to our institutions
has passed away. May we ever be under the Divine guidance
and protection!

Whilst it is the duty of the President, " from time to time,
to give to Congress information of the state of the Union," I
shall not refer in detail to the recent sad and bloody occurrences at Harper's Ferry. Still, it is proper to observe that these
events, however bad and cruel in themselves, derive their chief
importance from the apprehension that they are but symptoms
of an incurable disease in the public mind, which may break out
in still more dangerous outrages, and terminate, at last, in an
open war by the North to abolish slavery in the South.

Whilst, for myself, I entertain no such apprehension, they
ought to afford a solemn warning to us all to beware of the
approach of danger. Our Union is a stake of such inestimable
value as to demand our constant and watchful vigilance for its
preservation. In this view, let me implore my countrymen, North
and South, to cultivate the ancient feelings of mutual forbearance
and good will toward each other, and strive to allay the demon-
spirit of sectional hatred and strife now alive in the land. This
advice proceeds from the heart of an old public functionary whose
service commenced in the last generation, among the wise and
conservative statesmen of that day, now nearly all passed away,

---

[1] S. Ex. Doc. 2, 36 Cong. 1 Sess. I. 3–26.

and whose first and dearest earthly wish is to leave his country tranquil, prosperous, united, and powerful.

We ought to reflect that in this age, and especially in this country, there is an incessant flux and reflux of public opinion. Questions which in their day assumed a most threatening aspect have now nearly gone from the memory of men.   They are " volcanoes burnt out, and on the lava and ashes and squalid scoria of old eruptions grow the peaceful olive, the cheering vine, and the sustaining corn."   Such, in my opinion, will prove to be the fate of the present sectional excitement should those who wisely seek to apply the remedy continue always to confine their efforts within the pale of the Constitution.   If this course be pursued, the existing agitation on the subject of domestic slavery, like everything human, will have its day, and give place to other and less threatening controversies.   Public opinion in this country is all powerful, and when it reaches a dangerous excess, upon any question, the good sense of the people will furnish the corrective, and bring it back within safe limits.   Still, to hasten this auspicious result at the present crisis, we ought to remember that every rational creature must be presumed to intend the natural consequences of his own teachings.   Those who announce abstract doctrines subversive of the Constitution and the Union must not be surprised should their heated partisans advance one step further and attempt by violence to carry these doctrines into practical effect.   In this view of the subject it ought never to be forgotten that however great may have been the political advantages resulting from the Union to every portion of our common country, these would all prove to be as nothing should the time ever arrive when they cannot be enjoyed without serious danger to the personal safety of the people of fifteen members of the confederacy.   If the peace of the domestic fireside throughout these States should ever be invaded—if the mothers of families within this extensive region should not be able to retire to rest at night without suffering dreadful apprehensions of what may be their own fate and that of their children before the morning— it would be vain to recount to such a people the political benefits which result to them from the Union.   Self-preservation is the first instinct of nature, and therefore any state of society in which the sword is all the time suspended over the heads of the people must at last become intolerable.   But I indulge in no such gloomy forebodings.   On the contrary, I firmly believe that the events at Harper's Ferry, by causing the people to pause and reflect upon the possible peril to their cherished institutions, will be the means, under Providence, of allaying the existing excitement and preventing further outbreaks of a similar character. They will resolve that the Constitution and the Union shall not be endangered by rash counsels, knowing that should " the silver cord be loosed or the golden bowl be broken . . . at the fountain," human power could never reunite the scattered and hostile fragments.

I cordially congratulate you upon the final settlement, by the Supreme Court of the United States, of the question of slavery in the Territories, which had presented an aspect so truly formidable at the commencement of my administration.   The right has been established of every citizen to take his property of any kind, including slaves, into the common Territories belonging equally to all the States of the confederacy, and to have it protected there under the Federal Constitution.   Neither Congress, nor a territorial legislature, nor any human power, has any authority to annul or impair this vested right.   The supreme judicial tribunal of the country, which is a coördinate branch of the government, has sanctioned and affirmed these principles of constitutional law, so manifestly just in themselves, and so well calculated to promote peace and harmony among the States.   It is a striking proof of the sense of justice which is inherent in our people, that the property in slaves has never been disturbed, to my knowledge, in any of the Territories.   Even throughout the late troubles in Kansas, there has not been any attempt, as I am credibly informed, to interfere in a single instance with the right of the master.   Had any such attempt been made, the judiciary would doubtless have afforded an adequate remedy. Should they fail to do this hereafter, it will then be time enough to strengthen their hands by further legislation.   Had it been decided that either Congress or the territorial legislature possess the power to annul or impair the right to property in slaves, the evil would be intolerable.   In the latter event there would be a struggle for a majority of the members of the legislature at each successive election, and the sacred rights of property held under the Federal Constitution would depend, for the time being, on the result.   The agitation would thus be rendered incessant whilst the territorial condition remained, and its baneful influence would keep alive a dangerous excitement among the people of the several States.

Thus has the status of a Territory, during the intermediate period from its first settlement until it shall become a State, been irrevocably fixed by the final decision of the Supreme Court. Fortunate has this been for the prosperity of the Territories, as well as the tranquillity of the States. Now, emigrants from the North and the South, the East and the West, will meet in the Territories on a common platform, having brought with them that species of property best adapted, in their own opinion, to promote their welfare. From natural causes the slavery question will in each case soon virtually settle itself; and before the Territory is prepared for admission as a State into the Union, this decision, one way or the other, will have been a foregone conclusion. Meanwhile, the settlement of the new Territory will proceed without serious interruption, and its progress and prosperity will not be endangered or retarded by violent political struggles.

When, in the progress of events, the inhabitants of any Territory shall have reached the number required to form a State, they will then proceed in a regular manner, and in the exercise of the rights of popular sovereignty, to form a constitution preparatory to admission into the Union. After this has been done, to employ the language of the Kansas and Nebraska act, they " shall be received into the Union with or without slavery, as their constitution may prescribe at the time of their admission." This sound principle has happily been recognized, in some form or other, by an almost unanimous vote of both houses of the last Congress.

All lawful means at my command have been employed, and shall continue to be employed, to execute the laws against the African slave trade. After a most careful and rigorous examination of our coasts, and a thorough investigation of the subject, we have not been able to discover that any slaves have been imported into the United States except the cargo by the Wanderer, numbering between three and four hundred. Those engaged in this unlawful enterprise have been rigorously prosecuted, but not with as much success as their crimes have deserved. A number of them are still under prosecution.

Our history proves that the fathers of the republic, in advance of all other nations, condemned the African slave trade. It was, notwithstanding, deemed expedient by the framers of the Constitution to deprive Congress of the power to prohibit "the migration or importation of such persons as any of the States now existing shall think proper to admit" "prior to the year one thousand eight hundred and eight." It will be seen that this restriction on the power of Congress was confined to such States only as might think proper to admit the importation of slaves. It did not extend to other States or to the trade carried on abroad. Accordingly we find that so early as the 22d March, 1794, Congress passed an act imposing severe penalties and punishments upon citizens and residents of the United States who should engage in this trade between foreign nations. The provisions of this act were extended and enforced by the act of 10th May, 1800.

Again: the States themselves had a clear right to waive the constitutional privilege intended for their benefit, and to prohibit by their own laws this trade at any time they thought proper previous to 1808. Several of them exercised this right before that period, and among them some containing the greatest number of slaves. This gave to Congress the immediate power to act in regard to all such States, because they themselves had removed the constitutional barrier. Congress accordingly passed an act on 28th February, 1803, "to prevent the importation of certain persons into certain States where, by the laws thereof, their admission is prohibited." In this manner the importation of African slaves into the United States was to a great extent prohibited some years in advance of 1808.

As the year 1808 approached, Congress determined not to suffer this trade to exist even for a single day after they had the power to abolish it. On the 2d of March, 1807, they passed an act to take effect "from and after the first day of January, 1808," prohibiting the importation of African slaves into the United States. This was followed by subsequent acts of a similar character, to which I need not specially refer. Such were the principles and such the practice of our ancestors more than fifty years ago in regard to the African slave trade. It did not occur to the revered patriots who had been delegates to the convention, and afterwards became members of Congress, that in passing these laws they had violated the Constitution which they had framed with so much care and deliberation. They supposed that to prohibit Congress, in express terms, from exercising a specified power before an appointed day, necessarily involved the right to exercise this power after that day had arrived.

If this were not the case, the framers of the Constitution had expended much labor in vain. Had they imagined that Congress would possess no power to prohibit the trade either before or after 1808, they would not have taken so much care to protect the States against the exercise of this power before that period. Nay, more, they would not have attached such vast importance to this provision as to have excluded it from the possibility of future repeal or amendment, to which other portions of the Constitution were exposed. It would, then, have been wholly unnecessary to engraft on the fifth article of the Constitution, prescribing the mode of its own future amendment, the proviso, "that no amendment which may be made prior to the year one thousand eight hundred and eight shall in any manner affect" the provision in the Constitution securing to the States the right to admit the importation of African slaves previous to that period. According to the adverse construction, the clause itself, on which so much care and discussion had been employed by the members of the convention, was an absolute nullity from the beginning, and all that has since been done under it a mere usurpation.

It was well and wise to confer this power on Congress; because had it been left to the States its efficient exercise would have been impossible. In that event, any one State could have effectually continued the trade not only for itself, but for all the other slave States, though never so much against their will. And why? Because African slaves, when once brought within the limits of any one State in accordance with its laws, cannot practically be excluded from any other State where slavery exists. And even if all the States had separately passed laws prohibiting the importation of slaves, these laws would have failed of effect for want of a naval force to capture the slavers and to guard the coast. Such a force no State can employ in time of peace without the consent of Congress.

These acts of Congress, it is believed, have, with very rare and insignificant exceptions, accomplished their purpose. For a period of more than half a century there has been no perceptible addition to the number of our domestic slaves. During this period their advancement in civilization has far surpassed that of any other portion of the African race. The light and the blessings of Christianity have been extended to them, and both their moral and physical condition has been greatly improved.

Reopen the trade, and it would be difficult to determine whether the effect would be more deleterious on the interests of the master, or on those of the native born slave. Of the evils to the master, the one most to be dreaded would be the introduction of wild, heathen, and ignorant barbarians among the sober, orderly, and quiet slaves whose ancestors have been on the soil for several generations. This might tend to barbarize, demoralize, and exasperate the whole mass, and produce most deplorable consequences.

The effect upon the existing slave would, if possible, be still more deplorable. At present, he is treated with kindness and humanity. He is well fed, well clothed, and not overworked. His condition is incomparably better than that of the coolies which modern nations of high civilization have employed as a substitute for African slaves. Both the philanthropy and the self-interest of the master have combined to produce this humane result. But let this trade be reopened, and what will be the effect? The same, to a considerable extent, as on a neighboring island—the only spot now on earth where the African slave trade is openly tolerated; and this in defiance of solemn treaties with a power abundantly able at any moment to enforce their execution. There the master, intent upon present gain, extorts from the slave as much labor as his physical powers are capable of enduring; knowing that, when death comes to his relief, his place can be supplied at a price reduced to the lowest point by the competition of rival African slave-traders. Should this ever be the case in our country, which I do not deem possible, the present useful character of the domestic institution, wherein those too old and too young to work are provided for with care and humanity, and those capable of labor are not overtasked, would undergo an unfortunate change. The feeling of reciprocal dependence and attachment which now exists between master and slave would be converted into mutual distrust and hostility.

But we are obliged, as a Christian and moral nation, to consider what would be the effect upon unhappy Africa itself if we should reopen the slave trade. This would give the trade an impulse and extension which it has never had even in its palmiest days. The numerous victims required to supply it would convert the whole slave coast into a perfect pandemonium, for which this country would be held responsible in the eyes both of God and man. Its petty tribes would then be constantly engaged in predatory wars against each other for the purpose of seizing slaves to supply the American market. All hopes of African civilization would thus be ended.

On the other hand, when a market for African slaves shall no longer be furnished in Cuba, and thus all the world be closed against this trade, we may then indulge a reasonable hope for the gradual improvement of Africa. The chief motive of war among the tribes will cease whenever there is no longer any demand for slaves. The resources of that fertile but miserable country might then be developed by the hand of industry, and afford subjects for legitimate foreign and domestic commerce. In this manner Christianity and civilization may gradually penetrate the existing gloom.

The wisdom of the course pursued by this government towards China has been vindicated by the event. Whilst we sustained a neutral position in the war waged by Great Britain and France against the Chinese empire, our late minister, in obedience to his instructions, judiciously coöperated with the ministers of these powers in all peaceful measures to secure, by treaty, the just concessions demanded by the interests of foreign commerce. The result is, that satisfactory treaties have been concluded with China by the respective ministers of the United States, Great Britain, France, and Russia. Our "treaty, or general convention of peace, amity, and commerce," with that empire, was concluded at Tientsin on the 18th June, 1858, and was ratified by the President, by and with the advice and consent of the Senate, on the 21st December following. On the 15th December, 1858, John E. Ward, a distinguished citizen of Georgia, was duly commissioned as envoy extraordinary and minister plenipotentiary to China.

He left the United States for the place of his destination on the 5th of February, 1859, bearing with him the ratified copy of this treaty, and arrived at Shanghai on the 28th May. From thence he proceeded to Peking on the 16th June, but did not arrive in that city until the 27th July. According to the terms of the treaty the ratifications were to be exchanged on or before the 18th June, 1859. This was rendered impossible by reasons and events beyond his control, not necessary to detail; but still it is due to the Chinese authorities at Shanghai to state that they always assured him no advantage should be taken of the delay, and this pledge has been faithfully redeemed.

On the arrival of Mr. Ward at Peking he requested an audience of the emperor to present his letter of credence. This he did not obtain, in consequence of his very proper refusal to submit to the humiliating ceremonies required by the etiquette of this strange people in approaching their sovereign. Nevertheless, the interviews on this question were conducted in the most friendly spirit, and with all due regard to his personal feelings and the honor of his country. When a presentation to his Majesty was found to be impossible, the letter of credence from the President was received with peculiar honors by Kweiliang, " the emperor's prime minister and the second man in the empire to the emperor himself." The ratifications of the treaty were afterwards, on the 16th of August, exchanged in proper form at Pei-tsang. As the exchange did not take place until after the day prescribed by the treaty, it is deemed proper, before its publication, again to submit it to the Senate. It is but simple justice to the Chinese authorities to observe that, throughout the whole transaction, they appear to have acted in good faith and in a friendly spirit towards the United States. It is true this has been done after their own peculiar fashion; but we ought to regard with a lenient eye the ancient customs of an empire dating back for thousands of years, so far as this may be consistent with our own national honor. The conduct of our minister on the occasion has received my entire approbation.

In order to carry out the spirit of this treaty, and to give it full effect, it became necessary to conclude two supplemental conventions—the one for the adjustment and satisfaction of the claims of our citizens, and the other to fix the tariff on imports and exports, and to regulate the transit duties and trade of our merchants with China. This duty was satisfactorily performed by our late minister. These conventions bear date at Shanghai on the 8th November, 1858. Having been considered in the light of binding agreements subsidiary to the principal treaty, and to be carried into execution without delay, they do not provide for any formal ratification or exchange of ratifications by the contracting parties. This was not deemed necessary by the Chinese, who are already proceeding in good faith to satisfy the claims of our citizens, and, it is hoped, to carry out the other provisions of the conventions. Still I thought it was proper to submit them to the Senate, by which they were ratified on the 3d of March, 1859. The ratified copies, however, did not reach Shanghai until after the departure of our minister to Peking, and these conventions could not, therefore, be exchanged at the same time with the principal treaty. No doubt is entertained that they will be ratified and exchanged by the Chinese government should this be thought advisable; but, under the circumstances presented, I shall consider them binding engagements from their date on both parties, and cause them to be published as such for the information and guidance of our merchants trading with the Chinese empire.

It affords me much satisfaction to inform you that all our difficulties with the republic of Paraguay have been satisfactorily adjusted. It happily did not become necessary to employ the force for this purpose which Congress had placed at my command, under the joint resolution of 2d June, 1858. On the contrary, the president of that republic, in a friendly spirit, acceded promptly to the just and reasonable demands of the government of the United States. Our commissioner arrived at Assumption, the capital of the republic, on the 25th of January, 1859, and left it on the 17th of February, having in three weeks ably and successfully accomplished all the objects of his mission. The treaties which he concluded will be immediately submitted to the Senate.

In the view that the employment of other than peaceful means might become necessary to obtain " just satisfaction " from Paraguay, a strong naval force was concentrated in the waters of the La Plata to await contingencies whilst our commissioner ascended the rivers to Assumption. The Navy Department is entitled to great credit for the promptness, efficiency, and economy with which this expedition was fitted out and conducted.   It consisted of nineteen armed vessels, great and small, carrying two hundred guns and twenty-five hundred men, all under the command of the veteran and gallant Shubrick. The entire expenses of the expedition have been defrayed out of the ordinary appropriations for the naval service, except the sum of $289,000 applied to the purchase of seven of the steamers constituting a part of it, under the authority of the naval appropriation act of the 3d March last.   It is believed that these steamers are worth more than their cost, and they are all now usefully and actively employed in the naval service.

The appearance of so large a force, fitted out in such a prompt manner, in the far distant waters of the La Plata, and the admirable conduct of the officers and men employed in it, have had a happy effect in favor of our country throughout all that remote portion of the world.

Our relations with the great empires of France and Russia, as well as with all other governments on the continent of Europe, unless we may except that of Spain, happily continue to be of the most friendly character.

In my last annual message I presented a statement of the unsatisfactory condition of our relations with Spain; and I regret to say that this has not materially improved.

Without special reference to other claims, even the " Cuban claims," the payment of which has been ably urged by our ministers, and in which more than a hundred of our citizens are directly interested, remain unsatisfied, notwithstanding both their justice and their amount ($128,635.54) had been recognized and ascertained by the Spanish government itself.

I again recommend that an appropriation be made, " to be paid to the Spanish government, for the purpose of distribution among the claimants in the Amistad case."   In common with two of my predecessors, I entertain no doubt that this is required by our treaty with Spain of the 27th October, 1795.   The failure to discharge this obligation has been employed by the cabinet of Madrid as a reason against the settlement of our claims.

I need not repeat the arguments which I urged in my last annual message in favor of the acquisition of Cuba by fair purchase.   My opinions on that measure remain unchanged.   I therefore again invite the serious attention of Congress to this important subject.   Without a recognition of this policy on their part, it will be almost impossible to institute negotiations with any reasonable prospect of success.

Until a recent period there was good reason to believe that I should be able to announce to you on the present occasion that our difficulties with Great Britain, arising out of the Clayton and Bulwer treaty, had been finally adjusted in a manner alike honorable and satisfactory to both parties. From causes, however, which the British government had not anticipated, they have not yet completed treaty arrangements with the republics of Honduras and Nicaragua, in pursuance of the understanding between the two governments. It is nevertheless confidently expected that this good work will ere long be accomplished.

Whilst indulging the hope that no other subject remained which could disturb the good understanding between the two countries, the question arising out of the adverse claims of the parties to the island of San Juan, under the Oregon treaty of the 15th June, 1846, suddenly assumed a threatening prominence. In order to prevent unfortunate collisions on that remote frontier, the late Secretary of State, on the 17th July, 1855, addressed a note to Mr. Crampton, then British minister at Washington, communicating to him a copy of the instructions which he (Mr. Marcy) had given on the 14th July, to Gov. Stevens, of Washington Territory, having a special reference to an " apprehended conflict between our citizens and the British subjects on the island of San Juan." To prevent this, the governor was instructed " that the officers of the Territory should abstain from all acts on the disputed grounds which are calculated to provoke any conflicts. so far as it can be done without implying the concession to the authorities of Great Britain of an exclusive right over the premises. The title ought to be settled before either party should attempt to exclude the other by force, or exercise complete and exclusive sovereign rights within the fairly disputed limits."

In acknowledging the receipt, on the next day, of Mr. Marcy's note, the British minister expressed his entire concurrence " in the propriety of the course recommended to the governor of Washington Territory by your [Mr. Marcy's] instructions to that officer," and stating that he had " lost no time in transmitting a copy of that document to the governor general of British North America," and had " earnestly recommended to his excellency to take such measures as to him may appear best calculated to secure, on the part of the British local authorities and the inhabitants of the neighborhood of the line in question, the exercise of the same spirit of forbearance which is inculcated by you [Mr. Marcy] on the authorities and citizens of the United States."

Thus matters remained upon the faith of this arrangement until the 9th July last, when General Harney paid a visit to the island. He found upon it twenty-five American residents, with their families, and also an establishment of the Hudson's Bay Company, for the purpose of raising sheep. A short time before his arrival, one of these residents had shot an animal belonging to the company, whilst trespassing upon his premises, for which, however, he offered to pay twice its value, but that was refused. Soon after "the chief factor of the company at Victoria, Mr. Dalles, son-in-law of Governor Douglas, came to the island in the British sloop-of-war Satellite, and threatened to take this American (Mr. Cutler) by force to Victoria, to answer for the trespass he had committed. The American seized his rifle and told Mr. Dalles if any such attempt was made he would kill him upon the spot. The affair then ended."

Under these circumstances, the American settlers presented a petition to the general, "through the United States inspector of customs, Mr. Hubbs, to place a force upon the island to protect them from the Indians as well as the oppressive interference of the authorities of the Hudson Bay Company at Victoria, with their rights as American citizens." The general immediately responded to this petition, and ordered Captain George E. Pickett, 9th infantry, "to establish his company on Bellevue, or San Juan island, on some suitable position near the harbor at the southeastern extremity." This order was promptly obeyed, and a military post was established at the place designated. The force was afterwards increased, so that by the last return the whole number of troops then on the island amounted in the aggregate to six hundred and ninety-one men.

Whilst I do not deem it proper, on the present occasion, to go further into the subject, and discuss the weight which ought to be attached to the statements of the British colonial authorities, contesting the accuracy of the information on which the gallant general acted, it was due to him that I should thus present his own reasons for issuing the order to Captain Pickett. From these it is quite clear his object was to prevent the British authorities on Vancouver's island from exercising jurisdiction over American residents on the island of San Juan, as well as to protect them against the incursions of the Indians. Much excitement prevailed for some time throughout that region, and serious danger of collision between the parties was apprehended. The British had a large naval force in the vicinity; and it is but an act of simple justice to the admiral on that station to state that he wisely and discreetly forbore to commit any hostile act, but determined to refer the whole affair to his government and await their instructions.

This aspect of the matter, in my opinion, demanded serious attention. It would have been a great calamity for both nations had they been precipitated into acts of hostility, not on the question of title to the island, but merely concerning what should be its condition during the intervening period whilst the two governments might be employed in settling the question to which of them it belongs. For this reason Lieutenant General Scott was dispatched, on the 17th of September last, to Washington Territory, to take immediate command of the United States forces on the Pacific coast, should he deem this necessary. The main object of his mission was to carry out the spirit of the precautionary arrangement between the late Secretary of State and the British minister, and thus to preserve the peace and prevent collision between the British and American authorities pending the negotiations between the two governments. Entertaining no doubt of the validity of our title, I need scarcely add, that in any event, American citizens were to be placed on a footing at least as favorable as that of British subjects, it being understood that Captain Pickett's company should remain on the island. It is proper to observe that, considering the distance from the scene of action, and in ignorance of what might have transpired on the spot before the general's arrival, it was necessary to leave much to his discretion; and I am happy to state the event has proven that this discretion could not have been intrusted to more competent hands. General Scott has recently returned from his mission, having successfully accomplished its objects, and there is no longer any good reason to apprehend a collision between the forces of the two countries during the pendency of the existing negotiations.

I regret to inform you that there has been no improvement in the affairs of Mexico since my last annual message, and I am again obliged to ask the earnest attention of Congress to the unhappy condition of that republic.

The constituent congress of Mexico, which adjourned on the 17th of February, 1857, adopted a constitution and provided for a popular election. This took place in the following July, (1857,) and General Comonfort was chosen president almost without opposition. At the same election a new congress was chosen, whose first session commenced on the 16th of September, (1857.) By the constitution of 1857 the presidential term was to begin on the 1st of December, (1857,) and continue for four years. On that day General Comonfort appeared before the assembled congress in the city of Mexico, took the oath to support the new constitution, and was duly inaugurated as president. Within a month afterwards he had been driven from the capital, and a military rebellion had assigned the supreme power of the republic to General Zuloaga. The constitution provided that, in the absence of the president, his office should devolve upon the chief justice of the supreme court; and General Comonfort having left the country, this functionary, General Juarez, proceeded to form, at Guanajuato, a constitutional government. Before this was officially known, however, at the capital, the government of Zuloaga had been recognized by the entire diplomatic corps, including the minister of the United States, as the *de facto* government of Mexico. The constitutional president nevertheless maintained his position with firmness, and was soon established, with his cabinet, at Vera Cruz. Meanwhile, the government of Zuloaga was earnestly resisted in many parts of the republic; and even in the capital, a portion of the army having pronounced against it, its functions were declared terminated, and an assembly of citizens was invited for the choice of a new president. This assembly elected General Miramon; but that officer repudiated the plan under which he was chosen, and Zuloaga was thus restored to his previous position. He assumed it, however, only to withdraw from it; and Miramon, having become, by his appointment, "president substitute," continues, with that title, at the head of the insurgent party.

In my last annual message I communicated to Congress the circumstances under which the late minister of the United States suspended his official relations with the central government, and withdrew from the country. It was impossible to maintain friendly intercourse with a government like that at the capital, under whose usurped authority wrongs were constantly committed, but never redressed. Had this been an established government, with its power extending, by the consent of the people, over the whole of Mexico, a resort to hostilities against it would have been quite justifiable, and, indeed, necessary. But the country was a prey to civil war, and it was hoped that the success of the constitutional president might lead to a condition of things less injurious to the United States. This success became so probable that, in January last, I employed a reliable agent to visit Mexico and report to me the actual condition and prospects of the contending parties. In consequence of his report, and from information which reached me from other sources, favorable to the prospects of the constitutional cause, I felt justified in appointing a new minister to Mexico, who might embrace the earliest suitable opportunity of restoring our diplomatic relations with that republic. For this purpose a distinguished citizen of Maryland was selected, who proceeded on his mission on the 8th of March last, with discretionary authority to recognize the government of President Juarez, if, on his arrival in Mexico, he should find it entitled to such recognition, according to the established practice of the United States.

On the 7th of April following Mr. McLane presented his credentials to President Juarez, having no hesitation " in pronouncing the government of Juarez to be the only existing government of the republic." He was cordially received by the authorities at Vera Cruz, and they have ever since manifested the most friendly disposition towards the United States.

Unhappily, however, the constitutional government has not been able to establish its power over the whole republic.

It is supported by a large majority of the people and the States, but there are important parts of the country where it can enforce no obedience.

General Miramon maintains himself at the capital; and in some of the distant provinces there are military governors who pay little respect to the decrees of either government. In the meantime the excesses which always attend upon civil war, especially in Mexico, are constantly recurring. Outrages of the worst description are committed both upon persons and property. There is scarcely any form of injury which has not been suffered by our citizens in Mexico during the last few years. We have been nominally at peace with that republic, but " so far as the interests of our commerce, or of our citizens who have visited the country as merchants, shipmasters, or in other capacities, are concerned, we might as well have been at war." Life has been insecure, property unprotected, and trade impossible, except at a risk of loss which prudent men cannot be expected to incur. Important contracts, involving large expenditures, entered into by the central government, have been set at defiance by the local governments. Peaceful American residents, occupying their rightful possessions, have been suddenly expelled the country, in defiance of treaties, and by the mere force of arbitrary power. Even the course of justice has not been safe from control, and a recent decree of Miramon permits the intervention of government in all suits where either party is a foreigner. Vessels of the United States have been seized without law, and a consular officer who protested against such seizure has been fined and imprisoned for disrespect to the authorities. Military contributions have been levied, in violation of every principle of right, and the American who resisted the lawless demand has had his property forcibly taken away, and has been himself banished. From a conflict of authority in different parts of the country, tariff duties which have been paid in one place have been exacted over again in another place. Large numbers of our citizens have been arrested and imprisoned without any form of examination or any opportunity for a hearing, and even when released have only obtained their liberty after much suffering and injury, and without any hope of redress. The wholesale massacre of Crabbe and his associates, without trial, in Sonora, as well as the seizure and murder of four sick Americans who had taken shelter in the house of an American, upon the soil of the United States, was communicated to Congress at its last session. Murders of a still more atrocious character have been committed in the very heart of Mexico, under the authority of Miramon's government, during the present year. Some of these were only worthy of a barbarous age, and if they had not been clearly proven, would have seemed impossible in a country which claims to be civilized. Of this description was the brutal massacre in April last, by order of General Marquez, of three American physicians, who were seized in the hospital at Tacubaya while attending upon the sick and the dying of both parties, and without trial, as without crime, were hurried away to speedy execution. Little less shocking was the recent fate of Ormond Chase, who was shot in Tepic on the 7th of August by order of the same Mexican general, not only without a trial, but without any conjecture by his friends of the cause of his arrest. He is represented as a young man of good character and intelligence, who had made numerous friends in Tepic by the courage and humanity which he had displayed on several trying occasions, and his death was as unexpected as it was shocking to the whole community. Other outrages might be enumerated, but these are sufficient to illustrate the wretched state of the country and the unprotected condition of the persons and property of our citizens in Mexico.

In all these cases our ministers have been constant and faithful in their demands for redress, but both they and this government, which they have successively represented, have been wholly powerless to make their demands effective. Their testimony in this respect, and in reference to the only remedy which, in their judgments, would meet the exigency, has been both uniform and emphatic. "Nothing but a manifestation of the power of the government of the United States," wrote our late minister in 1856, "and of its purpose to punish these wrongs, will avail. I assure you that the universal belief here is, that there is nothing to be apprehended from the government of the United States, and that local Mexican officials can commit these outrages upon American citizens with absolute impunity." "I hope the President," wrote our present minister in August last, "will feel authorized to ask from Congress the power to enter Mexico with the military forces of the United States, at the call of the constitutional authorities, in order to protect the citizens and the treaty rights of the United States. Unless such a power is conferred upon him, neither the one nor the other will be respected in the existing state of anarchy and disorder, and the outrages already perpetrated will never be chastised; and, as I assured you in my No. 23, all these evils must increase until every vestige of order and government disappears from the country." I have been reluctantly led to the same opinion, and, in justice to my countrymen who have suffered wrongs from Mexico, and who may still suffer them, I feel bound to announce this conclusion to Congress.

The case presented, however, is not merely a case of individual claims, although our just claims against Mexico have reached a very large amount. Nor is it merely the case of protection to the lives and property of the few Americans who may still remain in Mexico, although the life and property of every American citizen ought to be sacredly protected in every quarter of the world. But it is a question which relates to the future as well as to the present and the past, and which involves, indirectly at least, the whole subject of our duty to Mexico as a neighboring state. The exercise of the power of the United States in that country to redress the wrongs and protect the rights of our own citizens is none the less to be desired, because efficient and necessary aid may thus be rendered at the same time to restore peace and order to Mexico itself. In the accomplishment of this result the people of the United States must necessarily feel a deep and earnest interest. Mexico ought to be a rich and prosperous and powerful republic. She possesses an extensive territory, a fertile soil, and an incalculable store of mineral wealth. She occupies an important position between the Gulf and the ocean for transit routes and for commerce. Is it possible that such a country as this can be given up to anarchy and ruin without an effort from any quarter for its rescue and its safety? Will the commercial nations of the world, which have so many interests connected with it, remain wholly indifferent to such a result? Can the United States, especially, which ought to share most largely in its commercial intercourse, allow their immediate neighbor thus to destroy itself and injure them? Yet, without support from some quarter, it is impossible to perceive how Mexico can resume her position among nations and enter upon a career which promises any good results. The aid which she requires, and which the interests of all commercial countries require that she should have, it belongs to this government to render, not only by virtue of our neighborhood to Mexico, along whose territory we have a continuous frontier of nearly a thousand miles, but by virtue, also, of our established policy, which is inconsistent with the intervention of any European power in the domestic concerns of that republic.

The wrongs which we have suffered from Mexico are before

the world, and must deeply impress every American citizen. A government which is either unable or unwilling to redress such wrongs is derelict to its highest duties. The difficulty consists in selecting and enforcing the remedy. We may in vain apply to the constitutional government at Vera Cruz, although it is well disposed to do us justice, for adequate redress. Whilst its authority is acknowledged in all the important ports and throughout the seacoasts of the republic, its power does not extend to the city of Mexico and the States in its vicinity, where nearly all the recent outrages have been committed on American citizens. We must penetrate into the interior before we can reach the offenders, and this can only be done by passing through the territory in the occupation of the constitutional government. The most acceptable and least difficult mode of accomplishing the object will be to act in concert with that government. Their consent and their aid might, I believe, be obtained; but if not, our obligation to protect our own citizens in their just rights, secured by treaty, would not be the less imperative. For these reasons I recommend to Congress to pass a law authorizing the President, under such conditions as they may deem expedient, to employ a sufficient military force to enter Mexico for the purpose of obtaining indemnity for the past and security for the future. I purposely refrain from any suggestion as to whether this force shall consist of regular troops or volunteers, or both. This question may be most appropriately left to the decision of Congress. I would merely observe that, should volunteers be selected, such a force could be easily raised in this country among those who sympathize with the sufferings of our unfortunate fellow-citizens in Mexico, and with the unhappy condition of that republic. Such an accession to the forces of the constitutional government would enable it soon to reach the city of Mexico, and extend its power over the whole republic.   In that event, there is no reason to doubt that the just claims of our citizens would be satisfied, and adequate redress obtained for the injuries inflicted upon them.   The constitutional government have ever evinced a strong desire to do justice, and this might be secured in advance by a preliminary treaty.

It may be said that these measures will, at least indirectly, be inconsistent with our wise and settled policy not to interfere in the domestic concerns of foreign nations. But does not the present case fairly constitute an exception? An adjoining republic is in a state of anarchy and confusion, from which she has proved wholly unable to extricate herself. She is entirely destitute of the power to maintain peace upon her borders, or to prevent the incursions of banditti into our territory. In her fate and in her fortune—in her power to establish and maintain a settled government—we have a far deeper interest, socially, commercially, and politically, than any other nation. She is now a wreck upon the ocean, drifting about as she is impelled by different factions. As a good neighbor, shall we not extend to her a helping hand to save her? If we do not, it would not be surprising should some other nation undertake the task, and thus force us to interfere at last, under circumstances of increased difficulty, for the maintenance of our established policy.

I repeat the recommendation contained in my last annual message, that authority may be given to the President to establish one or more temporary military posts across the Mexican line in Sonora and Chihuahua, where these may be necessary to protect the lives and property of American and Mexican citizens against the incursions and depredations of the Indians, as well as of lawless rovers on that remote region. The establishment of one such post at a point called Arispe, in Sonora, in a country now almost depopulated by the hostile inroads of the Indians from our side of the line, would, it is believed, have prevented much injury and many cruelties during the past season. A state of lawlessness and violence prevails on that distant frontier. Life and property are there wholly insecure. The population of Arizona, now numbering more than ten thousand souls, are practically destitute of government, of laws, or of any regular administration of justice. Murder, rapine, and other crimes are committed with impunity. I therefore again call the attention of Congress to the necessity for establishing a territorial government over Arizona.

The treaty with Nicaragua of the 16th of February, 1857, to which I referred in my last annual message, failed to receive the ratification of the government of that republic, for reasons which I need not enumerate. A similar treaty has been since concluded between the parties, bearing date on the 16th March, 1859, which has been already ratified by the Nicaraguan congress. This will be immediately submitted to the Senate for their ratification. Its provisions cannot, I think, fail to be acceptable to the people of both countries.

Our claims against the governments of Costa Rica and Nicaragua remain unredressed, though they are pressed in an earnest manner, and not without hope of success.

I deem it to be my duty once more earnestly to recommend to Congress the passage of a law authorizing the President to employ the naval force at his command for the purpose of protecting the lives and property of American citizens passing in transit across the Panama, Nicaragua, and Tehuantepec routes, against sudden and lawless outbreaks and depredations. I shall not repeat the arguments employed in former messages in support of this measure. Suffice it to say that the lives of many of our people, and the security of vast amounts of treasure passing and repassing over one or more of these routes between the Atlantic and Pacific, may be deeply involved in the action of Congress on this subject.

I would also again recommend to Congress that authority be given to the President to employ the naval force to protect American merchant vessels, their crews, and cargoes, against violent and lawless seizure and confiscation in the ports of Mexico and the Spanish American States, when these countries may be in a disturbed and revolutionary condition. The mere knowledge that such an authority had been conferred, as I have already stated, would of itself, in a great degree, prevent the evil. Neither would this require any additional appropriation for the naval service.

The chief objection urged against the grant of this authority is that Congress, by conferring it, would violate the Constitution —that it would be a transfer of the war-making, or, strictly speaking, the war-declaring power to the Executive. If this were well founded it would, of course, be conclusive. A very brief examination, however, will place this objection at rest.

Congress possess the sole and exclusive power, under the Constitution, " to declare war." They alone can " raise and support armies," and " provide and maintain a navy." But after Congress shall have declared war, and provided the force necessary to carry it on, the President, as commander-in-chief of the army and navy, can alone employ this force in making war against the enemy. This is the plain language, and history proves that it was the well known intention of the framers of the Constitution.

It will not be denied that the general "power to declare war" is without limitation, and embraces within itself not only what writers on the law of nations term a public or perfect war, but also an imperfect war, and, in short, every species of hostility however confined or limited. Without the authority of Congress the President cannot fire a hostile gun in any case except to repel the attacks of an enemy. It will not be doubted that under this power Congress could, if they thought proper, authorize the President to employ the force at his command to seize a vessel belonging to an American citizen which had been illegally and unjustly captured in a foreign port and restore it to its owner. But can Congress only act after the fact, after the mischief has been done? Have they no power to confer upon the President the authority in advance to furnish instant redress should such a case afterward occur? Must they wait until the mischief has been done, and can they apply the remedy only when it is too late? To confer this authority to meet future cases, under circumstances strictly specified, is as clearly within the war-declaring power as. such an authority conferred upon the President by act of Congress after the deed had been done. In the progress of a great nation many exigencies must arise imperatively requiring that Congress should authorize the President to act promptly on certain conditions which may or may not afterward arise. Our history has already presented a number of such cases. I shall refer only to the latest.

Under the resolution of June 2, 1858, "for the adjustment of difficulties with the republic of Paraguay," the President is "authorized to adopt such measures and use such force as in his judgment may be necessary and advisable in the event of a refusal of just satisfaction by the government of Paraguay." "Just satisfaction" for what? For "the attack on the United States steamer Water Witch," and "other matters referred to in the annual message of the President." Here the power is expressly granted upon the condition that the government of Paraguay shall refuse to render this "just satisfaction." In this and other similar cases Congress have conferred upon the President power in advance to employ the army and navy upon the happening of contingent future events; and this most certainly is embraced within the power to declare war.

Now, if this conditional and contingent power could be constitutionally conferred upon the President in the case of Paraguay, why may it not be conferred for the purpose of protecting the lives and property of American citizens in the event that they may be violently and unlawfully attacked in passing over the transit routes to and from California, or assailed by the seizure of their vessels in a foreign port? To deny this power is to render the navy in a great degree useless for the protection of the lives and property of American citizens in countries where neither protection nor redress can be otherwise obtained.

The thirty-fifth Congress terminated on the 3d of March, 1859, without having passed the " act making appropriations for the service of the Post Office Department during the fiscal year ending the 30th of June, 1860." This act also contained an appropriation " to supply deficiencies in the revenue of the Post Office Department for the year ending 30th June, 1859." I believe this is the first instance since the origin of the federal government, now more than seventy years ago, when any Congress went out of existence without having passed all the general appropriation bills necessary to carry on the government until the regular period for the meeting of a new Congress. This event imposed on the Executive a grave responsibility. It presented a choice of evils.

Had this omission of duty occurred at the first session of the last Congress, the remedy would have been plain. I might then have instantly recalled them to complete their work, and this without expense to the government. But on the 4th of March last there were fifteen of the thirty-three States which had not elected any representatives to the present Congress. Had Congress been called together immediately, these States would have been virtually disfranchised. If an intermediate period had been selected, several of the States would have been compelled to hold extra sessions of their legislatures, at great inconvenience and expense, to provide for elections at an earlier day than that previously fixed by law. In the regular course, ten of these States would not elect until after the beginning of August, and five of these ten not until October and November.

On the other hand, when I came to examine carefully the condition of the Post Office Department, I did not meet as many or as great difficulties as I had apprehended. Had the bill which failed been confined to appropriations for the fiscal year ending on the 30th June next, there would have been no reason of pressing importance for the call of an extra session. Nothing would become due on contracts (those with railroad companies only excepted) for carrying the mail for the first quarter of the present fiscal year, commencing on the 1st of July, until the 1st of December—less than one week before the meeting of the present Congress. The reason is, that the mail contractors for this and the current year did not complete their first quarter's service until the 30th September last; and by the terms of their contracts sixty days more are allowed for the settlement of their accounts before the department could be called upon for payment.

The great difficulty and the great hardship consisted in the failure to provide for the payment of the deficiency in the fiscal year ending the 30th June, 1859. The department had entered into contracts, in obedience to existing laws, for the service of that fiscal year, and the contractors were fairly entitled to their compensation as it became due. The deficiency, as stated in the bill, amounted to $3,838,728; but, after a careful settlement of all these accounts, it has been ascertained that it amounts to $4,296,009. With the scanty means at his command, the Postmaster General has managed to pay that portion of this deficiency which occurred in the first two quarters of the past fiscal year ending on the 31st December last. In the mean time, the contractors themselves, under these trying circumstances, have behaved in a manner worthy of all commendation. They had one resource in the midst of their embarrassments. After the amount due to each of them had been ascertained and finally settled according to law, this became a specific debt of record against the United States, which enabled them to borrow money on this unquestionable security. Still, they were obliged to pay interest, in consequence of the default of Congress, and, on every principle of justice, ought to receive interest from the government. This interest should commence from the date when a warrant would have issued for the payment of the principal, had an appropriation been made for this purpose. Calculated up to the 1st December, it will not exceed $96,660—a sum not to be taken into account when contrasted with the great difficulties and embarrassments of a public and private character, both to the people and the States, which would have resulted from convening and holding a special session of Congress.

For these reasons, I recommend the passage of a bill, at as early a day as may be practicable, to provide for the payment of the amount, with interest, due to these last-mentioned contractors, as well as to make the necessary appropriations for the service of the Post Office Department for the current fiscal year.

The failure to pass the post office bill necessarily gives birth to serious reflections. Congress, by refusing to pass the general appropriation bills necessary to carry on the government, may not only arrest its action, but might even destroy its existence. The army, the navy, the judiciary, in short, every department of the government, can no longer perform their functions if Congress refuse the money necessary for their support. If this failure should teach the country the necessity of electing a full Congress in sufficient time to enable the President to convene them in any emergency, even immediately after the old Congress has expired, it will have been productive of great good. In a time of sudden and alarming danger, foreign or domestic, which all nations must expect to encounter in their progress, the very salvation of our institutions may be staked upon the assembling of Congress without delay. If, under such circumstances, the President should find himself in the condition in which he was placed at the close of the last Congress, with nearly half the States of the Union destitute of representatives, the consequences might be disastrous. I therefore recommend to Congress to carry into effect the provisions of the Constitution on this subject, and to pass a law appointing some day previous to the 4th March in each year of odd number for the election of representatives throughout all the States. They have already appointed a day for the election of electors for President and Vice-President, and this measure has been approved by the country.

I would again express a most decided opinion in favor of the construction of a Pacific railroad, for the reasons stated in my two last annual messages. When I reflect upon what would be the defenceless condition of our States and Territories west of the Rocky mountains in case of a war with a naval power sufficiently strong to interrupt all intercourse with them by the routes across the isthmus, I am still more convinced than ever of the vast importance of this railroad. I have never doubted the constitutional competency of Congress to provide for its construction, but this exclusively under the war-making power. Besides, the Constitution expressly requires, as an imperative duty, that "the United States shall protect each of them [the States] against invasion." I am at a loss to conceive how this protection can be afforded to California and Oregon against such a naval power by any other means. I repeat the opinion contained in my last annual message, that it would be inexpedient for the government to undertake this great work by agents of its own appointment, and under its direct and exclusive control. This would increase the patronage of the Executive to a dangerous extent, and would foster a system of jobbing and corruption which no vigilance on the part of federal officials could prevent. The construction of this road ought, therefore, to be intrusted to incorporated companies, or other agencies, who would exercise that active and vigilant supervision over it which can be inspired alone by a sense of corporate and individual interest. I venture to assert that the additional cost of transporting troops, munitions of war, and necessary supplies for the army across the vast intervening plains to our possessions on the Pacific coast would be greater in such a war than the whole amount required to construct the road. And yet this resort would, after all, be inadequate for their defence and protection.

We have yet scarcely recovered from the habits of extravagant expenditure produced by our overflowing treasury during several years prior to the commencement of my administration. The financial reverses which we have since experienced ought to teach us all to scrutinize our expenditures with the greatest vigilance, and to reduce them to the lowest possible point. The executive departments of the government have devoted themselves to the accomplishment of this object with considerable success, as will appear from their different reports and estimates. To these I invite the scrutiny of Congress, for the purpose of reducing them still lower, if this be practicable, consistent with the great public interests of the country. In aid of the policy of retrenchment, I pledge myself to examine closely the bills appropriating lands or money, so that if any of these should inadvertently pass both houses, as must sometimes be the case, I may afford them an opportunity for reconsideration. At the same time we ought never to forget that true public economy consists, not in withholding the means necessary to accomplish important national objects confided to us by the Constitution, but in taking care that the money appropriated for these purposes shall be faithfully and frugally expended.

It will appear from the report of the Secretary of the Treasury that it is extremely doubtful, to say the least, whether we shall be able to pass through the present and the next fiscal year without providing additional revenue. This can only be accomplished by strictly confining the appropriations within the estimates of the different departments, without making an allowance for any additional expenditures which Congress may think proper, in their discretion, to authorize, and without providing for the redemption of any portion of the $20,000,000 of treasury notes which have been already issued. In the event of a deficiency, which I consider probable, this ought never to be supplied by a resort to additional loans. It would be a ruinous practice in the days of peace and prosperity to go on increasing the national debt to meet the ordinary expenses of the government. This policy would cripple our resources and impair our credit in case the existence of war should render it necessary to borrow money. Should such a deficiency occur as I apprehend, I would recommend that the necessary revenue be raised by an increase of our present duties on imports. I need not repeat the opinions expressed in my last annual message as to the best mode and manner of accomplishing this object, and shall now merely observe that these have since undergone no change.

The Report of the Secretary of the Treasury will explain in detail the operations of that department of the government.

The receipts into the treasury from all sources during the fiscal year ending June 30, 1859, including the loan authorized by the act of June 14, 1858, and the issues of treasury notes authorized by existing laws, were eighty-one million six hundred and ninety-two thousand four hundred and seventy-one dollars and one cent, ($81,692,471.01,) which sum, with the balance of six million three hundred and ninety-eight thousand three hundred and sixteen dollars and ten cents ($6,398,316.10) remaining in the treasury at the commencement of that fiscal year, made an aggregate for the service of the year of eighty-eight million ninety thousand seven hundred and eighty-seven dollars and eleven cents, ($88,090,787.11.)

The public expenditures during the fiscal year ending June 30, 1859, amounted to eighty-three million seven hundred and fifty-one thousand five hundred and eleven dollars and fifty-seven cents, ($83,751,511.57.) Of this sum seventeen million four hundred and five thousand two hundred and eighty-five dollars and forty-four cents ($17,405,285.44) were applied to the payment of interest on the public debt and the redemption of the issues of treasury notes. The expenditures for all other branches of the public service during that fiscal year were, therefore, sixty-six million three hundred and forty-six thousand two hundred and twenty-six dollars and thirteen cents, ($66,346,226.13.)

The balance remaining in the treasury on the 1st July, 1859, being the commencement of the present fiscal year, was four million three hundred and thirty-nine thousand two hundred and seventy-five dollars and fifty-four cents, ($4,339,275.54.)

The receipts into the treasury during the first quarter of the present fiscal year, commencing July 1, 1859, were twenty million six hundred and eighteen thousand eight hundred and sixty-five dollars and eighty-five cents, ($20,618,865.85.) Of this amount three million eight hundred and twenty-one thousand three hundred dollars ($3,821,300) was received on account of the loan and the issue of treasury notes—the amount of sixteen million seven hundred and ninety-seven thousand five hundred and sixty-five dollars and eighty-five cents ($16,797,565.85) having been received during the quarter from the ordinary sources of public revenue. The estimated receipts for the remaining three-quarters of the present fiscal year to June 30, 1860, are fifty million four hundred and twenty-six thousand four hundred dollars, ($50,426,400.) Of this amount it is estimated that five million seven hundred and fifty-six thousand four hundred dollars ($5,756,400) will be received for treasury notes which may be reissued under the fifth section of the act of 3d March last, and one million one hundred and seventy thousand dollars ($1,170,000) on account of the loan authorized by the act of June 14, 1858—making six million nine hundred and twenty-six thousand four hundred dollars ($6,926,400) from these extraordinary sources, and forty-three million five hundred thousand dollars ($43,500,000) from the ordinary sources of the public revenue—making an aggregate, with the balance in the treasury on the 1st July, 1859, of seventy-five million three hundred and eighty-four thousand five hundred and forty-one dollars and eighty-nine cents ($75,384,541.89) for the estimated means of the present fiscal year ending June 30, 1860.

The expenditures during the first quarter of the present fiscal year were twenty million seven thousand one hundred and seventy-four dollars and seventy-six cents, ($20,007,174.76.) Four million six hundred and sixty-four thousand three hundred and sixty-six dollars and seventy-six cents ($4,664,366.76) of this sum were applied to the payment of interest on the public debt and the redemption of the issues of treasury notes, and the remainder, being fifteen million three hundred and forty-two thousand eight hundred and eight dollars, ($15,342,808,) were applied to ordinary expenditures during the quarter. The estimated expenditures during the remaining three quarters, to June 30, 1860, are forty million nine hundred and ninety-five thousand five hundred and fifty-eight dollars and twenty-three cents, ($40,995,558.23.) Of which sum two million eight hundred and eighty-six thousand six hundred and twenty-one dollars and thirty-four cents ($2,886,621.34) are estimated for the interest on the public debt. The ascertained and estimated expenditures for the fiscal year ending June 30, 1860, on account of the public debt, are accordingly seven million five hundred and fifty thousand nine hundred and eighty-eight dollars and ten cents, ($7,550,988.10;) and for the ordinary expenditures of the government fifty-three million four hundred and fifty-one thousand seven hundred and forty-four dollars and eighty-nine cents, ($53,451,744.89,) making an aggregate of sixty-one million two thousand seven hundred and thirty-two dollars and ninety-nine cents, ($61,002,732.99;) leaving an estimated balance in the treasury on June 30, 1860, of fourteen million three hundred and eighty-one thousand eight hundred and eight dollars and forty cents, ($14,381,808.40.)

The estimated receipts during the next fiscal year ending June 30, 1861, are sixty-six million two hundred and twenty-five thousand dollars, ($66,225,000,) which, with the balance estimated, as before stated, as remaining in the treasury on the 30th June, 1860, will make an aggregate for the service of the next fiscal year of eighty million six hundred and six thousand eight hundred and eight dollars and forty cents, ($80,606,808.40.)

The estimated expenditures during the next fiscal year ending 30th June, 1861, are sixty-six million seven hundred and fourteen thousand nine hundred and twenty-eight dollars and seventy-nine cents, ($66,714,928.79.) Of this amount three million three hundred and eighty-six thousand six hundred and twenty-one dollars and thirty-four cents ($3,386,621.34) will be required to pay the interest on the public debt, leaving the sum of sixty-three million three hundred and twenty-eight thousand three hundred and seven dollars and forty-five cents ($63,328,-307.45) for the estimated ordinary expenditures during the fiscal year ending 30th June, 1861. Upon these estimates a balance will be left in the treasury on the 30th June, 1861, of thirteen million eight hundred and ninety-one thousand eight hundred and seventy-nine dollars and sixty-one cents, ($13,891,879.61.)

But this balance, as well as that estimated to remain in the treasury on the 1st July, 1860, will be reduced by such appropriations as shall be made by law to carry into effect certain Indian treaties, during the present fiscal year, asked for by the Secretary of the Interior, to the amount of five hundred and thirty-nine thousand three hundred and fifty dollars, ($539,350;) and upon the estimates of the Postmaster General for the service of his department the last fiscal year ending 30th June, 1859, amounting to four million two hundred and ninety-six thousand and nine dollars, ($4,296,009,) together with the further estimate of that officer for the service of the present fiscal year ending 30th June, 1860, being five million five hundred and twenty-six thousand three hundred and twenty-four dollars, ($5,526,-324)—making an aggregate of ten million three hundred and sixty-one thousand six hundred and eighty-three dollars, ($10,361,683.)

Should these appropriations be made as requested by the proper departments, the balance in the treasury on the 30th June, 1861, will not, it is estimated, exceed three million five hundred and thirty thousand one hundred and ninety-six dollars and sixty-one cents, ($3,530,196.61.)

I transmit herewith the reports of the Secretaries of War, of the Navy, of the Interior, and of the Postmaster General. They each contain valuable information and important recommendations well worthy of the serious consideration of Congress.

It will appear from the report of the Secretary of War that the army expenditures have been materially reduced by a system of rigid economy, which, in his opinion, offers every guarantee that the reduction will be permanent. The estimates of the department for the next have been reduced nearly two millions of dollars below the estimates for the present fiscal year, and half a million of dollars below the amount granted for this year at the last session of Congress.

The expenditures of the Post Office Department during the past fiscal year, ending on the 30th June, 1859, exclusive of payments for mail service, specially provided for by Congress out of the general treasury, amounted to $14,964,493.33, and its receipts to $7,968,484.07, showing a deficiency to be supplied from the treasury of $6,996,009.26, against $5,235,677.15 for the year ending 30th June, 1858. The increased cost of transportation, growing out of the expansion of the service required by Congress, explains this rapid augmentation of the expenditures. It is gratifying, however, to observe an increase of receipts for the year ending on the 30th of June, 1859, equal to $481,691.21, compared with those in the year ending on the 30th June, 1858.

It is estimated that the deficiency for the current fiscal year will be $5,988,424.04, but that for the year ending 30th June, 1861, it will not exceed $1,342,473.90, should Congress adopt the measures of reform proposed and urged by the Postmaster General. Since the month of March retrenchments have been made in the expenditures amounting to $1,826,471 annually, which, however, did not take effect until after the commencement of the present fiscal year. The period seems to have arrived for determining the question whether this department shall become a permanent and ever increasing charge upon the treasury or shall be permitted to resume the self-sustaining policy which had so long controlled its administration. The course of legislation recommended by the Postmaster General for the relief of the department from its present embarrassments, and for restoring it to its original independence, is deserving of your early and earnest consideration.

In conclusion, I would again commend to the just liberality of Congress the local interests of the District of Columbia. Surely the city bearing the name of Washington, and destined, I trust, for ages to be the capital of our united, free, and prosperous confederacy, has strong claims on our favorable regard.

JAMES BUCHANAN.

WASHINGTON CITY, December 19, 1859.

MESSAGE

ON A TREATY WITH PARAGUAY.[1]

[December 19, 1859.]

To THE SENATE OF THE UNITED STATES:

I transmit to the Senate, with a view to ratification, a treaty of friendship, commerce, and navigation concluded at Asuncion on the 4th of February last, between the plenipotentiaries of the United States and Paraguay.

JAMES BUCHANAN.

WASHINGTON, 19 December, 1859.

MESSAGE

ON A CONVENTION WITH PARAGUAY.[1]

To THE SENATE OF THE UNITED STATES:

I transmit to the Senate, with a view to ratification, the special convention concluded at Asuncion on the 4th of February last, between the plenipotentiaries of the United States and Paraguay, providing for the settlement of the claims of the United States and Paraguay Navigation Company.

JAMES BUCHANAN.

WASHINGTON, 19 December, 1858 [1859].

MESSAGE

ON A TREATY WITH NICARAGUA.[1]

[December 19, 1859.]

To THE SENATE OF THE UNITED STATES:

I transmit to the Senate, for consideration with a view to ratification, a treaty of friendship and commerce between the

---

[1] Senate Executive Journal, XI. 109.

United States and Nicaragua, signed by their respective plenipotentiaries at Managua on the 16th March last, together with
papers explanatory of the same, of which a list is herewith
furnished.

I invite attention especially to the last document accompanying the treaty, being a translation of a note of 26th September, ultimo, from Mr. Molina, chargé d'affaires *ad interim*
of Nicaragua, to the Secretary of State, together with the translation of the ratification of the treaty by the Nicaraguan Government thereto annexed.

The amendment stipulated in the second article of the decree
of ratification by Nicaragua is in conformity with the views of
this Government, to which the omitted clause was obnoxious, as
will be seen by reference to the note of the Secretary of State to
Mr. Irisarri of 26th May, 1859, a copy of which is among the
documents referred to.

JAMES BUCHANAN.

WASHINGTON, December 19, 1859.

1860.

TO MR. HOLT.[1]

Private and Confidential.

January 2, 1860.

MY DEAR SIR,

I would thank you to have a statement prepared immediately of the Troops on the Atlantic frontier and that of the
Gulf which could be rendered available for the defence of the
public property, and also of the force now in Fort Sumter.

Your friend very respectfully

JAMES BUCHANAN.

HON: MR. HOLT,
    Acting Secretary of War.

---

[1] Holt Papers, Library of Congress.

MESSAGE

ON A TREATY WITH MEXICO.[1]

[January 4, 1860.]

To THE SENATE OF THE UNITED STATES:

I transmit to the Senate, for consideration with a view to ratification, a "treaty of transit and commerce between the United States of America and the Mexican Republic," and also a "convention to enforce treaty stipulations" between the same parties, both of which were signed by the plenipotentiaries of the respective Governments at Vera Cruz on the 14th December ultimo.

I also transmit a copy of a despatch of the minister of the United States accredited to the Mexican Government, to the Secretary of State, relative to these instruments.

JAMES BUCHANAN.

WASHINGTON, 4 January, 1860.

MESSAGE

ON A TREATY WITH THE KANSAS INDIANS.[2]

To THE SENATE OF THE UNITED STATES:

I transmit herewith, for your constitutional action thereon, articles of agreement and convention made and concluded on the 5th day of October, 1859, with the Kansas Indians, and recommend that the same be ratified.

JAMES BUCHANAN.

WASHINGTON, January 10th, 1860.

---

[1] Senate Executive Journal, XI. 115.
[2] Senate Executive Journal, XI. 118.

MESSAGE

ON A TREATY WITH THE SAC AND FOX INDIANS.[1]

To the Senate of the United States:

I transmit herewith, for your constitutional action thereon, articles of agreement and convention made and concluded on the 1st day of October, 1859, with the Sacs and Foxes of the Mississippi, and recommend that the same be ratified.

JAMES BUCHANAN.

WASHINGTON, January 10, 1860.

MESSAGE

ON A TREATY WITH THE WINNEBAGO INDIANS.[2]

To the Senate of the United States:

I transmit herewith, for your constitutional action thereon, articles of agreement and convention made and concluded on the 15th day of April, 1859, with the Winnebagos, and recommend that the same be ratified.

JAMES BUCHANAN.

WASHINGTON, January 10, 1860.

MESSAGE

ON RELATIONS WITH MEXICO.[3]

[January 12, 1860.]

To the Senate of the United States:

In compliance with the resolution of the Senate in executive session of the 10th instant, I transmit herewith the report of the Secretary of State, and the papers accompanying it, relating to

[1] Senate Executive Journal, XI. 119.
[2] Senate Executive Journal, XI. 122.
[3] Senate Executive Journal, XI. 126.

the treaties lately negotiated by Mr. McLane, and to the condition of the existing Government of Mexico.

It will be observed from the report that these papers are originals, and that it is indispensable they should be restored to the files of the Department when the subject to which they relate shall have been disposed of.

JAMES BUCHANAN.

WASHINGTON, 12th January, 1860.

MESSAGE

ON TREATIES WITH THE INDIANS.[1]

[January 20, 1860.]

TO THE SENATE OF THE UNITED STATES:

I transmit herewith, for your constitutional action, articles of agreement and convention made and concluded on the 16th of July, 1859, with the Chippewas of Swan Creek and Black River, and the Christian Indians, and recommend that the same be ratified.

JAMES BUCHANAN.

WASHINGTON, January 20th, 1860.

MESSAGE

ON AN OCCURRENCE AT PERUGIA.[2]

[January 23, 1860.]

TO THE SENATE OF THE UNITED STATES:

In answer to the resolution of the Senate of the 12th instant, requesting information respecting an alleged outrage upon an

---

[1] Senate Executive Journal, XI. 129.
[2] S. Ex. Doc. 4, 36 Cong. 1 Sess.

American family at Perugia, in the Pontifical States, I transmit a report from the Secretary of State, and the documents by which it was accompanied.

JAMES BUCHANAN.

WASHINGTON, January 23, 1860.

MESSAGE

ON THE HEATING OF CERTAIN PUBLIC BUILDINGS.[1]

[January 25, 1860.]

TO THE SENATE OF THE UNITED STATES:

In compliance with the resolution of the Senate of the 11th June, 1858, requesting the President of the United States, if in his judgment compatible with the public interests, to communicate to that body " such information as the executive departments may afford of the contracts, agreements, and arrangements which have been made, and of proposals which have been received, for heating and ventilating the Capitol extension, the Post Office, and other public buildings in course of construction, under the management of Captain Meigs, and of the action of the Secretary of War and Captain Meigs thereon," I transmit herewith all the papers called for by the resolution.

JAMES BUCHANAN.

WASHINGTON, January 25, 1860.

---

[1] S. Ex. Doc. 20, 36 Cong. 1 Sess.

MESSAGE

ON SAN JUAN ISLAND.[1]

[January 30, 1860.]

To the Senate of the United States:

I transmit herewith a report of the Secretary of War, with accompanying papers, in answer to the resolution of the 9th instant, requesting the President " to communicate to the Senate the official correspondence of Lieutenant General Winfield Scott, in reference to the island of San Juan, and of Brigadier General William S. Harney, in command of the department of Oregon."

James Buchanan.

Washington, January 30, 1860.

VETO MESSAGE, FEBRUARY 1, 1860,

ON THE ST. CLAIR FLATS BILL.[2]

[February 1, 1860.]

To the Senate of the United States:

On the last day of the last Congress, a bill, which had passed both houses, entitled " An act making an appropriation for deepening the channel over the Saint Clair flats, in the State of Michigan," was presented to me for approval.

It is scarcely necessary to observe that during the closing hours of a session it is impossible for the President, on the instant, to examine into the merits or demerits of an important bill, involving, as this does, grave questions both of expediency and of constitutional power, with that care and deliberation demanded

---

[1] S. Ex. Doc. 10, 36 Cong. 1 Sess. 1; S. Ex. Doc. 29, 40 Cong. 2 Sess. 143

[2] S. Ex. Doc. 6, 36 Cong. 1 Sess. This was a case of a " pocket veto." The message was read and ordered to be printed and lie on the table. (Veto Messages: S. Mis. Doc. 53, 49 Cong. 2 Sess. 274.)

by his public duty, as well as by the best interests of the country. For this reason the Constitution has in all cases allowed him ten days for deliberation; because if a bill be presented to him within the last ten days of the session, he is not required to return it, either with an approval or a veto, but may retain it, " in which case it shall not be a law." Whilst an occasion can rarely occur when so long a period as ten days would be required to enable the President to decide whether he should approve or veto a bill, yet, to deny him even two days on important questions before the adjournment of each session for this purpose, as recommended by a former annual message, would not only be unjust to him, but a violation of the spirit of the Constitution. To require him to approve a bill when it is impossible he could examine into its merits, would be to deprive him of the exercise of his constitutional discretion and convert him into a mere registrar of the decrees of Congress. I therefore deem it a sufficient reason for having retained the bill in question that it was not presented to me until the last day of the session.

Since the termination of the last Congress, I have made a thorough examination of the questions involved in the bill to deepen the channel over the Saint Clair flats, and now proceed to express the opinions which I have formed upon the subject:

And 1. Even if this had been a mere question of expediency, it was, to say the least, extremely doubtful whether the bill ought to have been approved; because the object which Congress intended to accomplish by the appropriation which it contains of $55,000 had been already substantially accomplished. I do not mean to allege that the work had been completed in the best manner, but it was sufficient for all practical purposes.

The Saint Clair flats are formed by the Saint Clair River, which empties into the lake of that name by several mouths, and which forms a bar or shoal on which, in its natural state, there is not more than six or seven feet of water. This shoal is interposed between the mouth of the river and the deep water of the lake, a distance of six thousand feet, and in its natural condition was a serious obstruction to navigation. The obvious remedy for this was to deepen a channel through these flats by dredging, so as to enable vessels which could navigate the lake and the river to pass through this intermediate channel. This object had been already accomplished by previous appropriations, but without my knowledge, when the bill was presented to me. Captain Whipple, of the Topographical Engineers, to whom the expenditure of the last appropriation of $45,000 for this purpose in 1856 was intrusted, in his annual report, of the 1st October, 1858, stated that the dredging was discontinued on the 26th August, 1858, when a channel had been cut averaging two hundred and seventy-five feet wide, with a depth varying from twelve to fifteen and a half feet. He says: " so long as the lake retains its present height we may assume that the depth in the channel will be at least thirteen and a half feet." With this result, highly creditable to Captain Whipple, he observes that if he has been correctly informed, "all the lake navigators are gratified." Besides, afterwards, and during the autumn of 1858, the Canadian Government expended $20,000 in deepening and widening the inner end of the channel excavated by the United States. No complaint had been made, previous to the passage of the bill, of obstructions to the commerce and navigation across the Saint Clair flats. What, then, was the object of the appropriation proposed by the bill?

It appears that the surface of the water in Lake Saint Clair has been gradually rising, until, in 1858, it had attained an elevation of four feet above what had been its level in 1841. It is inferred, whether correctly or not it is not for me to say, that the surface of the water may gradually sink to the level of 1841; and in that event the water which was, when the bill passed, thirteen and a half feet deep in the channel, might sink to nine and a half feet, and thus obstruct the passage.

To provide for this contingency, Captain Whipple suggested "the propriety of placing the subject before Congress, with an estimate for excavating a cut, through the centre of the new channel, one hundred and fifty feet in width and four and a half feet deep, so as to obtain from the river to the lake a depth of eighteen feet during seasons of extreme high water, and twelve feet at periods of extreme low water. It was not alleged that any present necessity existed for this narrower cut in the bottom of the present channel, but it is inferred that for the reason stated it may hereafter become necessary. Captain Whipple's estimate amounted to $50,000, but Congress, by the bill, have granted $55,000. Now, if no other objection existed against this measure, it would not seem necessary that the appropriation should have been made for the purpose indicated. The channel was sufficiently deep for all practical purposes; but from natural causes constantly operating in the lake, which I need not explain, this channel is peculiarly liable to fill up. What is really required is, that it should at intervals be dredged out so as to preserve its present depth; and surely the comparatively trifling expense necessary for this purpose ought not to be borne by the United States. After an improvement has been once constructed by appropriations from the Treasury it is not too much to expect that it should be kept in repair by that portion of the commercial and navigating interests which enjoys its peculiar benefits.

The last report made by Captain Whipple, dated on the 13th September last, has been submitted to Congress by the Secretary of War, and to this I would refer for information, which is, upon the whole, favorable in relation to the present condition of the channel through the Saint Clair flats.

2.   But the far more important question is, does Congress possess the power under the Constitution to deepen the channels of rivers and to create and improve harbors for purposes of commerce?

The question of the constitutional power of Congress to construct internal improvements within the States has been so frequently and so elaborately discussed that it would seem useless on this occasion to repeat or to refute at length arguments which have been so often advanced. For my own opinions on this subject I might refer to President Polk's carefully considered message of the 15th December, 1847, addressed to the House of Representatives whilst I was a member of his Cabinet.

The power to pass the bill in question, if it exist at all, must be derived from the power " to regulate commerce with foreign nations and among the several States and with the Indian tribes."

The power " to regulate." Does this ever embrace the power to create or to construct? To say that it does is to confound the meaning of words of well-known signification. The word " regulate " has several shades of meaning, according to its application to different subjects, but never does it approach the signification of creative power. The regulating power necessarily presupposes the existence of something to be regulated. As applied to commerce, it signifies, according to the lexicographers, " to subject to rules or restrictions, as to regulate trade," &c.

The Constitution itself is its own best expounder of the meaning of words employed by its framers. Thus, Congress have the power " to coin money." This is the creative power. Then immediately follows the power " to regulate the value thereof "— that is, of the coined money thus brought into existence. The words " regulate," " regulation," and " regulations " occur several times in the Constitution, but always with this subordinate meaning. Thus, after the creative power " to raise and support armies " and " to provide and maintain the navy " had been conferred upon Congress, then follows the power " to make rules for the government and regulation of the land and naval forces " thus called into being. So the Constitution, acting upon the self-evident fact that " commerce with foreign nations and among the several States and with the Indian tribes " already existed, conferred upon Congress the power " to regulate " this commerce. Thus, according to Chief Justice Marshall, the power to regulate commerce " is the power to prescribe the rule by which commerce is to be governed." And Mr. Madison, in his veto message of the 3d March, 1817, declares that " the power to regulate commerce among the several States cannot include a power to construct roads and canals, and to improve the navigation of water-courses, in order to facilitate, promote, and secure such commerce without a latitude of construction departing from the ordinary import of the terms, strengthened by the known inconvenience which doubtless led to the grant of this remedial power of Congress." We know from the history of the Constitution what these inconveniences were. Different States admitted foreign imports at different rates of duty. Those which had prescribed a higher rate of duty for the purpose of increasing their revenue were defeated in this object by the legislation of neighboring States admitting the same foreign articles at lower rates. Hence, jealousies and dangerous rivalries had sprung up between the different States. It was chiefly in the desire to provide a remedy for these evils that the Federal Convention originated. The Constitution, for this purpose, conferred upon Congress the power to regulate commerce in such a manner that duties should be uniform in all the States composing the Confederacy; and moreover expressly provided that " no preference shall be given by any regulation of commerce or revenue to the ports of one State over those of another." If the construction of a harbor or deepening the channel of a river be a regulation of commerce, as the advocates of this power contend, this would give the ports of the State within which these improvements were made a preference over the ports of other States, and thus be a violation of the Constitution.

It is not too much to assert that no human being in existence, when the Constitution was framed, entertained the idea or the apprehension that, by conferring upon Congress the power to regulate commerce, its framers intended to embrace the power of constructing roads and canals, and of creating and improving harbors, and deepening the channels of rivers throughout our extensive Confederacy. Indeed, one important branch of this very power had been denied to Congress in express terms by the Convention. A proposition was made in the Convention to confer on Congress the power " to provide for the cutting of canals when deemed necessary." This was rejected by the strong majority of eight States to three. Among the reasons given for this rejection was, that " the expense in such cases will fall on the United States, and the benefits accrue to the places where the canals may be cut."

To say that the simple power of regulating commerce embraces within itself that of constructing harbors, of deepening the channels of rivers, in short, of creating a system of internal improvements for the purpose of facilitating the operations of commerce, would be to adopt a latitude of construction under which all political power might be usurped by the Federal Government. Such a construction would be in conflict with the well-known jealousy against Federal power which actuated the framers of the Constitution. It is certain that the power in question is not enumerated among the express grants to Congress contained in the instrument. In construing the Constitution, we must then next inquire, is its exercise " necessary and proper? "— not whether it may be convenient or useful " for carrying into execution " the power to regulate commerce among the States. But the jealous patriots of that day were not content even with this strict rule of construction. Apprehending that a dangerous latitude of interpretation might be applied in future times to the enumerated grants of power, they procured an amendment to be made to the original instrument, which declares that " the powers not delegated to the United States by the Constitution, nor prohibited by it to the States, are reserved to the States respectively, or to the people."

The distinctive spirit and character which pervades the Constitution is, that the powers of the General Government are confined chiefly to our intercourse with foreign nations, to questions of peace and war, and to subjects of common interest to all the States, carefully leaving the internal and domestic concerns of each individual State to be controlled by its own people and legislature. Without specifically enumerating these powers, it must be admitted that this well-marked distinction runs through the whole instrument. In nothing does the wisdom of its framers appear more conspicuously than in the care with which they sought to avoid the danger to our institutions which must necessarily result from the interference of the Federal Government with the local concerns of the States. The jarring and collision which would occur from the exercise by two separate governments of jurisdiction over the same subjects could not fail to produce disastrous consequences. Besides, the corrupting and seducing money influence exerted by the General Government in carrying into effect a system of internal improvements might be perverted to increase and consolidate its own power to the detriment of the rights of the States.

If the power existed in Congress to pass the present bill, then taxes must be imposed, and money borrowed to an unlimited extent to carry such a system into execution. Equality among the States is equity. This equality is the very essence of the Constitution. No preference can justly be given to one of the sovereign States over another. According to the best estimate, our immense coast on the Atlantic, the Gulf of Mexico, the Pacific, and the lakes, embraces more than 9,500 miles, and, measuring by its indentations and to the head of tide-water on the rivers, the distance is believed to be more than 33,000 miles. This, everywhere throughout its vast extent, contains numerous rivers and harbors; all of which may become the objects of congressional appropriation. You cannot deny to one State what you have granted to another. Such injustice would produce strife, jealousy, and alarming dissensions among them. Even within the same State improvements may be made in one river or harbor which would essentially injure the commerce and industry of another river or harbor. The truth is that most of these improvements are in a great degree local in their character, and for the especial benefit of corporations or individuals in their vicinity, though they may have an odor of nationality, on the principle that whatever benefits any part indirectly benefits the whole.

From our past history we may have a small foretaste of the cost of reviving the system of internal improvements.

For more than thirty years after the adoption of the Federal Constitution the power to appropriate money for the construction of internal improvements was neither claimed nor exercised by Congress. After its commencements, in 1820 and 1831, by very small and modest appropriations for surveys, it advanced with such rapid strides that, within the brief period of ten years, according to President Polk, "the sum asked for from the Treasury, for various projects, amounted to more than $200,-000,000." The vetoes of General Jackson and several of his successors have impeded the progress of the system and limited its extent, but have not altogether destroyed it. The time has now arrived for a final decision of the question. If the power exists, a general system should be adopted which would make some approach to justice among all the States, if this be possible.

What a vast field would the exercise of this power open for jobbing and corruption! Members of Congress, from an honest desire to promote the interests of their constituents, would struggle for improvements within their own districts, and the body itself must necessarily be converted into an arena where each would endeavor to obtain from the Treasury as much money as possible for his own locality. The temptation would prove irresistible. A system of "log-rolling" (I know no word so expressive) would be inaugurated, under which the Treasury would be exhausted, and the Federal Government be deprived of the means necessary to execute those great powers clearly confided to it by the Constitution for the purpose of promoting the interests and vindicating the honor of the country.

Whilst the power over internal improvements, it is believed, was "reserved to the States, respectively," the framers of the Constitution were not unmindful that it might be proper for the State legislatures to possess the power to impose tonnage duties for the improvement of rivers and harbors within their limits. The self-interest of the different localities would prevent this from being done to such an extent as to injure their trade. The Constitution, therefore, which had, in a previous clause, provided that all duties should be uniform throughout the United States, subsequently modified the general rule so far as to declare that " no State shall, without the consent of Congress, levy any duty of tonnage." The inference is, therefore, irresistible that, with the consent of Congress, such a duty may be imposed by the States. Thus, those directly interested in the improvement may lay a tonnage duty for its construction, without imposing a tax for this purpose upon all the people of the United States.

To this provision several of the States resorted until the period when they began to look to the Federal Treasury instead of depending upon their own exertions. Massachusetts, Rhode Island, Pennsylvania, Maryland, Virginia, North Carolina, South Carolina, and Georgia, with the consent of Congress, imposed small tonnage duties on vessels, at different periods, for clearing and deepening the channels of rivers and improving harbors where such vessels entered. The last of these legislative acts believed to exist is that of Virginia, passed on the 22d February, 1826, levying a tonnage duty on vessels for " improving the navigation of James River from Warwick to Rockett's Landing." The latest act of Congress on this subject was passed on the 24th of February, 1843, giving its consent to the law of the legislature of Maryland laying a tonnage duty on vessels for the improvement of the harbor of Baltimore, and continuing it in force until 1st June, 1850.

Thus a clear constitutional mode exists by which the legislature of Michigan may, in its discretion, raise money to preserve the channel of the Saint Clair River at its present depth, or to render it deeper. A very insignificant tonnage duty on American vessels using this channel would be sufficient for the purpose. And as the Saint Clair River is the boundary line between the United States and the province of Upper Canada, the provincial British authorities would doubtless be willing to impose a similar tonnage duty on British vessels to aid in the accomplishment of this object. Indeed, the legislature of that province have already evinced their interest on this subject by having but recently expended $20,000 on the improvement of the Saint Clair flats. Even if the Constitution of the United States had conferred upon Congress the power of deepening the channel of the Saint Clair River, it would be unjust to impose upon the people of the United States the entire burden, which ought to be borne jointly by the two parties having an equal interest in the work.   Whenever the State of Michigan shall cease to depend on the Treasury of the United States, I doubt not that she, in conjunction with Upper Canada, will provide the necessary means for keeping this work in repair in the least expensive and most effective manner, and without being burdensome to any interest.

It has been contended, in favor of the existence of the power to construct internal improvements, that Congress have, from the beginning, made appropriations for light-houses, and that, upon the same principle of construction, they possess the power of improving harbors and deepening the channels of rivers.   As an original question, the authority to erect light-houses under the commercial power might be considered doubtful; but even were it more doubtful than it is, I should regard it as settled after an uninterrupted exercise of the power for seventy years. Such a long and uniform practical construction of the Constitution is entitled to the highest respect, and has finally determined the question.

Among the first acts which passed Congress after the Federal Government went into effect, was that of August 7, 1789, providing " for the establishment and support of light-houses, beacons, buoys, and public piers."   Under this act, the expenses for the maintenance of all such erections then in existence were to be paid by the Federal Government; and provision was made for the cession of jurisdiction over them by the respective States to the United States.   In every case since, before a light-house could be built, a previous cession of jurisdiction has been required.   This practice doubtless originated from that clause of the Constitution authorizing Congress " to exercise exclusive legislation "   *   *   *   " over all places purchased by the consent of the legislature of the State in which the same shall be, for the erection of forts, magazines, arsenals, dock-yards, and other *needful buildings.*"   Among these *" needful buildings,"* light-houses must in fact have been included.

The bare statement of these facts is sufficient to prove that no analogy exists between the power to erect a light-house as a " needful building " and that to deepen the channel of a river.

In what I have said I do not mean to intimate a doubt of the power of Congress to construct such internal improvements as may be essentially necessary for defence and protection against the invasion of a foreign enemy. The power to declare war and the obligation to protect each State against invasion clearly cover such cases. It will scarcely be claimed, however, that the improvement of the Saint Clair River is within this category. This river is the boundary line between the United States and the British province of Upper Canada. Any improvement of its navigation, therefore, which we could make for purposes of war would equally inure to the benefit of Great Britain, the only enemy which could possibly confront us in that quarter. War would be a sad calamity for both nations; but should it ever unhappily exist, the battles will not be fought on the Saint Clair River or on the lakes with which it communicates.

JAMES BUCHANAN.

February 1, 1860.

MESSAGE

ON CONSULAR REGULATIONS IN CHINA.[1]

[February 6, 1860.]

TO THE SENATE AND HOUSE OF REPRESENTATIVES:

I transmit a copy of a letter of the 22d of April last from the chargé d'affaires *ad interim* of the United States in China, and of the regulations for consular courts which accompanied it,[2] for such revision thereof as Congress may deem expedient, pursuant to the sixth section of the act approved the 11th of August, 1848.

JAMES BUCHANAN.

WASHINGTON, February 6, 1860.

---

[1] S. Ex. Doc. 7, 36 Cong. 1 Sess.
[2] These regulations related to certain fees in the consular courts.

VETO OF A RESOLUTION

RELATING TO THE MISSISSIPPI RIVER.[1]

[February 6, 1860.]

To THE SENATE OF THE UNITED STATES:

On the last day of the last session of Congress, a resolution, which had passed both houses, " in relation to removal of obstructions to navigation in the mouth of the Mississippi River," was presented to me for approval. I have retained this resolution, because it was presented to me at a period when it was impossible to give the subject that examination to which it appeared to be entitled. I need not repeat the views on this point presented in the introductory portion of my message to the Senate of the 2d [1st] instant.

In addition, I would merely observe that, although at different periods, sums, amounting in the aggregate to six hundred and ninety thousand dollars, have been appropriated by Congress for the purpose of removing the bar and obstructions at the mouth of the Mississippi, yet it is now acknowledged that this money has been expended with but little, if any, practical benefit to its navigation.

JAMES BUCHANAN.

February 6, 1860.

MESSAGE

ON A CONVENTION WITH VENEZUELA.[2]

[February 9, 1860.]

To THE SENATE OF THE UNITED STATES:

I transmit for the approval of the Senate an informal convention with the Republic of Venezuela for the adjustment of claims of citizens of the United States on the Government of

---

[1] S. Ex. Doc. 8, 36 Cong. 1 Sess. This was a case of a " pocket veto." It was ordered that the message lie on the table and be printed. (Veto Messages: S. Misc. Doc. 53, 49 Cong. 2 Sess. 274.)

[2] Senate Executive Journal, XI. 142.

that Republic, growing out of their forcible expulsion by Venezuelan authorities from the guano island of Aves, in the Caribbean Sea.   Usually it is not deemed necessary to consult the Senate in regard to similar instruments relating to private claims of small amount when the aggrieved parties are satisfied with their terms.   In this instance, however, although the convention was negotiated under the authority of the Venezuelan Executive and has been approved by the National Convention of that Republic, there is some reason to apprehend that, owing to the frequent changes in that Government, the payments for which it provides may be refused or delayed upon the pretext that the instrument has not received the constitutional sanction of this Government.   It is understood that if the payments adverted to shall be made as stipulated, the convention will be acceptable to the claimants.

JAMES BUCHANAN.

WASHINGTON, 9 February, 1860.

MESSAGE

ON A TREATY WITH BOLIVIA.[1]

[February 9, 1860.]

TO THE SENATE OF THE UNITED STATES:

I transmit to the Senate, for its consideration with a view to ratification, a treaty of peace, friendship, commerce, and navigation between the United States and the Republic of Bolivia, signed by their respective plenipotentiaries, at La Paz, on the 13th of May, 1858.

JAMES BUCHANAN.

WASHINGTON, 9 February, 1860.

---

[1] Senate Executive Journal, XI. 142.

TO MR. VAIL.[1]

WASHINGTON, Feb. 11, 1860.

MY DEAR SIR,

I have received your favor of the [10th ultimo] and am rejoiced to learn, what, however, I never doubted, that your ancient feelings of friendship for myself remain unabated. I need scarcely assure you that on my part they are cordially reciprocated.

From other sources as well as from your letter I learn that the feeling on the Continent strongly favors the abolition of privateering upon the ocean. Whatever may be the policy of other Powers, the United States can never consent to this policy. We might with nearly the same propriety agree to abandon our system of volunteers and militia on the land and trust alone to the regular army as to deprive ourselves of the services of Privateers, which are our volunteers and militia upon the ocean. Neither would this abandonment of itself afford security to our commerce. If the right to blockade merchant vessels in our Ports should remain, we would have but few of them on the ocean to protect from privateering. A British fleet, by blockading the mouth of the Chesapeake, could effectually prevent any merchant vessel from going to sea from any port situated on that noble Bay or its tributary rivers. So in regard to New Orleans, New York, &c. &c. The truth is that we are comparatively with several of the nations of Europe a weak naval power, and our deficiency in guns can only be supplied by our Privateers, who would sweep the ocean as they did in our last war with England.

I have viewed with admiration the gigantic and successful struggles of your friend Louis Napoleon to overcome the difficulties of his situation. He is undoubtedly the man of the age. I am truly gratified that he thinks kindly of me. I have nothing more at heart than to preserve the most friendly relations with his Government during the brief remaining period of my administration. I have been in an inevitable storm since its commencement, and I shall retire from office on the 4th March, 1861, with much greater pleasure than when I assumed its cares on the 4th March, 1857. I have still, thank Providence, been generally

---

[1] Buchanan Papers, Historical Society of Pennsylvania.

successful, and hope to leave the Government in a better condition than I found it.

With my kindest regards to Mrs. Vail, I remain always sincerely and respectfully

Your friend

JAMES BUCHANAN.

HON. A. VAIL.

MESSAGE

ON MEMORIALS FROM THE EASTERN SLOPE OF THE
ROCKY MOUNTAINS.[1]

[February 20, 1860.]

To THE SENATE AND HOUSE OF REPRESENTATIVES
　　OF THE UNITED STATES:

Eight memorials, numerously signed by our fellow-citizens, "residents for the most part within the territorial limits of Kansas and Nebraska, at and near the eastern slope of the Rocky mountains," have been presented to me, containing the request that I would submit the condition of the memorialists to the two houses of Congress in a special message. Accordingly, I transmit four of these memorials to the Senate and four to the House of Representatives.

These memorialists invoke the interposition of Congress and the Executive for "the early extinguishment of the Indian title, a consequent survey and sale of the public lands, and the establishment of an assay office in the immediate and daily reach of the citizens of that region." They also urge "the erection of a new Territory from contiguous portions of New Mexico, Utah, Kansas, and Nebraska," with the boundaries set forth in their memorial. They further state, if this request should not be granted: "That (inasmuch as during this year a census is to be taken) an enabling act be passed, with provisions, upon condition that if, on the 1st day of July, 1860, thirty thousand resident

----

[1] S. Ex. Doc. 15, 36 Cong. 1 Sess.

inhabitants be found within the limits of the mineral region, then a territorial government is constituted by executive proclamation; or if, on the 1st day of September, 1860, one hundred and fifty thousand shall be returned, then a State organization to occur."

In transmitting these memorials to Congress, I recommend that such provision may be made for the protection and prosperity of our fellow-citizens at and near the eastern slope of the Rocky mountains, as their distance and the exigencies of their condition may require from their government.

JAMES BUCHANAN.

WASHINGTON, February 20, 1860.

MESSAGE

ON A LETTER OF THE FRENCH EMPEROR.[1]

[February 25, 1860.]

TO THE HOUSE OF REPRESENTATIVES:

In compliance with the resolution of the House of Representatives of the 16th instant, requesting a copy of a letter of the Emperor of France upon the subject of commerce and free trade, I transmit a report from the Secretary of State, to whom the resolution was referred.

JAMES BUCHANAN.

WASHINGTON, February 25, 1860.

---

[1] H. Ex. Doc. 30, 36 Cong. 1 Sess. The report of the Secretary of State, dated February 25, says "that the letter of the Emperor of the French referred to in the resolution has not been communicated to the Executive by the government of France, nor has it been officially communicated by the acting chargé d'affaires of the United States at Paris. With a despatch, however, of the 17th of January last, Mr. Calhoun transmitted, for the information of this department, a printed copy of the Emperor's letter, taken from the Moniteur of the 10th of that month, a translation of which accompanies this report."

TO MR. BAKER.[1]

WASHINGTON 28 February 1860.

MY DEAR SIR/

I am still decidedly of opinion that it would be wise to elect Gov: Bigler as a Delegate at large to Charleston. In his senatorial character he has ever been true & faithful to my administration, & has the warm regard of his brother Democratic Senators.

I need scarcely say that all allusion to myself as a Candidate for the Presidency ought to be avoided. Both my inclination & my judgment concur in the firm resolution I have adopted & proclaimed, not under any circumstances to be a Candidate.

I trust all things may go off well at the Reading Convention. I think it would be dangerous to select a Candidate for Governor who could not meet Curtin on the stump.

From your friend very respectfully

JAMES BUCHANAN.

J. B. BAKER, ESQUIRE.

MESSAGE

ON THE OREGON BOUNDARY.[2]

[February 29, 1860.]

TO THE SENATE OF THE UNITED STATES:

In answer to the resolution of the Senate of yesterday, requesting information with regard to the present condition of the work of marking the boundary, pursuant to the first article of the treaty between the United States and Great Britain of the 15th of June, 1846, I transmit a report from the Secretary of State, and the papers by which it was accompanied.

JAMES BUCHANAN.

WASHINGTON, February 29, 1860.

---

[1] Buchanan Papers, Historical Society of Pennsylvania.
[2] S. Ex. Doc. 16, 36 Cong. 1 Sess.

MESSAGE

ON THE HEATING OF CERTAIN PUBLIC BUILDINGS.[1]

WASHINGTON, March 1, 1860.

TO THE SENATE OF THE UNITED STATES:

I transmit herewith, in compliance with the resolution of the Senate of the 1st of February, 1860, a report from the Secretary of War, communicating the information desired relative to the payments, agreements, arrangements, etc., in connection with the heating and ventilating of the Capitol and Post Office extensions.

JAMES BUCHANAN.

MESSAGE

ON AFFAIRS ON THE RIO GRANDE.[2]

[March 5, 1860.]

TO THE SENATE OF THE UNITED STATES:

In compliance with the resolution of the Senate of the 23d of February, 1860,[3] I transmit to that body a communication of the Secretary of War, furnishing all the information requested in said resolution.

JAMES BUCHANAN.

WASHINGTON, March 5, 1860.

---

[1] Richardson's Messages and Papers of the Presidents, V. 581.

[2] S. Ex. Doc. 21, 36 Cong. 1 Sess.

[3] The resolution requested the transmission to the Senate of any communication from the Governor of Texas, and the documents accompanying it, concerning alleged hostilities existing on the Rio Grande between the citizens or the military authorities of Mexico and that State.

MESSAGE

ON A TREATY WITH MEXICO.[1]

[March 8, 1860.]

To THE SENATE OF THE UNITED STATES:

I transmit herewith a report from the Secretary of State, together with the papers accompanying it, in answer to the resolution of the Senate in executive session of the 28th ultimo, calling for the instructions to our minister or ministers in Mexico which resulted in the negotiation of the treaty with that country now before the Senate.

JAMES BUCHANAN.

WASHINGTON, 8th March, 1860.

MESSAGE

ON CORRESPONDENCE WITH CHINA.[2]

[March 12, 1860.]

To THE SENATE OF THE UNITED STATES:

In answer to the resolution of the Senate, of the 6th ultimo, requesting copies of the instructions to, and despatches from, the late and from the present minister of the United States in China, down to the period of the exchange of ratifications of the treaty of Tientsin; and also a copy of the instructions from the Department of State of February, 1857, to Mr. Parker, former commissioner in China, I transmit a report from the Secretary of State, and the papers by which it was accompanied.

JAMES BUCHANAN.

WASHINGTON, March 12, 1860.

---

[1] Senate Executive Journal, XI. 156.
[2] S. Ex. Doc. 30, 36 Cong. 1 Sess.

MESSAGE

ON AFFAIRS IN MEXICO.[1]

[March 15, 1860.]

To the Senate of the United States:

In compliance with the resolution of the Senate in executive session, on the 12th instant, I transmit a report from the Secretary of State, with the accompanying copies of Mr. Churchwell's correspondence.[2]

JAMES BUCHANAN.

WASHINGTON, March 15th, 1860.

MESSAGE

ON AFFAIRS ON THE RIO GRANDE.[3]

[March 15, 1860.]

To the Senate of the United States:

Referring to my communication of the 5th instant to the Senate, in answer to its resolution of the 23d February, calling for any communication which may have been received from the governor of Texas, and the documents accompanying it, concerning alleged hostilities now existing on the Rio Grande, I have the honor herewith to submit for the consideration of that body the following papers:

Despatch from the Secretary of War to the governor of Texas, dated 28th February, 1860.

Despatch from the governor of Texas to the Secretary of War, dated 8th March, 1860.

Despatch from the Acting Secretary of War to the governor of Texas, dated 14th March, 1860.

JAMES BUCHANAN.

WASHINGTON, March 15, 1860.

---

[1] Senate Executive Journal, XI. 160.

[2] The resolution of the Senate called for the report of the agent sent to Mexico to ascertain the condition of that country.

[3] S. Ex. Doc. 24, 36 Cong. 1 Sess.

MESSAGE

ON THE CAPITOL EXTENSION.[1]

[March 16, 1860.]

To THE SENATE OF THE UNITED STATES:

I transmit herewith a report from the Acting Secretary of War, with its accompanying papers, communicating the information called for by the resolution of the Senate, of the 9th instant, respecting the marble columns for the Capitol extension.

JAMES BUCHANAN.

WASHINGTON, March 16, 1860.

MESSAGE

ON A CONVENTION WITH PARAGUAY.[2]

[March 16, 1860.]

To THE SENATE AND HOUSE OF REPRESENTATIVES:

I transmit a copy of the convention between the United States and the republic of Paraguay, concluded on the 4th of February, 1859, and proclaimed on the 12th instant, and invite the attention of Congress to the expediency of such legislation as may be deemed necessary to carry into effect the stipulations of the convention relative to the organization of the commission provided for therein.

The commissioner on the part of Paraguay is now in this city, and is prepared to enter upon the duties devolved upon the joint commission.

JAMES BUCHANAN.

WASHINGTON, March 16, 1860.

---

[1] S. Ex. Doc. 22, 36 Cong. 1 Sess.
[2] H. Ex. Doc. 48, 36 Cong. 1 Sess. 1.

MESSAGE

ON A TREATY WITH NICARAGUA.[1]

[March 21, 1860.]

To the Senate of the United States:

In compliance with the request of the Senate contained in their resolution of yesterday, the 20th instant, I return to them the resolution of the 16th instant, " that the Senate do not advise and consent to the ratification of the treaty of friendship and commerce beween the United States and Nicaragua, signed at Managua on the 16th day of March, 1859." I also return the treaty itself, presuming that the Senate so intended.

James Buchanan.

Washington, 21 March, 1860.

MESSAGE

ON A TREATY WITH SWEDEN AND NORWAY.[2]

[March 22, 1860.]

To the Senate of the United States:

I transmit to the Senate, for its consideration with a view to ratification, a convention concluded on the 21st instant between the United States and His Majesty the King of Sweden and Norway for the mutual surrender of fugitive criminals.

James Buchanan.

Washington, March 22, 1860.

---

[1] Senate Executive Journal, XI. 165.
[2] Senate Executive Journal, XI. 167.

MESSAGE

ON THE COVODE INVESTIGATION.[1]

[March 28, 1860.]

To the House of Representatives of the United States:

After a delay which has afforded me ample time for reflection, and after much and careful deliberation, I find myself constrained by an imperious sense of duty, as a co-ordinate branch of the Federal Government, to protest against the first two clauses of the first resolution adopted by the House of Representatives on the 5th instant, and published in the Congressional Globe on the succeeding day. These clauses are in the following words: " *Resolved*, That a committee of five members be appointed by the speaker, for the purpose, 1st, of investigating whether the President of the United States, or any other officer of the Government, has, by money, patronage, or other improper means, sought to influence the action of Congress, or any committee thereof, for or against the passage of any law appertaining to the rights of any State or Territory; and 2d, ' also to inquire into and investigate whether any officer or officers of the Government have, by combination or otherwise, prevented or defeated, or attempted to prevent or defeat, the execution of any law or laws now upon the statute-book; and whether the President has failed or refused to compel the execution of any law thereof.' "

I confine myself exclusively to these two branches of the resolution, because the portions of it which follow relate to alleged abuses in post-offices, navy-yards, public buildings, and other public works of the United States. In such cases inquiries are highly proper in themselves, and belong equally to the Senate and the House as incident to their legislative duties, and being necessary to enable them to discover and to provide the appropriate legislative remedies for any abuses which may be ascertained. Although the terms of the latter portion of the resolution are extremely vague and general, yet my sole purpose in adverting to them at present is to mark the broad line of distinction between the accusatory and the remedial clauses of this resolution. The House of Representatives possess no power

---

[1] H. Ex. Doc. 50, 36 Cong. 1 Sess. See message of June 22, 1860, infra.

under the Constitution over the first or accusatory portion of the resolution, except as an impeaching body; whilst over the last, in common with the Senate, their authority as a legislative body is fully and cheerfully admitted.

It is solely in reference to the first or impeaching power that I propose to make a few observations. Except in this single case, the Constitution has invested the House of Representatives with no power, no jurisdiction, no supremacy whatever over the President. In all other respects he is quite as independent of them as they are of him. As a co-ordinate branch of the Government, he is their equal. Indeed, he is the only direct representative on earth of the people of all and each of the sovereign States. To them, and to them alone, is he responsible whilst acting within the sphere of his constitutional duty, and not in any manner to the House of Representatives. The people have thought proper to invest him with the most honorable, responsible, and dignified office in the world; and the individual, however unworthy, now holding this exalted position, will take care, so far as in him lies, that their rights and prerogatives shall never be violated in his person, but shall pass to his successors unimpaired by the adoption of a dangerous precedent. He will defend them to the last extremity against any unconstitutional attempt, come from what quarter it may, to abridge the constitutional rights of the Executive, and render him subservient to any human power except themselves.

The people have not confined the President to the exercise of executive duties. They have also conferred upon him a large measure of legislative discretion. No bill can become a law without his approval, as representing the people of the United States, unless it shall pass after his veto by a majority of two-thirds of both Houses. In his legislative capacity, he might, in common with the Senate and the House, institute an inquiry to ascertain any facts which ought to influence his judgment in approving or vetoing any bill.

This participation in the performance of legislative duties between the co-ordinate branches of the Government ought to inspire the conduct of all of them, in their relations towards each other, with mutual forbearance and respect. At least each has a right to demand justice from the other. The cause of complaint is, that the constitutional rights and immunities of the Executive have been violated in the person of the President.

The trial of an impeachment of the President before the Senate on charges preferred and prosecuted against him by the House of Representatives would be an imposing spectacle for the world. In the result, not only his removal from the presidential office would be involved, but, what is of infinitely greater importance to himself, his character, both in the eyes of the present and of future generations, might possibly be tarnished. The disgrace cast upon him would in some degree be reflected upon the character of the American people who elected him. Hence the precautions adopted by the Constitution to secure a fair trial. On such a trial it declares that " the Chief Justice shall preside." This was doubtless because the framers of the Constitution believed it to be possible that the Vice-President might be biased by the fact that, " in case of the removal of the President from office," " the same shall devolve on the Vice-President."

The preliminary proceedings in the House in the case of charges which may involve impeachment have been well and wisely settled by long practice upon principles of equal justice both to the accused and to the people. The precedent established in the case of Judge Peck, of Missouri, in 1831, after a careful review of all former precedents, will, I venture to predict, stand the test of time.

In that case, Luke Edward Lawless, the accuser, presented a petition to the House, in which he set forth minutely and specifically his causes of complaint. He prayed " that the conduct and proceeding in this behalf of said Judge Peck may be inquired into by your honorable body, and such decision made thereon as to your wisdom and justice shall seem proper." This petition was referred to the Judiciary Committee; such has ever been deemed the appropriate committee to make similar investigations. It is a standing committee supposed to be appointed without reference to any special case, and at all times is presumed to be composed of the most eminent lawyers in the House from different portions of the Union, whose acquaintance with judicial proceedings and whose habits of investigation qualify them peculiarly for the task. No tribunal, from their position and character, could in the nature of things be more impartial. In the case of Judge Peck the witnesses were selected by the committee itself, with a view to ascertain the truth of the charge. They were cross-examined by him, and everything was conducted in such a manner as to afford him no reasonable cause of complaint.

In view of this precedent, and, what is of far greater importance, in view of the Constitution and the principles of eternal justice, in what manner has the President of the United States been treated by the House of Representatives? Mr. John Covode, a Representative from Pennsylvania, is the accuser of the President. Instead of following the wise precedents of former times, and especially that in the case of Judge Peck, and referring the accusation to the Committee on the Judiciary, the House have made my accuser one of my judges.

To make the accuser the judge is a violation of the principles of universal justice, and is condemned by the practice of all civilized nations. Every freeman must revolt at such a spectacle. I am to appear before Mr. Covode, either personally or by a substitute, to cross-examine the witnesses which he may produce before himself to sustain his own accusations against me; and perhaps even this poor boon may be denied to the President.

And what is the nature of the investigation which his resolution proposes to institute? It is as vague and general as the English language affords words in which to make it. The committee is to inquire, not into any specific charge or charges, but whether the President has, by "money, patronage, or other improper means, sought to influence," not the action of any individual member or members of Congress, but "the action" of the entire body "of Congress" itself, "or any committee thereof." The President might have had some glimmering of the nature of the offence to be investigated, had his accuser pointed to the act or acts of Congress which he sought to pass or to defeat by the employment of "money, patronage, or other improper means." But the accusation is bounded by no such limits. It extends to the whole circle of legislation; to interference "for or against the passage of any law appertaining to the rights of any State or Territory." And what law does not appertain to the rights of some State or Territory? And what law or laws has the President failed to execute? These might easily have been pointed out, had any such existed.

Had Mr. Lawless asked an inquiry to be made by the House, whether Judge Peck, in general terms, had not violated his judicial duties, without the specification of any particular act, I do not believe there would have been a single vote in that body in favor of the inquiry.

Since the time of the Star Chamber and of general warrants there has been no such proceeding in England.

The House of Representatives, the high impeaching power of the country, without consenting to hear a word of explanation, have indorsed this accusation against the President, and made it their own act. They even refused to permit a member to inquire of the President's accuser what were the specific charges against him. Thus, in this preliminary accusation of " high crimes and misdemeanors " against a co-ordinate branch of the Government, under the impeaching power, the House refused to hear a single suggestion even in regard to the correct mode of proceeding, but, without a moment's delay, passed the accusatory resolution under the pressure of the previous question.

In the institution of a prosecution for any offence against the most humble citizen—and I claim for myself no greater rights than he enjoys—the Constitution of the United States, and of the several States, require that he shall be informed in the very beginning of the nature and cause of the accusation against him, in order to enable him to prepare for his defence. There are other principles which I might enumerate, not less sacred, presenting an impenetrable shield to protect every citizen falsely charged with a criminal offence. These have been violated in the prosecution instituted by the House of Representatives against the executive branch of the Government. Shall the President alone be deprived of the protection of these great principles which prevail in every land where a ray of liberty penetrates the gloom of despotism? Shall the Executive alone be deprived of rights which all his fellow-citizens enjoy? The whole proceeding against him justifies the fears of those wise and great men who, before the Constitution was adopted by the States, apprehended that the tendency of the Government was to the aggrandizement of the legislative at the expense of the executive and judicial departments.

I again declare, emphatically, that I make this protest for no reason personal to myself; and I do it with perfect respect for the House of Representatives, in which I had the honor of serving as a member for five successive terms. I have lived long in this goodly land, and have enjoyed all the offices and honors which my country could bestow. Amid all the political storms through which I have passed, the present is the first attempt which has ever been made, to my knowledge, to assail my personal or official integrity; and this as the time is approaching when I shall voluntarily retire from the service of my country. I feel proudly conscious that there is no public act of my life which will not bear the strictest scrutiny. I defy all investigation. Nothing but the basest perjury can sully my good name. I do not fear even this, because I cherish an humble confidence that the Gracious Being who has hitherto defended and protected me against the shafts of falsehood and malice will not desert me now, when I have become " old and gray-headed." I can declare, before God and my country, that no human being (with an exception scarcely worthy of notice) has, at any period of my life, dared to approach me with a corrupt or dishonorable proposition; and, until recent developments, it had never entered into my imagination that any person, even in the storm of exasperated political excitement, would charge me, in the most remote degree, with having made such a proposition to any human being. I may now, however, exclaim in the language of complaint employed by my first and greatest predecessor, that I have been abused " in such exaggerated and indecent terms as could scarcely be applied to a Nero, to a notorious defaulter, or even to a common pickpocket."

I do, therefore, for the reasons stated, and in the name of the people of the several States, solemnly protest against these proceedings of the House of Representatives, because they are in violation of the rights of the co-ordinate executive branch of the Government, and subversive of its constitutional independence; because they are calculated to foster a band of interested parasites and informers, ever ready, for their own advantage, to swear before *ex parte* committees to pretended private conversations between the President and themselves, incapable, from their nature, of being disproved, thus furnishing material for harassing him, degrading him in the eyes of the country, and eventually, should he be a weak or a timid man, rendering him subservient to improper influences, in order to avoid such persecutions and annoyances; because they tend to destroy that harmonious action for the common good which ought to be maintained, and which I sincerely desire to cherish between co-ordinate branches of the

Government; and, finally, because, if unresisted, they would establish a precedent dangerous and embarrassing to all my successors, to whatever political party they might be attached.

                                    JAMES BUCHANAN.

March 28, 1860.[1]

MESSAGE

ON THE SOUTHWESTERN FRONTIER.[2]

                                    [March 29, 1860.]

TO THE HOUSE OF REPRESENTATIVES:

I transmit herewith a report of the Secretary of War, with its accompaniments, communicating the information called for by the resolution of the House of Representatives of the 1st instant, concerning the difficulties on the southwestern frontier.

                                    JAMES BUCHANAN.

WASHINGTON, March 29, 1860.

---

[1] The House, after a protracted debate, passed, on the 8th day of June, by a vote of 87 yeas against 40 nays, the following resolutions:

"*Resolved,* That the House dissents from the doctrines of the special message of the President of the United States of March 28, 1860;

"That the extent of power contemplated in the adoption of the resolution of inquiry of March 5, 1860, is necessary to the proper discharge of the constitutional duties devolved upon Congress;

"That judicial determinations, the opinions of former Presidents, and uniform usage sanction its exercise; and

"That to abandon it would leave the executive department of the Government without supervision or responsibility, and would be likely to lead to a concentration of power in the hands of the President, dangerous to the rights of a free people." (Veto Messages: S. Misc. Doc. 53, 49 Cong. 2 Sess. 279.)

[2] H. Ex. Doc. 52, 36 Cong. 1 Sess.

MESSAGE

ON AFFAIRS ON THE MEXICAN COAST.[1]

[March 29, 1860.]

To the Senate of the United States:

In compliance with the resolution of the Senate of the 21st of March, 1860, requesting the President of the United States " to inform the Senate, if, in his opinion, it be not incompatible with the public interest, if any instructions have been given to any of the officers of the navy of the United States by which, in any event, the naval force of the United States, or any part thereof, were to take part in the civil war now existing in Mexico; and if the recent capture of two war steamers of Mexico by the naval force of the United States was done in pursuance of orders issued by this government; and also by what authority those steamers have been taken in possession by the naval force of the United States, and the men on board made prisoners," I transmit the inclosed report, with accompanying papers, from the Secretary of the Navy.

JAMES BUCHANAN.

WASHINGTON, March 29, 1860.

MESSAGE

ON THE IMPRISONMENT OF AN AMERICAN CITIZEN IN CUBA.[2]

[March 30, 1860.]

To the House of Representatives:

In answer to the resolution of the 26th instant, requesting information touching the imprisonment of an American citizen in the Island of Cuba, I transmit a report from the Secretary of State and the documents by which it was accompanied.

JAMES BUCHANAN.

WASHINGTON, March 30, 1860.

---

[1] S. Ex. Doc. 29, 36 Cong. 1 Sess.

[2] H. Ex. Doc. 54, 36 Cong. 1 Sess. The case referred to was that of a native of Spain who was naturalized in the United States, and who, upon visiting Cuba, was held for military service.

MESSAGE

ON DIPLOMATIC COSTUME.[1]

[April 2, 1860.]

To the Senate of the United States:

In compliance with the resolution of the Senate, of the 28th February last, relative to the uniform or costume of persons in the diplomatic or consular service, I transmit a report from the Secretary of State, and the papers by which it was accompanied.

JAMES BUCHANAN.

WASHINGTON, April 2, 1860.

MESSAGE

ON AFFAIRS IN UTAH.[2]

[April 3, 1860.]

To the Senate of the United States:

I herewith transmit to the Senate a report of the Attorney General, in answer to a resolution of the Senate of the 21st March, " that the President be· respectfully requested to communicate to the Senate the correspondence between the judges of Utah and the Attorney General or the President, with reference to the legal proceedings and condition of affairs in the Territory of Utah."

JAMES BUCHANAN.

WASHINGTON CITY, April 3, 1860.

---

[1] S. Ex. Doc. 31, 36 Cong. 1 Sess.
[2] S. Ex. Doc. 32, 36 Cong. 1 Sess.

TO MR. HOLT.[1]

WASHINGTON 4 April 1860.

MY DEAR SIR

I have received your favor of the 29 ultimo and regret deeply to learn the condition of Mrs. Holt. It cannot for a moment be questioned that you have adopted the proper course. Every feeling of my heart sanctions and approves it. I have no doubt we shall get along very well with the Department during your absence, though not nearly so well as if you were present. I beg you not to suffer your absence to give you the least uneasiness. Providence will direct all things right. With my kindest regards to Mrs. Holt, I remain always your friend

JAMES BUCHANAN.

HON : JOSEPH HOLT.

MESSAGE

ON A TREATY WITH HONDURAS AND ON INTEROCEANIC TRANSIT.[2]

[April 5, 1860.]

TO THE SENATE OF THE UNITED STATES :

I transmit, for the consideration of the Senate with a view to ratification, a treaty of friendship, commerce, and navigation between the United States and the Republic of Honduras, signed by the plenipotentiaries of the parties in this city on the 28th day of last month.

The fourteenth article of this treaty is an exact copy of the supplemental article of the " treaty of friendship, commerce, and navigation between Great Britain and the Republic of Honduras," dated 26th day of August, 1856, with the necessary changes in names and dates. Under this article the Government and people of the United States will enjoy, in the fullest and most satisfac-

---

[1] Holt Papers, Library of Congress.
[2] Senate Executive Journal, XI. 171.

tory manner, the use of the " Honduras Interoceanic Railway," in consideration of which the United States recognizes the rights of sovereignty and property of Honduras over the line of the road and guarantees its neutrality, and, when " the road shall have been completed, equally engages, in conjunction with Honduras, to protect the same from interruption, seizure, or unjust confiscation, from whatever quarter the attempt may proceed."

This treaty is in accordance with the policy inaugurated by the Government of the United States, and in an especial manner by the Senate, in the year 1846, and several treaties have been concluded to carry it into effect. It is simple, and may be embraced in a few words. On the one side a grant of free and uninterrupted transit for the Government and people of the United States over the transit routes across the Isthmus, and on the other, a guaranty of the neutrality and protection of these routes, not only for the benefit of the Republics through which they pass, but, in the language of our treaty with New Granada, in order to secure to themselves the tranquil and constant enjoyment of these interoceanic communications.

The first in the series of these treaties is that with New Granada, of the 12th·December, 1846. This treaty was concluded before our acquisition of California, and when our interests on the Pacific Coast were of far less magnitude than at the present day. For years before this period, however, the routes across the Isthmus had attracted the serious attention of this Government.

This treaty, after granting us the right of transit across the Isthmus of Panama in the most ample terms, binds this Government to guarantee to New Granada " the perfect neutrality of the before-mentioned Isthmus, with the view that the free transit from the one to the other sea may not be interrupted or embarrassed in any future time while this treaty exists."

In one respect it goes further than any of its successors, because it not only guarantees the neutrality of the route itself, but " the rights of sovereignty and property " of New Granada over the entire Province of Panama. It is worthy of remark that when it was sent to the Senate it was accompanied by a message of President Polk, dated February 10, 1847, in which the attention of that body was especially called to these important stipulations of the thirty-fifth article, and in which it was stated, moreover, that our chargé d'affaires who negotiated the treaty "acted in this particular upon his own responsibility and without instructions." Under these circumstances the treaty was approved by the Senate, and the transit policy to which I have referred was deliberately adopted. A copy of the executive document (confidential), Twenty-ninth Congress, second session, containing this message of President Polk, and the papers which accompanied it, is hereto annexed.

The next in order of time of these treaties of transit and guaranty is that of the 19th of April, 1850, with Great Britain, commonly called the Clayton and Bulwer treaty. This treaty, in affirmance of the policy of the New Granada treaty, established a general principle which has ever since, I believe, guided the proceedings of both Governments. The eighth article of that treaty contains the following stipulations: "The Government of the United States having not only desired in entering into this convention to accomplish a particular object, but also to establish a general principle, they hereby agree to extend their protection, by treaty stipulations, to any other practicable communications, whether by canal or railway, across the isthmus which connects North and South America, and especially to the interoceanic communications, should the same prove to be practicable, whether by canal or railway, which are now proposed to be established by the way of Tehuantepec or Panama." And the said "canals or railways shall also be opened on like terms to the citizens and subjects of every other State which is willing to grant thereto such protection as the United States and Great Britain propose to afford."

The United States, in a short time after the Clayton and Bulwer treaty was concluded, carried this stipulation in regard to the Tehuantepec route into effect by their treaty with Mexico of the 30th December, 1853. The eighth article of this treaty, after granting to us the transit privileges therein mentioned, stipulates that "the Mexican Government having agreed to protect with its whole power the prosecution, preservation, and security of the work, the United States may extend its protection, as it shall judge wise to use it, when it may feel sanctioned and warranted by the public or international law."

This is a sweeping grant of power to the United States which no nation ought to have conceded, but which, it is believed, has been confined within safe limits by our treaty with Mexico now before the Senate.

Such was believed to be the established policy of the Government at the commencement of this Administration, viz., the grant of transits in our favor, and the guaranty of our protection as an equivalent. This guaranty can never be dangerous under our form of government, because it can never be carried into execution without the express authority of Congress. Still, standing on the face of treaties, as it does, it deters all evil-disposed parties from interfering with these routes.

Under such circumstances the attention of the Executive was early turned to the Nicaragua route as in many respects the most important and valuable to the citizens of our country. In concluding a treaty to secure our rights of transit over this route, I experienced many difficulties, which I need not now enumerate, because they are detailed in different messages to Congress. Finally a treaty was negotiated exactly in accordance with the established policy of the Government and the views of the Executive, and clear from the embarrassments which might arise under the phraseology of previous treaties. The fourteenth article of the treaty contains a full, clear, and specific grant of the right of transit to the United States and their citizens, and is believed to be perfectly unexceptionable. The fifteenth article, instead of leaving one equivalent duty of protection, general and unlimited, as in our treaty with New Granada, and in the Clayton and Bulwer treaty, or instead of that general right assured to the Government in the Mexican treaty of extending its protection as it shall itself judge wise, when it may feel sanctioned and warranted by the public or international law, confines the interference conceded within just and specific limits.

Under the sixteenth article of this treaty, the Government of the United States has no right to interpose for the protection of the Nicaragua route, except with the consent or at the request of the Government of Nicaragua or of the minister thereof at Washington, or of the competent, legally appointed local authorities, civil or military; and when in the opinion of the Government of Nicaragua the necessity ceases, such force shall be immediately withdrawn. Nothing can be more carefully guarded than this provision. No force can be employed unless upon the request of the Government of Nicaragua, and it must be immediately withdrawn whenever in the opinion of that Government the necessity ceases.

When Congress shall come to adopt the measures necessary to carry this provision of the treaty into effect, they can guard it from any abuses which may possibly arise.

The general policy contained in these articles, although inaugurated by the United States, has been fully adopted by the Government of Great Britain and France. The plenipotentiaries of both these Governments have recently negotiated treaties with Nicaragua, which are but transcripts of the treaty between the United States and Nicaragua now before the Senate. The treaty with France has been ratified, it is understood, by both the French and Nicaraguan Governments, and is now in operation. That with Great Britain has been delayed by other negotiations in Nicaragua, but it is believed that these are now concluded and that the ratifications of the British treaty will soon, therefore, be exchanged.

It is presumed that no objection will be made to " the exceptional case " of the sixteenth article, which is only intended to provide for the landing of sailors or marines from our vessels which may happen to be within reach of the point of difficulty, in order to protect the lives and property of citizens of the United States from unforeseen and imminent danger.

The same considerations may be suggested with respect to the fifth article of the treaty with Mexico, which is also pending before the Senate. This article is an exact copy of the sixteenth article, just referred to, of the treaty with Nicaragua.

The treaty with Honduras, which is now submitted to the Senate, follows on this subject the language of the British treaty with that Republic, and is not, therefore, identical in its terms with the Nicaraguan and Mexican treaties. The same policy, however, has been adopted in all of them, and it will not fail, I am persuaded, to receive from the Senate all that consideration which it so eminently deserves. The importance to the United States of securing free and safe transit routes across the American Isthmus can not well be overestimated. These routes are of great interest, of course, to all commercial nations; but they are especially so to us, from our geographical and political position as an American State, and because they furnish a necessary communication between our Atlantic and Pacific States and Territories.

The Government of the United States can never permit these routes to be permanently interrupted, nor can it safely allow them to pass under the control of other rival nations. While it seeks no exclusive privileges upon them for itself, it can never consent to be made tributary to their use by any European power. It is worthy of consideration, however, whether, to some extent, it would not necessarily become so, if, after Great Britain and France have adopted our policy and made treaties with the Isthmian Governments, in pursuance of it, we should ourselves reconsider it and refuse to pursue it in the treaties of the United States. I might add that the opening of these transit routes can not fail to extend the trade and commerce of the United States with the countries through which they pass; to afford an outlet and a market for our manufactures within their territories; to encourage American citizens to develop their vast stores of mining and mineral wealth for our benefit; and to introduce among them a wholesome American influence calculated to prevent revolutions and to render their governments stable.

JAMES BUCHANAN.

WASHINGTON, April 5, 1860.

MESSAGE

ON THE EXPULSION OF AMERICANS FROM MEXICO.[1]

[April 10, 1860.]

TO THE HOUSE OF REPRESENTATIVES:

I communicate herewith a report from the Secretary of State, in reply to the resolution of the House of Representatives of the 6th instant, respecting the expulsion of American citizens from Mexico, and the confiscation of their property by General Miramon.

JAMES BUCHANAN.

WASHINGTON, April 10, 1860.

---

[1] H. Ex. Doc. 59, 36 Cong. 1 Sess.

MESSAGE

ON DUTIES ON TOBACCO.[1]

[April 10, 1860.]

TO THE HOUSE OF REPRESENTATIVES:

In compliance with the resolution of the House of Representatives of the 23d of December, 1858, requesting information in regard to the duties on tobacco in foreign countries, I transmit a report from the Secretary of State, and the documents by which it was accompanied.

JAMES BUCHANAN.

WASHINGTON, April 10, 1860.

———

MESSAGE

ON THE HARLEM RIVER.[2]

[April 11, 1860.]

TO THE HOUSE OF REPRESENTATIVES OF THE UNITED STATES:

In compliance with the resolution of the House of Representatives of March 26, 1860, requesting me " to transmit to the House all information in the possession of the officer in charge of the Coast Survey showing the practicability of making Harlem river navigable for commercial purposes, and the expenses thereof," I herewith transmit a report from the Secretary of the Treasury containing the desired information.

JAMES BUCHANAN.

WASHINGTON, D. C., April 11, 1860.

———

[1] H. Ex. Doc. 60, 36 Cong. 1 Sess.
[2] H. Ex. Doc. 64, 36 Cong. 1 Sess.

MESSAGE

ON COMPULSORY ENLISTMENTS IN PRUSSIA.[1]

[April 11, 1860.]

TO THE SENATE OF THE UNITED STATES:

In compliance with the resolution of the Senate of the 2d February, 1859, requesting information in regard to the compulsory enlistment of citizens of the United States in the army of Prussia, I transmit a report from the Secretary of State, and the documents by which it was accompanied.

JAMES BUCHANAN.

WASHINGTON, April 11, 1860.

MESSAGE

ON NAVASSA ISLAND.[2]

[April 12, 1860.]

In compliance with the resolution of the Senate, of the 23d of February last, requesting information in regard to the occupation by American citizens of the Island of Navassa, in the West Indies, I transmit a report from the Secretary of State and the documents by which it was accompanied.

JAMES BUCHANAN.

WASHINGTON, April 12, 1860.

---

[1] S. Ex. Doc. 38, 36 Cong. 1 Sess.
[2] S. Ex. Doc. 37, 36 Cong. 1 Sess. See Moore, International Law Digest, I. 266–267, 299, 577.

MESSAGE

ON INDIAN HOSTILITIES IN NEW MEXICO.[1]

WASHINGTON, April 12, 1860.

TO THE HOUSE OF REPRESENTATIVES:

I transmit, herewith, a report of the Secretary of War, with its accompaniments, communicating the information called for by the resolution of the House of Representatives of the 20th ultimo, respecting Indian hostilities in New Mexico.

JAMES BUCHANAN.

TO MR. PLUMER.[2]

WASHINGTON CITY 14 April 1860.

MY DEAR SIR/

I address you not only as a Delegate from Pennsylvania to the Charleston Democratic National Convention, but as an old & valued friend. Whilst trusting that no member of that Body will propose my name as a Candidate for re-election, yet lest this might possibly prove to be the case, I require you then immediately to inform the Convention, as an act of justice to myself, that in no contingency can I ever again consent to become a Candidate for the Presidency. My purpose to this effect was clearly indicated both in accepting the Cincinnati nomination & afterwards in my Inaugural address, & has since been repeated on various occasions, both public & private. In this determination neither my judgment nor my inclination has ever for a moment wavered. Deeply grateful to the great

---

[1] H. Ex. Doc. 69, 36 Cong. 1 Sess.

[2] Buchanan Papers, Historical Society of Pennsylvania; Curtis's Buchanan, II. 286. Arnold Plumer was a representative in Congress from 1837 to 1839, and again from 1841 to 1843. He was afterwards United States marshal for the Western District of Pennsylvania. Mr. Plumer was very influential in politics, and was a warm friend of Mr. Buchanan.

Democratic party of the Country, on whose continued ascendancy, as I verily believe, the prosperity & perpetuity of our Confederated Republic depend, & praying Heaven that the Convention may select as their Candidate an able, sound, and conservative Democrat in whose support we can all cordially unite, I remain

Very respectfully your friend

JAMES BUCHANAN.

HON: ARNOLD PLUMER.

MESSAGE

ON COMPULSORY ENLISTMENTS ABROAD.[1]

[April 16, 1860.]

TO THE SENATE OF THE UNITED STATES:

In compliance with the resolution of the Senate of the 4th instant, requesting information not heretofore called for relating to the claim of any foreign government to the military services of naturalized American citizens, I transmit a report from the Secretary of State and the documents by which it was accompanied.

JAMES BUCHANAN.

WASHINGTON, April 16, 1860.

---

[1] S. Ex. Doc. 38, 36 Cong. 1 Sess. 154.

MESSAGE

ON A TREATY BETWEEN FRANCE AND NICARAGUA.[1]

[April 17, 1860.]

To the Senate of the United States:

I transmit herewith, for the information of the Senate, the Paris Moniteur of the 4th February last, the official journal of the French Government, containing an imperial decree promulgating a treaty of friendship, commerce, and navigation, concluded on the 11th April, 1859, between France and the Republic of Nicaragua. It will be found in all respects similar to the treaty between the United States and Nicaragua now pending in the Senate.

JAMES BUCHANAN.

WASHINGTON, D. C., 17 April, 1860.

VETO OF A CLAIM BILL.[2]

[April 17, 1860.]

To the Senate of the United States:

I return, with my objections, to the Senate, for their reconsideration, the bill entitled "An act for the relief of Arthur Edwards and his associates," presented to me on the 10th instant.

This bill directs the Postmaster-General "to audit and settle the accounts of Arthur Edwards and his associates, for transporting the United States through mail on their steamers during the years 1849 and 1853 and intervening years," between Cleveland and Detroit, between Sandusky and Detroit, and between Toledo and Detroit, and "to allow and pay them not less than $28.60 for each and every passage of said steamers between said places during the aforementioned time, when the mails were on board."

---

[1] Senate Executive Journal, XI. 180.
[2] S. Ex. Doc. 40, 36 Cong. 1 Sess.

I have caused a statement to be made at the Post-Office Department of the least sum which can be paid to Mr. Edwards and his associates, under the bill, should it become a law, and from this it appears the amount will be $80,405.23.

Mr. Edwards and his associates, in 1854, a short time after the alleged services had been rendered, presented a claim to the Postmaster-General for $25,180 as compensation for these services. This claim consisted of nine items, setting forth, specifically, all the services embraced by the present bill. It is fair to presume that the parties best knew the value of their own service, and that they would not, by an under-estimate, do themselves injustice. The whole claim of $25,180 was rejected by the Postmaster-General, for reasons which it is no part of my present purpose to discuss.

The claimants next presented a petition to the Court of Claims, in June, 1855, " for a reasonable compensation " for these services, and " pray the judgment of your honorable court for the actual value of the service rendered by them, and received by the United States, which amounts to the sum of $50,000." Thus, the estimate which they placed upon their services had nearly doubled between 1854 and 1855; had risen from $25,180 to $50,000. On the 28 February, 1858, after a full hearing, the court decided against the claim, and delivered an opinion in support of this decision which cannot, I think, be contested on legal principles. But they state, in the conclusion of the opinion, that " for any compensation for their services beyond what they have received, they must depend upon the discretion of Congress."

This decision of the Court of Claims was reported to Congress on the 1st of April, 1858, and from it the present bill has originated. The amount granted by it is more, by upwards of $55,000, than the parties themselves demanded from the Postmaster-General in 1854, and is more, by upwards of $30,000, than they demanded when before the Court of Claims. The enormous difference in their favor between their own original demand and the amount granted by the present bill constitutes my chief objection to it. In presenting this objection, I do not propose to enter into the question whether the claimants are entitled, in equity, to any compensation for their services beyond that which it is alleged they have already received; or, if so, what would be " a reasonable and fair compensation." My sole purpose is to afford Congress an opportunity of reconsidering this case, on account of its peculiar circumstances.

I transmit to the Senate the reports of Horatio King, Acting Postmaster-General, and of A. N. Zevely, Third Assistant Postmaster-General, both dated on the 14th of April, 1860, on the subject of this claim.

JAMES BUCHANAN.

April 17, 1860.[1]

MESSAGE

ON THE TERRITORY OF MINNESOTA.[2]

[April 20, 1860.]

To THE HOUSE OF REPRESENTATIVES:

In answer to the resolution of the House of Representatives, " that the President be requested to communicate to the House, if not incompatible with the public service, all such information as he may possess in relation to the existence " of the Territory of Minnesota, he has to state that he possesses no information upon the subject except what has been derived from the acts of Congress and the proceedings of the House itself. Since the date of the act of the 11th of May, 1858, admitting a portion of the Territory of Minnesota as a State into the Union, no act has been performed by the Executive either affirming or denying the existence of such Territory. The question in regard to that portion of the Territory without the limits of the State remains for the decision of Congress, and is in the same condition it was when the State was admitted into the Union.

JAMES BUCHANAN.

WASHINGTON, April 20, 1860.

[1] The veto was read and its immediate consideration postponed from time to time until the 7th of June, when a vote was taken on the question, " Shall the bill pass, notwithstanding the objection of the President? "— which was determined in the negative, by a vote of 22 yeas against 30 nays. (Veto Messages: S. Misc. Doc. 53, 49 Cong. 2 Sess. 281.)

[2] H. Ex. Doc. 74, 36 Cong. 1 Sess.

MESSAGE

ON THE AFRICAN SQUADRON.[1]

[April 20, 1860.]

To the House of Representatives:

I transmit herewith a report of the Secretary of the Navy, to whom was referred the resolution of the House of Representatives of April 10, 1860, requesting the President to communicate to the House, in addition to the information asked in the resolution adopted in reference to the African slave trade, "the number of officers and men in the service of the United States, belonging to the African squadron, who have died in that service since the date of the Ashburton treaty up to the present time."

JAMES BUCHANAN.

WASHINGTON, D. C., April 20, 1860.

MESSAGE

ON A TREATY WITH NEW GRANADA.[2]

[April 22, 1860.]

To the Senate of the United States:

I return to the Senate the original convention between the United States and the Republic of New Granada, signed on the 10th September, 1857, and ratified by me as amended by the Senate on the 12th March, 1859.

The amendments of the Senate were immediately transmitted to New Granada for acceptance, but they arrived at Bogota three days after the adjournment of the Congress of

---

[1] H. Ex. Doc. 73, 36 Cong. 1 Sess. 1. The report of the Secretary of the Navy stated that, from an examination of the rolls of the vessels employed on the African coast since the Ashburton treaty (1842), it appeared that 86 persons in that squadron had died—9 officers and 77 men, or about five deaths per annum.

[2] Senate Executive Journal, XI. 182.

that Republic, notwithstanding the session had been protracted for twenty days, solely with a view to the consideration of the convention after it should have received the sanction of this Government.

At the earliest moment after the assembling of the New Granadian Congress, on the 1st of February last, the convention as amended and ratified was laid before that body, and on the 25th of the same month it was approved with the amendments. Inasmuch, however, as the period had expired within which by the third amendment of the Senate the ratifications should have been exchanged, the Congress of New Granada provided that " the convention should be ratified and the ratification should be exchanged at whatever time the Governments of the two Republics may deem convenient for the purpose, and therefore the period has been extended which the Senate of the United States had fixed."

The expediency of authorizing the exchange of ratifications at such time as may be convenient to the two Governments is, consequently, submitted to the consideration of the Senate.

JAMES BUCHANAN.

WASHINGTON, April 22, 1860.

MESSAGE

ON INSTRUCTIONS TO THE MINISTER TO CHINA.[1]

[April 23, 1860.]

TO THE SENATE OF THE UNITED STATES:

In answer to the resolution of the Senate of the 18th instant, requesting a copy of the instructions from the Department of State to Mr. McLane, when appointed minister to China, I transmit a report from the Secretary of State, with the instructions which accompanied it.

JAMES BUCHANAN.

WASHINGTON, April 23, 1860.

---

[1] S. Ex. Doc. 39, 36 Cong. 1 Sess.

MESSAGE

ON DISCRIMINATIONS AGAINST AMERICAN JEWS IN SWITZERLAND.[1]

[April 24, 1860.]

To the House of Representatives:

In compliance with the resolutions of the House of Representatives of the 2d March, 1859, and of the 26th ultimo, requesting information relative to discriminations in Switzerland against citizens of the United States of the Hebrew persuasion, I transmit a report of the Secretary of State, with the documents by which it was accompanied.

James Buchanan.

Washington, April 24, 1860.

MESSAGE

ON AN EXPULSION FROM PRUSSIA.[2]

Washington, April 25, 1860.

To the Senate of the United States:

In compliance with a resolution of the Senate of the 22d ultimo, calling for information concerning the expulsion from Prussia of Eugene Dullye a naturalized citizen of the United States, I transmit a report from the Secretary of State, dated the 24th instant.

James Buchanan.

---

[1] H. Ex. Doc. 76, 36 Cong. 1 Sess.
[2] Richardson's Messages and Papers of the Presidents, V. 592.

MESSAGE

ON AFFAIRS IN UTAH.[1]

[April 27, 1860.]

To THE HOUSE OF REPRESENTATIVES:

In compliance with the resolution of the House of Representatives of March 26, 1860, requesting "copies of all official correspondence between the civil and military officers stationed in Utah Territory, with the heads or bureaus of their respective departments, or between any of said officers, illustrating or tending to show the condition of affairs in said Territory since the 1st day of October, 1857, and which may not have been heretofore officially published," I transmit reports from the Secretaries of State and of War, and the documents by which they were accompanied.

JAMES BUCHANAN.

WASHINGTON, April 27, 1860.

MESSAGE

ON COMPULSORY ENLISTMENTS IN PRUSSIA.[2]

[April 30, 1860.]

To THE SENATE OF THE UNITED STATES:

In compliance with the resolution of the Senate of the 2d of February, 1859, requesting information in regard to the compulsory service of citizens of the United States in the Army of Prussia, I transmit an additional report from the Secretary of State, and the documents by which it was accompanied.

JAMES BUCHANAN.

WASHINGTON, April 30, 1860.

---

[1] H. Ex. Doc. 78, 36 Cong. 1 Sess.
[2] S. Ex. Doc. 38, 36 Cong. 1 Sess. 241.

MESSAGE

ON MASSACRES IN UTAH.[1]

[May 1, 1860.]

To the Senate:

In compliance with the resolution of the Senate, adopted March 19, 1860, calling for the correspondence, &c., in relation to the Mountain Meadow and other massacres in Utah Territory, I have the honor to transmit the report, with accompanying documents, of the Secretary of the Interior, who was instructed to collect the information.

JAMES BUCHANAN.

EXECUTIVE MANSION, May 1, 1860.

MESSAGE

ON A CONVENTION WITH SPAIN.[2]

[May 3, 1860.]

To the Senate of the United States:

I transmit to the Senate, for its consideration with a view to ratification, a convention between the United States and Spain for the settlement of claims signed at Madrid on the 5th of March, last.

JAMES BUCHANAN.

WASHINGTON, May 3, 1860.

---

[1] S. Ex. Doc. 42, 36 Cong. 1 Sess.
[2] Senate Executive Journal, XI. 183.

MESSAGE

ON CAPTURED AFRICANS.[1]

[May 19, 1860.]

To THE SENATE AND HOUSE OF REPRESENTATIVES:

On the 26th day of April last, Lieutenant Craven, of the U. S. steamer Mohawk, captured the slaver Wildfire on the coast of Cuba, with five hundred and seven African negroes on board. The prize was brought into Key West on the 31st April, and the negroes were delivered into the custody of Fernando J. Moreno, Marshal of the southern district of Florida.

The question which now demands immediate decision is, What disposition shall be made of these Africans? In the annual message to Congress of December 6, 1858, I expressed my opinion in regard to the construction of the act of 3d March, 1819, "in addition to the acts prohibiting the slave trade," so far as the same is applicable to the present case. From this I make the following extract:

'" Under the second section of this act, the President is ' authorized to make such regulations and arrangements as he may deem expedient for the safe-keeping, support, and removal beyond the limits of the United States, of all such negroes, mulattoes, or persons of color ' captured by vessels of the United States, as may be delivered to the marshal of the district into which they are brought; ' and to appoint a person or persons residing upon the coast of Africa, as agent or agents for receiving the negroes, mulattoes, or persons of color, delivered from on board vessels seized in the prosecution of the slave trade by commanders of the United States armed vessels.'

" A doubt immediately arose as to the true construction of this act. It is quite clear, from its terms, that the President was authorized to provide ' for the safe-keeping, support, and removal ' of these negroes up till the time of their delivery to the agent on the coast of Africa; but no express provision was made for their protection and support after they had reached the place of their destination. Still, an agent was to be appointed to receive them in Africa; and it could not have

---

[1] S. Ex. Doc. 44, 36 Cong. 1 Sess.

been supposed that Congress intended he should desert them at the moment they were received, and turn them loose on that inhospitable coast to perish for want of food, or to become again the victims of the slave trade.   Had this been the intention of Congress, the employment of an agent to receive them, who is required to reside on the coast, was unnecessary, and they might have been landed by our vessels anywhere in Africa, and left exposed to the sufferings and the fate which would certainly await them.

" Mr. Monroe, in his special message of the 17th December, 1819, at the first session after the act was passed, announced to Congress what, in his opinion, was its true construction.   He believed it to be his duty under it, to follow these unfortunates into Africa, and make provision for them there until they should be able to provide for themselves.   In communicating this interpretation of the act to Congress, he stated that some doubt had been entertained as to its true intent and meaning, and he submitted the question to them, so that they might, ' should it be deemed advisable, amend the same before further proceedings are had under it.'   Nothing was done by Congress to explain the act, and Mr. Monroe proceeded to carry it into execution according to his own interpretation.   This, then, became the practical construction."

Adopting this construction of President Monroe, I entered into an agreement with the Colonization Society, dated 7th September, 1858, to receive the Africans who had been captured on the slaver Echo from the agent of the United States in Liberia, to furnish them, during the period of one year thereafter, with comfortable shelter, clothing, and provisions, and to cause them to be instructed in the arts of civilized life suitable to their condition, at the rate of $150 for each individual.   It was believed that within that period they would be prepared to become citizens of Liberia, and to take care of themselves.

As Congress was not then in session, and as there was no outstanding appropriation applicable to this purpose, the society were obliged to depend for payment on the future action of that body.   I recommended this appropriation, and $75,000 were granted by the act of 3d March, 1859, [the consular and diplomatic bill,] " to enable the President of the United States to carry into effect the act of Congress of 3d March, 1819, and any subsequent acts now in force for the suppression of the slave trade." Of this appropriation, there remains unexpended the sum of $24,350.90, after deducting from it an advance made by the Secretary of the Interior, out of the judiciary fund, of $11,348.10.

I regret to say, that under the mode adopted in regard to the Africans captured on board the Echo, the expense will be large; but this seems, to a great extent, to be inevitable without a violation of the laws of humanity. The expenditure upon this scale for those captured on board the Wildfire will not be less than one hundred thousand dollars, and may considerably exceed that sum. Still, it ought to be observed that, during the period when the Government itself, through its own agents, undertook the task of providing for the captured, in Africa, the cost per head was much greater than that which I agreed to pay the Colonization Society.

But it will not be sufficient for Congress to limit the amount appropriated to the case of the Wildfire. It is probable, judging from the increased activity of the slave trade, and the vigilance of our cruisers, that several similar captures may be made before the end of the year. An appropriation ought, therefore, to be granted large enough to cover such contingencies.

The period has arrived when it is indispensable to provide some specific legislation for the guidance of the Executive on this subject. With this view, I would suggest that Congress might authorize the President to enter into a general agreement with the Colonization Society, binding them to receive, on the coast of Africa from an agent there, all the captured Africans which may be delivered to him, and to maintain them for a limited period, upon such terms and conditions as may combine humanity towards these unfortunates with a just economy. This would obviate the necessity of making a new bargain with every new capture, and would prevent delay, and avoid expense in the disposition of the captured. The law might then provide that in all cases where this may be practicable the captor should carry the negroes directly to Africa, and deliver them to the American agent there, afterwards bringing the captured vessel to the United States for adjudication.

The capturing officer, in case he should bring his prize directly to the United States, ought to be required to land the negroes in some one or more ports, to be designated by Congress, where the prevailing health throughout the year is good. At these ports, cheap but permanent accommodations might be provided for the negroes until they could be sent away, without incurring the expense of erecting such accommodations at every port where the capturing officer may think proper to enter. On the present occasion these negroes have been brought to Key West; and, according to the estimate presented by the Marshal of the southern district of Florida to the Secretary of the Interior, the cost of providing temporary quarters for them will be $2500, and the aggregate expenses for the single month of May will amount to $12,000. But this is far from being the worst evil. Within a few weeks the yellow fever will most probably prevail at Key West; and hence the marshal urges their removal from their present quarters at an early day, which must be done, in any event, as soon as practicable. For these reasons, I earnestly commend this subject to the immediate attention of Congress. I transmit, herewith, a copy of the letter and estimate of Fernando J. Moreno, Marshal of the southern district of Florida, to the Secretary of the Interior, dated 10th May, 1860, together with a copy of the letter of the Secretary of the Interior to myself, dated 16th May.

It is truly lamentable that Great Britain and the United States should be obliged to expend such a vast amount of blood and treasure for the suppression of the African slave trade, and this when the only portions of the civilized world where it is tolerated and encouraged are the Spanish Islands of Cuba and Porto Rico.

JAMES BUCHANAN.

WASHINGTON, May 19, 1860.

MESSAGE

ON THE CAPTURE OF THE SLAVER "WILLIAM."[1]

[May 22, 1860.]

To the Senate and House of Representatives:

I transmit herewith the copy of a letter, dated yesterday, from the Secretary of the Interior, communicating the copy of a letter addressed to him, on the 13th instant, by Fernando J. Moreno, marshal of the southern district of Florida. From this it appears that Lieutenant Stanley, of the United States steamer Wyandotte, captured the bark William, with about five hundred and fifty African negroes on board, on the south side of Cuba, near the Isle of Pines, and brought her into Key West on the 12th instant. These negroes have doubtless been delivered to the marshal, and, with those captured on board the Wildfire, will make the number in his custody about one thousand. More may be daily expected at Key West, which, both on account of a deficiency of water and provisions, and its exposure to the yellow fever, is one of the worst spots for an African negro depot which could be found on the coast of the United States.

JAMES BUCHANAN.

WASHINGTON, May 22, 1860.

MESSAGE

ON LAND CLAIMS IN CALIFORNIA.[2]

[May 22, 1860.]

To the House of Representatives:

In answer to the resolution passed on the 26th of March last, calling for a detailed statement of the expenditures from the " appropriations made during the first session of the 34th

---

[1] H. Ex. Doc. 83, 36 Cong. 1 Sess.
[2] H. Ex. Doc. 84, 36 Cong. 1 Sess.

Congress and the first and second sessions of the 35th Congress, for legal assistance and other necessary expenditures in the disposal of private land claims in California, and for the service of special counsel and other extraordinary expenses of such land claims, amounting in all to $114,000," I have the honor to transmit to the House of Representatives a report of the Attorney General, which with the accompanying documents contains the information required.

JAMES BUCHANAN.

WASHINGTON, May 22, 1860.

MESSAGE

ON THE CHINESE COOLIE TRADE.[1]

[May 26, 1860.]

TO THE HOUSE OF REPRESENTATIVES:

In compliance with the resolution of the House of Representatives of the 21st instant, requesting any information recently received respecting the Chinese coolie trade, which has not been heretofore communicated to Congress, I transmit a report from the Secretary of State, with the documents which accompanied it.

JAMES BUCHANAN.

WASHINGTON, May 26, 1860.

---

[1] H. Ex. Doc. 88, 36 Cong. 1 Sess.

TO QUEEN VICTORIA.[1]

WASHINGTON CITY, June 4, 1860.

To HER MAJESTY QUEEN VICTORIA:—

I have learned from the public journals that the Prince of Wales is about to visit your Majesty's North American dominions. Should it be the intention of His Royal Highness to extend his visit to the United States, I need not say how happy I shall be to give him a cordial welcome to Washington. You may be well assured that everywhere in this country he will be greeted by the American people in such a manner as cannot fail to prove gratifying to your Majesty. In this they will manifest their deep sense of your domestic virtues, as well as the conviction of your merits as a wise, patriotic, and constitutional sovereign.

Your Majesty's most obedient servant,

JAMES BUCHANAN.

---

[1] Curtis's Buchanan, II. 229. The reply of the Queen was as follows:

BUCKINGHAM PALACE, June 22, 1860.

MY GOOD FRIEND:—

I have been much gratified at the feelings which prompted you to write to me inviting the Prince of Wales to come to Washington. He intends to return from Canada through the United States, and it will give him great pleasure to have an opportunity of testifying to you in person that those feelings are fully reciprocated by him. He will thus be able at the same time to mark the respect which he entertains for the Chief Magistrate of a great and friendly state and kindred nation.

The Prince will drop all royal state on leaving my dominions, and travel under the name of Lord Renfrew, as he has done when travelling on the continent of Europe.

The Prince Consort wishes to be kindly remembered to you.

I remain ever your good friend,

VICTORIA RA.

TO MR. STANTON.[1]

[June 10, 1860.]

MY DEAR SIR/

Mr. Winslow sent me word through James Buchanan that Forney would be examined before the Committee to-morrow. His cross-examination is all-important. In his violent speech after Pennington's election he foreshadowed the course of the Covode Committee. The President himself was to be attacked, not the members of the Cabinet. That speech ought to be found, & he ought to be examined upon it seriatim. God knows what he may swear. If he should tell anything like the truth, I have nothing to fear.

Your friend very respectfully

JAMES BUCHANAN.

MR. STANTON.

MESSAGE

ON A CONVENTION WITH THE DELAWARE INDIANS.[2]

[June 14, 1860.]

TO THE SENATE OF THE UNITED STATES:

I submit, for the consideration of the Senate, articles of agreement and convention with the Delaware Indians, concluded May 13, 1860. I concur in the recommendation of the Secretary of the Interior, that the treaty should be ratified with the amendments suggested by the Commissioner of Indian Affairs.

JAMES BUCHANAN.

WASHINGTON, June 14, 1860.

---

[1] Buchanan Papers, Historical Society of Pennsylvania.
[2] Senate Executive Journal, XI. 206.

TO MR. BENNETT.[1]

(Private & Confidential.)

WASHINGTON 18 June 1860.

MY DEAR SIR/

I thought I never should have occasion to appeal to you on any public subject & I knew if I did I could not swerve you from your independent course. I therefore now only ask you as a personal friend to take the trouble of examining yourself the proceedings of the Covode Committee & the reports of the majority & minority, & then to do me what you may deem to be justice. That Committee were engaged in secret conclave for nearly three months in examining every man, *ex parte,* who from disappointment or personal malignity would cast a shade upon the character of the Executive. If this dragooning can exist, the Presidential office would be unworthy of the acceptance of a gentleman.

In performing my duties I have endeavored to be not only pure but unsuspected. I have never had any concern in awarding contracts, but have left them to be given by the Heads of the appropriate Departments. I have ever detested all jobs, & no man at any period of my life has ever approached me on such a subject. The testimony of Wendell contains nothing but falsehoods, whether for or against me, for he has sworn all round.

I shall send a message to the House in a few days on the violation of the Constitution involved in the vote of censure & in the appointment & proceedings of the Covode Committee. I am glad to perceive from the Herald that you agree with me on the Constitutional question. I shall endeavor to send you a copy in advance.

With my kindest regards to Mrs. Bennett, I remain very respectfully your friend

JAMES BUCHANAN.

JAMES GORDON BENNETT, ESQ.

------

[1] Buchanan Papers, Historical Society of Pennsylvania; Curtis's Buchanan, II. 260.

MESSAGE

ON THE COVODE INVESTIGATION.[1]

[June 22, 1860.]

To the House of Representatives:

In my message to the House of Representatives of the 28th March last, I solemnly protested against the creation of a committee, at the head of which was placed my accuser, for the purpose of investigating whether the President had, " by money, patronage or other improper means, sought to influence the action of Congress, or any committee thereof, for or against the passage of any law appertaining to the rights of any State or Territory." I protested against this because it was destitute of any specification, because it referred to no particular act to enable the President to prepare for his defence, because it deprived him of the constitutional guards, which, in common with every citizen of the United States, he possesses for his protection, and because it assailed his constitutional independence as a coördinate branch of the Government.

There is an enlightened justice, as well as a beautiful symmetry, in every part of the Constitution. This is conspicuously manifested in regard to impeachments. The House of Representatives possesses " the sole power of impeachment; " the Senate " the sole power to try all impeachments; " and the impeachable offences are " treason, bribery, or other high crimes or misdemeanors." The practice of the House, from the earliest times, had been in accordance with its own dignity, the rights of the accused, and the demands of justice. At the commencement of each judicial investigation which might lead to an impeachment, specific charges were always preferred; the accused had an opportunity of cross-examining the witnesses, and he was placed in full possession of the precise nature of the offence which he had to meet. An impartial and elevated standing committee was charged with this investigation, upon which no member inspired with the ancient sense of honor and justice would have

---

[1] H. Ex. Doc. 102, 36 Cong. 1 Sess. For a history of the so-called Covode Investigation, see Curtis's Buchanan, II. 246–260. See, also, Message of March 28, 1860, supra.

served, had he ever expressed an opinion against the accused. Until the present occasion, it was never deemed proper to transform the accuser into the judge, and to confer upon him the selection of his own committee.

The charges made against me, in vague and general terms, were of such a false and atrocious character that I did not entertain a moment's apprehension for the result. They were abhorrent to every principle instilled into me from my youth, and every practice of my life; and I did not believe it possible that the man existed who would so basely perjure himself as to swear to the truth of any such accusations. In this conviction I am informed I have not been mistaken.

In my former protest, therefore, I truly and emphatically declared that it was made for no reason personal to myself, but because the proceedings of the House were in violation of the rights of the coördinate executive branch of the Government, subversive of its constitutional independence, and, if unresisted, would establish a precedent dangerous and embarrassing to all my successors. Notwithstanding all this, if the committee had not transcended the authority conferred upon it by the resolution of the House of Representatives, broad and general as this was, I should have remained silent upon the subject. What I now charge is, that they have acted as though they possessed unlimited power, and, without any warrant whatever in the resolution under which they were appointed, have pursued a course not merely at war with the constitutional rights of the Executive, but tending to degrade the presidential office itself to such a degree as to render it unworthy of the acceptance of any man of honor or principle.

The resolution of the House, so far as it is accusatory of the President, is confined to an inquiry whether he had used corrupt or improper means to influence the action of Congress or any of its committees on legislative measures pending before them. Nothing more, nothing less. I have not learned through the newspapers, or in any other mode, that the committee have touched the other accusatory branch of the resolution, charging the President with a violation of duty in failing to execute some law or laws. This branch of the resolution is therefore out of the question. By what authority, then, have the committee undertaken to investigate the course of the President in regard to

the convention which framed the Lecompton constitution? By
what authority have they undertaken to pry into our foreign
relations, for the purpose of assailing him on account of the
instructions given by the Secretary of State to our minister in
Mexico relative to the Tehuantepec route? By what authority
have they inquired into the causes of removal from office, and
this from the parties themselves removed, with a view to prejudice his character, notwithstanding the power of removal belongs
exclusively to the President under the Constitution, was so decided by the first Congress in the year 1789, and has accordingly
ever since been exercised? There is in the resolution no pretext
of authority for the committee to investigate the question of
the printing of the post-office blanks, nor is it to be supposed that
the House, if asked, would have granted such an authority,
because this question had been previously committed to two other
committees, one in the Senate and the other in the House.
Notwithstanding this absolute want of power, the committee
rushed into this investigation in advance of all other subjects.

The committee proceeded for months, from March 22d,
1860, to examine *ex parte,* and without any notice to myself,
into every subject which could possibly affect my character.
Interested and vindictive witnesses were summoned and examined before them; and the first and only information of their
testimony which, in almost every instance, I received, was obtained from the publication of such portions of it as could
injuriously affect myself, in the New York journals. It mattered
not that these statements were, so far as I have learned, disproved
by the most respectable witnesses who happened to be on the spot.
The telegraph was silent respecting these contradictions. It was
a secret committee in regard to the testimony in my defence, but
it was public in regard to all the testimony which could by
possibility reflect on my character. The poison was left to produce its effect upon the public mind, whilst the antidote was
carefully withheld.

In their examinations the committee violated the most sacred
and honorable confidences existing among men. Private correspondence, which a truly honorable man would never even
entertain a distant thought of divulging, was dragged to light.
Different persons in official and confidential relations with myself,
and with whom it was supposed I might have held conversations,

the revelation of which would do me injury, were examined. Even members of the Senate and members of my own cabinet, both my constitutional advisers, were called upon to testify, for the purpose of discovering something, if possible, to my discredit.

The distribution of the patronage of the Government is by far the most disagreeable duty of the President. Applicants are so numerous, and their applications are pressed with such eagerness by their friends both in and out of Congress, that the selection of one for any desirable office gives offence to many. Disappointed applicants, removed officers, and those who for any cause, real or imaginary, had become hostile to the administration, presented themselves, or were invited by a summons to appear before the committee. These are the most dangerous witnesses. Even with the best intentions they are so influenced by prejudice and disappointment that they almost inevitably discolor truth. They swear to their own version of private conversations with the President without the possibility of contradiction. His lips are sealed and he is left at their mercy. He cannot, as a coördinate branch of the Government, appear before a committee of investigation to contradict the oaths of such witnesses. Every coward knows that he can employ insulting language against the President with impunity, and every false or prejudiced witness can attempt to swear away his character before such a committee without the fear of contradiction.

Thus for months, whilst doing my best at one end of the avenue to perform my high and responsible duties to the country, has there been a committee of the House of Representatives in session at the other end of the avenue, spreading a drag-net, without the shadow of authority from the House, over the whole Union, to catch any disappointed man willing to malign my character; and all this in secret conclave. The lion's mouth at Venice, into which secret denunciations were dropped, is an apt illustration of the Covode committee. The Star Chamber, tyrannical and odious as it was, never proceeded in such a manner. For centuries there has been nothing like it in any civilized country, except the revolutionary tribunal of France, in the days of Robespierre. Now, I undertake to state and to prove that should the proceedings of the committee be sanctioned by the House, and become a precedent for future times, the balance of the Constitution will be entirely upset, and there will no longer remain the three coördinate and independent branches of the Government—legislative, executive, and judicial. The worst fears of the patriots and statesmen who framed the Constitution in regard to the usurpations of the legislative on the executive and judicial branches will then be realized. In the language of Mr. Madison, speaking on this very subject, in the forty-eighth number of the *Federalist:* " In a representative republic, where the executive magistracy is carefully limited both in the extent and duration of its power, and where the legislative power is exercised by an assembly which is inspired, by a supposed influence over the people, with an intrepid confidence in its own strength, which is sufficiently numerous to feel all the passions which actuate a multitude, yet not so numerous as to be incapable of pursuing the objects of its passions by means which reason prescribes, it is against the enterprising ambition of this department that the people ought to indulge all their jealousy and exhaust all their precautions." And in the expressive and pointed language of Mr. Jefferson, when speaking of the tendency of the legislative branch of Government to usurp the rights of the weaker branches: " The concentrating these in the same hands is precisely the definition of despotic government. It will be no alleviation that these powers will be exercised by a plurality of hands, and not by a single one. One hundred and seventy-three despots would surely be as oppressive as one. Let those who doubt it turn their eyes on the Republic of Venice. As little will it avail us that they are chosen by ourselves. An elective despotism was not the government we fought for, but one which should not only be founded on free principles, but in which the powers of government should be so divided and balanced among several bodies of magistracy as that no one could transcend their legal limits without being effectually checked and controlled by the others."

Should the proceedings of the Covode committee become a precedent, both the letter and spirit of the Constitution will be violated. One of the three massive columns on which the whole superstructure rests will be broken down. Instead of the Executive being a coördinate it will become a subordinate branch of the Government. The presidential office will be dragged into the dust. The House of Representatives will then have rendered the Executive almost necessarily subservient to its wishes, instead of being independent.   How is it possible that two powers in the State can be coördinate and independent of each other, if the one claims and exercises the power to reprove and to censure all the official acts and all the private conversations of the other, and this upon *ex parte* testimony before a secret inquisitorial committee—in short, to assume a general censorship over the others? The idea is as absurd in public as it would be in private life. Should the President attempt to assert and maintain his own independence, future Covode committees may dragoon him into submission by collecting the hosts of disappointed office-hunters, removed officers, and those who desire to live upon the public treasury, which must follow in the wake of every administration, and they, in secret conclave, will swear away his reputation. Under such circumstances, he must be a very bold man should he not surrender at discretion and consent to exercise his authority according to the will of those invested with this terrific power. The sovereign people of the several States have elected him to the highest and most honorable office in the world.   He is their only direct representative in the Government.   By their Constitution they have made him commander-in-chief of their army and navy.   He represents them in their intercourse with foreign nations.   Clothed with their dignity and authority, he occupies a proud position before all nations, civilized and savage.   With the consent of the Senate, he appoints all the important officers of the Government.   He exercises the veto power, and to that extent controls the legislation of Congress.   For the performance of these high duties he is responsible to the people of the several States, and not in any degree to the House of Representatives.

Shall he surrender these high powers, conferred upon him as the representative of the American people, for their benefit, to the House, to be exercised under their overshadowing influence and control?   Shall he alone of all the citizens of the United States be denied a fair trial?   Shall he alone not be " informed of the nature and cause of the accusation " against him?   Shall he alone not " be confronted with the witnesses " against him? Shall the House of Representatives, usurping the powers of the Senate, proceed to try the President through the agency of a secret committee of the body where it is impossible he can make any defence, and then, without affording him an opportunity of being heard, pronounce a judgment of censure against him?

The very same rule might be applied for the very same reason, to every judge of every court of the United States. From what part of the Constitution is this terrible secret inquisitorial power derived? No such express power exists. From which of the enumerated powers can it be inferred? It is true the House cannot pronounce the formal judgment against him of " removal from office," but they can, by their judgment of censure, asperse his reputation, and thus, to the extent of their influence, render the office contemptible. An example is at hand of the reckless manner in which this power of censure can be employed in high party times. The House, on a recent occasion, have attempted to degrade the President by adopting the resolution of Mr. John Sherman, declaring that he, in conjunction with the Secretary of the Navy, " by receiving and considering the party relations of bidders for contracts, and the effect of awarding contracts upon pending elections, have set an example dangerous to the public safety, and deserving the reproof of this House."

It will scarcely be credited that the sole pretext for this vote of censure was the simple fact that in disposing of the numerous letters of every imaginable character which I daily receive, I had, in the usual course of business, referred a letter from Colonel Patterson, of Philadelphia, in relation to a contract, to the attention of the Secretary of the Navy, the head of the appropriate department, without expressing or intimating any opinion whatever on the subject; and to make the matter, if possible, still plainer, the Secretary had informed the committee that *" the President did not in any manner interfere in this case, nor has he in any other case of contract since I have been in the department."* The absence of all proof to sustain this attempt to degrade the President, whilst it manifests the venom of the shaft aimed at him, has destroyed the vigor of the bow.

To return, after this digression. Should the House, by the institution of Covode committees, votes of censure, and other devices to harass the President, reduce him to subservience to their will, and render him their creature, then the well-balanced Government which our fathers framed will be annihilated. This conflict has already been commenced in earnest by the House against the Executive. A bad precedent rarely, if ever, dies. It will, I fear, be pursued in the time of my successors, no matter what may be their political character. Should secret committees be appointed with unlimited authority to range over all the words and actions, and, if possible, the very thoughts of the President, with a view to discover something in his past life prejudicial to his character, from parasites and informers, this would be an ordeal which scarcely any mere man since the fall could endure. It would be to subject him to a reign of terror from which the stoutest and purest hearts might shrink. I have passed triumphantly through this ordeal. My vindication is complete. The committee have reported no resolution looking to an impeachment against me; no resolution of censure; not even a resolution pointing out any abuses in any of the executive departments of the Government to be corrected by legislation. This is the highest commendation which could be bestowed on the heads of these departments. The sovereign people of the States will, however, I trust, save my successors, whoever they may be, from any such ordeal. They are frank, bold, and honest. They detest delators and informers. I therefore, in the name and as the representative of this great people, and standing upon the ramparts of the Constitution which they " have ordained and established," do solemnly protest against these unprecedented and unconstitutional proceedings.

There was still another committee raised by the House on the 6th of March last, on motion of Mr. Heard, to which I had not the slightest objection. The resolution creating it was confined to specific charges, which I have ever since been ready and willing to meet. I have at all times invited and defied fair investigation upon constitutional principles. I have received no notice that this committee have ever proceeded to the investigation.

·Why should the House of Representatives desire to encroach on the other departments of the Government? Their rightful powers are ample for every legitimate purpose. They are the impeaching body. In their legislative capacity it is their most wise and wholesome prerogative to institute rigid examinations into the manner in which all departments of the Government are conducted, with a view to reform abuses, to promote economy, and to improve every branch of the administration. Should they find reason to believe, in the course of their examinations, that any grave offence had been committed by the President or any officer of the Government, rendering it proper, in their judgment, to resort to impeachment, their course would be plain. They would then transfer the question from their legislative to their accusatory jurisdiction, and take care that in all the preliminary judicial proceedings, preparatory to the vote of articles of impeachment, the accused should enjoy the benefit of cross-examining the witnesses, and all the other safeguards with which the Constitution surrounds every American citizen.

If, in a legislative investigation, it should appear that the public interest required the removal of any officer of the Government, no President has ever existed who, after giving him a fair hearing, would hesitate to apply the remedy.

This I take to be the ancient and well-established practice. An adherence to it will best promote the harmony and the dignity of the intercourse between the coördinate branches of the Government, and render us all more respectable both in the eyes of our own countrymen and of foreign nations.

JAMES BUCHANAN.

WASHINGTON, June 22, 1860.[1]

VETO OF THE HOMESTEAD BILL.[2]

[June 22, 1860.]

TO THE SENATE OF THE UNITED STATES:

I return, with my objections, to the Senate, in which it originated, the bill entitled "An act to secure homesteads to actual settlers on the public domain, and for other purposes," presented to me on the 20th instant.

This bill gives to every citizen of the United States "who is the head of a family," and to every person of foreign birth residing in the country who has declared his intention to become a citizen, though he may not be the head of a family, the privilege of appropriating to himself one hundred and sixty acres

---

[1] This message was referred to a select committee, with instructions to report at the next session. No report was ever made.
[2] S. Misc. Doc. 53, 49 Cong. 2 Sess. 281.

of Government land, of settling and residing upon it for five years; and should his residence continue until the end of this period, he shall then receive a patent on the payment of twenty-five cents per acre, or one-fifth of the present Government price. During this period, the land is protected from all the debts of the settler.

This bill also contains a cession to the States of all the public lands within their respective limits " which have been subject to sale at private entry, and which remain unsold after the lapse of thirty years." This provision embraces a present donation to the States of twelve million two hundred and twenty-nine thousand seven hundred and thirty-one acres, and will, from time to time, transfer to them large bodies of such lands which, from peculiar circumstances, may not be absorbed by private purchase and settlement.

To the actual settler, this bill does not make an absolute donation; but the price is so small that it can scarcely be called a sale. It is nominally twenty-five cents per acre; but, considering this is not to be paid until the end of five years, it is, in fact, reduced to about eighteen cents per acre, or one-seventh of the present minimum price of the public lands. In regard to the States, it is an absolute and unqualified gift.

1. This state of the facts raises the question whether Congress, under the Constitution, has the power to give away the public lands either to States or individuals. On this question, I expressed a decided opinion in my message to the House of Representatives of the 24th February, 1859, returning the agricultural college bill. This opinion remains unchanged. The argument then used applies, as a constitutional objection, with greater force to the present bill. There it had the plea of consideration, growing out of a specific beneficial purpose; here it is an absolute gratuity to the States without the pretext of consideration. I am compelled, for want of time, in these the last hours of the session to quote largely from this message.

I presume the general proposition will be admitted that Congress does not possess the power to make donations of money already in the Treasury, raised by taxes on the people, either to States or individuals.

But it is contended that the public lands are placed upon a different footing from money raised by taxation, and that the proceeds arising from their sale are not subject to the limitations of the Constitution, but may be appropriated or given away by Congress, at its own discretion, to States, corporations, or individuals, for any purpose they may deem expedient.

The advocates of this bill attempt to sustain their position upon the language of the second clause of the third section of the fourth article of the Constitution, which declares that " the Congress shall have power to dispose of and make all needful rules and regulations respecting the territory or other property belonging to the United States." They contend that, by a fair interpretation of the words " dispose of " in this clause, Congress possesses the power to make this gift of public lands to the States for purposes of education.

It would require clear and strong evidence to induce the belief that the framers of the Constitution, after having limited the powers of Congress to certain, precise, and specific objects, intended by employing the words " dispose of," to give that body unlimited power over the vast public domain. It would be a strange anomaly, indeed, to have created two funds, the one by taxation, confined to the execution of the enumerated powers delegated to Congress, and the other from the public lands, applicable to all subjects, foreign and domestic, which Congress might designate. That this fund should be " disposed of," not to pay the debts of the United States, nor " to raise and support armies," nor " to provide and maintain a navy," nor to accomplish any one of the other great objects enumerated in the Constitution, but be diverted from them to pay the debts of the States, to educate their people, and to carry into effect any other measure of their domestic policy. This would be to confer upon Congress a vast and irresponsible authority, utterly at war with the well-known jealousy of Federal power which prevailed at the formation of the Constitution. The natural intendment would be that, as the Constitution confined Congress to well-defined specific powers, the funds placed at their command, whether in land or money, should be appropriated to the performance of the duties corresponding with these powers. If not, a government has been created with all its other powers carefully limited, but without any limitation in respect to the public lands.

But I cannot so read the words " dispose of " as to make them embrace the idea of " giving away." The true meaning of words is always to be ascertained by the subject to which they are applied, and the known general intent of the law-giver. Congress is a trustee under the Constitution for the people of the United States to " dispose of " their public lands; and I think I may venture to assert with confidence, that no case can be found in which a trustee in the position of Congress has been authorized to " *dispose of* " property by its owner, where it has ever been held that these words authorized such trustee to give away the fund intrusted to his care. No trustee, when called upon to account for the disposition of the property placed under his management before any judicial tribunal, would venture to present such a plea in his defence. The true meaning of these words is clearly stated by Chief Justice Taney in delivering the opinion of the court (19 Howard, p. 436). He says, in reference to this clause of the Constitution: " It begins its enumeration of powers by that of disposing, in other words, making sale of, the lands, or raising money from them, which, as we have already said, was the main object of the cession (from the States), and which is the first thing provided for in the article." It is unnecessary to refer to the history of the times to establish the known fact that this statement of the Chief Justice is perfectly well-founded. That it never was intended by the framers of the Constitution that these lands should be given away by Congress is manifest from the concluding portion of the same clause. By it Congress has power not only " to dispose of " the territory, but of the " other property of the United States." In the language of the Chief Justice (p. 437): " And the same power of making needful rules respecting the territory is in precisely the same language applied to the other property of the United States, associating the power over the territory, in this respect, with the power over movable or personal property—that is, the ships, arms, or munitions of war which then belonged in common to the State sovereignties."

The question is still clearer in regard to the public lands in the States and territories within the Louisiana and Florida purchases. These lands were paid for out of the public Treasury from money raised by taxation. Now, if Congress had no power to appropriate the money with which these lands were purchased, is it not clear that the power over the lands is equally limited? The mere conversion of this money into land could not confer upon Congress new power over the disposition of land which they had not possessed over money. If it could, then a trustee, by changing the character of the fund intrusted to his care for special objects from money paid into land, might give the land away, or devote it to any purpose he thought proper, however foreign from the trust. The inference is irresistible that this land partakes of the very same character with the money paid for it, and can be devoted to no objects different from those to which the money could have been devoted. If this were not the case, then, by the purchase of a new territory from a foreign Government out of the public Treasury, Congress could enlarge their own powers, and appropriate the proceeds of the sales of the land thus purchased, at their own discretion, to other and far different objects from what they could have applied the purchase money which had been raised by taxation.

2. It will prove unequal and unjust in its operation among the actual settlers themselves.

The first settlers of a new country are a most meritorious class. They brave the dangers of savage warfare, suffer the privations of a frontier life, and with the hand of toil bring the wilderness into cultivation. The "old settlers," as they are everywhere called, are public benefactors. This class have all paid for their lands the Government price, or $1.25 per acre. They have constructed roads, established schools, and laid the foundation of prosperous commonwealths. Is it just, is it equal, that, after they have accomplished all this by their labor, new settlers should come in among them and receive their farms at the price of twenty-five or eighteen cents per acre? Surely the old settlers, as a class, are entitled to at least equal benefits with the new. If you give the new settlers their land for a comparatively nominal price, upon every principle of equality and justice you will be obliged to refund out of the common treasury the difference which the old have paid above the new settlers for their land.

3. This bill will do great injustice to the old soldiers who have received land warrants for their services in fighting the battles of their country. It will greatly reduce the market value of these warrants. Already their value has sunk, for one hundred and sixty acre warrants, to sixty-seven cents per acre, under an apprehension that such a measure as this might become a law.

What price would they command, when any head of a family may take possession of a quarter section of land and not pay for it until the end of five years, and then at the rate of only twenty-five cents per acre? The magnitude of the interest to be affected will appear in the fact that there are outstanding unsatisfied land warrants reaching back to the last war with Great Britain, and even Revolutionary times, amounting, in round numbers, to seven and a half millions of acres.

4. This bill will prove unequal and unjust in its operation, because, from its nature, it is confined to one class of our people. It is a boon exclusively conferred upon the cultivators of the soil. Whilst it is cheerfully admitted that these are the most numerous and useful class of our fellow-citizens, and eminently deserve all the advantages which our laws have already extended to them, yet there should be no new legislation which would operate to the injury or embarrassment of the large body of respectable artisans and laborers. The mechanic who emigrates to the West and pursues his calling must labor long before he can purchase a quarter section of land, whilst the tiller of the soil who accompanies him obtains a farm at once by the bounty of the Government. The numerous body of mechanics in our large cities cannot, even by emigrating to the West, take advantage of the provisions of this bill without entering upon a new occupation, for which their habits of life have rendered them unfit.

5. This bill is unjust to the old States of the Union in many respects; and amongst these States, so far as the public lands are concerned, we may enumerate every State east of the Mississippi, with the exception of Wisconsin and a portion of Minnesota.

It is a common belief, within our limits, that the older States of the Confederacy do not derive their proportionate benefit from the public lands. This is not a just opinion. It is doubtful whether they could be rendered more beneficial to these States under any other system than that which at present exists. Their proceeds go into the common treasury to accomplish the objects of the Government, and in this manner all the States are benefited in just proportion. But to give this common inheritance away would deprive the old States of their just proportion of this revenue without holding out any, the least, corresponding advantage. Whilst it is our common glory that the new States have become so prosperous and populous, there is no good reason why the old States should offer premiums to their own citizens to emigrate from them to the West. That land of promise presents in itself sufficient allurements to our young and enterprising citizens, without any adventitious aid. The offer of free farms would probably have a powerful effect in encouraging emigration, especially from States like Illinois, Tennessee, and Kentucky, to the west of the Mississippi, and could not fail to reduce the price of property within their limits. An individual in States thus situated would not pay its fair value for land when, by crossing the Mississippi, he could go upon the public lands and obtain a farm almost without money and without price.

6. This bill will open one vast field for speculation. Men will not pay $1.25 for lands when they can purchase them for one-fifth of that price. Large numbers of actual settlers will be carried out by capitalists upon agreements to give them half of the land for the improvement of the other half. This cannot be avoided. Secret agreements of this kind will be numerous. In the entry of graduated lands the experience of the Land Office justifies this objection.

7. We ought ever to maintain the most perfect equality between native and naturalized citizens. They are equal, and ought always to remain equal before the laws. Our laws welcome foreigners to our shores, and their rights will ever be respected. Whilst these are the sentiments on which I have acted through life, it is not, in my opinion, expedient to proclaim to all the nations of the earth that whoever shall arrive in this country from a foreign shore and declare his intention to become a citizen shall receive a farm of one hundred and sixty acres at a cost of twenty-five or twenty cents per acre, if he will only reside on it and cultivate it. The invitation extends to all; and if this bill becomes a law, we may have numerous actual settlers from China and other Eastern nations enjoying its benefits on the great Pacific slope. The bill makes a distinction in favor of such persons over native and naturalized citizens. When applied to such citizens, it is confined to such as are the heads of families, but when applicable to persons of foreign birth recently arrived on our shores, there is no such restriction. Such persons need not be the heads of families, provided they have filed a declaration of intention to become citizens. Perhaps this distinction was an inadvertence, but it is, nevertheless, a part of the bill.

8. The bill creates an unjust distinction between persons claiming the benefit of the pre-emption laws. Whilst it reduces the price of the land to existing pre-emptors to sixty-two and a half cents per acre, and gives them a credit on this sum for two years from the present date, no matter how long they may have hitherto enjoyed the land, future pre-emptors will be compelled to pay double this price per acre. There is no reason or justice in this discrimination.

9. The effect of this bill on the public revenue must be apparent to all. Should it become a law, the reduction of the price of land to actual settlers to twenty-five cents per acre, with a credit of five years, and the reduction of its price to existing pre-emptors to sixty-two and a half cents per acre, with a credit of two years, will so diminish the sale of other public lands as to render the expectation of future revenue from that source, beyond the expenses of survey and management, illusory. The Secretary of the Interior estimated the revenue from the public lands for the next fiscal year at $4,000,000, on the presumption that the present land system would remain unchanged. Should this bill become a law, he does not believe that $1,000,000 will be derived from this source.

10. This bill lays the axe at the root of our present admirable land system. The public land is an inheritance of vast value to us and to our descendants. It is a resource to which we can resort in the hour of difficulty and danger. It has been managed heretofore with the greatest wisdom under existing laws. In this management the rights of actual settlers have been conciliated with the interests of the Government. The price to all has been reduced from $2 per acre to $1.25 for fresh lands, and the claims of actual settlers have been secured by our pre-emption laws. Any man can now acquire a title in fee-simple to a homestead of eighty acres, at the minimum price of $1.25 per acre, for $100. Should the present system remain, we shall derive a revenue from the public lands of $10,000,000 per annum, when the bounty-land warrants are satisfied, without oppression to any human being. In time of war, when all other sources of revenue are seriously impaired, this will remain intact. It may become the best security for public loans hereafter, in times of difficulty and danger, as it has been heretofore. Why should we impair or destroy the system at the present moment? What necessity exists for it?

The people of the United States have advanced with steady but rapid strides to their present condition of power and prosperity. They have been guided in their progress by the fixed principle of protecting the equal rights of all, whether they be rich or poor. No agrarian sentiment has ever prevailed among them. The honest poor man, by frugality and industry, can, in any part of our country, acquire a competence for himself and his family, and in doing this he feels that he eats the bread of independence. He desires no charity, either from the Government or from his neighbors. This bill, which proposes to give him land at an almost nominal price, out of the property of the Government, will go far to demoralize the people, and repress this noble spirit of independence. It may introduce among us those pernicious social theories which have proved so disastrous in other countries.

JAMES BUCHANAN.

June 22, 1860.[1]

MESSAGE

ON THE CALIFORNIA MAIL SERVICE.[2]

[June 23, 1860.]

TO THE SENATE AND HOUSE OF REPRESENTATIVES:

GENTLEMEN: I feel it my duty to communicate to you that it has been found impracticable to conclude a contract for the transportation of the mails between our Atlantic and Pacific ports on the terms authorized by the fourth section of an act entitled

[1] This message was considered by the Senate at once. A motion was made that the further consideration of the bill be postponed until the first Monday in the following December, which was lost by a vote of 19 yeas against 26 nays. The question was then taken upon "the passage of the bill, the President's objections notwithstanding," and it was determined in the negative by a vote of 28 yeas against 18 nays. So the bill was not passed. (Veto Messages: S. Misc. Doc. 53, 49 Cong. 2 Sess. 287.)

[2] H. Ex. Doc. 99, 36 Cong. 1 Sess. 1.

" An act making appropriations for the service of the Post Office Department during the fiscal year ending June 30, 1861," approved June 15, 1860. The Postmaster General has offered the California mails to the several companies and ship-owners engaged in the trade with the Pacific, *viâ* the Isthmus, but they have all declined carrying them for the postages. They demand a higher rate of compensation, and unless power is given to the Postmaster General to accede to this demand, I am well satisfied that these mails cannot be forwarded. It should not be forgotten that, in consequence of the diversion of a large part of the letter mail to the overland route, the postage derived from the California service has been greatly reduced, and affords a wholly inadequate remuneration for the ocean transportation. The weight of these mails, averaging from twelve to fifteen tons semi-monthly, renders it, in view of the climate and character of the road, manifestly impossible to forward them overland without involving an expenditure which no wise administration of the Government would impose upon the Treasury. I therefore earnestly recommend that the act referred to be so modified as to empower the Postmaster General to provide for carrying the California mails at a rate of compensation which may be deemed reasonable and just.

JAMES BUCHANAN.

June 23, 1860.

MESSAGE

ON AN APPROPRIATION FOR THE WASHINGTON AQUEDUCT.[1]

[June 25, 1860.]

TO THE HOUSE OF REPRESENTATIVES:

I have approved and signed the bill entitled " An act making appropriation for sundry civil expenses of the Government for the year ending the 30th June, 1861."

---

[1] H. Ex. Doc. 101, 36 Cong. 1 Sess.

In notifying the House of my approval of this bill, I deem it proper, under the peculiar circumstances of the case, and in accordance with precedent, to make a few explanatory observations, so that my course in relation to it may not hereafter be misunderstood.

Amid a great variety of important appropriations, this bill contains an appropriation " for the completion of the Washington Aqueduct, $500,000, to be expended according to the plans and estimates of Captain Meigs, and under his superintendence: Provided, That the office of engineer of the Potomac waterworks is hereby abolished, and its duties shall hereafter be discharged by the chief engineer of the Washington Aqueduct." To this appropriation for a wise and beneficial object I have not the least objection. It is true I had reason to believe, when the last appropriation was made, of $800,000, on the 12th June, 1858, " for the completion of the Washington Aqueduct," that this would have been sufficient for the purpose. It is now discovered, however, that it will require half a million more " for the completion of the Washington Aqueduct; " and this ought to be granted.

The Captain Meigs to whom the bill refers is Montgomery C. Meigs, a captain in the corps of engineers of the Army of the United States, who has superintended this work from its commencement, under the authority of the late and present Secretary of War.

Had this appropriation been made in the usual form, no difficulty could have arisen upon it. This bill, however, annexes a declaration to the appropriation that the money is to be expended under the superintendence of Captain Meigs.

The first aspect in which this clause presented itself to my mind was, that it interfered with the right of the President to be " Commander-in-Chief of the Army and Navy of the United States." If this had really been the case, there would have been an end to the question. Upon further examination, I deemed it impossible that Congress could have intended to interfere with the clear right of the President to command the army and to order its officers to any duty he might deem most expedient for the public interest. If they could withdraw an officer from the command of the President, and select him for the performance of an Executive duty, they might, upon the same principle, annex to an appropriation to carry on a war a condition requiring it not to be used for the defence of the country unless a particular person of its own selection should command the army. It was impossible that Congress could have had such an intention. According to my construction of the clause in question, it merely designated Captain Meigs as its preference for the work, without intending to deprive the President of the power to order him to any other army duty for the performance of which he might consider him better adapted. Still, whilst this clause may not be—and I believe is not—a violation of the Constitution, yet, how destructive it would be to all proper subordination, and how demoralizing its effect upon the *morale* of the army, if it should become a precedent for future legislation. Officers might then be found, instead of performing their appropriate duties, besieging the halls of Congress for the purpose of obtaining special and choice places by legislative enactment. Under these circumstances, I have deemed it but fair to inform Congress that, whilst I do not consider the bill unconstitutional, this is only because, in my opinion, Congress did not intend, by the language which they have employed, to interfere with my absolute authority to order Captain Meigs to any other service I might deem expedient. My perfect right still remains, notwithstanding the clause, to send him away from Washington to any part of the Union to superintend the erection of a fortification, or any other appropriate duty.

It has been alleged, I think, without sufficient cause, that this clause is unconstitutional because it has created a new office, and has appointed Captain Meigs to perform its duties. If it had done this it would have been a clear question, because Congress have no right to appoint to any office, this being specially conferred upon the President and Senate. It is evident Congress intended nothing more by this clause than to express a decided opinion that Captain Meigs should be continued in the employment to which he had been previously assigned by competent authority.

It is not improbable that another question of grave importance may arise out of this clause. Is the appropriation conditional, and will it fall provided I do not deem it proper that it shall be expended under the superintendence of Captain Meigs?

This is a question which shall receive serious consideration;

because upon its decision may depend whether the completion of the water-works shall be arrested for another season. It is not probable that Congress could have intended that this great and important work should depend upon the various casualties and vicissitudes incident to the natural or official life of a single officer of the army. This would be to make the work subordinate to the man, and not the man to the work, and to reverse our great axiomatic maxim of " principles and not men." Upon the true and correct decision of the clause in this respect I desire to express no opinion. I repeat that this question shall be carefully considered, should its decision ever become necessary.

JAMES BUCHANAN.

WASHINGTON, June 25, 1860.

PROCLAMATION

CALLING AN EXTRA SESSION OF THE SENATE.[1]

[June 25, 1860.]

BY THE PRESIDENT OF THE UNITED STATES OF AMERICA.

A PROCLAMATION.

Whereas an extraordinary occasion has occurred, rendering it necessary and proper that the Senate of the United States shall be convened, to receive and act upon such communications as have been or may be made to it on the part of the Executive:

Now, therefore, I, James Buchanan, President of the United States, do issue this my proclamation, declaring that an extraordinary occasion requires the Senate of the United States to convene for the transaction of business at the Capitol, in the city of Washington, on the 26th day of June instant, at 12 o'clock at noon of that day, of which all who shall then be entitled to act as members of that body are hereby required to take notice.

---

[1] United States Statutes at Large, XII. 1257.

Given under my hand and the seal of the United States,
     at Washington, this 25th day of June A. D. 1860, and
[Seal.] of the Independence of the United States the eighty-
     fourth.

JAMES BUCHANAN.

By the President:
     LEWIS CASS, Secretary of State.

TO MR. HOLT.[1]

28 June 1860.

MY DEAR SIR

I would thank you to call and see me this morning on the
subject of the transportation of the Mails to California.

Yours very respectfully

JAMES BUCHANAN.

HON: MR. HOLT.

TO MR. COMSTOCK.[2]

WASHINGTON, 5 July, 1860.

DEAR SIR,

I have received yours of the 3d Instant, & although I do not
write letters on the subject to which it refers, I have determined
to address you a few lines.

The equality of the States in the Territories is a truly Democratic doctrine which must eventually prevail. This is all for
which I have ever contended. The Supreme Court of the United

---

[1] Holt Papers, Library of Congress.
[2] Buchanan Papers, Historical Society of Pennsylvania; Curtis's
Buchanan, II. 289.

States,—a co-ordinate branch of the Government, to which the decision of this question constitutionally belongs, have affirmed this equality, & have placed property in slaves upon the same footing with all other property. Without self-degradation the Southern States cannot abandon this equality, & hence they are now all in a flame. Non-intervention on the part of Congress with Slavery in the Territories, unless accompanied by non-intervention on the part of the Territorial Legislatures, amounts to nothing more in effect than to transfer the Wilmot Proviso from Congress to these Legislatures. Whilst the South cannot surrender their rights as co-equal States in the Confederacy, what injury can it possibly do to the Northern States to yield this great Democratic principle? If they should not do this, then we will have the Democratic party divided, South & North, by a geographical line, just as the Methodist Church has been divided, & another link binding the Union together will be broken. No person can fairly contend that either assemblage at Baltimore at the time the nominations were made was a Democratic National Convention; hence every Democrat is free to choose between the two candidates. These are in brief my sentiments. I regret that they so widely differ from your own. You have taken your own course, which you had a perfect right to do, & you will, I know, extend a similar privilege to myself.

Yours very respectfully,

JAMES BUCHANAN.

C. COMSTOCK, ESQUIRE.

SPEECH, JULY 9, 1860.[1]

I have ever been the friend of regular nominations. I have never struck a political ticket in my life. Now, was there anything done at Baltimore to bind the political conscience of any sound Democrat, or to prevent him from supporting Breckinridge

[1] Curtis's Buchanan, II. 290. This speech was made from the portico of the White House to a great crowd which had assembled there. It was the only public speech made by President Buchanan on the issues of the campaign.

or Lane? ["No! no!"]   I was contemporary with the abandonment of the old Congressional convention or caucus.   This
occurred a long time ago; very few, if any, of you remember it.
Under the old Congressional convention system, no person was
admitted to a seat except the Democratic members of the Senate
and House of Representatives.   This rule rendered it absolutely
certain that the nominee, whoever he might be, would be sustained at the election by the Democratic States of the Union.
By this means it was rendered impossible that those States which
could not give an electoral vote for the candidate when nominated, should control the nomination and dictate to the Democratic States who should be their nominee.

This system was abandoned—whether wisely or not, I shall
express no opinion.   The National Convention was substituted
in its stead.   All the States, whether Democratic or not, were
equally to send delegates to this convention according to the
number of their Senators and Representatives in Congress.

A difficulty at once arose which never could have arisen
under the Congressional convention system.   If a bare majority
of the National Convention thus composed could nominate a
candidate, he might be nominated mainly by the anti-Democratic
States against the will of a large majority of the Democratic
States.   Thus the nominating power would be separated from
the electing power, which could not fail to be destructive to the
strength and harmony of the Democratic party.

To obviate this serious difficulty in the organization of a
National Convention, and at the same time to leave all the States
their full vote, the two-thirds rule was adopted.   It was believed
that under this rule no candidate could ever be nominated without embracing within the two-thirds the votes of a decided
majority of the Democratic States.   This was the substitute
adopted to retain, at least in a great degree, the power to the
Democratic States which they would have lost by abandoning
the Congressional convention system.   This rule was a main
pillar in the edifice of national conventions.   Remove it and the
whole must become a ruin.   This sustaining pillar was broken to
pieces at Baltimore by the convention which nominated Mr.
Douglas.   After this the body was no longer a national convention, and no Democrat, however devoted to regular nominations,
was bound to give the nominee his support; he was left free to

act according to the dictates of his own judgment and conscience. And here, in passing, I may observe that the wisdom of the two-thirds rule is justified by the events passing around us.   Had it been faithfully observed, no candidate could have been nominated against the will and wishes of almost every certain Democratic State in the Union, against nearly all the Democratic Senators, and more than three fourths of the Democratic Representatives in Congress.   [Cheers.]

I purposely avoid entering upon any discussion respecting the exclusion from the convention of regularly elected delegates from different Democratic States.   If the convention which nominated Mr. Douglas was not a regular Democratic convention, it must be confessed that Breckinridge is in the same condition in that respect.   The convention that nominated him, although it was composed of nearly all the certain Democratic States, did not contain the two-thirds; and therefore every Democrat is at perfect liberty to vote as he thinks proper, without running counter to any regular nomination of the party. [Applause and cries of "three cheers for Breckinridge and Lane."]   Holding this position, I shall present some of the reasons why I prefer Mr. Breckinridge to Mr. Douglas.   This I shall do without attempting to interfere with any individual Democrat or any State Democratic organization holding different opinions from myself.   The main object of all good Democrats, whether belonging to the one or the other wing of our unfortunate division, is to defeat the election of the Republican candidates; and I shall never oppose any honest and honorable course calculated to accomplish this object.

To return to the point from which I have digressed, I am in favor of Mr. Breckinridge, because he sanctions and sustains the perfect equality of all the States within their common Territories, and the opinion of the Supreme Court of the United States, establishing this equality.   The sovereign States of this Union are one vast partnership.   The Territories were acquired by the common blood and common treasure of them all.   Each State, and each citizen of each State, has the same right in the Territories as any other State and the citizens of any other State possess.   Now what is sought for at present is, that a portion of these States should turn around to their sister States and say, " We are holier than you are, and while we will take our property to the Territories and have it protected there, you shall not place your property in the same position." That is precisely what is contended for. What the Democratic party maintain, and what is the true principle of Democracy is, that all shall enjoy the same rights, and that all shall be subject to the same duties. Property —this Government was framed for the protection of life, liberty, and property. They are the objects for the protection of which all enlightened governments were established. But it is sought now to place the property of the citizen, under what is called the principle of squatter sovereignty, in the power of the Territorial legislature to confiscate it at their will and pleasure. That is the principle sought to be established at present; and there seems to be an entire mistake and misunderstanding among a portion of the public upon this subject. When was property ever submitted to the will of the majority? [" Never."] If you hold property as an individual, you hold it independent of Congress or of the State legislature, or of the Territorial legislature —it is yours, and your Constitution was made to protect your private property against the assaults of legislative power. [Cheers.] Well, now, any set of principles which will deprive you of your property, is against the very essence of republican government, and to that extent makes you a slave; for the man who has power over your property to confiscate it, has power over your means of subsistence; and yet it is contended, that although the Constitution of the United States confers no such power—although no State legislature has any such power, yet a Territorial legislature, in the remote extremities of the country, can confiscate your property!

[A Voice. " They can't do it; they ain't going to do it."]

There is but one mode, and one alone, to abolish slavery in the Territories. That mode is pointed out in the Cincinnati platform, which has been as much misrepresented as anything I have ever known. That platform declares that a majority of the actual residents in a Territory, whenever their number is sufficient to entitle them to admission as a State, possess the power to " form a constitution with or without domestic slavery, to be admitted into the Union upon terms of perfect equality with the other States." If there be squatter sovereignty in this resolution, I have never been able to perceive it. If there be any reference in it to a Territorial legislature, it has entirely escaped my notice.   It presents the clear principle that, at the time the people form their constitution, they shall then decide whether they will have slavery or not.   And yet it has been stated over and over again that, in accepting the nomination under that platform, I endorsed the doctrine of squatter sovereignty.   I suppose you have all heard this repeated a thousand times.

[A VOICE.   " We all knew it was a lie! "]

Well, I am glad you did.

How beautifully this plain principle of constitutional law corresponds with the best interests of the people!   Under it, emigrants from the North and the South, from the East and the West proceed to the Territories.   They carry with them that property which they suppose will best promote their material interests; they live together in peace and harmony.   The question of slavery will become a foregone conclusion before they have inhabitants enough to enter the Union as a State.   There will then be no " bleeding Kansas " in the Territories; they will all live together in peace and harmony, promoting the prosperity of the Territory and their own prosperity, until the time shall arrive when it becomes necessary to frame a constitution.   Then the whole question will be decided to the general satisfaction. But, upon the opposite principle, what will you find in the Territories?   Why, there will be strife and contention all the time. One Territorial legislature may establish slavery and another Territorial legislature may abolish it, and so the struggle will be continued throughout the Territorial existence.   The people instead of devoting their energies and industry to promote their own prosperity, will be in a state of constant strife and turmoil, just as we have witnessed in Kansas.   Therefore, there is no possible principle that can be so injurious to the best interests of a Territory as what has been called squatter sovereignty.

Now, let me place the subject before you in another point of view.   The people of the Southern States can never abandon this great principle of State equality in the Union without self-degradation.   [" Never! "]   Never without an acknowledgment that they are inferior in this respect to their sister States.   While it is vital to them to preserve their equality, the Northern States surrender nothing by admitting this principle.   In doing this they only yield obedience to the Constitution of their country as expounded by the Supreme Court of the United States.   While for the North it is comparatively a mere abstraction, with the South it is a question of co-equal State sovereignty in the Union.

If the decrees of the high tribunal established by the Constitution for the very purposes are to be set at naught and disregarded, it will tend to render all property of every description insecure. What, then, have the North to do? Merely to say that, as good citizens, they will yield obedience to the decision of the Supreme Court, and admit the right of a Southern man to take his property into the Territories, and hold it there just as a Northern man may do; and it is to me the most extraordinary thing in the world that this country should now be distracted and divided because certain persons at the North will not agree that their brethren at the South shall have the same rights in the Territories which they enjoy. What would I, as a Pennsylvanian, say or do, supposing anybody was to contend that the legislature of any Territory could outlaw iron or coal within the Territory? [Laughter and cheers.] The principle is precisely the same. The Supreme Court of the United States have decided,—what was known to us all to have been the existing state of affairs for fifty years,—that slaves are property. Admit that fact, and you admit everything. Then that property in the Territories must be protected precisely in the same manner with any other property. If it be not so protected in the Territories, the holders of it are degraded before the world.

We have been told that non-intervention on the part of Congress with slavery in the Territories is the true policy. Very well. I most cheerfully admit that Congress has no right to pass any law to establish, impair, or abolish slavery in the Territories. Let this principle of non-intervention be extended to the Territorial legislatures, and let it be declared that they in like manner have no power to establish, impair or destroy slavery, and then the controversy is in effect ended. This is all that is required at present, and I verily believe all that will ever be required. Hands off by Congress and hands off by the Territorial legislature. [Loud applause.] With the Supreme Court of the United States I hold that neither Congress nor the Territorial legislature has any power to establish, impair or abolish slavery in the Territories. But if, in the face of this positive prohibition, the Territorial legislature should exercise the power of intervening, then this would be a mere transfer of the Wilmot proviso and the

Buffalo platform from Congress, to be carried into execution in the Territories to the destruction of all property in slaves. [Renewed applause.]

An attempt of this kind, if made in Congress, would be resisted by able men on the floor of both houses, and probably defeated. Not so in a remote Territory. To every new Territory there will be a rush of free-soilers from the Northern States. They would elect the first Territorial legislature before the people of the South could arrive with their property, and this legislature would probably settle forever the question of slavery according to their own will.

And shall we for the sake of squatter sovereignty, which, from its nature, can only continue during the brief period of Territorial existence, incur the risk of dividing the great Democratic party of the country into two sectional parties, the one North and the other South? Shall this great party which has governed the country in peace and war, which has raised it from humble beginnings to be one of the most prosperous and powerful nations in the world—shall this party be broken up for such a cause? That is the question. The numerous, powerful, pious and respectable Methodist Church has been thus divided. The division was a severe shock to the Union. A similar division of the great Democratic party, should it continue, would rend asunder one of the most powerful links which bind the Union together.

I entertain no such fearful apprehensions. The present issue is transitory, and will speedily pass away. In the nature of things it cannot continue. There is but one possible contingency which can endanger the Union, and against this all Democrats, whether squatter sovereigns or popular sovereigns, will present a united resistance. Should the time ever arrive when Northern agitation and fanaticism shall proceed so far as to render the domestic firesides of the South insecure, then, and not till then, will the Union be in danger. A united Northern Democracy will present a wall of fire against such a catastrophe!

There are in our midst numerous persons who predict the dissolution of the great Democratic party, and others who contend that it has already been dissolved. The wish is father to the thought. It has been heretofore in great peril; but when divided for the moment, it has always closed up its ranks and become more powerful, even from defeat. It will never die whilst the Constitution and the Union survive. It will live to protect and defend both. It has its roots in the very vitals of the Constitution, and, like one of the ancient cedars of Lebanon, it will flourish to afford shelter and protection to that sacred instrument, and to shield it against every storm of faction. [Renewed applause.]

Now, friends and fellow-citizens, it is probable that this is the last political speech that I shall ever make. [A VOICE. " We hope not! "] It is now nearly forty years since I first came to Washington as a member of Congress, and I wish to say this night, that during that whole period I have received nothing but kindness and attention from your fathers and from yourselves. Washington was then comparatively a small town; now it has grown to be a great and beautiful city; and the first wish of my heart is that its citizens may enjoy uninterrupted health and prosperity. I thank you for the kind attention you have paid to me, and now bid you all a good-night. [Prolonged cheering.]

TO MR. WALL.[1]

WASHINGTON 14 July 1860.

MY DEAR SIR/

I have received your favor of the 10th Instant & am happy to learn that you wish me to forget & forgive the " many very harsh things " you have said of me. This I do with all my heart. It would be a vain labor to review the past, because we should never agree in relation to the occurrences to which you have so often referred. Let them all pass into oblivion.

With a single exception, I was as much attached to your excellent father as to any man living; & it has always been a source of deep regret to me that I should ever have had any misunderstanding with his son.

Yours very respectfully

JAMES BUCHANAN.

JAMES W. WALL, ESQ.

---

[1] Buchanan Papers, Historical Society of Pennsylvania.

TO MR. HENRY ET AL.[1]

WASHINGTON 17 July 1860.

GENTLEMEN/

I have received, through the kindness of Isaac Lawrence, Esquire, the Resolutions adopted on the 12th Instant by "the National Volunteers" of New York. In these you are pleased to say that the speech delivered by me on the night of the 9th Instant, when serenaded by the Ratification meeting of the friends of Breckinridge & Lane in this City, "is so clear, paternal, & statesmanlike a remonstrance against the spirit of disunion" that your association accept it as an expression of your own views. For this token of your kindness, as well as for the expression of your "personal regard & individual esteem & respect," I feel deeply grateful.

I am one of the last survivors of a race of men who were in their day the faithful guardians of the Constitution & the Union. This sacred duty has now descended to a new generation: & I am happy to believe that they will prove themselves to be worthy of the momentous trust. In this view I hail with sincere satisfaction the establishment of "the National Volunteers," & cordially wish them prosperity & usefulness.

May the kind Providence which has watched over our Country from the beginning restore the ancient friendship & harmony among the different members of the Confederacy, & render the Constitution & the Union perpetual!

Yours very respectfully

JAMES BUCHANAN.

JOHN T. HENRY, ESQUIRE, President, GIDEON I. TUCKER, 1st Vice President, HENRY J. CLARK, Treasurer, & JAMES MONROE, Secretary, &c. &c.

----

[1] Buchanan Papers, Historical Society of Pennsylvania.

TO MR. HALLOCK.[1]

Private and Confidential.

WASHINGTON, August 11, 1860.

MY DEAR SIR:

I have received your favor of the 5th instant, and in acknowledging it embrace the opportunity of expressing my warm and sincere acknowledgments to the Journal of Commerce for the able and valuable support which it has voluntarily given to my administration.

In regard to Mr. Comstock: the difficulties of retaining him in office, I can assure you, are almost insurmountable. I do not indulge a proscriptive spirit, and have not removed one in twenty of the Douglas officeholders. His father-in-law (Cutts) and his brother-in-law (Granger) are still in lucrative offices in this city, and I have no present intention of removing either. There are peculiar cases, however, which I cannot overlook, and it appears to me that Mr. Comstock is within this category. Whilst holding one of the best offices in my gift, he is at the same time, as you say, "at the head of the leading Democratic organ" in your State. This organ not only does not sustain the principles of my administration, but is in direct antagonism to them. It maintains political doctrines in violation of the Constitution of the United States as expounded by the Supreme Court. Unless these doctrines can be overthrown, there never will be a reunion between the Democratic party North and the Democratic party South,—or, in other words, a Democratic party co-extensive with the Union. Without this, the Constitution and the Union cannot be perpetuated. Under these circumstances, how can I remove any other officeholder, who is at the same time the Editor of a Journal, using it to oppose my administration on questions which I consider momentous & even vital, should I retain Mr. Comstock? I assure you I have no feeling against that gentleman, but directly the reverse, although his journal has classed the friends of Breckinridge, and of course including myself, as disunionists.

---

[1] Buchanan Papers, Historical Society of Pennsylvania.

This is the very first letter of the kind I have ever written. I intended to write but a few lines when I commenced; but my pen has run on. I remain

Very respectfully your friend

JAMES BUCHANAN.

GERARD HALLOCK, ESQRE.

TO MISS LANE.[1]

BEDFORD SPRINGS, 22 Aug: '60.

MY DEAR HARRIET/

I have only time to write a line before Mr. Wagoner, the messenger of Mr. Thompson, leaves. I am well & the water is producing its usual good effect. The company is reduced very much though what remains is agreeable & respectable. My visitors from the neighbourhood are numerous. I think I shall leave here on Monday or Tuesday next; but by what route I shall return home I have not yet determined. I shall telegraph at the proper time.

Mr. Magraw is doing well. Mr. Taylor has improved very much by the use of the waters. I am truly sorry Mr. Riggs has not come.

I found Judge Black here. He went to Somerset on Monday & will return here on Saturday.

Give my love to Lily. If things proceed as from appearances we might anticipate, she will soon be in the diplomatic corps; but I yet entertain doubts whether she will stand fire at the decisive moment.

Many inquiries have been made about you here & regrets expressed that you did not accompany me. In haste, yours affectionately,

JAMES BUCHANAN.

MISS LANE.

---

[1] Buchanan Papers, private collection. Imperfectly printed in Curtis's Buchanan, Il. 244.